Made in Egypt

MADE IN EGYPT

Gendered Identity and Aspiration on the Globalised Shop Floor

Leila Zaki Chakravarti

berghahn
NEW YORK • OXFORD
www.berghahnbooks.com

First published in 2016 by
Berghahn Books
www.berghahnbooks.com

© 2016, 2019 Leila Zaki Chakravarti
First paperback edition published in 2019

All rights reserved. Except for the quotation of short passages
for the purposes of criticism and review, no part of this book
may be reproduced in any form or by any means, electronic or
mechanical, including photocopying, recording, or any information
storage and retrieval system now known or to be invented,
without written permission of the publisher.

Library of Congress Cataloging-in-Publication Data
Names: Chakravarti, Leila Zaki, author.
Title: Made in Egypt: gendered identity and aspiration on the globalised shop floor / by Leila Zaki Chakravarti.
Description: New York : Berghahn Books, 2016. | Includes bibliographical references and index.
Identifiers: LCCN 2015046390| ISBN 9781785330773 (hardback: alk. paper) | ISBN 9781785330780 (ebook)
Subjects: LCSH: Clothing trade--Egypt. | Women clothing workers--Egypt. | Clothing workers--Egypt. | Organizational behavior. | Organizational sociology.
Classification: LCC HD9940.E32 C43 2016 | DDC 331.4/8870962--dc23
LC record available at http://lccn.loc.gov/2015046390

British Library Cataloguing in Publication Data
A catalogue record for this book is available from the British Library

ISBN 978-1-78533-077-3 hardback
ISBN 978-1-78920-511-4 paperback
ISBN 978-1-78533-078-0 ebook

*For my father,
in gratitude*

Contents

Illustrations, Maps and Figures ... ix
Acknowledgements ... xi
A Note on Transliteration ... xiv
Map of the Nile Delta ... xv

Chapter 1 The factory as crucible ... 1
Port Said – the nation's 'Dual Frontier'
Space and order: the factory as blueprint –
and as lived experience
Issues, inspiration and method
Ordering and animating the ethnography

Chapter 2 Firm as family – control and resistance ... 49
Il-kebir: the role of the proprietor-patriarch
Ikhlaas: filial loyalty and sibling rivalry
Ihtiram: performing respectability
Taraabut: articulations of community and entitlement
Entekhbo Qasim Fahmy! – the workers endorse
their *kebir*

Chapter 3 Shop floor as marketplace – love and consumption ... 98
Sexualising the workplace – the struggle for love
'Love in a world ruled by money' (*il-hub fi zaman il-felus*)
Hub il-shibak: love matches
Commodifying the shop floor – trading in dreams
Celebrating dreams – a picture says a thousand words

Chapter 4 Daughters of the factory – discipline and nurture   139
Discipline as performance
Performing efficiency
Mishmish alley cats – distinctive femininities
Nurturing and performing male power

Chapter 5 Globalised takeover – performance and resistance   172
Refashioning the labour landscape
Retrieving the firm as family
The end of the road?

Chapter 6 Domination and resistance   194
Globalisation and localisation
Co-optation and appropriation
The revolution that wasn't

Appendix The Fashion Express workforce   213

Select Glossary   217

Bibliography   221

Index   247

Illustrations, Maps and Figures

Illustrations

Illustration 1.1	Early Port Said – Quartier des Affaires	8
Illustration 1.2	Early Port Said – Rue du Commerce	8
Illustration 1.3	Early Port Said – Quartier Residentielle	9
Illustration 1.4	Early Port Said – Quartier Arabe	9
Illustration 1.5	Port Said Today – Tarh el Bahr (Commercial District)	14
Illustration 1.6	Port Said Today – the *souk* (market)	14
Illustration 1.7	Port Said Today – Hay el Afrangi (the 'Foreign Quarter')	15
Illustration 1.8	Port Said Today – lower-income housing	15
Illustration 1.9	Cutting	19
Illustration 3.1	*Shabaab riwish* ('cool youth'): pop star Amr Diab	111
Illustration 3.2	The *minagid* (quilt fluffer) at work	134
Illustration 3.3	A *tangid* (quilt fluffing) party getting into gear	135

Maps

Map 0.1	The Nile Delta	xv
Map 1.1	Port Said and the Suez Canal	6
Map 1.2	Antique map of the Suez Canal (1897)	7
Map 1.3	Port Said Today	13

Figures

Figure 1.1	Industrial labour actions in Egypt	2
Figure 1.2	Official plan of the Port Said Export Processing Zone (EPZ)	17
Figure 1.3	Schematic plan of the factory (ground floor)	18
Figure 1.4	Schematic plan of the factory (mezzanine gallery)	22
Figure 2.1	The *Marakiz il Quwa* ('Centres of Power')	67
Figure 4.1	Schematic location of *kawadir* (supervisory cadres)	142
Figure A1	Monthly fluctuations in total workforce numbers	213
Figure A2	Gender mix of workforce	214
Figure A3	Age distribution of workforce	214
Figure A4	Number of workers by age and gender	215
Figure A5	Proportion of males/female workers by age group	215
Figure A6	Education levels of workforce	216
Figure A7	Proportion of male and female workers by educational level	216

Acknowledgements

Five months after I left my fieldwork site in December 2004, the factory which had been my daily workplace ceased all production, its gates locked, and its premises empty and silent. Yet the clatter and din of industrial sewing machines on the hot shop floor, the piercing female voices of supervisors ringing out across the assembly lines, the flirtatious laughter of the young workforce, are some of the enduring images that remain vivid in my mind and heart, and have sustained me through the years of writing-up and completion.

I am indebted first of all to my gatekeepers: without their advice and assistance I would never have come near a shop floor, let alone had the chance of enjoying the type of fieldwork site I had longed to experience. Mr Ahmed Genedi, Senior Consultant at the Friedrich Ebert Stitfung in Cairo, introduced me to key contacts in Port Said. I especially thank Eng. Fuad Sabet, NGO and business consultant in Port Said, and Mr Magdi Kamal, Director General of the Port Said's Investors' Association, for opening doors to the factory where I worked, and facilitating my access by drafting the Arabic paperwork needed for legal and official purposes. I also extend my thanks to Mr Ahmed Sarhan, Chairman of Port Said's Investors' Association, and his successor, Mr Mahmud Abbud, for their gracious hospitality throughout my stay and subsequent visits.

Within the academic community, I am deeply indebted to Professor Deniz Kandiyoti, whose intellectual rigour as a scholar of the Middle East region, and whose patience and insights during the course of my research preparation and writing-up, have been pivotal in assisting me to see analytical connections that would otherwise have escaped me. I am also grateful to colleagues in the Centre for Gender Studies and the Department of Anthropology and Sociology at SOAS. Dr Myriem Naji and Dr Anna Portisch are among the close friends whose enthusiasm, creativity and warmth have sustained me since we were postgraduate students together, as has the friendship and encouragement I have received from Prof. Sami Zubeida. The academic list would be incomplete without mentioning the late Professor Cynthia

Nelson, who guided me throughout my undergraduate years at the American University in Cairo, taught me the value of keeping detailed descriptive field-notes during my first experiences of fieldwork, and encouraged and supported me when I returned to anthropology later on in life.

On the home front, I owe Bhaskar more than words can say. He turned the scribbled workforce statistics in my notebook and data tables from various reports into the graphs in chapter 1 and the appendix; prepared the illustrations (with invaluable professional photography services provided by David Cutts at thedpc.com); and has generally been a tower of strength all through my fieldwork, my thesis writing-up and the long stages of getting my manuscript ready for publication, with its endless drafts (many of which he painstakingly proof-read) and moments of doubt. I won't go further, as I know what I have written will already embarrass him.

There is no easy way to end these brief acknowledgements without wishing, at this point, that the course of events in 'Fashion Express' (the fictitious name I have used to protect the identity of the factory) had turned out to be different. Its future was uncertain from the outset, and as such no different from other garment factories elsewhere encountering the tough and punishing realities of both global and local competition. Those to whom I accordingly feel the greatest debt are, inevitably and regrettably, precisely the individuals whose names I am required to omit in order to preserve their anonymity.

My most profound gratitude is reserved for the proprietor of Fashion Express, whose generosity of spirit remains unrivalled. Given the financial problems besetting his firm, granting me research access must have been a far from easy decision. With hindsight, it was an act that took immense courage, motivated by a deep personal conviction that the factory exposes – in his phrase "without *retouche*" – the strengths and painful contradictions found in Egypt a decade ago, and still part of its living reality. On occasions his subdued mutterings made me only too aware of his opinion of the seemingly ridiculous lengths to which ethnographic methods of fieldwork seemed required to go. This was mingled with silent admiration of, and support for, the unusual requirements of an educational system that dispatches students to work on a shop floor in order to earn their degrees!

To the workers in all the units I have been part of, and to their supervisors, my affection speaks for itself. In my mind, as much as in theirs, Fashion Express connected us, and gave us an *ism* (name), a shop floor language of our own making, and a collective identity that set us apart from others in the Zone. The resilience of the shop floor's fiercely independent spirit – mandated by physical space, production, webs of social relationships and the economic necessity of making a living – is what this ethnography aspires to capture. I am proud to share the spirit in which Lévi-Strauss concluded his 1960 Inaugural Lecture to the Collège de France, paying tribute to the

Amazonian and other peoples amongst whom he had done his early seminal fieldwork, when he said:

> To them, I have incurred a debt, which I can never repay, even if ... I were able to give some proof of the tenderness which they inspire in me and of the gratitude which I feel towards them by continuing to be as I was among them, and ... as I would hope never to cease from being: their pupil, their witness. (Levi-Strauss 1967: 53)

Leila Zaki Chakravarti
Port Said, Cairo and London

A Note on Transliteration

All transliterated words are in italics throughout the text. It is well known that transliterating Arabic into English is far from straightforward. The system of transliteration used in this study largely follows that recommended by the International Journal of Middle East Studies. I have also taken the liberty of modifying aspects of the system when the speech being reported varies considerably from colloquial Cairene, modern standard, or classical Arabic – as in the distinctive shop floor slang used in the factory, or the different dialects used in Port Said and its surrounding regions. In such cases I have tried to transliterate the Arabic words as closely as possible to how they were actually uttered by the players involved. In particular, long/short vowels and emphatic/non-emphatic sounds are not differentiated. An apostrophe ' is used for the glottal stop.

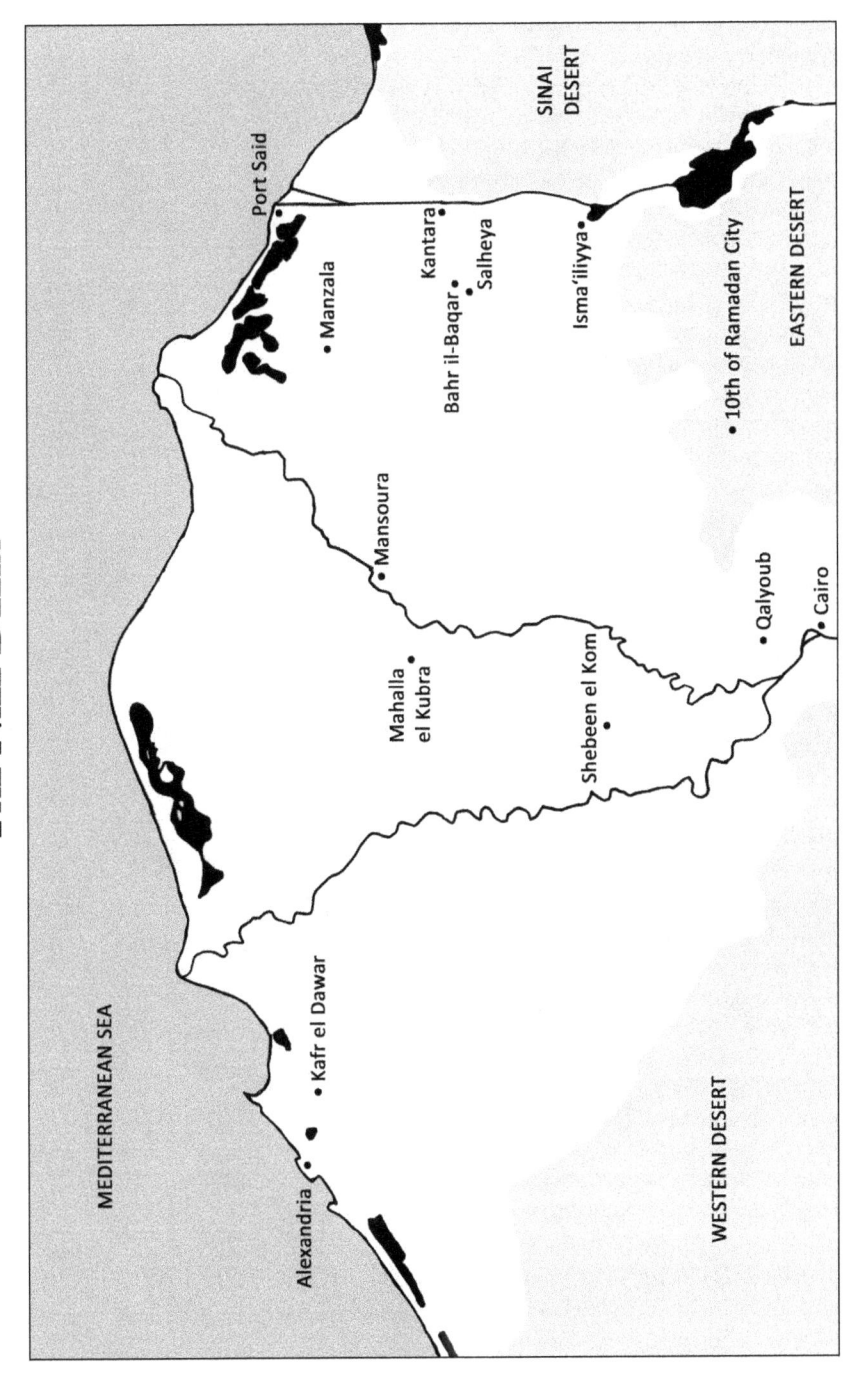

Chapter 1

THE FACTORY AS CRUCIBLE

> 'So this is phase two of the revolution ... what we need
> to do now is to take Tahrir to the factories.'

In May 2011, some three months after huge crowds in Cairo's Tahrir Square had jubilantly celebrated the forced removal of Egypt's long-serving President Hosni Mubarak, the *Guardian* newspaper's online series 'The new Egypt: 100 days on' carried a guest column by Hossam al-Hamalawy.[1] al-Hamalawy had long been a prolific blogger and tweeter on Egypt's Arab Spring upheavals, using a wide gamut of social media.[2] Writing in English as well as in Arabic, he was amongst the most prominent of Egypt's representatives of what Thomas Friedman later came to call the 'Square People',[3] characterised as 'mostly young, aspiring to a higher standard of living and more liberty, seeking either reform or revolution (depending on their existing government), connected to one another either by massing in squares or through virtual squares or both'.

Taken at face value, al-Hamalawy's 'To the factories!' exhortations might easily be dismissed as the trendy musings of a Westernised urban intellectual, disconnected from the realities of everyday life outside Egypt's e-savvy enclaves of privilege. In fact, though, he had been one of the first to draw explicit attention to the 'crucial but under-researched' (Gunning and Baron 2013: 59) role which widespread labour unrest played in the build-up to Mubarak's downfall. Blogging in its immediate aftermath on his '3arabawy' website, he wrote:

In Tahrir Square you found sons and daughters of the Egyptian elite ... But remember that it's only when the mass strikes started three days ago that's when the regime started crumbling ... Some have been surprised that the workers started striking. I really don't know what to say. The workers have been staging the longest and most sustained strike wave in Egypt's history, triggered by the Mahalla strike in December 2006. It's not the workers' fault that you were not paying attention to their news.[4]

The distinguished labour historian Joel Beinin and others (Abdalla 2012; Achcar 2013; Gunning and Baron 2013; Tripp 2013; Abdelrahman 2014; Gerges 2014; Schenker 2016) have published collated data on the overall scale and nature of labour unrest in Egypt,[5] showing a pattern of successive waves building to the denouement highlighted by al-Hamalawy (Figure 1.1). Beinin had also been assiduous in chronicling many of these labour disputes at the time they were unfolding (2005, 2006, 2007; Beinin and al-Hamalawy 2007a,b). His accounts of the 2006–7 Mahalla strikes vividly describe how workers had become embittered towards their managers, as, for example, when they held aloft placards saying '*Ilhaquna*! (Come to our rescue!) *Il-haramiyya saraquna*! (These thieves have robbed us blind!)' (Beinin 2007).[6] In other instances criticisms were more personalised, as when in 2007 striking textile workers in a factory in Kafr el Dawar publicly excoriated their Chairman with the expletive 'Ali *gazma*! (Ali is a shoe i.e. worthless)'.[7] And in 2005 workers at a recently privatised factory in Qalyoub openly complained to the press about their new proprietor and his allies:[8]

> We are dealing with a regular mafia here. Do you think we're joking? This man tried to wipe out all our rights. He really showed us the ugly face of privatisation.

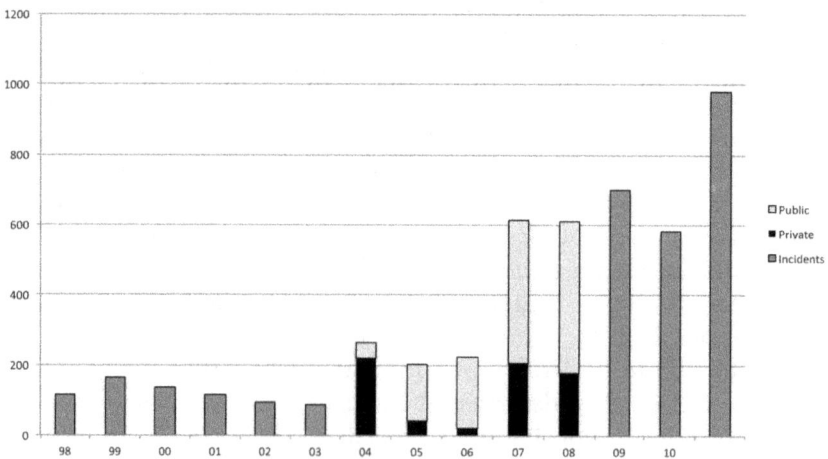

Figure 1.1 Industrial labour actions in Egypt

Yet it was in the preceding year of 2004, on a hot summer afternoon in the Mediterranean city of Port Said, that I had found myself experiencing a radically different kind of labour demonstration, as the employees of the privately owned garment manufacturing company to whose shop floor I had secured participant-observer research access drove around in electorally festooned factory buses, supporting their own proprietor's candidacy in the elections then underway for the Upper House of Egypt's Parliament shouting slogans such as '*Entikhbo* (vote for) *Qasim Fahmy*! *Ism Allah 'aleh* (the name of Allah be upon him)! *Hami rayetna* (the protector of our flag)!' From my seat, jammed in among the giggling, cheering female workers, there was nothing forced about the demonstration. These workers were as enthusiastic in support of their proprietor as the workers of Qalyoub, Kafr el Dawar and Mahalla were in repudiation and condemnation of theirs. As I look back on my time on the shop floor from February to December 2004, inevitably now through the prism of all that has happened in Egypt since then, I am still struck by the totality of the contrast and intrigued by the underlying causes and factors which might explain it.

These go deeper than obvious factors such as the presence or absence of organised trade unions. When Nasser nationalised the most important sectors of the Egyptian economy in the state socialism of the 1950s, the only unions that were legally permitted were a limited number of national, sector-specific unions (including the General Union of Textile Workers), all of which were branches of the Egyptian Trade Union Federation (Posusney 1997; Pratt 1998). From its inception in 1957 the ETUF operated as, in effect, an arm of the security state, controlling its millions of registered workers in state-owned enterprises, and frequently marshalling them in active political support of the Nasser-Sadat-Mubarak regimes. Though strikes were, in theory, permitted, they could only legally take place with the authorisation of a two-thirds majority of ETUF's Board (which consisted of regime appointees) – and in its entire history the ETUF only ever authorised a total of two strikes. The wildcat strikers of the state-owned enterprises and recently privatised firms who galvanised and made up the waves of labour unrest charted above were, as a result, almost invariably as vehement in their denunciations of their ETUF representatives as they were towards their management. And as Figure 1.1 shows, the fact that private sector company employees were legally forbidden (and sometimes beaten up and physically prevented) from forming independent trade unions did not in any way mean that private factories and firms were free from labour unrest. In my own fieldwork site, my time on the shop floor was marked by a seemingly endless series of management–labour arguments, fights and disputes. Yet my co-workers evidently had fostered a social contract with their proprietor that was honoured on terms different from those which the striking workers of Mahalla and other factories had with theirs.

At the time of my fieldwork in 2004, Fashion Express (as I will call the firm, using a pseudonym) was an export-orientated garment manufacturing enterprise, located within Port Said's Export Processing Zone (EPZ) at the northern mouth of the Suez Canal. The EPZ was one of nine such onshore tax havens established by the Egyptian government to enable export-orientated garment and other manufacturing to boost local economies and employment opportunities. The firm was run as a family business by Qasim Fahmy, who was also its local investor, employing a workforce of 450 male and female employees. In seeking to understand the management–labour dynamics in play, I have focused my ethnographic research on ways in which categories of gender, class and religion intersect on a labour-intensive shop floor which, because of the export profile of the firm, provides a nexus where myriad global and local economic forces interact to influence the environment of the workplace.

My research also aims to break new ground in the literature of gender and work in the Middle East by providing an ethnographic account of the public and visible economic activities of women in an institutional workplace within the formal economy. For although issues relating to women and gender have received considerable attention in Middle East studies (Meriwether and Tucker 1999; Keddie 2007; Whitlock 2007), when it comes to women's increasing economic roles it is the informal sector that most studies have emphasised. Even here, with the exception of a handful of ethnographies covering women's economic activity in home-based work and related areas (Rugh 1985; Hoodfar 1997a; el-Kholy 2002; Rugh 1985; Sonbol 2003), most studies have taken as their focus communities where women's educational backgrounds have not qualified them to seek work in the formal economy, causing them to rely primarily on self-help initiatives and informal networks (Early 1993a,b; Singerman and Hoodfar 1996; Bibars 2001; Barsoum 2002; Assad 2003; Ismail 2006; Assad and Barsoum 2009). This study aims to address this lacuna with an ethnography which recognises women as active economic actors within the public workplace. The research thus has dual, intertwined objectives: on the one hand, to provide an ethnography of a hitherto 'hidden' community, and on the other to interrogate the ethnographic data in order to explore issues of gender, class and religion in a context that has not yet been analysed.

In this introductory chapter I 'set the scene' for Fashion Express, the factory that was my research setting, and summarise the main points of focus, inspiration and methodological challenge for my research. In doing so, I first of all describe the distinctive urban environment of Port Said, highlighting the continuities between the present and the past which inform the city's daily life. Next I focus on Fashion Express, describing 'the factory as blueprint', the type of ordered, efficient enterprise which any management would wish to present to prospective international clients within the complex subcontracting chain that characterises the globalised garment industry (Lim 1990; Cairoli 1999; Rofel 1999; Kabeer 2000; Collins 2003; Hale and Willis 2005; Hewamanne 2008). An immediate dislocation, however, becomes apparent between the 'smoothly humming machine' that the factory is designed to operate as, and the stop-go production cycle it is forced to operate by 'famine and feast' peaks and troughs in the orders actually coming in.

I then describe the workforce which populates the blueprint, deliberately adopting the technocratic, de-humanised perspective of the official 'manpower statistics' which I was given. From there I shift my focus to the human beings behind the raw labour statistics, who were my colleagues, my informants and my guides during my time on the shop floor. It is the lived experience of their daily lives which provides, in Lévi-Strauss' ringing formulation, 'a means of assigning to human facts their true dimensions' (Lévi-Strauss 1967: 52). A sharp contrast emerges between the anonymous, dehumanised, smoothly efficient perspective of the factory as blueprint, and the chaotic, raucous social experience of the human beings who populate it.

This contrast provides the basis for identifying the research questions which guided this study, and which I set out in the following section. I move on to reflect on some of the theoretical insights and understandings from other scholars that inspired and challenged me as I fought to make sense of the welter of impressions and insights in which I was submerged, and highlight the principal methodological challenges and ethical issues that I found myself facing. Finally, I end this introductory chapter by setting out the sequence of the chapters that follow.

Port Said – the nation's 'Dual Frontier'

Port Said (Map 1.1) is one of Egypt's more modern cities, built on previously empty desert in the 1860s (Modelski 2000; Karabell 2003) at the time of the construction of the new canal named after the port city of Suez, located at its opposite end (Map 1.2). Egypt is a land whose centres of human habitation typically trace their origins hundreds – sometimes thousands – of years into the historical past: Suez, for example, traces its history as a city back at least to the 8th century AD (CE). By contrast, Port Said has always been one of Egypt's most enduring icons of modernisation, industrialisation and internationalisation – the nation's 'Dual Frontier', both spatially to the outside world and temporally to a modern, globally engaged and prosperous future.

From the city's foundation through to the overthrow of the monarchy by Gamal Abdel Nasser's Free Officers Revolution of 1952, Port Said maintained a reputation (global as well as domestic) for its commercial elan and European elegance – along with a parallel notoriety for its somewhat

6 • Made in Egypt

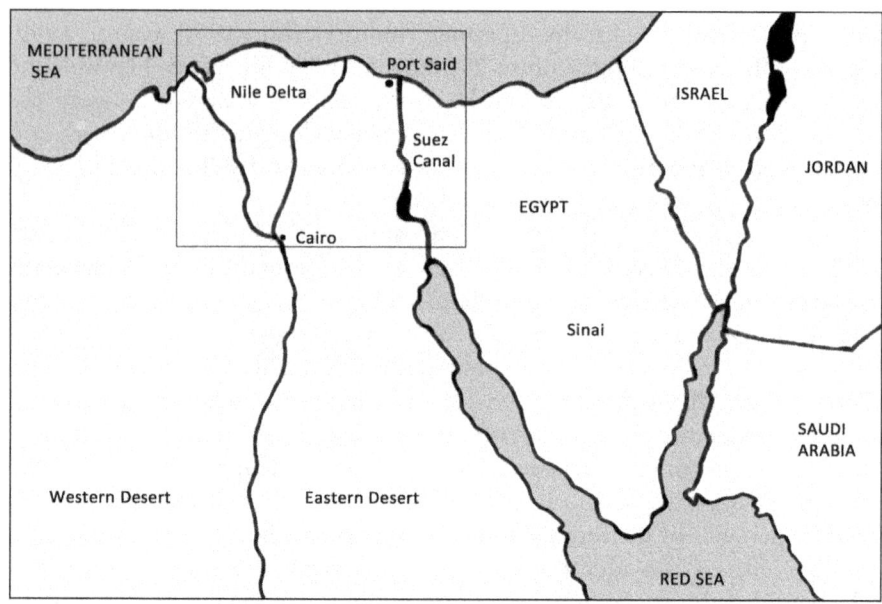

Map 1.1 Port Said and the Suez Canal

raffish docklands lifestyle. Urban planning and development was deliberately modern, on a rigorously rectangular grid of roads and boulevards. Along the northern corner of the west bank of the Canal stretched the Quartier des Affaires (what we would now call the Central Business District), with its bustling shops, offices, diplomatic representations, cafes, restaurants and hotels (see Illustration 1.1). These shared an architectural template distinctive to the city, and in particular very different from the multi-storey Parisian-style buildings of *belle époque* Cairo (Myntti 2015). The Port Said style was low-rise, and marked by the elegant wooden, often intricately carved, balconies and frontages to be seen adorning the different buildings (Illustration 1.2).

A few blocks inland was the Quartier Residentielle, its elegant villas and apartment blocks maintaining the Port Said aesthetic along tree-lined boulevards and garden squares (Illustration 1.3). Further west was the designated 'Village Arabe', which, though visibly less affluent than the modern European city, nevertheless maintained organisational and aesthetic continuity with it (Illustration 1.4).

Even during the austere years of Nasserist state socialism, the passage of foreign ships, goods and people through the newly nationalised canal (underpinned by the continuing vigour of local traditions of smuggling, contraband commercialism and other forms of shady or illegal business activity) enabled Port Said to sustain its reputation as Egypt's point of

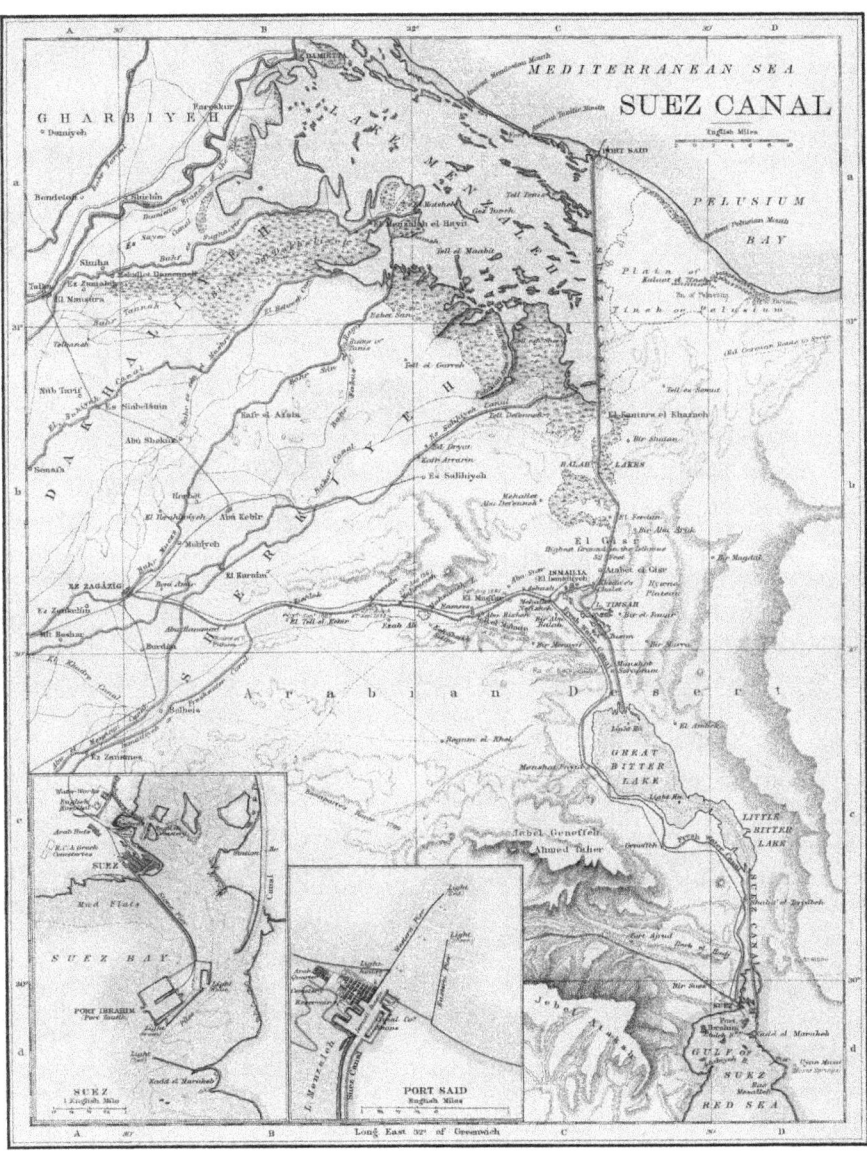

Map 1.2 Antique map of the Suez Canal (1897)

Illustration 1.1 Early Port Said – Quartier des Affaires (1910s Postcard)

Illustration 1.2 Early Port Said – Rue du Commerce

The Factory as Crucible • 9

Illustration 1.3 Early Port Said – Quartier Residentielle

Illustration 1.4 Early Port Said – Quartier Arabe

engagement with the excitement, glamour, temptation and consumer choice with which the outside world continued to beguile the nascent Republic. The abortive 1956 British-French invasion brought into focus the port-city's strategic military significance, adding to its self-consciously modernist self-image a strong sense of pride in its reputation for fiercely defending the motherland against British, French and later Israeli forces (Farnie 1969; Hamrush 1970; Najm 1987; Hewedy 1989; Kyle 1991; El-Kilsh 1997; Turner 2006).

Following Egypt's defeat in the 1967 Six Day War, the bustling port fell on hard times. The opposing armies facing each other across the Canal converted it into what Moshe Dayan is reputed to have called 'one of the best anti-tank ditches in the world', with the Egyptians blockading all traffic, and the Israelis building a twenty metre high fortified wall of sand along the length of its Eastern bank. At the same time the Egyptian government forcibly evacuated all civilian residents from the city, dispersing them across urban and rural centres throughout the country in what locals still refer to as their years of *hijra* (deliberately borrowing the term in Islamic history for the Prophet Mohamed's temporary retreat from Mecca to regroup in the city of Medina).

In 1975, riding high on Egypt's military breakthrough in the 1973 Yom Kippur War and the cessation of hostilities with Israel, the newly consecrated *Batal il-Ubur* (Hero of the Crossing i.e. of the Canal, by Egyptian forces) President Anwar Sadat led the reversal of decades of Nasserite state-socialism by declaring his new economic *infitah* (opening) policy to reinvigorate and develop international trade and commerce, and so end decades of socialist austerity, war and economic difficulties. A key measure was the re-opening of the Canal to international traffic in 1975. A year later, as part of his ambitious plans for economic regeneration of the war-blighted *mudun il-qanal* (cities of the Canal – namely Port Said at the north, Suez at the south, and Isma'iliyya in the middle) a Free Trade Zone was established in Port Said to encourage international trade and commerce. These steps were offered in the spirit of a reward (and compensation) for the sacrifices of the citizens of Port Said, and to provide an economic incentive for locals to return to their homes in the city.

In the laissez-aller spirit of *infitah*, the re-opening of the city was quickly recognised as one of the fastest routes to making money from the peace bonanza with Israel, triggering an influx of 'carpetbaggers' with no previous connections with Port Said. As one local official responsible for resettling the city's residents said to me, when I asked him – thirty years later – about those heady, chaotic days:

> Securing residency in this town was a once in a lifetime opportunity to hit the jackpot. Many individuals without the remotest links to Port Said rushed to

declare themselves its lost descendants, even as they exploited this town. No criteria existed to say who was allowed in or left out. The entire experiment was about survival, personal politics, rivalry, credibility and money. The newcomers remained suspect, despite the fortunes made. Let's put it another way – although everyone was fashioning a living and doing well, we lost the hospitable social infrastructure of the past.

The duty-free imported goods that suddenly flooded the city's shops and street bazaars were immediately seen to be cementing Port Said's reputation as the spearhead for making Egypt a more 'open' country, one that had finally turned to the world and the future. A huge number of small-scale family shops sprang up, which flourished by tapping the enormous pent-up appetite for all kinds of consumer goods, luxuries, cars and the unexpected opportunities that such consumerism reinvigorated. In a short space of time, the new-look Port Said, complete with Customs barriers on all roads leading into it from the rest of the country, captured the hearts, minds and imaginations of most Egyptians as a *madinet il-tuggar* (town of petty shopkeepers) and 'Egypt's first supermarket' (Heikal 1986).

The new duty-free entrepot was quick to embrace the fashion sector in particular, a development which was well in keeping with the reputation that Port Said had previously developed as the only region in Egypt to trade in second-hand clothes. As one local said to me, recalling what for her were 'the good old days':

> I can't think of a time when second-hand clothes weren't all the rage. The trade was born from ships passing through the Canal. The harbour is part of life in this town, and as locals we always knew which ship was disembarking where. The sealed containers of clothes were known as *palletta*. Traders were charged by weight, and the cash had to be paid on the spot, without any detailed information about what was inside. It was the luck of the draw as to which items were excavated as the contents of each *palletta* were sifted and separated, and in no time at all the flea markets would be awash with everything from leather jackets to trendy jeans. And once the clothes started to come with specific brand labels the flea markets prospered even more – nobody guessed which market you got your Levis from, or how much you'd forked out for them! Every family here had a member involved in the recycling business. This is the sector credited with giving us Port Saidians our first experience of imported goods, and what you might call *il-mazhar* (a dress sense). Through these widening horizons, we locals became more discerning.

The city, however, experienced a major setback with the abrupt cancellation in 2002 of its duty-free status, reputedly at the personal order of Sadat's successor, President Mubarak, as the latest – and harshest – of a stream of economic 'punishments' inflicted on Port Said in reprisal for an assassination attempt on him during an official visit in 1999. Port Saidians, however, dismiss this account as an excuse, concocted either to mitigate the brutal manner in which state security agents shot dead a local resident with a history of mental instability, who wandered too close to the Presidential motorcade or – at an even darker level of conspiracy – to eliminate competition for a potentially lucrative project which Mubarak's son Gamal and his business associates were promoting to construct a new harbour on the Canal's eastern bank. The Presidential decision dealt a devastating blow to the livelihoods of the many locals who, in the two decades since their return from evacuation, had come to regard gaining income from trade (both informal and formal, legal as well as dubious) as their right, and for whom the prospects that took off in the 1980s could not have been bettered.

With the city's duty-free commercial lifeblood choked off, local businessmen had little option but to turn their focus from trade and retail to manufacturing, focusing on the investment incentives available in the new Export Processing Zone (EPZ) recently established within the walls of what had been a cargo storage area adjacent to the port. *Malabis gahza* (ready-made clothes) was only one of a range of sectors officially approved for investment breaks within the Port Said EPZ;[9] yet virtually all newly invested factories turned to garment assembly work. The rapid development of the Zone into 'one big tailoring shop' (*mahal khiyata kebir*), as one of the the locals called it, provided further compelling testimony to the centrality of fashion and clothing in Port Said's history. As my informant about the *palletta* trade went on to put it:

> The *istithmar* (EPZ) was for us just the latest face of the world for these transactions: garments, fashion and the West turning up at our doorstep.

At the time of my 2004 fieldwork, in the late Mubarak neoliberalist heyday, the city was suffering something of a loss of its commercial vim and vigour, beset by a loss of international investment to competitor supply chain countries (notably in East Asia) and the general sense of stagnation besetting the domestic economy. Attempts to promote tourism were yielding at best partial success, with international cruise liners pausing only to decant their passengers directly into special buses for day excursions to Cairo and the Pyramids, and domestic tourists favouring the more well-established and upmarket seaside resorts along the Mediterranean coast to Alexandria and further west.

Yet under the somewhat desultory atmosphere, the city's distinctive heritage continued to be very visible in everyday contemporary life – as, indeed, it still does. North of the three original port basins – as clearly recognisable today as they were in early maps of the city (see inset in Map

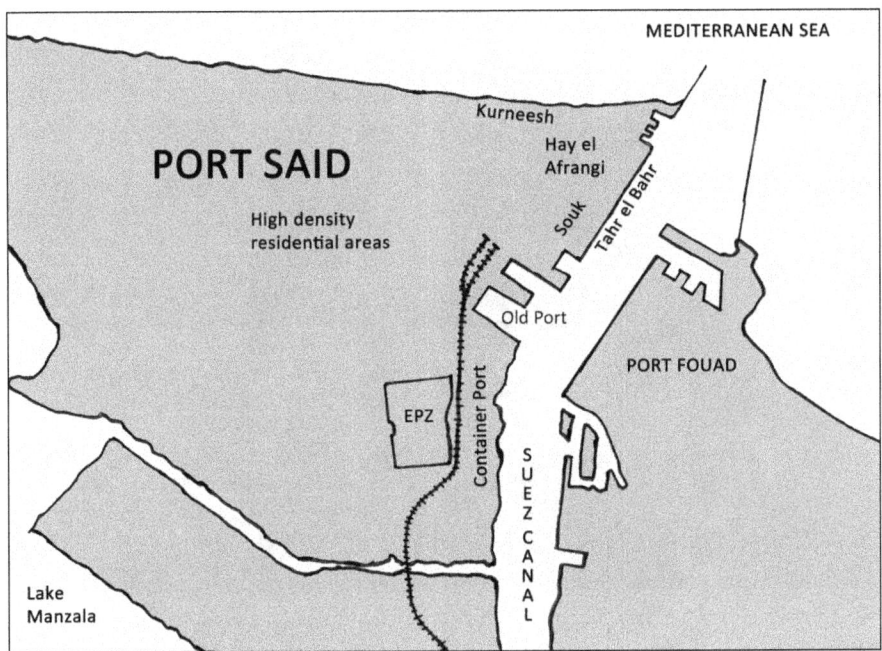

Map 1.3 Port Said Today

1.2) – stretches the district now known as Tarh il-Bahr (First Fruitbuds of the Sea), its upmarket boutiques, shops and cafes (see Illustration 1.5) retaining many of the original architectural features of the original Commercial District's business/recreational facilities (see Illustration 1.2). A few streets inland, their fading elegance rapidly gives way to the downmarket hustle and bustle of the local *souk* (market/shopping/social area – see Illustration 1.6), with its profusion of household stores, eateries and garment emporiums so characteristic of the busy *madinet il-tuggar*.

Further inland on the site of the old Quartier Residentielle, but now extending north to the expensive hotels and restaurants along the Kurneesh (Corniche), is the upmarket residential area now known as Hay el Afrangi (Foreign Quarter), many of its elegant apartment blocks continuing, more or less, to hold their own against a clutter of illegal rooftop extensions and commercial add-ons (see Illustration 1.7), as well as the constant threat of demolition for redevelopment.[10] Just as in the old postcards, the contrast continues to be vivid with the city's lower-income housing areas (see Illustration 1.8), which stretch out westwards from the site of the old Village Arabe. The inhabitants of this high-density housing make their feelings clear in their slang designation of the posher residential quarter as Hay il-Bodra (Cocaine Quarter).

14 • Made in Egypt

Illustration 1.5 Port Said Today – Tarh el Bahr (Commercial District) (Photo: Jamie Furlong)

Illustration 1.6 Port Said Today – the *souk* (market)

Illustration 1.7 Port Said Today – Hay el Afrangi (the 'Foreign Quarter') (Photo: The Egyptian at the English language Wikipedia)

Illustration 1.8 Port Said Today – lower-income housing (Photo: Jamie Furlong)

Immediately to the west of the railway line serving the new container port, and running though to the city's railway station, is the prominently visible rectangular grid of the Export Processing Zone – and it is onto this that I now zoom for a closer look at the location of the factory which was my workplace for fifteen transformative months of my life.

Space and order: the factory as blueprint – and as lived experience

The Port Said Export Processing Zone was one of the first to be established by the Egyptian government under its newly passed Investment Law 8 of 1997, aimed at attracting both local and international private sector investors to reinvigorate the country's struggling manufacturing sector, and so counterbalance the economy's overwhelming reliance on tourism, Canal revenues from international shipping, and remittances from the large numbers of expatriate Egyptians working in the Gulf and other parts of the Middle East. Incentives included providing subsidies for the cost of feasibility and related studies, facilitating loans from banks at favourable rates, granting rebates on the duties paid on imported equipment, and setting up tax relief windows for extended periods of time (Hinnebusch 1990; Hill 2003). In 2005 the site was described glowingly on an official government website (www.bmentp.gov.eg) as 'the hub of trade between Middle East, Europe and Far East'.

The official plan of the EPZ (see Figure 1.2) shows its origins as a walled compound that had previously been a storage zone for the adjacent container docking area, with its factories laid out in a neat and orderly grid. The plan graphically captures the impression the enterprise seeks to make on potential international clients, presenting itself as an oasis of ordered, modern efficiency – with raw materials flowing in and finished garments flowing out, virtually without setting foot in the hustle, bustle and hassle of 'real Egypt', and its tenants overflowing into adjacent compounds as testament to its bustling popularity as an investment choice. Needless to say, the official presentation masks inconvenient realities which get in the way of the desired impression, e.g. the fact that, at the time of my fieldwork, only seventeen of the more than one hundred units shown were actually operating as working factories – all the others were either used as warehouses for cloth and other raw materials, or were completely shuttered and locked. Over thirty units are highlighted in the plan as *Malabis Gahza* (ready-made clothes, i.e. garment) factories, the sector which is awarded top place in the key at the bottom left of the plan: the others are for chemicals, foods or engineering industries, and for ancilliary services such as refrigeration and storage.[11]

The Factory as Crucible • 17

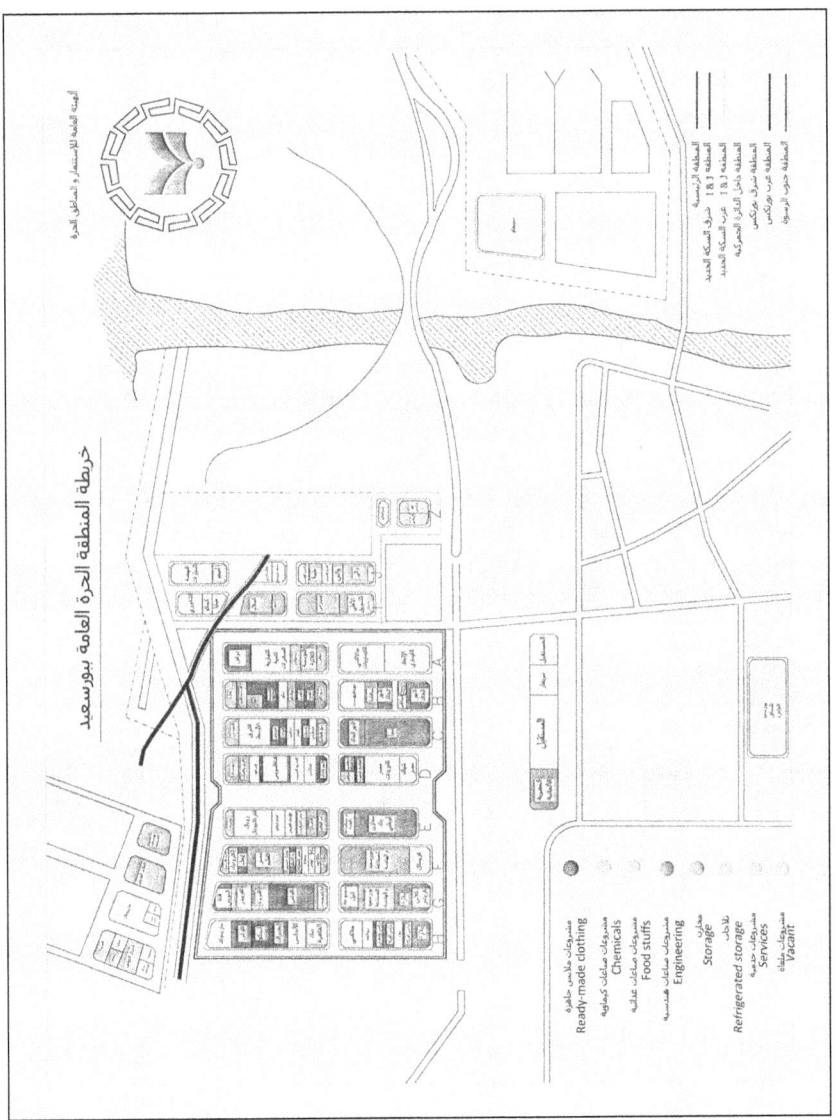

Figure 1.2 Official plan of the Port Said Export Processing Zone (EPZ)

18 • Made in Egypt

One of the roofs that make up the grid is that of Fashion Express. The factory offers clients the facility for 'Cut and Make' (C&M) garment assembly.[12] The C&M client provides the design specifications, the material and accessories – along with a specimen of the finished garment. Production works through the set stages of cutting, assembly, quality control, laundry, ironing and packing so that the finished goods can be despatched in compliance with strict completion deadlines. The ground-floor plan of the factory provided in Figure 1.3 shows how its physical layout is structured around the production process and its stages, which in effect runs from bottom-right to top-left of the diagram, in the sequence described below.

The Production Process

Cutting

The process begins when the large corrugated iron doors tucked away at the rear of the building are unlocked and pulled back for trucks to unload rolls of cloth into the warehouse attached to the Cutting Unit. Six male workers known as *faraddin* (rollers) load the cloth onto rollers, then work in pairs to run these up and down the length of the twenty-metre cutting tables, spreading the fabric until the number of layers specified by the Planning Department has been achieved. Preparations are complete when the unit supervisor unrolls over the top layer a large paper pattern, which the Design

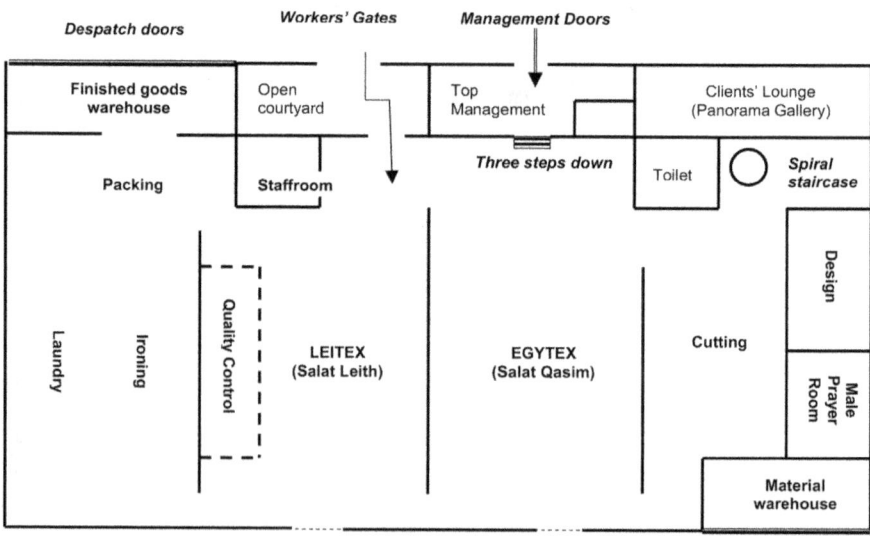

Figure 1.3 Schematic plan of the factory (ground floor)

Department has printed out from a computer disk provided by the client, and ensures that it is stapled securely to the material. At each table skilled workers then wield industrial cutters, hanging from electric cables in the ceiling, to slice through the layers of material according to the pattern marked. It requires skill, strength and concentration to guide the heavy, vibrating implements round the contours of each component, as if using a fretsaw to cut wood.

Illustration 1.9 Cutting

Two supervisors inspect the cut components for defects, before they are moved to a nearby *tarqim* (marking) table where three female workers swing into action. Marking is a standing job that requires a rapid wrist movement to flick through the layers of materials with one hand (rather like a bank teller counting notes), while with the other using a marking pistol to attach a sticker printed with a unique serial number to each item in the pile. The number identifies both the component and the layer of material from which it has been cut. This ensures that each assembled garment will be made up of components cut from the same layer of cloth, so that any variations in dyeing are matched (something of particular importance for finished denim garments). The marked items are tied into bundles using long strips of leftover material from the cutting tables, recorded in the supervisor's notebook, and moved to metal stands ready for transfer to the assembly lines.

Assembly

The two Assembly Halls (*salat* in Arabic, deliberately differentiated from the standard *qism* used for all other units or departments) form the heart of the entire operation. The one nearest Cutting is the more recent, originally sectioned off from the main *sala* to fulfil contracts under a commercial partnership (long since defunct) with another firm from elsewhere in the Middle East. A sign hanging in the centre of the hall that announces its name as Salet Qasim (i.e. Qasim Hall, after the proprietor) – although in the daily language of the shop floor it is known simply as Egytex, after the name of the vanished partner firm. The remaining area of the main hall takes pride in being the original shop floor from the time when the factory was bought by the current proprietor in 1996. Its sign declares its name to be Salet Leith (after the owner's son), yet it is universally known as Leitex (the original name of the factory). Leitex houses three assembly lines, Egytex a single line.

The process in Assembly is organised according to two principles: *tahdir* (preparation), and *tagmi'* (assembling), along with in-line quality control inspection. *Tahdir* is stationed towards one end of the hall, where a group of industrial sewing machines are clustered together, demarcated visually as well as spatially from the long, vertical rows of *tagmi'* machines in the hall. *Tahdir* is engaged in stitching and piecing together small components, such as pockets and loops, which will be stitched into the complete garment further down the *tagmi'* lines. Each machine on a *tagmi'* line is engaged in a single *marhala* (sewing task), after which the garment is folded and passed to the next machine. Depending on the design, a garment can easily pass through thirty separate stages of being unfolded, worked and folded again before *tagmi'* is complete. Monitors at in-line quality control stations (*gawdit khutut*) closely scrutinise each partially assembled garment at regular stages, using both qualitative and quantitative measures (such as visually assessing whether a seam looks puckered, or using a tape measure to check the width of a belt loop). Finished garments finally pile up in *gawda niha'i* (final quality control), whose metal tables are located to one side of Leitex. Pre-final checks include *tashtib* (focusing on removing, with small scissors, threads hanging loose from seams) and *tagwid* (removing finer threads protruding from the stitching itself). A final quality control known as *muraga* gives each finished garment a holistic inspection, checking that it is accurately put together as well as aesthetically pleasing, before it is finally recorded in the QC (quality control) supervisor's notebook.

Laundry and ironing

Maghsala (laundry) occupies the far corner of the factory, its rows of industrial-sized washing and drying machines lined up against an external wall. There is also a special machine for distressing denim and making it look fashionably well worn. Closer to Leitex is *makwa* (ironing) with rows of tables equipped with electric steam pressers. Garments are unfolded, pressed, steamed and folded in a uniform manner, before they are piled up for collection.

Packing

Ta'bi'a (packaging) is the final stage of the process. It involves fitting the garments with all the accessories that prepare them for final retail, including brand-name/size tags, shop barcodes, and prices in the foreign currency of the market for which they are destined. On a large table the finished garments are folded, wrapped in polythene (on hangers if appropriate), and then meticulously packed into cartons, which are then sealed with a record of the number contained inside. The sealed cartons are piled up neatly, awaiting final tally by the contractor, before they are loaded into the *hawiyya* (containers) of trucks ready to export them from the Zone to ships waiting at the nearby waterside.

Conception and execution: Edara and Entag

In a seminal work which continues to inform critical labour studies (e.g. Baran and Teegarden 1987), Harry Braverman famously analysed the structural separation between conception and execution in an industrial set-up, and the way in which this is arranged so as to be perceived as both 'logical' and 'natural' in a large-scale factory enterprise and workplace:

> Both in order to ensure management control and to cheapen the worker, conception and execution must be rendered separate spheres of work, and for this purpose the study of work processes must be reserved to management and kept from the workers, to whom its results are communicated only in the form of simplified job tasks governed by simplified instructions which it is thenceforth their duty to follow unthinkingly and without comprehension of the underlying technical reasoning or data. (1974: 118)

This separation operates in Fashion Express, much as in other factories in the Zone. The whole of the productive labour landscape described up until now is collectively referred to as *entag* (production). Responsibility for recruiting the workforce, planning production, monitoring progress and processing the paperwork associated with export is the separate prerogative of *edara* (administration). The fact that *edara* is entirely invisible within Figure 1.3 (the ground floor plan) is no coincidence. In a vivid demonstration of Braverman's principle of separation, *edara* have their own separate suite of offices – complete with segregated prayer and toilet facilities – located on a mezzanine floor specially constructed for them above the Cutting Department and reached by a single, spiral staircase (as shown in Figure 1.4).

Managerial space is divided into half-walled compartments, separated by large glass panels that allow visual access to all offices and individuals within the 'gallery', as the middle managers of *edara* uniformly refer to their segregated area. Four main departments dominate the gallery, lending weight and authority to the *takhassusat* (specialisations) of managerial work: Planning, Production Studies, Workers' Affairs, and Commercial Affairs. The remaining cubicles stand empty and disused, reminders of the days when, with production booming, there was a need for greater numbers of managerial staff.

Top management's initiation document for any new order, as transmitted to *edara*, specifies the nature of the items to be produced, the production volume required for each, and – most importantly for *shuhna* (export orders) – the deadline for completion of the contract. Armed with this mandate, the Planning Department steps in by applying its expertise to draw up a detailed plan that lays out with clarity the separation of individual stages of *entag* (production), allocating the time each will take according to self-declared scientific methods such as stopwatch measurements of how long a worker takes to complete a section of a garment. Planning's computer files store figures and charts, used to generate averages and norms which support its

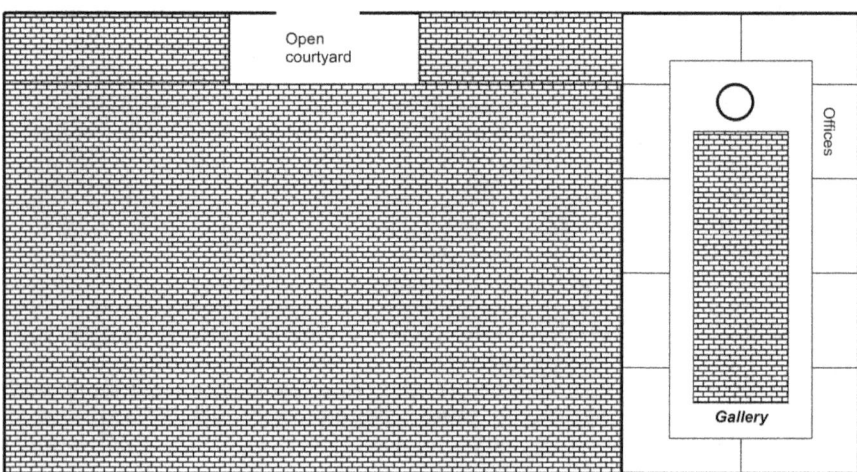

Figure 1.4 Schematic plan of the factory (mezzanine gallery)

planning assumptions for how rapidly *entag* can complete an order. Teams of *mutab'in* (monitors) from Planning visit the shop floor every hour to help build a profile of *entag*'s progress in completing each order according to plan.

Planning's expertise is deployed and demonstrated on paper. Production Studies however relies on visual inspection of the *mudilat* (models, i.e. specimen samples) despatched with each new order. All these are carefully scrutinised, favouring *il-mudilat il-sahala* (easy patterns) that characterise orders of *kaswil* (casual, i.e. leisure wear). A knowledge of the realities of earlier production orders gives the exercise a practical edge, with each new order evaluated against other similar orders that have already gone through the production circuit. It is for this reason that when bottlenecks in production disrupt Planning's smooth timelines, it is Production Studies who are called upon to come up with adjustments to the *tazbitat il-shughl* (work arrangements).

Workers' Affairs is responsible for the recruitment of new workers, for monitoring the attendance and performance of existing workers, for keeping records of all fines and penalties issued by supervisors and, in the last resort, for processing the departure of workers who leave the firm.

Commercial Affairs concerns itself with the paperwork associated with completed orders, notably those destined for export – the scale and complexity of which have long made Egypt's customs authorities famous all over the world.

Top management

Top management's role at the apex of the firm, overseeing the structural divide between conception and execution, is explicitly reflected in its physical separation from both *edara* and *entag*. As shown in Figure 1.3, top management's dedicated entrance at the front of the factory leads directly into a lounge where a leather sofa and several armchairs reflect the hierarchical pre-eminence of the space. Office doors lead to the rooms of the Chairman (as the proprietor is officially known) and the General Manager, while a secretarial space guards access to them. A separate small kitchen is used to prepare refreshments for top management and their visitors. At the far end of the top management lounge, a set of opaque glass doors, carefully watched over by the security guard stationed at the main entrance, opens onto a short flight of three stairs leading down to the *entag* halls. The effect is to ensure that top management is both separate from, and yet in some sense 'close to' the workers, most especially by contrast with the more distant, elevated offices of *edara*.

The machine in operation – famine and feast

These details found in the 'blueprint' view of the factory are geared to presenting the image of a well-oiled, gently humming machine, effortlessly converting computerised designs and bales of limp fabric into meticulously finished garments, neatly labelled and packed, ready for export on the next stage of their journey along the international supply chains of the globalised garment industry. In this view, even as the loading bays at the front end of the factory are being emptied of their piles of cartons of completed garments for one order, new rolls of fabric for the next order are being unrolled in the materials warehouse at the opposite corner, so that the relentless cycle of production spins smoothly and efficiently, to the mutual satisfaction of client and contractor alike.

Realities on the ground, however, are somewhat different. To begin with, the relationship between client and contractor is far from one of equal bargaining power. In the globalised garment industry, assembly plants are placed in a dependent position as suppliers of labour to foreign clients, who are themselves linked to foreign markets in a complex subcontracting chain (Lim 1991; Cairoli 1999; Kabeer 2000; Collins 2003). As well as inequality in such vertical relationships, assembly plants are also forced into competition with other firms in their geographical location (Hale and Wills 2005). Firms that are more successful in securing clients have to produce finished garments to demanding contractual deadlines – which means that they, in turn, often need to subcontract part of their work to other firms in their localities, resulting in horizontal relationships that are equally divisive. And since clients have both the discretion and the power to move orders around the globe from one location to another, as well as from one assembly plant to another within the same location, assembly firms can experience rapid changes in fortune – from being recipients of export orders from clients, and prime suppliers of subcontracting orders to others, to finding themselves at the receiving end of the hierarchy.

I was told that, in the not so distant past, Fashion Express had regularly undertaken work directly for international clients, who had provided a steady set of orders for each new season. At the time I undertook my research this was, however, no longer the case, as it was common knowledge that the factory no longer had any *'umala* (clients) with which to liaise directly. Instead, the current orders were labelled as *shughl min il-batin* (under the counter work), i.e. subcontracting orders from other local firms such as Lafayette, Transnational and Top Fashion, who having secured orders that exceeded their production capabilities were unable to meet their pressing deadlines (and so sustain their reputation within the global supply chain) without subcontracting some of the work to other firms. Securing subcontracts of this type for Fashion Express depended heavily on the proprietor's social and professional networks with other local investors in and outside the Zone, and his skill in mobilising these networks to extract orders. It was also common knowledge in the Zone that the proprietor's current economic difficulties meant that his factory was obliged to operate on an almost ad hoc basis, abandoning long-term planning in favour of taking whatever orders it could grab, often for short durations of time.

The result was an uneven and unpredictable production cycle, oscillating between weeks when assembly lines would fall silent, drained of orders, followed by sudden bursts of work to complete orders for limited quantities of garments within short timescales. The common seasonal slumps to hit the garment assembling plants at specific points in the year also accentuated this particular dimension. It formed a 'famine and feast' pattern of production, contrasting dramatically with the ideal presentation of the smooth-running, uninterrupted functioning of the 'factory as blueprint' – a pattern which, I came to discover, was a major determinant of many of the work practices on the shop floor.

Populating the blueprint – the factory's workforce

Blueprints contain no symbols for the human beings who operate the processes they represent. Yet any visitor to Fashion Express passing through the smoked glass doors at the far end of the top management suite would be overwhelmed, as I was, by the scale and intensity of human activity and interaction taking place in the factory space that is revealed, and the din generated, by humans as much as by machines, on the shop floor. The workforce is mixed male and female. This mixing of genders runs contrary to sociocultural proscriptions and, even in itself, is a relatively recent phenomenon in Egypt's industrial workplaces.

When it comes to divisions between male and female labour, the rigid public gender boundaries that operate in Islamic cultures and societies have been widely recorded and analysed (Minai 1981; Macleod 1991; Poya 1999; Hijab 2001; Sonbol 2003; Keddie 2007). Although Egypt's initial wave of Nasserist state industrialisation gave prominence to employment for women, it respected wider religious, social and cultural gender boundaries by arranging for certain industrial sectors to be understood as suitable for – and restricted to – female employment (Nassar 2003). Garment manufacturing was one such industry, in contrast to the spinning and textile-weaving industry, where the workforce remained wholly male. The same feminised view of the garment industry carried through into the early stages of Sadat's *infitah* programme of economic liberalisation, where garment manufacturing for export was one of the industries prioritised for private sector development.

The history of the company where I did my fieldwork was no exception. Some of the long-serving workers, who had been with the firm since its inception in 1982 and had stayed with it as it relocated three times[13] before settling in its present location in Port Said's Export Processing Zone, had vivid memories of the times when virtually the factory's entire labour-force was female. Apart from the ironing unit and the small maintenance crew who carried heavy equipment around, only supervisory and management roles were open to men. By the time I came to work in the factory the position had changed dramatically, with men now accounting for 60 per cent of the workforce[14] (though, perhaps contrary to stereotypical expectations of factory labour, the firm honoured the public-sector principle of 'equal pay for equal work' – in terms of wages, bonuses and incentives – for workers of both sexes). The workforce was overwhelmingly young, with nearly three-quarters of all workers under thirty (and only two employees over sixty – both of whom were long-serving men working in the laundry unit). It was also well educated, with only a quarter of employees having failed to complete high school (and over 10 per cent having graduated from university). There were more young men with post-intermediate or university level qualifications than there were young women. This profile confirms recent studies carried out on gender, employment and the gendered nature of the segmented and changing labour market in Egypt (Assad 2003; Nassar 2003). The relatively recent integration of educated male labour in previously all-female sectors is related to unemployment rates and the changing expectations of male graduates, who are willing to enter the private sector whilst pursuing the coveted *wazifa* (civil service) appointment-for-life. By contrast, the obstacles young educated women encounter in obtaining private-sector jobs relate to balancing their economic need to earn wages with what is still perceived as their primary socio-religious responsibility of starting a family, compelling them to confine their employment expectations to 'traditionally' marked areas of work (Assad and Barsoum 2009).

Even such a statement immediately takes us beyond neat and tidy 'workforce statistics', and into the lived reality of the human beings who populate and animate the blueprint. Workers are not simply cogs in the production blueprint, or points on a statistical graph. They have their own perspectives on the operations of the factory, their own experiences of their daily sojourn within its walls. It is these human beings who are the focus of my ethnography, and it is to their daily experiences that I now turn for the remainder of this study.

The factory as lived experience

The day starts well before dawn for the many Fashion Express workers who live outside Port Said, in the villages and towns of surrounding provinces. They need to have left their homes in the dark so as to be waiting at their designated pick-up points for the factory bus that will take them to work. A favourite shop floor joke tells how the buses are programmed to arrive punctually all the time, saving their equally 'programmed' breakdowns for the return journey home. Male workers sit at the front of the bus, female workers at the rear – with the middle benches occupied by shop floor *mushrifat* (female supervisors), ever vigilant in ensuring that none of the boys are tempted to turn round and chat up the girls. Friends typically sit next to each other in informally allotted places, catching up on the factory gossip about co-workers' romances, engagements and wedding parties.

As the buses arrive in Port Said after journeys of up to a couple of hours, the city streets are still quiet. But the main gate of the *istithmar* (EPZ) is a honking melee of buses bringing workers from other provinces and for other factories, their exhaust fumes choking the taxis and private cars which have brought management staff and local workers from their homes within the city. Since buses are not allowed into the Zone, workers have to walk through its narrow alleys to the factory, where Security ticks their names in a large, bound register confirming their arrival before the all-important 8 A.M. deadline (late-comers will have their wages docked). As they arrive, the factory's cleaners will still be sweeping up the previous day's debris from the shop floor: sweet papers, chewing gum packets, pieces of thread and blunt sewing needles. Lockers are provided for workers to store their personal belongings, along with separate prayer rooms for men and women to use before taking up their work stations in time for the loud electric bell that rings punctually at 8.30 A.M. to mark the start of morning production.

The early moments provide an opportunity for workers to prepare their stations, while at the same time organising lunch orders for one of their colleagues (typically the youngest male worker) to go out and buy from the food stalls outside the factory gates. Close notice is taken of the outfits everybody has come to work in for the day. Single young men are frequently turned out in designer T-shirts tucked into tight, pre-faded jeans, set off by thick leather belts with studs and dangling silver key-rings, mobile phones, and the latest gelled hairstyles modelled after the best known pop star faces of *aghani shababiyya* (songs of youth), as featured in video clips on TV. Women, by unspoken convention (the factory has no formal dress code), wear a variety of different styles of *hijab* (veil), ranging from the brightly patterned nylon headscarves worn by young, single girls to the austere *niqab* (covering the whole body, including the face) worn by some of the more self-consciously religious women.

Shop floor workers are required to remain at their stations and not walk about. Even visits to the toilet can only be made by first getting hold of one of the two plastic-covered *tasarih* (permits) that circulate around the shop floor. Supervisors (both male and female), by contrast, fulfil their roles by incessantly moving about in what shop floor argot calls *yi-wir* (literally 'going round in circles'). As the noise levels from working machines steadily rise, the supervisors move about waving their arms and shouting dramatically – at their workers, and at each other. They pounce on anyone who seems to be slacking, push garments from one station to the next, and count and note on sheets the *entag* (production) quotas churned out on an hourly basis. Every hour monitors from *edara* (middle management) are on the shop floor to collect these statistics, to feed them into their computers upstairs. In the frenzy of meeting quotas, it is easy for order to collapse, as workers along the rows of assembly lines take matters into their own hands, shouting at each other above the deafening clatter of the industrial sewing machines and the penetrating voices of supervisors continuously yelling criticism. Undisciplined scenes can easily evolve, with workers calling, whistling and throwing garments at each other, the din pierced by their mobile phones ringing with the latest *raqs sharqi* (belly dancing) ring-tones. Sometimes calm can only be restored by one of the supervisors switching on the factory's PA system and playing a cassette recording of the Koran.

Eventually the electric bell rings again, signalling the noon start of *il-rest*, the half hour lunch-break which divides the working day. The factory lights dim, and all workers are required to leave the shop floor under the watchful eye of Security. As most of the Zone's factories share a common lunch-hour, the rest area outside the factory's gates becomes a lunchtime promenade for the *istithmar*, allowing workers to review the passing fashion parade of ensembles, veils, footwear and accessories, and catch up on news of former colleagues who, as happens from time to time, have decamped to other employers in the Zone.

Within a few minutes of the bell ringing to signal the end of break, all are back at their stations and work rapidly resumes its earlier hectic pace. However, there always seems to be time for discussion of the latest catalogues of consumer goods to be circulated around the shop floor (offering anything from cosmetics to ready-made desserts to lingerie), or to consult *masader* (sources, informants) about the latest rumours of new orders that Qasim Bey might have managed to secure to keep the firm viable. Animated work-station chit chat however falls silent as soon as anyone suspected of being a *gusus* (spy) for *edara* or *amn* (Security) – say one of the boys who push around trolleys transferring garments from one stage of production to another – hoves into view. At times of deadline-driven pressure, the PA microphone can be heard to click on again late in the afternoon, as the voice of *edara* announces the names of workers required for *sahra* (staying on late for compulsory overtime). As the Arabic word is also a pun for 'a fun evening out', it provokes risqué banter between the men and women on the nominated list.

The long, hot afternoon's work continues until at last, promptly at 4.30 P.M., the bell rings again down the length of shop floor to mark the end of the working day. Female workers retrieve their handbags from their lockers, change into their outdoor slippers and stand in line – there is a separate line for the men – to be inspected by *amn* to ensure that no garments are being illegally smuggled off the premises. Workers make their way back to the main gates of the *istithmar*, where their waiting buses are surrounded by hawkers doing a brisk trade in small polythene bags of drinks and hot snacks for the road. The dusk ride home provides a chance for discussion of all that has happened in the busy working day, and quiet reflection on the future and the next working day to come.

Issues, inspiration and method

Issues

There is evidently a sharp dislocation between, on the one hand, the dehumanised efficiency of the 'factory as blueprint' view of Fashion Express with its dry charts and tables of workforce statistics, and, on the other, the social energy and emotional intensity of its employees' human experience of their daily workplace. And it was my deepening understanding of the range and depth of this dislocation which, as my work progressed, enabled me to formulate specific questions on which to focus my ethnography of women as economic actors, namely:

- In what ways do globalised economic forces and local factors interact to determine the distinctive environment of the factory?
- In the face of this, does management invoke or manipulate (and, if so, in what ways) categories of class, gender and religion in order to recruit and retain a viable workforce – and to exert control over it in order to meet contractual deadlines, quality standards and cost ceilings?
- Do workers comply with, resist or contest these management control strategies – and what are the effects of their actions on categorisations of class, gender and religion within the factory?

As I became drawn into exploring these issues, I grew increasingly aware that, while self-consciously seeking to break new ethnographic ground in terms of content, I was nevertheless able to draw deeply on previous research in a range of disciplines. In this section I outline my prime sources of inspiration, showing how the twists and turns of my developing empirical research drew me into particular engagements with a range of insights drawn from the rich scholarly heritage which they represent.

Inspiration

Right from the start of scoping my proposed research, and long before specific research issues and questions started to come into focus for me, I was clear that the 'field' for my intended fieldwork was to be the workplace environment of a factory engaged in industrial production. One of the sources of prior scholarship to which initially I turned was the established body of work by social and cultural historians of the growth and development of Egypt's formal industrial sector which, reflecting the intellectual climate in which it originated in the late sixties, has maintained a strong focus on Egyptian working-class history (Goldberg 1986, 1994; Beinin and Lockman 1987; Lockman 1994a, 1994b; Posusney 1997; Beinin 2001; Chalcraft 2007). Beginning from Egypt's industrialisation and integration into the capitalist economy in the late nineteenth century, the available literature documents a comprehensive chronological account of different periods of labour economics, unionisation, conflict and political involvement. The account is rich in details of wages, working conditions, instances of strikes, the formation of unions, and relations between unions, assorted political movements (including the Wafd, the communists and the Muslim Brotherhood) and the changing attitudes, policies and responses of successive Egyptian regimes. Many studies are founded, if only implicit, on a classically Marxist 'objectivist' conception of class, resulting in a teleological narrative (generally with a male gender bias) of working-class consciousness, exploitation and resistance determined by economic structural processes. One of the field's leading scholars, reflecting on its development and his own part in it, helped orientate and focus my own intended research with his comment that:

> To be most useful … future research will need to be guided by theoretical perspectives different from those that have hitherto largely dominated the field of labor history. Among other things, instead of using 'experience' as a way of directly linking objective circumstances with specific forms of worker consciousness, we will need to look at the discursive field within which there were available to workers several different (though interacting) ways of comprehending (or perhaps more precisely, structuring) their circumstances,

their experiences, and themselves ... including craft identities, gender identities and relations, kinship ties, loyalties to neighbourhoods, and what might be called popular-Islamic conceptions of justice and equity. (Lockman 1994a: 102)

When, after considerable vicissitudes, I was finally able to gain access to my intended 'field' of shop floor production and engaged in garment assembling work, I was struck by the *spatial* organisation of the workplace as a physical setting. My initial memory of joining a workplace of such size and complexity is best described as a mixture of shock and bewilderment as I look out on the vast open-plan layout, filled by row upon row of machinery and inhabited by a large workforce serving a relentless production process. A welter of sensory perceptions give the spatial landscape its manufacturing definition – the intensity of the clattering sounds; the distinctive colour schemes of the garments being put together for the subcontracting orders in hand; the oppressive heat; and the swirl and turbulence of large numbers of individual bodies in motion. Within this welter of sensory data, the visual cortex initially registers the production process as a range of discrete locations on the shop floor. As pieces of work get churned out in bulk by various units, each group appears much like any other, except in the nature of the particular item they produce, and any individual worker appears as just another anonymous face on the crowded shop floor.

As the days grow into weeks, these first overwhelming impressions subside and several issues become clearer. Firstly, the position of different units with respect to each other becomes better defined, as one unit's output becomes another's input, and the directional flow along the overall production process becomes apparent. At the same time, the finer division of labour within each unit emerges, as one begins to understand how the subdivision of skills is the structuring principle underlying the organisation of the workplace (Edwards 1979). Thus Cutting ceases to appear as a single team deploying homogeneous skills, but rather as a number of sub-units each specialising in a particular skill such as *fard* (rolling), *qas* (cutting) and *tarqim* (numbering). And within each unit, both the characters of individual workers, and the social relations between them, start to acquire clarity and granularity – so that what at first appeared simply as a sea of anonymous faces comes into focus as a social network between distinctive personalities. In these ways each unit in the division of shop floor labour becomes a *takhassus* (specialisation), distinct in itself and yet also an integral part of the intensive production process, and of the whole enterprise as firm and community.

As I came to relate my growing experience of the hurly-burly of the spatial organisation of the three-dimensional workplace to the neat and tidy, two-dimensional paper plans and shop floor layout diagrams that I had been given on arrival, the most powerful theoretical aid to my understanding was Henri Lefebvre's articulation and exploration of 'social space' (1997). Lefebvre sought to challenge abstracted methods of representation that turned social space into fetishised abstractions (space as blueprint), and to emphasise instead 'the lived experience of space'. The critique he developed distinguishes between three interrelated and mutually conditioned aspects of spatial practice: the experienced, the perceived and the imagined. 'Experienced spatial practice' refers to the physical and material flows and interactions that occur in and across space to assure material production as well as social reproduction; 'perceived spatial practice' includes all codes and 'knowledges' about spaces that allow the experienced spatial practices to be articulated and understood; and the 'imagined' dimension refers to the mental inventions that generate new meanings of possible spatial practices.[15] From this perspective, my emerging understanding of the spatial organisation of the factory workspace began to develop a multi-dimensional resonance with aspects of Lefebvre's analysis of 'the monument', in which, as he elaborated:

> The affective level – which is to say, the level of the body, bound to symmetries and rhythms – is transformed into a 'property' of monumental space, into symbols which are generally intrinsic parts of a politico-religious whole, into co-ordinated symbols. The component elements of such wholes are disposed according to a strict order for the purposes of the use of space: some at a first level, the level of the affective, bodily, lived experience ... some at a second level, that of the perceived, of socio-political signification; and some at a third level, the level of the conceived, where the dissemination of ... knowledge welds the members of society into a 'consensus', and in so doing confers upon them the status of 'subject'. Monumental space permits of continual back-and-forth between the private speech of ordinary conversations and the public speech of discourses, lectures, sermons, rallying-cries, and all theatrical forms of utterance. (1997: 142)

I could easily relate Lefebvre's first dimension of 'experienced spatial practice' to the flow of raw materials and part-completed garments along the production process according to which the shop floor was arranged. In my understanding, his concept of the second dimension of 'perceived space' was most readily apparent in management's 'lived experience' of the spatial arrangement of the factory shop floor. From management's perspective, the 'codes' and 'knowledges' by which the spatial ordering of the factory is articulated relate primarily to issues of control over a production process driven by tight deadlines and cost ceilings, set through intense competition for subcontracting orders from external clients. From this perspective the neat, black-and-white floor plan diagrams make perfect sense as technocratic representations of an efficient, orderly production process.

From the workers' point of view, however, things can be seen to be different. Their experience of the shop floor workspace seemed to me to be much more in line with what Lefebvre (1997: 142) described as 'sojourning in a poetic world', as they accommodated management's 'codes and knowledges' and used this understanding to move to Lefebvre's third level of 'imagined space', actively generating new meanings and possibilities for spatial practice, through which they challenged spatial domination by transforming it into an 'imagined community' and arena for the realisation of their wider hopes and aspirations.

Yet management was in no position simply to allow the workers a free hand in this respect. Management was driven by the need to maintain demanding quality standards, whilst also meeting tight deadlines for the completion of orders. Issues of power and control were therefore a central preoccupation, not only over the production process, but also over the predominantly young, mixed-gender workforce so actively engaged in their own imagined spatial experiences of the shop floor. During my initial months on the shop floor I was, however, at something of a loss to see where and how power and control were being exercised by management. Instead, production appeared to move effortlessly and apparently under its own volition, as I saw sheets of paper with order specifications appear from management offices, bales of cloth delivered at one gate, and the entire production process swing into action with supervisors governing production as a seamless operation until the assembled garments were packed and ready for collection.

With increasing familiarity with the work environment I came to realise that the rules and practices of the factory were designed to organise the institutional domain into two fundamental, clearly demarcated strata, *edara* (management) and *entag* (production), and give the working day of each its distinctive 'order'. *Edara* was responsible for paperwork, processed in separated spaces fitted out with equipment that define their nature of work: for example, desks and computer screens. *Entag* was designated to carry out the 'labouring' procedures, in separate spaces equipped with machinery appropriate to the stratum. This initial realisation led me to an engagement with Michel Foucault's celebrated studies of the nature of institutional power in prisons and mental asylums in nineteenth-century Europe (Foucault 1979b, 1997). It was Foucault's analyses of the regimentation of such institutions that strengthened my attempts to get beneath the surface of the operations of the factory. In particular, his 'eye of power' analysis of Jeremy Bentham's design for the ideal prison of the Panopticon (Foucault 1997a,b) resonated powerfully with my emerging understanding of the physical organisation of Fashion Express. It helped me see how the open-plan layout of the production landscape was principally organised for maximum visibility in both strata: the offices of *edara*, divided from one another by glass partitions; the well-marked exit and entry points to the factory; and the internal connecting passages, staircases and corridors all fell into place as 'strategic' resources utilised by management to expose developments in both *edara* and *entag* landscapes.

Armed with this insight, the human dimension to the regimentation of the institution also began to become more apparent. When I joined the production landscape, it was not difficult to identify the faces of 'law and order' as the security staff and supervisors who ceaselessly monitored the production landscape to detect 'irregularities' and who had the power to enforce fines. As I spent more time on the shop floor as a worker in the production lines, the internal system that integrated middle management to the production landscape revealed other more subtle forces that policed and exerted different levels of control. These included the relays of monitors 'sent down' from *edara* to collect hourly production figures from each assembly line, with the recorded totals collated and carefully drawn out in neat graphs and charts to be reviewed by authorised figures for the purpose of producing 'scientific' assessments. They also included visits by top management to the production zones at unpredictable or critical moments.

It was only later that a more extreme instance started to become clear of the intention of unseen, ceaseless, universal control which motivates Foucault's concept of the 'eye of power'. This took the form of an all-pervasive system of surveillance that rested on *gawasis* (spies), who informed top management of developments that they had had occasion to observe, overhear or hear about from others. Its effect was that I began to identify a radically different hierarchical arrangement cutting across the formal ordering of the production and managerial landscape, and revealing the power individual workers and middle management acquired through exercising their roles as informers (reporting across the formal lines and chains of command of line-management) to enable top management to exercise more intimate levels of control. As an established 'work practice', surveillance re-shaped the organisation of the production landscape quite differently from the straightforward hierarchical relationships I had found in the neat organograms with which I was presented when I first started my fieldwork.

This understanding of the ways in which this all-pervasive system of surveillance functioned led me to engage with another of Foucault's insights, namely his analysis of power as 'more a verb than a noun', essentially something that is performed in a micro-context and serves as a strategy, rather than something that is 'possessed' by one party in a unidirectional power relationship (as in the conventional Marxist model of power as a straightforward relationship between oppressor and oppressed). In *Power/Knowledge* (1988), Foucault describes how:

> I am not referring to Power with a capital P, dominating and imposing its rationality upon the totality of the social body. In fact, there are power

relations. They are multiple; they have different forms, they can be in play in family relations, or within an institution, or an administration ... Power must be analyzed as something which circulates, or something which only functions in the form of a chain ... Power is employed and exercised through a netlike organisation ... Individuals are the vehicles of power, not its points of application. (Foucault 1982: 38, 98)

This analysis provided me with a theoretical framework within which to pursue an analysis of the covert networks of power relationships – not simply between managers, supervisors and workers, but perhaps even more so within each of these groups and the many sub-groups and individuals that constituted them – the empirical results of which form a central feature of my ethnography.

When I came to examine how power was asserted, exerted and resisted, I soon saw that the factory's formal systems and processes formed only part of the picture. Power emerged as many other mutations within the factory. Ties of kinship between workers exerted their own power dynamics on the shop floor, not dissimilar to those in operation in the wider sociocultural world outside. Experience of sharing a common geography (e.g. travelling on the bus to work from a particular neighbouring province, or having been evacuated from Port Said during the war years to a particular city elsewhere in Egypt) also created bonds between the individuals concerned, which were amenable to the interplay of power. Religion exerted its own power in different ways, ranging from strongly conservative positions imported from the wider world, to the more tolerant interpretations of tradition of the shop floor. Underlying much of it was a gender dynamic which grew more multifaceted and complex the more I became immersed in it. This growing understanding of the multidimensionality of power within the workplace environment led me to engage with another of Foucault's central insights, namely his distinctive development of the analytical principle of 'discourse'. Although the concept is difficult to pin down, discourse can perhaps best be understood as a mix of images, cultural products and social practice which comprise systems whose meanings are expressed not only in language but also in other signifying practices (Lockman 1994a).

Far from being a reflection of an already existing reality, in Foucault's view discourse is the medium through which reality is ordered. Discourses are normative in the sense that they convey norms of behaviour and standards of what counts as desirable or undesirable, proper or improper. So as well as ordering reality, discourse also defines difference. 'Subjects' are formed – in many ways form themselves – in terms of what they come to recognise and understand from the discourses in which they are involved. And since any individual will be involved in a multiplicity of discourses, and linked to other discourses, there is an inherent subjectivity and openness in the process of subject formation which renders the outcomes essentially open-ended.

Foucault has also explored the complicity of both parties within any power relationship, emphasising that:

> Discourses are tied up with power and serve to reinforce or undermine relations of power between people ... Discourse can be both an instrument and an effect of power, but also a hindrance, a stumbling block, a point of resistance and a starting point for an opposing strategy ... Discourse transmits and produces power, it reinforces it, but also undermines and exposes it, renders it fragile and makes it possible to thwart it. (Foucault 1978: 100–1)

The more the complex dynamics of control and resistance in operation on the shop floor came into view, the more I could see discourse as relevant not only to the exercise of power, but also to its contestation. This stimulated an engagement with de Certeau's exploration (1984) of ways the supposedly 'powerless' have of seizing opportune moments to 'trick the order of things', and Scott's analysis (1990) of how public performances of deference towards power can incorporate 'hidden transcripts' which are themselves critiques of power expressed in action and language.

Foucault's multi-layered exposition of discourse facilitated an analysis of the unspoken, tacit rules of behaviour that I could see in operation all around me, which together framed the *modus vivendi* of the workplace. As I will show, concepts of *ihtiram* (respectability) and *ikhlaas* (loyalty) ordered reality for the inhabitants of the factory workspace. They also prescribed norms of behaviour, defined difference, and fostered the generation of multiple subjective identities – all within the complex web of power relations, energised by a two-way dynamic involving attempts both to enforce power and to contest it, that formed the framework of an overarching paradigm of the 'firm as family'.

As I applied these insights to my particular interest in issues of gender, I began to notice how it was relevant not only to *actions* individuals were taking on the shop floor but also to the distinctive workplace *personas* some were crafting for themselves. Examples of gendered actions of which I became conscious often related to the recent introduction of male workers within a previously all-female shop floor: these included the exaggeratedly masculinised swagger with which a male cutter would wield the heavy electrical cutters that were the tools of his trade, or the almost caricatured panache with which some of the runners responsible for transferring garment components from one point of the assembly line to another would 'drive' their trolleys, swerving to a halt with the air of a young man showing off his first sports car. Examples of gendered workplace personas included the changes which female supervisors crafted whilst at work, in their bodily posture, the register and modulation of their voices, their gait and their clothing (Chakravarti 2011).

Presentation of self on the one hand, and action on the other, are both aspects of performance. My growing appreciation of how this played out within the workplace environment resonated with Judith Butler's 'performative' theory of gender (1990, 1993). Building on Foucault's analysis of discourses as productive of the identities they are representing, Butler argues that the notion of performance does not separate the doer from the doing, since 'we become subjects from our performances and the performances of others towards us' (1990: 140).

Butler argues that gender differences and gendered meanings are effects of contingent social practices, and so opens up the possibility that they can be remade in multiple ways. Her emphasis on gender as performative also has the effect of focusing on the ways in which the performance of masculinity and femininity is contextual, and is interdependent with the performance of other aspects of identity such as class and ethnicity. It follows that what is drawn out is a script that can be variable, and that the ideals of femininity and masculinity which it lays out can change over time. This aspect of 'iterability' is significant in Butler's work, insisting that meaning is not fixed by its position in a system or structure, but acquires a temporal dimension which can be captured in language and its relation to gender norms. Its repetition in different contexts allows different meanings to emerge. As she argues:

> If we repeat performances in different contexts then different meanings can emerge which can undermine and subvert dominant ones [so that] the coherence of a unified package of gender/sex/sexuality is pulled apart. (1993: 226)

Gender was a central focus of my interest from the outset, and led me to an early engagement with studies of women in the globalised economy. These issues came into focus through accounts of how globalisation's reallocation of labour between developed and developing countries resulted in manufacturing sectors which are 'female-led and export-led' (Joekes 1987). Economic issues were brought to the forefront of early debates on gender through focusing on the demand side of labour, and the economic relations through which women were incorporated in the employment opportunities made available to them.[16]

These analyses of the systematic exploitation of women within globalised capitalism's need for labour efficiency and flexibility had limitations derived from their treating gender as a given, with history something that is 'added on'. The results helped construct an image of the 'type' of worker best suited to capitalism's evolving needs, in the shape of a myth of a global productive femininity that is homogenous in its low levels of skill, and passive and docile in the face of rampant capitalist management (Lim 1990; Kabeer 2000). The 'nimble-fingered docility' image of women workers in the garment industry has however been contested by more recent ethnographies which, by exploring the gendering processes of the workplace, show that how gender works is indeed central, but not in the ways established in the earlier literature. Salzinger's (1997, 2002, 2003) research in four of Mexico's *maquila* factories interrogates the global myth of the 'docile and dextrous' icon, and exposes this as the construction of a contemporary trans-nationally produced fantasy. While gender continues to be a fundamental feature of global production, Salzinger reveals femininity as a trope – a structure of meaning – through which workers drawn into the industry are understood, and production is designed.

In a similar vein, Lee's (1993, 1995, 1997) ethnographic work in two electronic assembling plants belonging to the same company but operating in different locations in south China, along with Yelvington's (1995) factory ethnography in a Caribbean workplace and Hewamanne's study of Sri Lanka's EPZs (2008), have looked at how categories such as class and ethnicity are endemic to the ways in which power is constructed and contested in the material productive arrangements of specific contexts. Their pioneering insights reveal that within a culture of domination, local features and attributes are used in the exercise of power as much as in its resistance. Moreover, given that domination for the most part is also insidious, hidden and contorted, the roles these categories play become more significant in understanding the perpetuation and reinforcement of patterns of domination and its links to production politics.

I also gained insights from recent ethnographies looking at women and employment in Egypt and elsewhere in the Middle East, even though these have tended to focus on the growing informal labour force into which an increasing number of women are drawn either as home-based workers, wage workers or as workers in small family-run workshops and ateliers (White 1994; El-Kholy 2002; Secor 2003; Dedeoglu 2004). El-Kholy's (2002) community study in Cairo found that different forms of employment corresponded with life-cycle phases, so that piecework and home-based work attracted married women, while unmarried adolescents were drawn to relatively better paid wage-work in *warshas* (small sweatshops). The strategic trade-off between wage-labour and the patriarchal expectations of their communities expresses itself in social practices such as the ostentatious display of defloration, through which female respectability and reputation are publicly reaffirmed.

The ethnographies by White (1994) and Dedeoglu (2004) focus more on how family-run, small-scale garment-making firms appear to have resolved the gender paradox of allowing women to work among strangers by restricting their mobility within a strictly familial enterprise. Their social and gender identity carefully disguises their labour and financial contribution to household budgets. A common theme is the ambivalence which arises around women's categorisation as wage-workers, and the inherent gender paradox between income-generating activities and the complexities associated with working with total strangers. These issues have been interrogated more recently in Ismail's research (2006) in Bulaq, one of Cairo's new quarters. She shows how state practices of heavy surveillance have altered gender relations, leading the women of Bulaq to become more mobile, and to challenge men's fear of community gossip, and their demands for increased Islamic observance, as patriarchal social control practices and masculine enactment stemming from their poor economic prospects.

Inspired as I was by these accounts of Middle Eastern women's labour, I could see from an early stage that my study was going to be different. I was taking as my setting a workplace where women were not merely provisional members of an informal labour force, but instead an integral part of the operations of a formal industrial sector – one that, moreover, had long been identified as female-dominated. Yet the sources summarised above provided me with inspiration and material for reflection through my exploration and analysis of the issues I encountered, which I relate in the following ethnography. In my conclusion I return to these sources, and reflect on how my findings led me to reinforce, contend with, and on occasions even to refute, aspects of the scholarly body which they constitute.

Method

Gaining research access to a factory turned out to be a lengthy and laborious process involving seven dispiriting months of approaches, negotiations, rebuffs and false starts with a range of companies and institutions (including the Egyptian Trade Union Federation). The wary, defensive and sometimes hostile reactions I received showed me the suspicion with which my proposed research subject (blue-collar factory workers) and proposed research method (qualitative participant observation) were widely viewed. At various times I found myself being suspected of being an undercover tax inspector, a spy for the competition, and even a secret agent for U.S./British intelligence. It was made clear to me that factory workplaces and their workforces constituted an *'alam khaas* (separate, distinctive world), which would be impossibly difficult if not downright dangerous (morally as well as physically) for anyone from *hita tanya* (some far-removed place).

The extent to which gaining research access in institutional settings and organisations can turn out to be, to borrow a phrase, 'a game of chance, not skill' (Buchanan, Boddy and McCalman 1988: 56) was confirmed when a passing comment from a personal friend (herself unconnected with manufacturing, labour or government) put me in touch with one of her acquaintances in the NGO sector, who unexpectedly opened the way to my eventual research site in Port Said. The Export Processing Zone's overt reasons for accepting a researcher from a U.K.-based university turned out to be closely tied to its specific economic conditions, as described above, and ambitions to boost the legitimacy and status of its new garment-for-export enterprises 'in the eyes of the world'.

In addition, although there was a common consensus among Zone officials that, as one of them put it to me, 'the hoarding mentality of the *nouveau riche* has turned us into an inward-looking insular society', the decisive factor proved to be the personally supportive attitude of the proprietor of Fashion Express. As I came to understand the dynamics of the firm more fully, I formed my own thoughts as to what might have motivated him in going against the prevailing winds and allowing me into his factory – points to which it will be more appropriate for me to return to in my conclusion. It nevertheless soon became clear to me that his personal interest in, and support for, my work and my well-being was registered throughout the factory as bestowing a special status known as *il-brestij* (prestige), providing a license to operate and the extra leverage that came from operating under his *awamir* (direct orders, personal commands). A flavour of his behind-the-scenes interventions on my behalf is provided by the reports I received of his reply to complaints from *edara* that I was letting the class side down by engaging in shop floor *entag* labour:

> She's doing her *bahth* (research project) – and she knows what she's doing. If tomorrow morning you see her taking 'Am Naguib's ('Uncle' Naguib, the old cleaner's) broomstick and sweeping the floor in *Qas* (Cutting), you're to just leave her to it!

Not that I was being given carte blanche access to all areas of the factory's or the Fahmy family's operations. I soon found out that the proprietor's and his top management colleagues' contracting and subcontracting deals were firmly out of bounds, and only *edara* and *entag* were to be available for research. As a member of Top Management explained to me during my very last month in the factory, visibly relishing his insider knowledge and status:

> Qasim gave us the green light to offer assistance and be cooperative. But [with an enigmatic chuckle] you do understand, don't you? There are two kinds of green lights – one with results, and the other without.

Even armed with this degree of top-level personal support, I nevertheless found that Gellner and Hirsch's insights (2001) into how access, even once granted, has to be continuously renegotiated (and also continuously scrutinised for ways in which it may be transforming the research) remained highly relevant right until I concluded my fieldwork in 2005. My expressed interest in getting involved in the production side of shop floor labour led to my being launched on the standard trajectory for any new female entrant joining the firm with no previous experience. I moved from one stage of production to the next, starting with unskilled work in the Cutting Department (such as counting garments and doing simple arithmetical calculations) until I built up some basic skills that qualified me to join other labour units as a quality control (QC) worker. This progression involved acquiring shop floor experience across a spectrum of diverse *takhasusat* (specialisations) and produced its own insights into how varied the experience of work was in separate labour units. Each labour unit had, I found, developed its own unique style and 'system' for the orderly arranging of work relations, and was vigilant in guarding its territory and distinctive social environment.

For the workers, my insistence on participation went further than simply seeking to experience the work, or get a feel for production. It was rather taken as showing a commitment to take part in the working environment and put up, as everyone did, with the conditions of labour, day in and day out, for months on end. It was about enduring the heat on the shop floor, the deafening din of the sewing machines, the yelling of supervisors, the flaring of tempers, the hours of boredom, the shop floor games, the vigorous trade in sweets, chewing gum and lollipops, and the complicated trail of fights over love entanglements. It mattered to them that I 'stuck at it' when work shifted to late hours, or when I was moved to other units to meet pressing deadlines, and at weekends when not all the workforce was required to be present. As I built up rapport with my co-workers through this progression, I came to recognise sub-groups within the 450-strong workforce differentiated by their regions of origin, as well as their specific workstations.

The factory's *salat* (Assembly Halls) were the most prestigious units of labour, the lifeline of the factory, with the highest wages (and potential for fines) and where all levels of skill were spoken of as requiring 'an eye' (*il-ayyn* – implying smart, experienced working). *Il-ayyn* became a metaphor that, in multiple senses of the word, coloured my experience of labour as a worker. The deafening din in the halls made it difficult to hear workers during the course of the working day and left me lip-reading machinists, a task that became easier with time. From where I was standing on the shop floor, watching doors and exits, I would identify a new face, and speculate if the visitor was a client, an official from the Zone or a new recruit. If my curiosity was aroused then, prevented from leaving my station, I resorted to asking for information from cleaners, supervisors and monitors who were licensed to walk around. At other times, a small and soft 'pssst' sound (which strangely enough was audible over the din) would be enough for others closer to the visiting party to relay the news back to me. Watching people's movements on the shop floor, and simultaneously carrying on with the repetitive task of folding and unfolding garments in rapid succession, my eyes gliding over seams, zippers and lines of sewing stitches, bending forward to mark faulty garments with chalk or stickers, returning them to machinists facing me or passing them to the machinists behind me, I watched the world go by. I saw how social and work scenarios were played out, how new developments unfolded, how old *aflam* (romantic shop floor gossip) could resume with a new twist, and my insatiable curiosity was aroused just like everybody else's.

Cultivating a 'watchful eye' also enabled me to see the garments I was inspecting in a new light – not simply as piles of material cut and stitched in set stages, but as products with a 'life' of their own. Each *marka* (brand order from an international client) was intended for a specific market, demonstrated visually in the range of sizes required, with the U.S. commanding particularly gigantic sizes and the Far East the smallest. Each order was considered to have a 'spirit', referred to in shop floor slang as its *irfa*, infusing the garment in question with its own distinct shop floor personality and history. There was one order (subcontracted from factory T) that left a stubborn black dye on everyone's hands that was difficult to wash off; another that brought an infestation of fleas to the shop floor; a third that had to be sent back to the assembly halls after the zippers burst in the laundry (where the machines had mistakenly been set to the wrong temperature); and a fourth, even more unfortunate order which when sent to be stone-washed had come out *fatafit* (in shreds), a calamity that brought Qasim Bey to the shop floor to 'see with his own eyes'. The range and variety of adjectives given to the *irfa* of each garment order created the *khanqa* (jittery and suffocating) atmosphere of one working day if not the next. It was the unpredictability of each *irfa*, set against the repetitive movement of hands and eyes and stationary positions of shop floor, that plunged me into the rhythms of *entag* as a dynamic process. In the constant rush to meet quotas and keep close tabs on figures, and through the ties cemented between workers in each line and station, the captivating and almost addictive nature of assembling work became real to me as in the supervisors' proud description as the factory's *shughl il-matbakh* (kitchen work, implying the heart of its operation).

'Watchful eye' observation also became an invaluable tool for identifying the implicit rules that governed developments in the internal politics of the shop floor, especially its close entanglements with production issues. It enabled me to gain a deeper grasp of how territorial membership in different shop floor labour units and networks was a vital survival skill deployed in negotiations with management, and understand how the dynamic interplay of gender and class was instrumental in shaping specific outcomes – issues I discuss at length in chapters 2 and 4. I saw how the sharing of the latest snippets of news was part of an intricate and all-absorbing web of 'insider' knowledge, operating as a surveillance machine in which the entire workforce were the prime participants. I found much truth in the commonly repeated saying that *il-masna' malush asrar* (the factory has no secrets). The underpinning dual function of 'observing while being observed' demanded the skills to read any signs of change, to keep up to date with new developments, to evaluate how the analysis of any single episode fits with other agendas and, finally, whether to wait or to take more assertive action to affect developments, judging who was best qualified to mobilise others to undertake this task.

Reading about the instability of garment work (Phizachlea 1990; Green 1996, 2002; Rath 2002; Collins 2003; Hale and Wills 2005) and experiencing it first-hand on the shop floor formed two separate realities. Under the wildly fluctuating 'famine and feast' rhythms of external demand for labour on the shop floor, I came to understand how the perennially vexing issue of the delayed payment of wages was a double-edged sword. On the one hand, it was exploited by management to discourage workers from leaving the premises during periods of contractless 'famine' (which could extend for as long as three months), and was deeply troubling in the brutality with which it exacerbated workers' financial difficulties. But, on the other hand, paying workers on time simply gave them a window of opportunity to decamp to other factories where there was work to be had, emphasizing the stark shortages of skilled labour within the Zone. I came to understand that I had to accept, in the same way as other workers with more experience of dealing with it, the economic environment as inherently unstable and unpredictable, and focus my attention on whatever issues turned up, however unexpectedly, each day. As it was not feasible to identify clear patterns in the cycles of feast and famine, and as there were evident contradictions between internal rumours explaining the causes of any particular slump and what could be seen to be taking place outside the factory, fears of closure were always real and pervasive. In the flux of unpredictable work orders and continually fluctuating workforce numbers, everyone involved in production was left trying to make sense of chaos, not knowing whether to stay with the firm or explore other employment avenues.

Periods of slump allowed me to carry out semi-structured interviews with groups of workers. These threw into sharp relief the different provinces and locations from which 'migrant' workers came, and the way in which, under normal conditions of production, they were dispersed across different shop floor units. Girls, and at times boys, from the same region would sit together and participate in these informal gatherings. Each would chip in with her or his version of events. Some were comparatively forthcoming in their views, others preferred to listen quietly, speaking up only on other occasions, or preferring to arrange one-to-one sessions later on. They gained more confidence once they recognised that they had the option to rephrase an answer or a question. Often they would correct me by reflecting on the question, rephrasing it in different ways for greater precision, and adding new dimensions to the different details that would personalise their account. It was possible in this way to explore how recruitment operated through regional networks, and to develop my understanding of the importance of *taraabut* (togetherness, solidarity) within the workplace, issues which I explore in detail in chapter 2.

Other group conversations were organised according to the hierarchical structure of the workplace. The female supervisors' staffroom was one such distinct hierarchical space to which I was eventually granted 'honorary membership' access. The room was formally known as *odit il-ishraf* (supervisors' room) though it was given by *edara* upstairs more pejorative names such as *wikr il-dababir* (the beehive, implying where plots are laid and conspiracies hatched). It was like the teachers' staffroom in any educational institution. It was the only room in the factory with a fan (though all it did was blow hot air), and the *mushrifat*'s (female supervisors') daily lunch of choice was also a mark of their status. Their strong sense of forming a *shilla* (a group of peers) was vital to their sense of status and rank in *entag* and in the overall structure of the firm. Their many topics of 'staffroom chitchat' covered a range of themes from their personal lives and relations with one another. They also discussed current issues regarding the work environment, sharing the latest snippets of information to have reached any one of them, what to make of it, the best way to keep themselves up to date with all the goings on, and whether to wait or to intervene – their conversation revolving around playing and shaping politics on the shop floor. Many of the decisions they took were based on their intensive observation of the individual circumstances of workers on the shop floor, striking a balance between their dual roles as shop floor controllers and social workers on the scene, which I discuss in greater detail in chapter 4.

Material derived from the *odit il-ishraf*, with its mix of the personal and professional, revealed much about appropriate gender roles and the assumptions underlying them. Whereas I was inclined to take any worker's request at face value, the female supervisors did the reverse. They categorically assumed the worst, trying to fathom the 'real' reason behind the declared one, adamant in their conviction that some hidden interest was lurking there, and in their strong suspicions over the ways subordinates tried to trick them. Female nature was construed as a customised *tarkiba* (mix, as ingredients in a dish) of tactics. Even displays of meek docility in the face of authority (whether hierarchical or patriarchal) were instantly suspected as put-ons, performances staged for other, ulterior motives. Often this declared female characteristic of being *adra* (capable, implying trickery) was admired, especially when it came to pranks the girls staged on unsuspecting male co-workers, as when a male worker arrived pleading to be relieved of the unsigned heated love letters they had stuffed into his jacket pockets signed with the letter N (there were four girls in the line with the same initial). These anecdotes provided rich material for reading the complex gender dynamics at play on the mixed-gender shop floor, and led me to contest enduring images in the literature characterising female workers in the globalised garment industry as passive, dutiful exemplars of 'nimble-fingered docility'.

Other activities conducted during slack periods of production involved day outings organised by different teams, with the supervisors ever present to keep an eye on their workers. These involved trips to the seaside or to one of Port Said's many street markets, with the girls scouring the range of clothes and scarves on offer for the most sought-after items. I was intrigued and amused to see how the skills acquired in Quality Control were deployed to scrutinise potential purchases, turning girls into shrewd shoppers. The array of objects they bought for their *gihaaz* (prenuptial purchases to furnish the marital home) were up-market products that led me to identify with greater clarity how marriage and prospects of social mobility were part of the class struggle to escape the poverty trap, making real their aspirations as working women. These were also evident on the shop floor itself in the ways in which the landscape of production easily shifted into a space of avid consumption, with different workers hawking and snapping up a wide range of products through *commerce a la valise* transactions or catalogue purchases (activities which I describe in chapter 3), all to improve marriage prospects and, through investing in the collective spirit of *taraabut* (togetherness), to keep the dreams of change alive. Getting invited to attend engagement and wedding functions drove home to me how far these workers had come towards reaching these rising expectations and new heights of consumerism in relations of their choice.

The most serious ethical issue I encountered arose during a major shake-up of Fashion Express's operations by a new firm that was said to be British. For the first time, this rekindled the issue of access – throwing into disarray the process of renegotiating permission to continue the project. While the much-emphasised special status bestowed by the family firm and the proprietor had provided me with some degree of covert protection and a deeper insight into the complex blend of 'real' and 'metaphorical' kinship, I suddenly found myself in a changed and more hostile climate. As a researcher from a British university, I was suspected of being an undercover 'spy' employed to provide the new (purportedly British) firm with data that jeopardised *asrar il-masna* (the secrets of the firm). However, in the intricate entanglements of power and opportunity, not all workers saw my potential 'mole' function in negative terms. If anything, they associated me, in their down-to-earth way, with bringing *il-kheir* (blessings) to the firm, with the resulting opportunity to gain more shop floor power an advantage to be exploited. After my months of rapport building, it was hard to tell whether the contradictory rumours and speculations spreading like wildfire were having the effect of making me more of an 'insider' and one of them – or a total 'stranger'. I eventually chose not to treat the episode of 'regime change' as a distraction to my research, but to analyse ways in which the encounter between two visions of change in labour relations highlighted the tacit rules that governed the social contract of the 'firm as family', and the distinctive work environment this discourse had carefully and purposefully cultivated in difficult economic times.

Ordering and animating the ethnography

'Writing up' is a deceptively short and simple term for the transformation of fieldwork research into an academic text. After I returned from Port Said, I could not immediately think of a way of arranging my research material so as to convey both the immediacy and the complexity of my fieldwork immersion in the manufacturing world of the factory.

At first, I attempted to order my material according to the 'life story' of a garment making its way along the production line, from raw material to finished, boxed product – rather as Snyder (2008) traces the journey of a pair of jeans from raw denim to manufactured garment to retail commodity, in order to analyse the globalised garment economy. This offered the merit of allowing me to structure my material according to the different production units in which I worked while collecting data. But the fluidity of labour, with workers being switched from one unit to another according to the demands of production, or coming and going according to their own priorities, meant that 'characters' and their issues were refusing to stay neatly in boxes marked cutting, assembly, quality control, etc. This approach also made it impossible to capture the multi-dimensional nature of the working relationships I had experienced, which were 'vertical' (linking *entag* to *edara* to top management and the proprietor) as much as 'horizontal' (within and between production units). It also ran the risk of impoverishing my material, giving prominence to anything and everything to do with production, but leaving no space for consideration of all the activity over and above production which also characterised the factory environment.

I have finally settled on a thematic approach, organising my ethnography according to what seem to me to be the main principles and personalities that combine to create the distinctive world of Fashion Express, and the ways in which class, gender and religion are interwoven within it. The first of my thematic chapters, chapter 2, is built around the stratagems and principles through which the proprietor of Fashion Express, faced with intense competition from other factory owners for scarce labour, moves beyond the 'family firm' to craft a distinctive workplace environment of 'firm as family', with himself at its head as 'proprietor-patriarch'. I explore the various control mechanisms he and his management team seek to deploy in order to meet demanding contractual deadlines and quality standards, and the forms of workforce resistance with which these are met. Chapter 3 switches the focus to the workforce, describing ways in which, accommodating management's chosen principles of 'firm as family', and in many cases turning these back on themselves, they appropriate the workplace and convert it into a zone for the realisation of their aspirations for romantic and material fulfilment. Chapter 4 focuses on a particular sub-group of the workforce-family, the 'daughters and sons of the factory' as the shop floor supervisors have been christened by the patriarch-proprietor. Their role is crucial in disciplining and nurturing the workforce, in maintaining production through all the interruptions and hiccups that beset the shop floor on a daily basis, and in reinforcing the working culture of 'firm as family'. I highlight ways in which they perform this critical, multi-dimensional role, including the creation and performance of distinctive gendered labour personalities – and how these can come into conflict with socioreligious norms (and what happens when they do). Chapter 5 examines the factory's encounter with a foreign organisational scheme that attempts to modernise the factory. It pulls together the major themes analysed previously, and, by demonstrating how the workforce reassert their preferred paradigm of 'firm as family', draws into sharper focus the issues relevant to the identity and raison d'être of a workplace caught between global and local forces. In conclusion I summarise my findings by referring back to the research questions I had defined at the outset, and reflect on possible resonances between my localised experience of labour unrest in 2004 and all that followed in Egypt's Arab Spring uprising of 2011 and its aftermath.

Notes

1. 'Now Overthrow the Workplace Mubaraks, Urges Labour Activist', *Guardian* 20 May 2011.
2. *www.arabawy.org*; *https://twitter.com/3arabawy*; *http://www.youtube.com/user/3arabawy*; *http://www.youtube.com/user/3arabawy*.
3. *http://www.nytimes.com/2014/05/14/opinion/friedman-the-square-people-part-1.html*.
4. *http://www.arabawy.org/2011/02/12/permanent-revolution.html*.
5. Beinin 2010: 16, 2012a: 93, 2012b; Abdalla 2012: 2; Gunning and Baron 2013: 61. Beinin cautions that 'these statistics should be considered approximations'. For the five

years for which data is available I have – for indicative purposes – split the total number of collective incidents pro rata to the number of individual workers who took part in them.
6. The pivotal role of the Mahalla textiles complex in Egypt's labour history, and in the events leading up to the January 2011 revolution, is examined in the the Aljazeera TV documentary *The Factory: A Glimpse into Life inside Egypt's Mahalla Textile Factory – A Cauldron of Revolt where Workers Inspired an Uprising* (Bocchialini and El Gazwy 2012).
7. 'Unprecedented strike wave sweeps Egypt', posted by Ed on *https://libcom.org/news/unprecedented-strike-wave-sweeps-egypt-this-week-14022007*.
8. 'Esco ordeal ends', *Al-Ahram* (745), 2–8 June 2005, *(http://weekly.ahram.org.eg/2005/745/eg9.htm)*; 'We are not for sale – ignored by the press and sidelined by the authorities the Esco textile workers are on strike' *Al-Ahram* (732), 2–9 March 2005 *(http://weekly.ahram.org.eg/2005/732/eg63.htm.)*
9. Others included chemicals, leather goods, food processing, agricultural processing machinery and electrical appliances manufacturing, as well as petroleum and maritime services.
10. *http://www.egyptindependent.com/news/ngos-and-activists-protest-save-architecture-port-said*
11. English gloss added by author.
12. The alternative 'Free on Board' (FOB) system is a different arrangement, as described in my concluding chapter, under which the contractor is required to purchase all materials and components in advance, and only recoups these outlays once the client has paid for the finished garments.
13. The firm initially opened for business in the 10th of Ramadan City, then subsequently relocated to Isma'iliyyaa and then to Mansura (Map 0.1).
14. Detailed workforce statistics are provided in the Appendix.
15. Lefebvre's 'imagined dimension' relates to de Certeau's complementary challenge to abstract conceptions of space, which emphasises the ways in which the subjective experience of everyday practices imbue a space with its distinctive inhabited quality (de Certeau 1984). It also links with Anderson's development of an 'imagined community' (Anderson 1983).
16. See for example, Fernandez-Kelly 1983; Kung 1983; Lim 1983, 1990; Elson 1986, 1992; Leacock and Safa 1986; Mies 1986; Safa 1986, 1995; Enloe 1989; Ong 1990; Salaff 1990; Ward 1990; Wolf 1992; Tiano 1994; Chhachhi and Pittin 1996; Fernandes 1997a; Mills 1999.

Chapter 2

FIRM AS FAMILY – CONTROL AND RESISTANCE

Five months after I returned to London I learned that Fashion Express had succumbed to the financial problems besetting it, and finally ceased production. Concerned for the welfare of my former co-workers, I was reassured to learn from phone calls that many had found jobs in other factories in the Export Processing Zone. The Director General of the Zone told me that, although their wages there were higher, they nevertheless complained bitterly about their change of fortune. The explanation for this was concise: 'Whereas at one time we thought Qasim was spoiling them, we now see that he had *'amal gaw usari* (nurtured a family)'.

In this chapter I draw on my participant-observer fieldwork notes from the time before the factory had closed, to describe how the proprietor of Fashion Express, faced with intense competition from other factory owners for scarce labour, builds on the management model of the 'family firm' to craft a distinctive workplace environment of 'firm as family', with himself at its head as 'patriarch-proprietor'.

The circumstances in which he does this are, however, turbulent and challenging. Although the Export Processing Zone projects an external image which emphasises its stable, well-trained workforce it is not, in reality, well regarded as a source of employment, and so suffers from chronic labour shortages. The different garment factories located within it are therefore in a constant state of cut-throat competition for workers to man their production lines in order to deliver contract orders to tight deadlines and demanding quality standards. In this struggle, Fashion Express is at an inherent disadvantage owing to its widespread reputation as a 'fallen factory' which, though once humming with orders for prestigious international clients, has since fallen on hard times.

In these circumstances, Qasim Bey's response is to invoke the Fahmy family's reputation as one of Port Said's elite families, closely associated with its social, economic and political developments both before and after its economic restructuring following the 1973 war. His further, crucial, stratagem is to extend the mantle of the family image to include not only his blood kin, but also the entire workforce of his factory. This construction of a metaphorical 'firm as family', with himself both proprietor and patriarch, is the foundation of Qasim Bey's strategy for attracting workers into his production lines.

It is seen in action in the codified (though implicit) rules according to which he appoints close relatives to top management positions in the firm, and fosters among them an ethos that emphasises both filial loyalty and sibling rivalry. I identify *ikhlaas* (loyalty) as one of the underpinning principles according to which Fashion Express operates, as each member of top management sets up his own network of *mukhlis* (loyal) employees in *edara* and *entag*. I show how they are engaged in a constant, pervasive exercise in surveillance, vying with each other to demonstrate their loyalty to the person of the patriarch-proprietor, whose chosen persona is in turn reinforced through his all-seeing, all-knowing presence.

A second principle I identify is that of *ihtiram* (respectability), which Qasim Bey draws from the reputation of his *'aila* (family, in the sense of lineage) and extends to his metaphorical *beit* (family, in the sense of current household). I describe how the construction of *ihtiram* in the sense of social respectability can be seen to be in operation in the recruiting practices of the firm. *Ihtiram* is also extended to moral respectability, a critical issue for a 'fallen firm' seeking to recruit a predominantly young, mixed-gender labour force to work in the sort of close physical proximity prohibited under wider social and religious norms. Enforcing moral respectability is seen to be a second purpose of the all-pervading system of surveillance, reinforced by the religiosity in which the workplace is seeped.

The metaphor of 'firm as family' is taken up by the workforce, most literally through the widespread practice of informal recruitment. The metaphorical 'firm as family' is further strengthened by the ways in which workers turn the system of surveillance on itself, transforming it from an instrument of management control into a mechanism for reinforcing their sense of solidarity, expressed in the central principle of *taraabut* (togetherness). The family metaphor adds a dimension of meaning to *taraabut* that takes on quasi-religious overtones in the workforce's chosen means of articulating entitlement.

Throughout the discussion I highlight the ways in which issues of class, gender and religion intersect, as proprietor-patriarch and workforce-family collaborate to identify their shared interests in the firm. A coda to the chapter, describing how the entire workforce throws itself into Qasim Bey's campaign in 2004 for election to the Upper House of the Egyptian Parliament, shows the family-as-firm in operation.

Il-kebir: the role of the proprietor-patriarch

The Export Processing Zone's official shop-window to the world of globalised trade invokes Port Said's heritage to explain, in idiosyncratic English, how 'Port Said had suffered a lot from all wars in Egypt since Pharos till Islamic conquest and at the end the 6th October war. So all the governments rolled [ruled] Egypt believed they must compensate Port Said. So, in 1975 Port Said was declared a free zone...'[1] and emphasise how, as a consequence, '... it prepared thousands of trained workers and administrators ... Of course, the Free Zone was the key to find the treasure called Egyptians...' so that its current advantages prominently include '...ampleness of trained and ordinary labor with low salaries than other free zones'. The official narrative of a stable and well-qualified workforce is also one which the owners and managers of the firms in the Zone seek every opportunity to reinforce.

This became clear at a seminar I attended in August 2004 organised by a local NGO. Its purpose was to affirm the suitability of Port Said for inclusion in a new U.S. government initiative called the Qualified Industrial Zone (QIZ) programme. The programme aimed to promote trade and economic relations between Israel and other countries in the Middle East by giving access to U.S. markets for garments manufactured in Middle Eastern countries with at least 11.7 per cent of their components sourced from Israeli accessory manufacturers. The seminar (held in a conference room on the first floor of one of Port Said's poshest five star hotels) was presided over by the Chairman of a local NGO, known affectionately by his Port Said business colleagues as *Embirator il-sina'at il-saghira* (the Emperor of small-scale industries) – an informal title stemming not only from his dominance of the NGO scene, but also his access to foreign NGO funding to cover the costs of such events (including generous refreshments and meals, as well as substantial per diems for all participants). He had recently led a fact-finding delegation to study established QIZs already in operation in Jordan and Dubai. The delegation had reported back in glowing terms on the 'unprecedented prosperity' that these were bringing about 'in areas previously desert', in terms of an increase in the number of factories, a rise in the supply and participation of skilled labour (though whether these were nationals or migrant workers was left unsaid), and the profits being made by investors in the QIZs.[2]

At the seminar were representatives of twelve of the seventeen garment factories of the *istithmar*, seated round a U-shaped table, draped with green felt and laden with a generous array of refreshments. My field notes record how, noting the high turnout, the General Manager of a Yemeni clothing enterprise (himself an Egyptian) turns to me to explain in a private aside:

> We've made a point of taking time to attend this conference. We don't want to appear party poopers in the face of a debate that is expected to change the industrial features of the Zone. There are implications that will affect us especially that the crucial decisions are made elsewhere – in the government offices in Cairo.

With the microphone moving around the U-shaped table, the representatives deploy economic rhetoric – much of it picked up from sugar-coated government press releases – to project Port Said as a forward-looking and exemplary zone, with specific features that mark it as possessing a competitive edge against other zones in Egypt, and therefore deserving of winning a seat in the first round of the national QIZ competition. The EPZ's qualified and stable workforce feature prominently in these accounts. The speech made on behalf of the Zone's investors' association highlights the *gawda* (efficiency/ performance) and *se'r* (cost) which the Zone's *'emala mu'ahala* (qualified workforce) delivers, enabling Port Said's garment industry to 'prove its technical credentials' in competing on the world stage for export markets.

Formal public events of this kind also provide opportunities for *il-lama wil akl* (gathering and free food), and a chance to catch up with news and local gossip during the obligatory lunch and tea breaks. Some of the conversation is evidently social rather than entrepreneurial, as high on the agenda is the way in which the overwhelmingly masculine presence in both the ownership and management of the garment firms of the EPZ (well indicated by the faces attending the symposium) has been disrupted by its latest entrant, the Mina Clothing Firm. The new owner, Madame S, has earlier appeared at the conference in a white tracksuit, with matching white sneakers and chiffon headscarf-style *hijab*, clutching a stack of papers and talking animatedly on her mobile phone. Reputed to have inherited her capital of seven million Egyptian pounds from her late husband, a famous footballer from Isma'iliyya (one of the Canal governorates from which firms get their migrant workers), she is attacked over lunch for lacking *khibra* (expertise) and *tagarub* (experience) and for being, as one of the (male) participants puts it, 'insensitive to the Zone's masculine sensitivities. For example, driving her posh cars in the Zone at all hours of the day is *istifzaz* (provocative). One day it is the white Mercedes, the next the black Cherokee, or her BMW. It's the only car seen driving around the streets with speed'.

The conversation also turns to more pressing business issues, including the current state of the labour market in the Zone. In this informal setting, the picture provided diverges sharply from the glossy public presentations made during the formal seminar sessions. Sipping his steaming bowl of *fawakih il-bahr* (Arabic for *fruits de mer*, a popular local dish), one firm's General Manager, himself a retired military officer of high rank, explains how acute shortages of labour are well known to many garment factories, and how the competition for skilled workers is intense. Indeed, the steady expansion in the number of factories in the Zone has created a brewing resentment over the increasingly underhand ways in which firms 'poach' the workforce of neighbouring factories:

> The ready-made garment factory is like a house of cards. Each stage is the foundation of the next: a delicate balance of layers that fold on top of each other. When a newcomer arrives in the Zone, as Madame S lately has, and helps herself to five skilled workers from one factory, and another five from a second, until she completes her workforce, the disruption affects all seventeen factories in the zone – not just one or two of us. QIZ may bring much prosperity and an increase in the orders we are taking – but my expectations are that a yet more ferocious war will be fought over the workforce. We are all going to pay a hefty price.

The General Manager of Top Fashion concurs, adding that the workers have become adept at hopping from job to job to get the best deal they can at any moment: 'I am less inclined to view the worker in this Zone as a stable worker with a secure job, and more as a *sawah* (wanderer)' he tells me, the closing lilt in his voice invoking the image of the rootless wanderer popularised in a famous 1960s love song which most Egyptians know by heart (*Sawah mashi fil bilad sawah* 'Wanderer, rootlessly roaming the land'). Together my companions enjoy a play on words in agreeing that the Zone's labour is not so much *'emala mu'ahala* (a qualified workforce, as lauded in the official presentations) as *'emalat foras* (an opportunity-seeking workforce).

During my time in Port Said I was able to piece together the main reasons for this difficult labour reality, so different from the 'stable and well-qualified workforce' celebrated in the Zone's external presentations. The first reason is that public sector employment overwhelmingly remains the first preference for fresh graduates seeking a job. Public sector jobs are perceived as being 'for life'; prestigious, with social standing; undemanding, in many cases only requiring workplace attendance of a few hours each week; and, though paying low salaries, offering generous allowances and related benefits which increase steadily with length of service (Kerr 1965; Doumato and Posusney 2002; Elgeziri 2012). Private sector jobs are seen as comparing unfavourably on all counts. More importantly, once formally registered in a private sector employment insurance scheme, a citizen ceases to be eligible for employment in the public sector, in practice meaning that there is no opportunity to change one's mind in the future.

Port Said's economy, as I have pointed out in the previous Chapter, has nonetheless always had a vigorous private sector, with seemingly every one of the local citizenry engaged in 'wheeler-dealer' transactions for the provision of a range of goods and services, most of them related to the city's entrepôt heritage, and frequently shading into tax evasion and illegality, with smuggling drugs and counterfeit goods popularly recognised as livelihoods in their own right. The desired ideal, however, remains combining any such activity with a permanent public sector position. Manual labour of any kind is widely seen as more 'arduous', and therefore inherently less attractive, than freewheeling commerce, and the Zone is notorious for requiring workers to work unsocial hours to meet contractual deadlines, and for an unreliable pipeline of orders from international or local clients. Furthermore, in contrast to the instant cash-in-hand readily available from freewheeling commerce and trade, delayed and irregular payment of wages is rife in the Zone's factories. There is an additional dimension to the Zone's unfavourable image as a source of employment opportunity, one which is both social and moral. Inviting in migrant workers from neighbouring provinces is considered by locals to 'lower the tone'; and this is compounded by the migrant female workers' reputed propensity, away from their rural villages and exposed to the bright city lights, for racy and flirtatious (*lewna*) behaviour.

The result is that, within Port Said's local economic context, the Zone has to struggle hard to attract workers to take up jobs in its factories – as, indeed, it always had. The early days of the EPZ in the 1990s, when local Port Saidians could not be found to man the production lines, are still fresh in the minds of many current officials. The Director General of the EPZ remembers those days vividly, raising the issue of gender preferences:

> We came up with a plan. We hired a minibus and drove to the rural areas of Manzala, Kantara and Bahr il-Baqar (see Map 0.1). We sought the assistance of the local mosques and the *sheyukh* (clergymen – plural of *sheikh*) there to spread word and to assure local families that these were respectable jobs for their daughters. We wanted to assure them that factories were safe places to send their daughters to work, from where they could bring good incomes at the end of the month. I recall a family with four daughters, and as an example I pointed that employing four young girls could mean a sum of LE 1,200 (£120) a month. In paper money, this was a fortune. One man was so taken by the idea that he wanted to send his wife along with the girls!

Even if attracted to the prospect of employment within the Zone, recruits seldom approach a particular factory without having some idea of the firm's reputation, since the reputation of each firm is well known to all employed in the *istithmar*. During break periods, when workers from neighbouring factories mix and mingle on the streets outside, I overheard on several occasions Fashion Express spoken of as *fawda* (chaotic), a *masna' waqe'* (fallen factory), *il-'amaliyya nayma* (a dead end), or as being in a state of *hargala* (disorganisation). These views stigmatise the current conditions of Fashion Express and its workforce, a point explicitly recognised by the General Manager when he expressed to me his sense of frustration at how things currently were with the factory:

> If we're to talk honestly, we're just surviving. The options are limited. To get back on track to our more productive days means living with, and facing up to, the constraints that hold the factory back – the debts that have piled up. I cannot escape from how, all the time, the firm's present financial crises dictate the conditions of the workplace and the employment of workforce. I would love to break free from these constraints, but my ankles are shackled.[3]

Given its stigmatised reputation as a 'fallen factory', and in the face of intense competition both within and from outside the Zone, Fashion Express would normally stand little chance of attracting workers – and so drastic remedial action is required. It is here that the proprietor, Qasim Bey, moves centre stage, as the architect and prime mover of a strategy to counter and overcome these disadvantages. His chosen strategy is to build on the well-established business model of the 'family firm', and construct within Fashion Express a distinctive workplace environment of 'firm as family', crafting for himself, at its head, an equally distinctive role as proprietor-patriarch.

The 'family firm' is a consistent framework resonating through the literature of the Middle East, which stresses the survival and intensification of kinship ties through major social changes, and the enduring centrality of the family as a basic social and economic unit (Zaalouk 1989; Zubaida 1989; Gilsenan 1996; Haddad 2002; Rosen 2002; Borneman 2005). As Kandiyoti (2001: 57) succinctly puts it: 'There exists ... no autonomous associational arena between state and society that is not thoroughly permeated by both the reality and the idiom of kinship and family relations'. Although comparatively little has been written on how the family as an institution is organised and operates (Tucker 1993; Joseph 1999a), one feature that is frequently highlighted is its hierarchical structure, with the patriarchal figure at its apex. In this view, vertical and horizontal relationships within family networks are geared to cementing the stratified and hierarchical features of the patriarchal structure, constructing and upholding the dominant image of the male patriarch as the *kebir* (the head of the household and its most powerful authority) whose presence and authority defines, legitimises and controls the *kayaan* (structure and form) of the family. Religion is seen to further reinforce these structures by stressing the sanctity of *silat il-rahim* (relations of the womb), to the point where parallels are invoked between the religious conception of the father and of God, where the one becomes an extension or abstraction of the other (Barakat 1985: 45–46, 1993: 116; Hammoudi 1997: 78–84; Borneman 2005).

The literature is even thinner when it comes to providing explicit illustrations of how rule by the father is constituted in different contexts and changes over time. Instead, social science literature seems to have relied on defining and elaborating patriarchal figures through recourse to literature rather than ethnography (Barakat 1993; Altorki 1999; Al-Nowaihi 1999; van Leeuwen 2000; Rizzo 2014). The result is that an essentialist view of patriarchy as the central principle of Arab family structures and dynamics has taken hold. For example, Hisham Sharabi (1988a: 35) provides an interesting analysis of the patriarchal structures of Arab society to develop a theory of neopatriarchy, explaining how these structures are further strengthened by modernisation, and appropriated to legitimise authoritarian sociopolitical structures (whether secular or religious). In his view such modern authoritarian discourses create 'a distorted and inverted modernity' (Sharabi 1988a: 5) by invoking an ostensible tradition that legitimises authoritarian structures as stemming from largely untransformed patriarchal schemata that have persistently regulated interpersonal relations at all levels – from the family to the state (Gilsenan 1996; Hammoudi 1997; Shehata 2003; Glass 2006; Borneman 2005). Suad Joseph, by contrast, has developed the more multidimensional concept of patriarchal connectivity, which, while stressing the role of the patriarchal family over the individual, nevertheless allows for the existence of a multiplicity of connective relationships that are essential for social existence through the definition of fluid selves. In her view the latter are appropriated to the service of the former, so that:

> Intertwined, connectivity and patriarchy have helped produce selves trained in the psychodynamics of domination, knowing how to control and be controlled … I caution, however, against seeing men or fathers as prime movers or causes of these complex relationships. Each person, including women and juniors, is an active participant, both caused and causative of the relations of inequality in patriarchal systems. (1999a: 13–14)

Other studies comparing the relationship of the family to other social institutions have also highlighted the complementary and contradictory nature of kin relationships, especially where issues of loyalty are involved

(Springborg 1982; Rugh 1986; Singerman 1995; Hopkins 2001). And although structural socioeconomic changes were initially thought to have undermined some of the roles traditionally undertaken by the family (for example in education and employment), the family has nevertheless continued to maintain its centrality. This is evidenced by the concerted lengths to which the family, as a specific type of dominant informal group and a primary socioeconomic unit, is prepared to go in cooperating and pooling its resources to secure its livelihood (Singerman 1995; Rosen 2002). There is also the well-established claim in the literature that enterprises such as shops, factories, or businesses are 'commonly owned and operated for the benefit of all … where the success or failure of an individual member becomes that of the family as a whole. Every member of the family is held responsible for the acts of every other member' (Barakat 1985: 28).

This is reflected in Port Said's Export Processing Zone, where for most firms the owner is also the prime investor. Hiring *arayib* (relatives) is considered to be in the best interest of the firm, promoting and securing the interests of the *sahib il-'amal* (owner of the firm) from real or perceived dangers, while simultaneously promoting the economic well-being of family members. As one local NGO official put it to me:

> This is not an issue only found in Port Said. The whole of Egypt operates on this principle. It is an accepted practice that putting one's whole savings in a project is not just to reap the expected profits from the enterprise. It is also a way of getting one's offspring on their feet and securing their future. Bringing relatives into any enterprise applies to the local saying *eli ne'rafu ahsan min ili-mane'rafush* ('those we know are better than those we don't').

These principles of kinship govern appointments to the managerial positions within Fashion Express. Each of the three *tob man* (top man)[4] positions generally considered as being *asasi* (special, in the sense of vital to the overall management of the firm) are occupied by relatives of the proprietor, Qasim Bey. The Vice-Chairman is Leith Fahmy, his son. The General Manager is Imam Azmi, his brother-in-law (who is also seen to occupy a position of special proximity, through sharing a residence with the proprietor and his son); and the Head of Security is Tewfik Saleh, a second cousin on the maternal side who is classed as belonging to the same age group and *shilla*[5] as the sons of Qasim Bey. By strategically placing his *arayib* across the firm's organisational landscape, with specific and sharply differentiated roles to oversee separate areas of management, the proprietor creates a supportive force which provides stability and continuity through the factory's fluctuating economic circumstances and fluid workforce. Its permanence enhances the solidarity of family in the firm, and attests to the cohesive and tenacious nature of the kinship group of the *sahib il-'amal* and his *arayib*, perceived as crucial to protecting the private interests of the firm's head.

Yet far from simply occupying a pre-defined and accepted position of *sahib il-'amal* (proprietor) of a 'family firm', Qasim Bey is continually engaged in an active process of extending the meaning of 'kinship' from the literal to the metaphorical, and broadening its application to take in *all* the workers in his firm (whether blood relatives or not) so as to develop a distinctive construct of 'firm as family'. And as the *kebir* at its apex, he simultaneously constructs a specific, defined and equally distinctive role for himself as proprietor-patriarch of the 'firm as family'. Indeed, right since the time Fashion Express was founded, Qasim Fahmy appears to have chosen to construct his role as a generous and benevolent *rab usrit il-masna'* (father of the factory family). Deep within the collective memory of the workers who had been with the firm since its formative years is an abiding image of a glorious past, and an employer with rich economic resources. What comes to the mind of long-serving workers is not simply that delayed wages were unheard of during these early years, but also how Qasim Fahmy's personal generosity was evident on special occasions. Their tales recount how the factory's completion of its first ever export order was celebrated by slaughtering a dozen sheep, with each worker given two kilos of meat. Also recalled is his active use of his personal connections in the government bureaucracy to help individual workers in their times of emergency. As Kimo, a long-standing machinist in Leitex recalls:

> He often reminded us that we are his *beit* (family, household), and how close we were. There is much truth in his statement. Working in this firm was for many of us like working in our homes. We did not feel like we were hired workers in the same way as the working experience is in other factories. Before the economic crisis hit us he was an exemplary employer – and he has remained a good employer, not *muftari* (despotic).

Other proprietors behave differently towards their workforce. Mr Ansari of Lafayette, for example, is spoken of as a *mu'assis* (founder), who skilfully uses financial incentives to *yerabi* (breed – used in the sense of to multiply) his workforce by encouraging workers to marry, and then support the role of the working wife. His generosity is focused on recipients outside the workplace, as he is well known for regularly feeding two hundred disadvantaged families. The religious dimension to his external charitable patriarchal image is explicit in his devotion to ensuring that, every year without fail, he performs both the major and the minor *haj* pilgrimage to Mecca. This provides a vivid instance of the tendency, astutely noted by Ismail in her recent study of urban communities in Cairo, for businessmen who have made their money through *infitah* policies to resort to religious traditions of charity, citing the slogan 'The heart of the private sector beats for the community' as an example of their welfare commitments (Ismail 2006: 82). Their chosen narratives become significant drivers in establishing the credibility of their firms, and of themselves as individual members of the class of investors.

These narratives are not only articulated by the investors/proprietors who construct them: they are taken up and actively articulated by each firm's workforce. Thus Mr Ansari – originally a taxi driver – is spoken of among his workforce as *'esami* (a self-made man), providing proof that anybody with determination and insight can 'make it big'. Qasim Fahmy's choice of defining narrative however provides a contrasting profile, drawing on codes of class and family standing which form part of the existing social capital so as to portray himself as coming from an *'aila* (a patrician lineage) that is *muhtaramin* (respectable). This has the added effect of deliberately differentiating him from the EPZ *ashab il-'amal* who have risen from more humble origins. A vivid example of this is to be found in his choice of portraits hung in the central lounge of the top management suite, where international clients and other important visitors wait for their appointments. On the walls, two portraits serve as significant markers of class and political persuasion. One is that of Egypt's long-serving President Mubarak, confirming the current political allegiance of the proprietor. The other, given equal prominence in an ornate gilded frame, is an enlarged reproduction of an old black and white photograph of the proprietor's father, taken in the 1940s,[6] which imparts a regal image of a man in the prime of life, dressed in the ceremonial outfit of the monarchical *Majlis il-Nuwab* (Chamber of Deputies). The image highlights the historical roots of the family's political involvement in Port Said, and its solid standing among the local haute-bourgeoisie.

In choosing to base his defining narrative on these foundations, Qasim Bey is exploiting the extent to which the Fahmy family name has a distinctive resonance in the history and living memory of the local community, which has bestowed on them the titular status of *shurafa'* (honourable). The family's *shurafa'* status appears to derive from the shifting mix within its history of political activism on the one hand, and economic power on the other. The family's political prominence goes back to active nationalist politics in the 1940s, and is associated in particular with the reconstruction of Port Said after the 1973 war with Israel. In the heyday of the Egyptian independence struggle, Qasim Fahmy's father was a prominent Saadist (a member of a reformist faction of the Wafd party, which emphasised industrialisation over reliance on inherited wealth – as favoured by the landed gentry involved in the party's origins) after whom a street is named in the commercial district. In the 1970s Qasim Fahmy was part of Sadat's inner circle, reputedly instrumental in persuading the President to establish the first Free Zone in Port Said.

With the arrival of the Mubarak era he became, by Presidential appointment (*tazkiyya*), a prominent member of the Port Said branch of the ruling National Democratic Party. This continuing involvement in politics (both within the local community and on the national scene) resonates with Hourani's classic formulation of a 'politics of the notables' (Hourani 1983), as well as with historical analyses characterising early twentieth-century Egyptian politics as an inherited vocation associated with land-owning and mercantile urban elites, born into privilege, who assume political office, and then expect their male children and grandchildren to continue to preserve this entitlement (Smith 1984; Abdalla 1985; Khalidi 1988; Baron 2005). Even if, by current standards, such associations appear remote and somewhat idyllic, Qasim Fahmy articulates this profile further within the local community through his frequent appearances on local TV, especially on chat shows publicising local figures and their achievements, where his involvement reinforces the Fahmy family's pedigree and influential reputation.

Yet although their social and political pedigree is well-established, the economic fortunes of the Fahmy family have been less settled, and at the time of my fieldwork it was common knowledge that they were staggering under colossal debts. In a community where wealth is valued, and quick money has seen families rise and fall, the decline of a family's financial assets is cause for much rumour and 'bad mouthing'. It was accordingly taken for granted that the family needed to consolidate its resources to maintain its name and status within the community, including keeping a family firm in operation even when the enterprise did not make visible profits. A clear statement of this came from one of its prominent members, Tewfik Saleh:

> It's the family name, its reputation, that is of utmost importance to all of us *as a family*. This is a small community where the word of a man, and his reputation, counts. Port Saidians are renowned for positive qualities like courage – but they are also fickle. The pendulum swings, and our community is predominantly self-serving, with members surviving by grabbing what they can through personal connections and favours. Without financial resources, and unable to keep up with resources others are accumulating fast, it turns into a race of moving sands.

In this race, Qasim Bey's chosen strategy is to reach back into the period before his current economic woes set in, invoke the distinguished reputation of his *'aila*, and by constructing the metaphorical 'firm as family', extend this aura to employees who gain employment in Fashion Express. The extent to which this strategy is successful in winning the competition to recruit and retain labour is what I move on to explore in the remainder of this chapter.

Ikhlaas: filial loyalty and sibling rivalry

The three people to whom Qasim Bey has delegated overall control of the workforce by appointing them to *asasi* (key) management positions are, as mentioned, members of his immediate family. Having appointed them, Qasim Bey reinforces his power through a public dynamic in which he invests each of them with his patriarchal trust, and at the same time demands from each of them complete loyalty to himself as *kebir* of both the Fahmy family and the metaphorical Fashion Express 'firm as family'. Thus when, one day, I ask Imam Azmi about his *kebir*'s expectations of him, he wryly quotes an old Arabic saying: *Wa itha rabu il-beit bil dofi dareban, fashimat ahl il-beit il-raqs* (when the head of the *beit* beats the tambourine, its members identify themselves by dancing). Qasim Bey is explicit in even associating the loyalty he demands with the essence of manhood, having been frequently heard to declare publicly that: '*Il-insan il-mukhlis ragil qawi* (the loyal person is a strong – in the sense of 'real macho' – man)'. The family is expected to stand together to counter the financial turbulence of the factory – not only as a self-sustaining economic enterprise, but also as an extension of the Fahmy family entity. Family members in the firm are expected to engage in continual demonstrations of *ikhlaas* (loyalty) to the *kebir*. This requires being within easy reach of the patriarch, running all sorts of errands for him, dealing with issues that weigh on his mind, and seizing opportunities to show family solidarity as *rigaltu* ('his men' i.e. the men of his family). Through these opportunities the position of the family is secured and, equally if not more importantly, the position of the *kebir* is upheld, accentuated and continually reaffirmed. It is, however, also evident that there are differences in the level of patriarchal trust invested in each *tob man* family member. This is made known through differences in their salary packages. Even more evident are variations in the degree of social and physical proximity to the person of the patriarch which each is known to enjoy. Day-to-day work in the firm provides a succession of opportunities for each of them to demonstrate their assigned degree of intimacy with the absent figure of the patriarch.

Thus, locked in his office and away from the *entag* and *edara* zones, Imam Azmi looks stressed as he fields a succession of phone calls confirming arrangements for cloth to be delivered, or for a completed order to be collected, or as part of the difficult search for a replacement for a suddenly cancelled order. Several times a day, calls from Qasim Bey arrive on his personal mobile. These tend to be short and to the point, alerting him that his performance on the job is being continually monitored and is expected to be close to perfection. These calls from the patriarch are occasions for others in the room to witness the powerful interaction of the *kebir* with family members in the firm. As his personal mobile identifies the caller, Imam Azmi hushes the room with a wave of his hand. The room falls silent, complicit in giving the impression that the General Manager is on his own. Answering the call, Imam rises from his chair and paces the room as, in a loud and more assertive voice, he gives verbal assurances of how the production situation stands at the moment, and vigorously nods his head as he listens to Qasim Bey's responses. Once the phone call is over, he sits back in his chair to resume the more mundane conversation it had interrupted, his loyalty and proximity to the patriarch reinforced.

By contrast, Qasim Bey's son Leith provides little demonstrated evidence of paternal intimacy. His role appears to be confined to networking in the Zone and bringing in some of the local subcontracting orders. He is only occasionally seen on the factory premises, his office in the top management suite standing empty most of the time. His inconspicuous presence in the firm, which contrasts sharply with the role of the proprietor's blood-sons in other factories in the Zone, is widely attributed to generational differences within Beit Fahmy. Tewfik Saleh's relationship with the patriarch is the least intimate of the three, in line with his more distant kin *sila* (relationship), and by virtue of his being a comparative late-comer to the firm. Yet he appears to have been assigned the role of briefing and communicating not only with other members of top management, but also directly with the patriarch.

Claiming *nasab* (ties of ancestry) reinforces the ascriptive social status an individual enjoys when claiming descent from, or belonging to, a prominent family, and is relevant to *all* family members (Barakat 1993; Gilsenan 1996; Hammoudi 1997). However, in the context of the firm, the sense of belonging co-exists with conflicting affiliations stemming from their differing personal relationships – not only with each other but also, and most especially, with the person of the *kebir*. In this way the structure of the firm places these family members within an essentially divisive dynamic, modulating the notion of the kin group as one entity. Each is publicly and visibly invested with patriarchal trust; yet the demonstrated differentials between them set them apart, distinguishing each as a member of Beit Fahmy in his own right. The workplace situation thus sets up a dynamic of mutual rivalry between the three family members of top management. They are active in continually reinforcing, through their actions, their positions as senior male members of the Fahmy family – and they are equally active in vying with each other to demonstrate the degree of their personal loyalty to the figure of the patriarch.

Each builds his own profile through narratives of acts of bravura performance that circulate among them. These include details of interventions in the working environment of the firm, such as thwarting an attempted theft, or catching an actual thief, or closing the deal on a tricky subcontracting order, or heading off a shop floor strike before it takes place. Ideally these acts of bravura also need to show that the performer is well-connected in the Zone and the wider Port Saidian community, and that his broader social network has been mobilised *bisor'a* ('with speed') – a point particularly noted in the course of conversation – whenever the need arises to break a bureaucratic impasse that threatens an export deadline, or to reverse papers that have been dispatched erroneously, and so protect the tight budget within which the patriarch is forced to operate.

These acts of bravura are intended not only for the eyes or ears of the patriarch, but also for the workforce to witness. They attempt to demonstrate a 'natural male disposition' to accomplish heroic feats, providing proof of both a high degree of professionalism and deep personal loyalty to the *kebir* and firm. These performances are carefully observed and commented on by the workforce. As one non-kin member of *edara* commented on the hostilities between the *tob men*: '*Il-ana* (the personal pronoun 'I') is a big part of the show. It is inflated at times to the point of exaggeration, and comes across as *khart* (fictitious)'.

Any such feat appears all the greater if an error can be traced to professional mistakes made by a rival. Thus hidden tensions in the relationship between Tewfik Saleh and Imam Azmi are exposed when each *tob man* recounts a litany of faults he has uncovered about the other, pointing to the *istighlal* (exploitative, manipulative) nature of his relationship to the *kebir*. Yet any such complaint is instantly concluded with the standard and sweeping phrase of '*ehna aila wahda* (we are one family)', closing the ranks firmly around the concept of kin as a cohesive entity.

Given the mutual rivalry between them, it is in the interest of each *tob man*, even while professing that he is working in the interests of the patriarch-proprietor, to draft as many allies as he can secure within the wider workforce. So each family-occupied post cultivates within the firm its own separate cadre of allies and supporters, drafted from three prime locations: *amn* (Security), *edara* (middle-management) and *entag* (shop floor production). The resulting cliques are known on the shop floor as the factory's *marakiz il-quwa* (centres of power),[7] and there is constant tension, rivalry and competition between them. Appointments, transfers and promotions are a key means through which each *tob man* reinforces and strengthens his own *markaz*. Any such appointment instantly frames the individual as having secured admission to a faction personally protected and backed by a top member of the Fahmy family. The extension of metaphorical kinship which Qasim Bey bestows on members of the Fashion Express workforce is thus refined, within the factory, into the allegiance structure of the factions within the 'firm as family'.

Opportunities to use the power of appointment as a means of reinforcing the rival *marakiz il-quwa* only arise when vacancies occur and require filling, or new positions are created within the enterprise. On a more continual basis, the process is sustained by the flow of information along an all-pervading system of surveillance that is in operation throughout the firm. At the most obvious level, the entire physical layout of the factory constitutes a landscape organised, like Bentham's 'Panopticon', for visibility. Within this open-plan design, visibility becomes paramount to the control of production, with the physical boundaries between the different units often only evident to an eye familiar with the processes and stages of production involved in garment work. One physical separation that is clear and distinct is the segregation of the heads of the competing *marakiz il-quwa* behind the smoked-glass doors that separate the top management suite of offices from the heat and clutter of the factory floor. Since their visits to the shop floor are sporadic, they must perforce have other means of gathering information to nourish and sustain their own *markaz*, and to perform their competitive demonstrations of *ikhlaas* to the patriarch. My first clue as to the existence of this all-pervading system of surveillance came several weeks into my fieldwork, when one of the junior workers confided a warning about the presence of *gawasis* (spies) on the shop floor. Although at first I assumed her use of the word to be rhetorical, it did not take me long to work out that there existed, within the formal hierarchy of the firm, entire networks of *gawasis*. Almost every employee (whether worker, supervisor or *edara* manager) had a dual function of watching the production scene on someone else's behalf, and reporting 'significant events' across a variety of selected pathways.

This incessant monitoring of the labour landscape through a complex web of individuals and factions constitutes the principal means of management control of the workforce. It is through these diverse channels that management is able to identify which units in production drag their feet and which are relatively trouble-free; get access to developments in shop floor moods and the latest circulating shop floor rumours; obtain news of unusual developments (such as the infestation of fleas that came with a subcontracting order from a neighbouring firm, or production disruptions in the packaging units in the tense run up to a tight deadline for an export order); or pick up early signs of restlessness due to late wages, including spotting trouble-makers instigating other workers. The overt uses of surveillance for the purposes of management control thus involve 'keeping a finger on the pulse' of the workplace. In particular, surveillance is used to assess the mood of the workforce to determine the timing of top management's visits to the shop floor or announcements over the factory's microphone. An example of the system in operation was provided during a lean production spell, when, as fears of no forthcoming work grew steadily worse, rumours of outright closure began to circulate around the factory. Getting to hear of murmurs amongst some workers about the need to look for employment elsewhere, Imam Azmi made straight for the microphone to provide assurances of 'strong leadership' and the *kebir*'s personal commitment to 'every worker in this firm'.

Yet the scope of all the information that is amassed, analysed, collated and reported goes well beyond such 'obvious' foci of management interest. It provides an illustration of James Scott's analysis of the power of hidden transcripts within the discourse of power relationships, especially those relating to gossip and rumours among subordinates regarding others more senior in the hierarchical ladder (Scott 1990). Fashion Express's management seeks not only to obtain information that may call for personal action on their part, but also to gain easy access to the hidden transcripts of the shop floor. This all-pervasive, invisible surveillance system, commonly referred to as *'eyun il-sherka* (the eyes of the firm), was taken as an essential element of management's duty to protect *kayaan il-sherka* (the structure of the firm – though the use of the term *kayaan* also evokes a strong association with the family as an entity) and constantly reinforce the message that top management is *mudrika* (vigilant).

The entire system of the *'eyun il-sherka* rests on the specific role of the *gawasis*, which is to convey *ma'lumat* (information) to the *ashab il-qarar* (decision makers). It requires a concerted organisational effort to amass on a daily basis the volume of information needed to fulfil management's requirements. For this reason, *gawasis* are 'known' to operate everywhere around the factory premises. Some are figures (such as cleaners) whose work routinely moves around the premises, whom the predominantly stationary production workers give names such as *'asfura* (bird) and *reuter wi wasil* (a radio with a strong signal). Others are employees whose work ties them to fixed positions, such as certain supervisors who are observed to disappear periodically from their workstations before they resurface after these mysterious absences.

Some *gawasis* are overt and explicit in their roles as informants for senior staff: these are popularly referred to as *rasmi* (official). There are indisputable benefits to be gained from being physically close to *il-solta* (the seat of power). These informers closest to the person of the patriarch are accorded the greatest influence within the surveillance system, and also appear to be the most feared and least liked. Thus a well-known figure whom *entag* identified as *rasmi* is Om Makram, the cleaner who attends to the needs of top management in their suites of offices. In her early fifties, Om Makram dons a conservative *khumar* veil in toned down colours of deep grey or navy blue. Her age and matriarchal appearance in the traditional fashion of *awlad il-balad* (sons of the soil) are important features of the image she projects. Despite her *khadamat* (service) role, the lowest rank within the factory hierarchy, she wields enormous power in the firm. She grants herself the sole authority to enter the chambers of top management unannounced, either to produce the coffee they have requested or remove the dirty cups and ashtrays filled with cigarette butts. At the start of each morning, her tasks are more precise. These include supervising the cleaning of Qasim Bey's office, having memorised by heart where everything is supposed to lie and the order it is expected to be in. Clearing ashtrays, dusting family photographs of smiling grandchildren and the patriarch shaking hands with dignitaries, and laying open the pages of the Koran to the *sura* (verse) which Qasim Bey particularly likes to see, are the small details that show how her work is attuned to the details of the personal likes and dislikes of her employer. Every day she concludes her morning chores by burning several sticks of incense to bring blessings for the day to come. She is fierce in declaring her personal support for the figure of the patriarch:

> When God knows you are a good person, you shall be victorious. Qasim Bey is a good person. He has not risen from rags to riches, like others you see around you these days. If that were the case, he would not be good – he would be *muftari* (despotic), just like all the rest of them.

Om Makram is aware that a significant part of her profile and power within the firm comes from demonstrating that she is fulfilling the need of the *kebir* for reassurance that she *khayfa 'aleh* (cares for him as a person) with *albaha 'aleh* (his interests at heart) – significant markers of 'firm as family' loyalty. She is also active in gathering intelligence through her networks both on the shop floor and in *edara*. Her right of unrestricted entry to the top management offices, and her physical proximity to their inhabitants, mark her status in the firm as possessing unparalleled advantages and powers, her words described as '*il-hot line*' travelling directly into the ears of the patriarch.

In other instances, despite the absence of physical proximity, the channels can leap over hierarchical layers and lead directly to the *kebir*. Thus Shaker, the head of the Planning Unit in *edara*, is spoken of as the 'right-hand man' of Qasim Bey himself, without the mediation of any particular *tob man*. Having been with the factory since its relocation to Port Said in 1996, Shaker started as a junior clerk in Planning, a job he describes as involving filling in forms requesting storeroom items such as tags and zippers for use in production. Working closely with the then Head of Planning enabled him to come to grips with the logistics involved in planning, and within a span of three years he himself rose to the post of Unit Head. Shaker's current status, and the power that comes with it, are evident from the frequent telephone calls he receives from *il-rayis* (the boss) – the term Shaker uses when answering calls from Qasim Bey – and the time he spends in top management's chambers. Shaker has staffed his unit predominantly with young male graduates, freshly recruited from his own kin network. All identify more directly with Shaker than they do with any other manager in the firm, referring to themselves as 'Shaker's men'. Members of his unit are keen to show that they are *mukhlissin* (loyal) and 'standing by Shaker'. The central requirement of *ikhlaas* (loyalty) is demonstrated through labour tasks which capitalise heavily on the advantages their gender provides, such as a license to work late, not leaving until a vital *shahn* (shipment) has been checked several times over, or even to spend the whole night on-site if duty calls – activities in which the 'masculine as performative' is exhibited as a demonstration of personal allegiance. Shaker reciprocates by sustaining the unity of his faction so as not to be defeated in disputes with other *edara* factions operating on a similar principle.

Om Makram and Shaker are unusual in that they are known to be direct agents of the patriarch. The extent to which other networks cut across hierarchical department/unit boundaries, family kinship groups and other axes within the workspace is indicated by the partial mapping of *gawasis* relations shown in Figure 2.1 below. Within this spaghetti-like tangle of grapevine reporting, the head of each power centre has a distinctive style in collecting the snippets of information, sifting the interesting items,

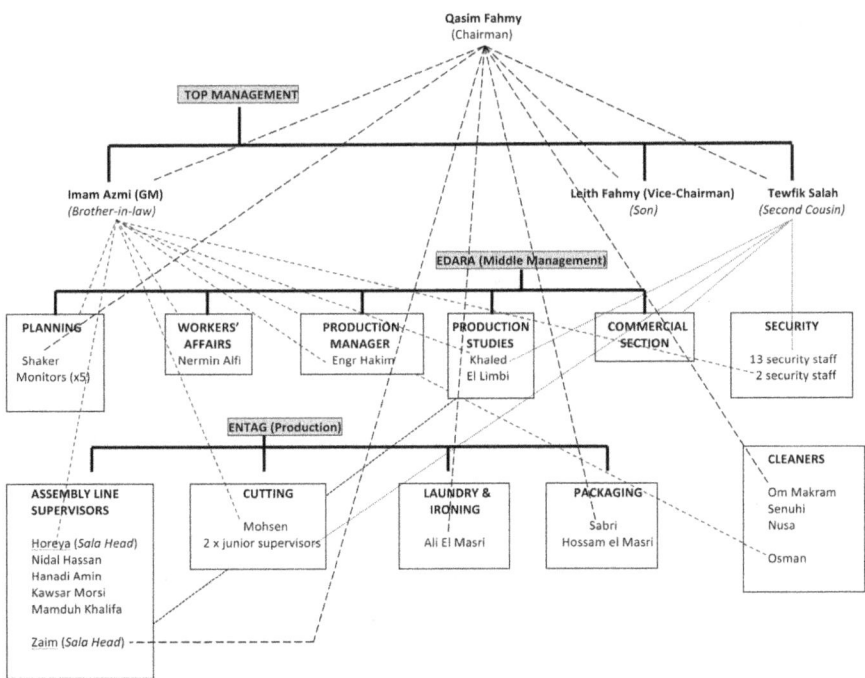

Figure 2.1 The *Marakiz il Quwa* ('Centres of Power')

and then collating them into comprehensive intelligence reports. In this context Tewfik Saleh's position as Head of Security provides him with a natural advantage, since each security point in the factory serves as a multi-purpose point for collecting information from assorted sources. The main security desk (the centre for *gawasis rasmi* – the 'official' i.e. overt spies) is the point where workers' skirmishes on buses are reported; workers not on talking terms with their supervisors are sent to cool down; workers acting 'suspiciously' (for example by extolling employment conditions in competing factories) are reported; conversations and phone calls made to *entag* workers are overheard; ambulances are called for sudden emergencies; or sweets are distributed in celebration of an engagement. Both the labour-related and the wider social data that passes through each security point are collected, classified, and converted into material that is deemed as 'worthy' of 'notifying the authorities'.

The task of gathering information on such a scale comes naturally to Tewfik Saleh. He has an astute sense of social observation, and his social skills are deployed during the long morning coffee breaks he spends with the security boys in the factory. He is well-connected to the more mundane side of Port Said's social life, with extensive contacts in the local police force. His personal mobile, the latest brand and a prized status symbol, has police siren ringtones set to distinguish his police contact callers and signify the easy access he enjoys to official government channels. In his view, the job of excavating news is greatly facilitated in the firm by Port Saidians' reputation within Egypt for *feduliyya,* which means gossip and idle-talk by busybodies. Within this fertile environment, Tewfik Saleh's approach to intelligence gathering typifies the determination of the *'eyun il-sherka* to monitor factory life. As he explains:

> Given that Security extends throughout the factory, any information that reaches us can be counter-checked. So if a worker drops, in an indirect way, information that he had previously worked in another factory or Zone, it is easy enough to use contacts, which are part of our social network outside the factory, to confirm whether this is true. We may then proceed through leaks and tips from these sources to find out all there is to know about this person. Nothing is too minor or insignificant, as anything might turn out to be important in the future ... We have here before our gaze the whole panorama of Egyptian society in capital letters. Years of experience allow us to penetrate *il-aqne'a* (the masks) people wear.

A principal technique for determining the truth behind *il-aqne'a* involves collecting as many different accounts and viewpoints as possible about any single incident or person. All the data that pours in is screened, collated and analysed with a view to defining the positions of individuals and groups through the reiteration of the *mawaqif* (situations) of labour. *Mawaqif* becomes a vital concept that makes reference to the specific set of circumstances associated with an event that encapsulates actions which, when turned into a narrative, sheds light on *il-haqiqa* (the 'true' nature) of the individuals on the scene – thus performing the unmasking job referred to by Tewfik Saleh.

Similar thoughts are echoed by the head of the rival *markaz il-quwa*, Imam Azmi, who is explicit that his position of General Manager of the firm requires him to know *kul sha'ra* (every hair on the head i.e. 'every last detail of what's going on in the factory'). Unlike Tewfik, who receives reports up the line from his network, Imam's preferred mode of operation is to work face-to-face with a wide range of individuals, giving the personal encounter a special significance to his work relations. The personalised aspect of his relationships is highly valued by workers and supervisors alike. The General Manager's preference for hearing from people at first-hand grants them entry privileges into the separate spatial terrain of top management. It allows them to be seated or left standing when spelling out their work issues, eliciting an instant response of support or advice, and enabling them to sense that the issues that they deem problematic will be sorted out by the personal intervention of the General Manager. They thus share a feeling that there is a *dahr* (support) in the firm to back them in the person of the General Manager, who has within his power the capacity to overrule formal procedures, to reinstate workers caught up in shop floor disputes, and to diffuse the frustrations of labour issues. Accessibility to this sort of support has helped shape Imam's image as an approachable *tob man* close to the *kebir*, with a style of firm management seen as 'humane', concerned for the welfare of the firm's workers as well as for production.

Information gathered in the framework of a personalised working relationship is usually voluntarily and willingly given, and therefore projected as more reliable. Imam Azmi nevertheless sees testing the information also to be an essential part of the job, working on the premise that not everybody approaching the General Manager 'with a *film* (tale)' is necessarily telling the whole truth. The General Manager's thirst for accumulating fragments of news has earned him, among the Planning Unit, the nickname 'Mossad', after the infamous Israeli intelligence service. The term serves as a label and metaphor for the efficiency, accuracy and speed with which news of any scale is accumulated, classified and stored in the mind of an individual who makes clear his compulsive need to have within his grasp '*kul il-khuyyut*' (all the threads, a phrase which acquires greater resonance in the context of a sewing-based industry) of the factory.

Within the rival networks and *marakiz il-quwa* each 'discovery' is jealously guarded and not shared with a rival or a faction that may jeopardise the claiming of the excavation as its own. Most prized of all is intelligence which *yeharak il-mawdu'* (changes the story, in the sense of radically changing the nature of the understanding being developed) and constitutes *asrar il-masna'* (the classified information of the firm), which the *marakiz il-quwa* know to be cards closely held by the proprietor. The system thus serves to monitor and reinforce the principle of *ikhlaas* around which the 'firm as family' is constructed. The same principle which operates in the rivalry found between the heads of the competing centres of power also extends to the central role of the *gawasis*. Each demonstrates loyalty so that the act of informing on others is undertaken to *ye'arafo* (notify) the Head of their *markaz il-quwa* and in this manner demonstrate most explicitly that he/she is *mukhlis/mukhlisa* (loyal) to the firm as an entity and to the person of the *kebir*.

When it comes to the competition to demonstrate loyalty, there is never an outright winner in the rivalry between the heads of the different *marakiz il-quwa* (centres of power). And, indeed, it is a key element of Qasim Bey's strategy that there never should be. For as each vies ever harder to express and demonstrate his loyalty to the *kebir*, the legitimacy of the patriarch is continually strengthened. Family members are exposed to personal recriminations if found to be lacking in their surveillance duties. Thus Tewfik Salah vividly remembers the instance when Qasim Bey heard from his 'sources' that garments made in the factory had been discovered on sale in the local market, and gave his security team a tongue-lashing.

It is far from unusual for Qasim Bey to 'get to hear' of developments not reported to him by the top management family members. In one of my first shop floor interviews Zizi, in the Cutting Department, volunteered the opinion that: 'Qasim Bey is an excellent employer. He has a knack of knowing everything that goes on in the factory. I'm not sure how the news gets to him, but he is aware of *everything* that goes on – up in *edara* and right down here'. The 'all-seeing, all-knowing' image adds a further important dimension to the role Qasim Bey has constructed for himself. This plays on a central feature of Middle Eastern kinship dynamics to which Bill and Springborg (1994) have drawn attention – namely the way in which it becomes crucial that the head of the network has within his grasp as much personal information as possible about others. Indeed, it is the 'ever-present, ever-watchful eye' which constitutes a key element of the patriarch's *solta* (power) 'to shape and control the behaviour of others' (Bill and Springborg 1994: 117).

While his reputation with the workforce is thus to be 'all-seeing', Qasim Bey also maintains a deliberately low profile within the factory itself. In many other of the Zone's factories the proprietor is present on the premises more often than not. For example Mr Ammar, of Sphinx Clothing, is well known for standing at his factory's gates each morning to personally take the register of workers reporting for duty, and for subsequently maintaining close personal supervision of the day's production, including firing workers on the spot. Qasim Bey, by contrast, is known to be firm but self-effacing, delegating the control of the workforce to other family members. However, the low profile is recognised as part of his personal strategy, and seldom interpreted as 'absence' even on days when he is away from the firm. The entire system of surveillance continually transmits the message that as *akbar ras fil sherka* (top head of the firm), *ragil teqil* (a man with power and connections), *sahib il-qarar* (the man of decision) and *ragul il-sa'a* (the man of the hour), the patriarch 'sees' and is aware of all happenings on the shop floor and in *edara* – part of the practise of knowing and controlling others in the social hierarchy of the workplace.

His carefully constructed persona as 'the all-seeing unseen' is powerfully reinforced through two supporting stratagems he adopts. One relates to his reputation amongst the workforce for operating behind-the-scenes to solve seemingly impossible problems with sudden masterstrokes of unanticipated action; and the other to the meticulous staging of his rare, carefully timed, physical appearances on the shop floor. In cultivating the former image, Qasim Bey is exploiting a commonly shared association stemming from the days when he was a close confidant of the former President Anwar Sadat, who also took pride in adopting a bold, 'cutting the Gordian knot' approach to solving intractable problems – as, most famously, when he broke decades of hostile political stalemate with Israel by unilaterally deciding to go in person to Tel Aviv to address the Knesset. Qasim Bey is not hesitant in encouraging the belief that his years in Sadat's political circle have shaped his personal style of running the firm, leading the workforce to believe that, from his mentor, he has assimilated much of Sadat's *tariqit il-tafkir* (way of thinking). Thus they speak of the way he suddenly produces surprising solutions to seemingly dead end situations – what they often describe as *sadamat kahraba'iyya* (electric shock treatment), where underneath a calm demeanour is a person who is sufficiently skilled to play 'the game' with the 'stroke of a master'. Thus when, via a flurry of mobile phone calls to managers in the factory, the absent Qasim Bey unexpectedly breaks a critical deadlock in production that is threatening failure to meet an export order deadline, a worker triumphantly shouts across the shop floor, *'le'ebha sah!'* ('Smart move!' – implying Machiavellian wisdom). Similarly whenever slumps in production threaten to extend beyond periods that are tolerable, and the risk of workers declaring a *naksa* (calamity) and walking off becomes critical, the power of *il-kebir* is invariably seen in the way in which subcontracts suddenly appear on the shop floor.

These powerful interventions are made more dramatic on the occasions when Qasim Bey makes a rare physical appearance on the shop floor. These are never announced in advance. Instead, his presence is sensed by a flying whisper in the din of the assembly halls as the smoked glass doors open and the proprietor is suddenly found standing in Egytex. In an immaculate dark tailored suit, the silent and soft spoken figure of *il-kebir* stands still for a few moments before commencing a tour of *entag*. The presence of the proprietor watching the production scene creates a stir, running quickly down assembly lines. The postures of work are almost uniform, as movement of bodies on the shop floor shift with only slight variations here and there. Ancillary workers, who usually stand around waiting for garments to pile up, abruptly pick up scissors and, heads industriously bent, apply themselves busily to tidying up loose threads. Quality control inspection continues as usual, through the mechanical unfolding, checking and folding of piles of garments on table tops. The QC workers' posts enable them to watch the visit with greater clarity than the operators seated at their sewing machines, with their backs to the doors from which Qasim Bey has just emerged.

The visit is watched by the shop floor with interest and, at the same time, an assumed air of indifference. Those stationed in quality control stations give a running commentary to the group before them, highlighting any peculiarities that stand out in the visit. Each visit represents an unfolding drama before them. The figure of the Production Manager is never far. Certain supervisors are called to have a word with the *kebir* and join the touring party as, accompanied by senior *edara* members, he is seen to acknowledge his long-serving workers by name – attesting in this way to the personalised atmosphere of the firm-as-family and his own personal ties with the workforce. The content of the conversation amidst the din of the assembly hall can be discerned from the sign language of arms moving in one direction rather than the other, the nodding or shaking of heads, or the sound of raised nervous laughter when a finished sample of the garment is brought out for review.

Supervisors return to resume their work with what appears like added vigour. Workers stationed close to the visiting party may have insights to add from phrases picked up from the encounter. As the inspection party moves to *Salet Leith* (Leitex), the hall has been notified in advance by workers stationed close to Egytex. Leitex's assembly halls are engaged in a similar process of watching, with the first instalment of a news bulletin flying back to Egytex and other *entag* units via the junior assistants wheeling trolleys of garments and cleaners walking with their buckets and broomsticks. As the *kebir* departs, what is left in the assembly halls is the lingering scent of his powerful eau de toilette that belongs to *il-hagat il-ghalyya* (the expensive brands). The visits of the patriarch are interpreted as an auspicious sign – wages are most certainly to be paid within the next forty-eight hours.

Ihtiram: performing respectability

In the previous section I explored how the proprietor-patriarch of Fashion Express demands continual demonstrations of *ikhlaas* (loyalty) to his person from each and every member of the metaphorical 'firm as family', and establishes systems and procedures that set members of the workforce in competition with each other, and at the same time mobilises the entire workforce, to this end. In this way, as the *kebir* of the family-factory, he impresses his presence and authority throughout the factory. In this section I move on to explore the ramifications of this for the strategy through which the proprietor contests the external image of Fashion Express as a *masna' wake'* ('fallen factory'). This involves invoking the *ihtiram* (respectability) which he embodies, and extending it to his metaphorical *beit* (family in the sense of current household). The personalised authority of *il-kebir* permeates the entire production landscape – and so, as a consequence, does the aura of *ihtiram* with which his persona is infused. As Tewfik Saleh once emphatically declared to me: '*Il-makan eli fi kebir, makan muhtaram* ('it's the firm which has its own *kebir* that is a respectable place'). In this section I explore how this effect is re-created and reinforced through the distinctive workplace practices of Fashion Express. I begin with the social aspects of *ihtiram*, and then move on to its moral features, highlighting how issues of class, gender and religion are deployed within discursive aspects of labour practices.

One of the most visible demonstrations of the construction of social respectability can be seen in the factory's formal recruitment procedures. The seasonal timing of these is shared with other factories in the Zone. Twice a year, with unvarying regularity, banners of white cloth are hung at the entrance of the *istithmar* gates to publicly announce vacancies in the EPZ's clothing firms. This marks the seasons of *bab il-ta'inat* (Door of Appointments), when the garment factories in the zone officially declare open their formal channels for the taking of new recruits. The twice-yearly operation of the scheme is determined principally by the movements of young people still engaged in education: April marks the beginning of the summer vacation when students can take up holiday jobs in the Zone; August marks the end of the holidays, when those leaving the Zone to return to their schools leave production positions vacant for new entrants. The gaudy clusters of banners at the gate of the EPZ fit well with Port Said's reputation as *balad il-yufat* ('city of banners'), derived from the propensity of the locals to hang out large banners (or even fly them from tethered hot air balloons) on a wide range of occasions, including the opening of new shops or enterprises, the inauguration of commercial fairs, conferences or wedding celebrations. The brightly coloured recruitment banners also seek to evoke the image of a festival of abundant job opportunities in the labour market of the *istithmar* – though the extent to which the locals are not impressed is shown when the taxi driver taking me to the factory one day in early April remarks dismissively, 'All that just shows that nobody wants to work there!'.

As we drive past, I recognise Fashion Express's banner. Its design and display is the responsibility of the Production Studies Department. Sawsan Etrebi – Head of Department – fiercely guards her professional authority in the matter of official recruitment. She is proud to declare her professional neutrality, uninfluenced by both top management and their power games, and by the shop floor politics with which she is familiar. 'The heads of the *salat* and their *mushrifat* (female supervisors) can shout and yell as much as they want', she declares as she straightens herself in her office chair, 'they don't have a say in how many workers they need, or over whom they want to appoint'. She is adamant that it is only her personal managerial authority that counts when it comes to the selection of new recruits, and to assigning new entrants to the assembly lines of production. And it rapidly becomes evident that the defining theme of *ihtiram* (respectability) comes into operation as soon as the official recruitment procedures begin to generate responses on the day the banner is hung out, and a few would-be applicants arrive at the factory gates and are told to wait at Security.

A brief phone call to Sawsan Etrebi's desk from the gate announces the presence of the new arrivals. Mongid, her assistant, is dispatched to take a look at the new recruits and returns twenty minutes later. First he verbally conveys the basic facts: the number of recruits, male or female, and whether they have arrived from other neighbouring factories or are total newcomers to the Zone. Volunteering to summarise *il-hala il-igtima'iyya* (the social profile), Mongid next describes the reasons new arrivals have expressed for pleading at the door to be given a chance to be tried out. These conditions range from having an ailing husband or a bedridden parent in need of costly medical care, to being a divorcee with three young children to educate. Sawsan Etrebi listens without showing much sympathy to the litany of *il-hala il-igtima'iyya*. Mongid's assessment, putting issues of *il-haga* (economic need) before questions of ability and skill, is dismissed as being due to his inexperience in the factory environment. In an impatient mood, Sawsan Etrebi declares that his views on who should be allowed into the firm are going to change the factory into a charitable home. 'The front steps of Fashion Express will be like the il-Abbas mosque![8] This makes me look like a *sharira* (witch) in my more rigorous questioning of recruits – I have developed a hard heart when listening to these accounts'. In a ringing affirmation of her role in enforcing the central principle of *ihtiram*, she continues:

My prime duty is to select and pick *ashkal nedifa* (untarnished characters) – it's not just anyone that can breeze in. In the past the factory had hired almost all recruits who turned up asking for jobs. The result was appalling. We were exposed on a daily basis to *ashkal tikhawif* (unsavoury characters) lurking in *entag*. Some male workers were addicts, who left whiffs of *bango*[9] in the *salat* in the morning; others were *sawabiq* (slang for people with 'previous' ie criminal records). It was not the sort of environment any of us wanted to be associated with. The factory as it stands today has been cleansed. It is a *makan mohtaram* (place of respectability).

Sawsan Etrebi's rigorous questioning is widely recognised to be a skill, involving deploying *il-'ayyn* (the eye), of seeing through the recruits to detect, through a series of pointed questions, whether they are lying or telling the truth, and from astute first impressions intuiting each would-be recruit's potential for employment in the firm. Her first glance at a group of recruits arriving upstairs and crowding into her office shows her preference to be instantly directed at young-looking women. As she explains, it is while still young that the individual is impressionable and open to *is-ti'aab* (absorption), a critical factor in the acquisition of skills and speed, which the untrained recruit is expected to develop within a few weeks on the shop floor. Older women, presumed to be married with children, are 'less suitable': they are preoccupied with 'the burdens of the world', inhibiting their potential for picking up the requisite skills, and are therefore less successful candidates in the recruitment process. A 'respectful attitude' and 'neat appearance' are also critical to success, especially in the case of outsiders with no previous work experience. A neat appearance is taken to reflect a person who is, by extension, meticulous in her personal habits and will give any task the care and attention it requires. The desired attitude is a non-confrontational manner when answering questions, and showing a measure of deference towards authority.

Once the recruit has been identified as suitable, Fashion Express is not fussy in its paperwork procedures. A copy of the individual's ID card is all that is needed to land a new entrant, whether skilled or unskilled, with a job on the shop floor. Indeed, an interesting practical feature of the entire selection process is that no one seems, at this stage, to get turned away. In economic terms this can readily be explained by the factory's overwhelming need to fill vacancies. Yet if this were the only driver underpinning the recruitment process, there would be no need for the elaborate construction of a rigorous process of spotting 'unsuitable' elements before they reach the shop floor. The care and energy that go into the construction of this image of the zealous guardianship of respectability suggests that it is not merely economic rationale which is driving this stage of recruitment, but the construction and performance of *ihtiram* as a defining characteristic of the factory.

Once an applicant has been formally employed, the next stage is her or his assignment to a particular work unit. New recruits are sent downstairs, in a group, where they are 'claimed' by individual supervisors of the factory's various work units, with first choice given to the supervisors of the assembly lines. When I asked about the basis on which workers employed upstairs by *edara* were assigned to different work units, shop floor supervisors asserted that it was 'all to do with skills'. In their view *edara*'s selection of recruits is based on an undifferentiated view of the production landscape – applicants either have the potential to be trained in this single, homogeneous 'skill', or they do not. Supervisors on the shop floor however produce their own criteria for evaluating the recruit, adopting a more specific, nuanced approach to *kifa'at* (skills) assessment. Thus for example different skills have come to be associated with particular areas from which migrant workers come. So in this way a Salheya girl's 'hand' in sewing is considered unmatched for its accuracy, while Manzala girls' 'precision' in quality control is much sought after.

Newcomers with previous work experience in other factories are given a brief ten minute practical test, to evaluate the experience they claim to have already gained. In sewing, the test entails being seated in a *sala* and timed with a stop-watch to see how many garments can be stitched per minute. For quality control work, the test involves a particular method of unfolding a finished garment – a process that entails knowing the steps that machinists have taken in the assembling process. Untrained recruits are drafted according to the need of the units of *entag* for labour, with physical attributes openly declared as the principal criterion. Horeya, the female foreman of both Assembly Halls, explains how this dates back to an earlier time when the workforce was predominantly female, and is explicit as to how it continues even with the current mixed-gender workforce:

> In the past, when we were all girls – there was a different classification system. If a girl looked broad with a large frame, she was sent to Cutting. If however she looked neat and tiny, she was given quality control work. And if she looked intelligent, from the way her eyes glowed, she was destined to be a machinist. Even today a neat appearance remains significant.

All supervisors are involved in assessing female recruits for their neatness and suitability. Untrained male workers, by comparison, are assessed only by male supervisors – and once again on the basis of their appearance. Certain signs indicate whether the male recruit is a *sawabiq*: these include tattoos, bruises or scars from physical cuts on the face and arms. These are read as signs of young males who carry a *silah* (blade), usually leading directly into the assumption that many of them are also drug addicts and involved in gangs and crime (Ismail 2006). The need to exclude such direct threats to the respectability of the shop floor (not only by their simple presence, but also because of the dangerous temptation they represent for female co-workers) is vividly articulated by the views expressed by girls who had worked with *sawabiq* types in the past. Thus Rasha, for example, remembers them from her early days on the assembly lines:

> They had wild nicknames like *Masura* (pipe) and *Zumara* (whistle) and a certain aura about them, tough and ready to get into a fight. They were feared. But they were *gid'aan* (chivalrous), especially where girls were concerned. We liked them a lot.

Nowadays, within mixed-gender work units, it is left to the supervisor's personal discretion to determine the gender of the new recruit, though they often take into account the preferences expressed by long-serving workers in their teams. Thus *Bashmuhandis* Mohsen, who heads the Cutting Unit, is clear that hiring girls is greatly preferable:

> Girls are much better than boys. Girls are by nature obedient and shy to say no. They say *hader, hader, hader* ('Yes I obey' [nodding his head when repeating the 'yes' word]), without arguing back. Boys are the complete opposite, always arguing over the detailed logistics of any task expected of them, rather than just getting on with it.

This gender preference, and the interaction between the workers in a team and their supervisor, was seen in practice when a *tarqim* position became vacant in Cutting. Zizi, the supervisor, announced to the *tarqim* unit how, despite being 'of the same professional standing' as Mohsen, she was not consulted over the decision to fill the vacant position: 'Mohsen, as you all know by now, is in favour of recruiting a *bint* (girl) with the usual noises he makes about girls bringing a sense of *roh* (spirit) to the place – unlike the boys, who give him stress'. The news was received in silence, as the girls in the unit continued to bang stickers on different garment components. Aware that their new member is likely to be from the latest recruits, they watch the stream of new faces ascending and descending the staircase. Those whose appearance qualifies as *kwayisa* (good) or *hadya* (subdued) are favoured – even though, as Zeinab, speaking from bitter past experience, whispers 'looks can be deceptive'. The girls settle on their preferred candidates, identifying them by the different colours and styles of their *hijab*, and then draw the boys working with them into their deliberations to benefit from their 'experienced eye' before the carefully hand-picked newcomers are officially drawn into the unit. The intense interest provoked by recruitment through formal channels indicates each unit's own initiative to exercise a measure of control over members drawn from the outside pool.

Given the apparent rigour and discrimination, which goes into this second, 'downstairs' stage of the recruitment process, it remains the case that, in practice, no one ever seems to get turned away without being assigned to a unit. The construction and performance of *ihtiram* is, however, further strengthened by the public explanations given for the occasional instances when, after having been given a work unit assignment and started work, an individual recruit is found, after all, not to be up to the job. This invariably occurs at the individual's own volition: he or she just 'leaves' of their own accord. And the explanation offered, and accepted, is that they were never properly 'respectable' in the first place, but somehow slipped through due to lapses in vigilance and failure to recognise aspects of the individual's unsuitability. Sawsan Etrebi uses an example to show up the inexperience of her assistant in recruiting the 'wrong' worker:

> I was away on that day, and Mongid hired a machinist drafted into *Khat Zaim* (an assembly line). Three days into the factory job, she turned up to hand in her resignation and complained that she found the atmosphere in *entag* insulting. For starters her face was a *kharita* ('a map' signifying too much make-up) and we found her talking to us *bil 'ayn wil hagib* ('with the eye and the eyebrow' ie giving herself airs). We brought Zaim over for questioning to find out if there were any grounds for the displeasure she had expressed. It was all *kalam awanta* (an emphatic colloquialism denoting 'bullshit'). If it was left to me, I would never have allowed her to set foot in this place even had she claimed she had all the skills of the *istithmar* under her belt. She was never right for this place.

The moral aspects of *ihtiram* are visible in a number of workplace practices. Some of these relate directly to the aura of *ihtiram* which infuses the environment as a consequence of Qasim Bey's all pervasive, if unseen, presence. Continuing reminders of Qasim Bey's moral force are provided by the religiosity in which the factory premises are steeped, reportedly at his personal behest. Large religious inscriptions such as *ma sha'allah* (Praise be to God) and *la hawla wala quwat ila billah* (There is no Power without Him) are painted on the factory's white-washed walls in bold green Kufi calligraphy, alongside large posters which instruct workers on health and safety measures. These bold, impressive scripts give the workplace a deeply conservative outlook. Other religious prints can be found at the entry points to different units of production. Most common are the last three verses of the Koran, believed to offer divine protection to the believer, which hang in gilded frames. Decorative worry beads inscribed with the ninety-nine names of God also hang from nails in different corners of *salat*, to allow divine protection to permeate the production zones of the workplace, and provide protection from any individual who, knowingly or unknowingly, has the potential to endanger it.

The religious aura saturating the workplace is accompanied by the visits every Monday week by Sheikh 'Yassin'. This is understood to be a personal *'ada* (tradition) close to the heart of Qasim Bey and the Fahmy family. Every week, at the same hour, the smoked glass doors to the top management suite open and Sheikh Soliman, an elderly clergyman known to be a personal friend of the family, appears. Dressed in his long Azharite gown and traditional turban with a deep burgundy shawl on one shoulder, he steps across the shop floor carrying the Holy Koran, to recite, at precisely 11.45 A.M., *Surit Yassin*, the 'Heart of the Holy Koran' and the source of the nickname, Sheikh 'Yassin', that the workforce have given him. After concluding his recitation he quietly commands a communal reading of the *fatha* (the opening chapter of the Koran).

Other measures taken to reinforce the image of Fashion Express as a *makan mohtaram* (respectable area) are related more directly to the mixed-gender setting. So, for example, great emphasis is placed on ensuring that none of the female workers are seen by the factory's gates, or are otherwise visible from outside the premises, during working hours. Yet for male workers to be given ready access to the factory's entry and exit gates is considered to be simply a matter of 'able-bodied men being where they are supposed to be'. At one level these restrictions on the movement of female workers, long adopted by the firm from the days when the entire labour force was female, can trace their enduring internal logic to the sexual division of labour common in traditional rural households, where women's work is to stay indoors and 'transform' what the men 'bring in' (Hopkins 1988). In Port Said, such sensitivity to women's mobility and visibility can however be further heightened, also evoking unacceptable parallels with the notorious houses of ill repute, which, though now long gone, once did a vigorous trade serving sailors from ships passing through the Suez Canal (Modelski 2000).

The present-day risks of potential immorality are, nevertheless, recognised as both real and immediate. This is because the majority of the Fashion Express workforce is young and single, and comes from a mixed urban and rural background where gender mixing (other than with one's blood relatives) is strictly proscribed on socioreligious grounds. As one perceptive observer has put it:

> Muslim sexuality is territorial: its regulatory mechanisms consist primarily in a strict allocation of space to each sex and an elaborate ritual for resolving the

contradictions arising from inevitable intersections of spaces … Interaction(s) between unrelated men and women … violate the spatial rules that are the pillars of the Muslim sexual order. (Mernissi 1987: 137)

The factory therefore provides the young men and women from a mixed rural and urban background with a space in which to interact at closer quarters. Top management are highly sensitive to the potential this opens up for breaches of the central principle of *ihtiram* in its moral aspects. Tewfik Saleh explains it in a matter of fact way:

> *Il-mam-nu' marghub* (that which is forbidden is desired) – over here it's an unmistakable feature of the local mentality. Sex is on everybody's mind. Its presence can almost be said to be palpable in the factory, as elsewhere. In your West, it's less intense because it is not forbidden – but here it is heightened.

As a result, the all-pervading system of surveillance which I described earlier as designed for the collection, collation, confirmation and transmission of information as a continual demonstration of *ikhlaas* (loyalty) to the person of *il-kebir*, is also turned to a second purpose, namely the prevention of breaches of the moral aspects of *ihtiram* (respectability). In the following chapters I describe in detail the extent to which the workplace is sexualised, and the ways in which romantic interactions are monitored. To conclude this section I will therefore confine myself to describing how the episodes excavated through surveillance, even when related to labour issues, are often overlaid with a narrative of morality. Tewfik Saleh illustrates this when recounting a case he remembers particularly vividly:

> We had employed a woman in Security who claimed her father was some bigwig in the Isma'iliyya police force. One morning I received news that the original model of a pair of jeans, provided by the contractor for us to copy, had gone missing. We turned the factory upside down in search of it, and I went berserk – the template couldn't just disappear into thin air. Who in their right mind would *steal* the original sample? The hours of the day were ticking away fast. The lads in Security had noticed that the woman in question had reported to work that day in a black skirt – not the jeans she was seen wearing later. I began to have my suspicions, and if my doubts were correct we'd have to find the black skirt before the shift ended 4.30 or else it would be too late! I got the lads to search the place a second and third time, and personally went into the Planning Unit where she was seen to have spent a few hours. As I sat on Shaker's desk with my head in my hands, feeling defeated by the futile search, it was as if a divine inspiration prompted me to look into the bin right next to me. Underneath sheets of newspapers, I found the skirt. With this evidence, I had to confront her. On these occasions there need to be at least two of us confronting her, as some women get up to pranks. She could tear her clothes,

scream or claim I attempted to sexually assault her. I ordered her to undergo a personal search, at which she defensively shouted, 'I'm not the thief'. Quick as a flash I answered, 'How did you know it was a theft case we are investigating?' In searching her handbag we found a packet of cigarettes and contraceptive pills (implying incriminating evidence of loose female morality).'

This episode shows how the excavated material reinforces the system's raisons d'être. The two principles most vital to the firm's image, namely *ihtiram* and *ikhlaas*, are woven into the narrative, providing the fundamental axes on which the organisation of the 'firm as family' is constructed. The *'eyun il-sherka* ('eye of the firm') is the instrument and system which distinguishes between individuals who demonstrate loyalty to the patriarch and personify the respectability that he epitomises, and others who show they have abandoned the standards demanded by, and the salt and bread shared with, the *kebir*. This constant monitoring of the workforce, and classification of individuals as loyal and respectable – or the reverse – provides a mechanism not simply for management control of the workforce, but also for constant reaffirmation of the metaphorical kinship dynamic of the 'firm as family'.

Taraabut: articulations of community and entitlement

In previous sections of this chapter I have shown how issues of class, gender and religion are intertwined in management's stratagems to recruit and retain workers in the face of fierce external competition for skilled labour, and to control the factory's workforce in the face of an uncertain and wildly fluctuating production pipeline. I now move on to consider the workforce's responses to these management control strategies, and in particular to explore how issues of accommodation and resistance manifest themselves in the workplace.

I begin by returning to the factory's recruitment practices, as described earlier. It is clear that the twice-yearly formal recruitment process of *bab il-ta'inat* is, by itself, inadequate to meet the day-to-day labour demands of the shop floor. Sawsan Etrebi sees the acute disjuncture between externally presented image and hard economic reality, as it is her responsibility to receive each day's attendance register. She takes a single glance at the daily attendance sheet Mongid hands her to sign, and looks up disgusted. On this particular day the total figure of 105 workers present in two assembly *salat* yields a tally of 80 absentees (i.e. over 40 per cent of the required manpower). Daily fluctuations on this scale are not unusual in the working environment of *entag*. When I ask for some basic workforce statistics, she declares herself defeated in her basic duty of maintaining a definitive database of workforce numbers:

Keeping a database of a steady workforce has not been possible for quite some time now. We're simply watching figures of workforce numbers rise and fall. This is a constant losing battle and at the heart of it is the problem all factories face, which is that of retaining its workforce on a permanent basis. We find our work pattern taking on the form of *takdiz* (pile-ups – as in traffic jams), where one work order turns up and pressure is placed on the existing workforce of limited size. When the order is large, we are stretching our resources to the limit, only to face an indefinite slump later. The sense of security is absent.

Given these uncertainties, other informal, more flexible processes of recruitment need to be brought into operation in order to fill ad hoc vacancies that regularly arise on the shop floor. A clue to what these might involve emerged during the first three weeks of my fieldwork, which I spent in the Planning Department. I rapidly discovered that Rasmeya was a close girlfriend of Shaker's ex-fiancée; Hamed was Shaker's first cousin; Sawsan Etrebi was married to Zeiko; and Mongid, her new assistant, was the Production Manager's cousin. In sum, everybody was 'known' to somebody in the firm and identified as either a direct blood relation, a distant relative, or a family tie of friendship that counts as a *me'rifa* (an acquaintance). When I later moved to *entag* I found a similar pattern. Around every worker in *entag*, a cluster of neighbours, siblings, friends and acquaintances could be found either in the same unit, or dispersed in other units of production, exposing a kinship network that was far more intricate and extended than in the smaller units of *edara*.

So it soon became evident that the basis on which the flexible, informal channels of ad hoc recruitment are structured is one of kinship in its literal sense. When vacancies arise in any unit, the preferred channel of making up numbers is for existing workers to 'bring in' kin. This practice is most pronounced among the factory's migrant workers from neighbouring provinces. Immediately vacancies become available, they act as brokers for their local communities by offering a chance to join the EPZ labour market to other members of their network who are searching for employment, with wages higher than those available in their rural home bases. These networks extend well beyond 'blood relative' kinship ties. Some date back to the 1967–1975 years of *hijra* when families from the three Canal Governorates (Port Said, Isma'iliyya and Suez) were evacuated to other regions of Egypt. The ties formed there, which helped them survive the years of estrangement from their home areas, have come over the four decades since then to be regarded as equivalent to genuine kin relationships. Several Isma'ilawi and Port Saidian families in *entag* are 'related' in this manner, and speak explicitly of one another as *ikhwat il-hijra* (diaspora siblings).

Relatives introduced to the factory through these informal recruitment channels are hired with briefer interviews than in the formalities of *bab il-ta'inat*. Vacancies seem almost to be there for the taking, and kin members brought in are on the shop floor within ten minutes of arrival. As a result, it is common to find that the first questions asked about any new face in the labour pool is '*arib min?*' ('whose relative are they?'), long before any curiosity is expressed about their skills, experience or the production unit to which they have been assigned. The speed with which they settle into their new working environment, and their acquisition of skills, is facilitated by the informal networks I have described, giving the kinship relationship an important register through which new recruits become accepted in the working environment (Safa 1995; Fernandes 1997a; Rofel 1999; Toth 1999). Through these practices the workplace begins to take on some of the familial features of sheltered community life, as members of each external community who join the factory as individuals network together to personalise the collective working environment of *entag*.

For management, this widespread reliance on formal and informal kinship networks has several advantages. Firstly, it enables vacancies to be filled speedily, outside the formal *bab il-ta'inat* channels, which, in order to project an external image of regularity and stability, can only operate at fixed periods in the year. Secondly, it provides built-in assurance that the central principle of *ihtiram* (respectability) will not be undermined by each new recruit brought in through these informal channels. Since the sponsoring worker is already known to the firm, their kinship or acquaintance with each newcomer serves to vouch for their character, be they male or female. And thirdly, the reliance on kinship networks enables management to achieve labour flexibility – essential for meeting tight production deadlines – within a cultural context determined by gender rigidity.

As production deadlines for export orders loom, *takdiz* (pile-ups) tend to build up towards the final stages of production, especially in the laundry and packaging departments. Management thus needs to redeploy workers from units engaged in earlier stages of production (such as cutting, marking and assembly) to help clear the backlogs. Since the laundry and packaging departments are seen as exclusively male domains of labour, drafting female workers into these units poses significant risks to embedded socioreligious proscriptions against gender mixing, with potentially negative implications of violating codes of proper female behaviour by generating income (supposedly a male prerogative), and doing so through working with total strangers (White 1994; El-Kholy 2002; Dedeoglu 2005). The risks are further heightened by the way in which tight deadlines demand extending working hours well into the night, a time when all respectable women are required to be in their homes, not mixing with men in public spaces, whether this be the workplace or the nocturnal bus ride home.[10] The extensive kinship networks (both formal and informal) operating in the factory, however, mean that, in most cases, one or more of a female worker's *mehrem* (religiously sanctioned male relatives) will be present in the unit into which she is being drafted. And since mixing with *mehrem* is exempted from proscription, this enables such temporary drafting of female labour to other units to take place without risk to the individual's *sira* (reputation), or to the factory's carefully crafted image as a *makan mohtaran*. In this way, what might easily be interpreted as management exploiting the kinship dimension of labour for their own ends is carefully disguised: what is instead fashioned is the image of a 'respectable' workplace, one that zealously guards the reputation of its female workforce. This 'disguising' strategy contrasts with more explicit management strategies for regulating a mixed-gender workforce through social groups and communities, which can be seen to operate in the informal sector and family-run sweatshops (Secor 2003).

Yet it is by no means only management who benefit from the informal process of ad hoc recruitment through kinship networks. This arrangement also provides advantages for the workers involved. To begin with, it provides existing workers with a parallel assurance that each additional newcomer in their midst is reinforcing, rather than diluting, the principle of *ihtiram*, which is central not only to the construction of Fashion Express' image as a workplace, but also to their own vested interest in being seen to be working in, and affiliated with, a 'respectable' establishment. It also provides the newcomer, especially if she is female, with an important degree of reassurance about the character of the work environment into which she is entering. This not only applies to her own perceptions of the perils and pitfalls of an environment characterised by a workforce that is both young and of mixed gender. More importantly, it encourages her family and community to see the factory setting as a more appropriate area for female employment for single girls – especially since they are also allowed to bring in male kin as extra *mehrem*. Notions of social acceptability are important to the rural communities, especially as most female recruits in Fashion Express are first-generation waged and single workers. A frequent comment made by rural migrant girls was that in their communities working in alternative service sectors, such as shops, is considered as *'aiba* (shameful). Undertaking the journeys backwards and forwards as teams of girls and boys, many of them siblings and relatives, gives factory work greater social acceptability as an avenue of employment. A management policy that actively supports the recruitment of kin is perceived as the 'good' employer practice of *'ye-melo lil-nas ili 'andohom khater'* ('taking care of their own people'), echoing the perceptive comment made by Anna Secor in her study of migrant women workers in Istanbul that 'the meaning of work depends not only on the place where it is performed but also on the neighbourhood and community within which these practices are negotiated' (Secor 2003: 2218).

Evidently it is not only the proprietor-patriarch of Fashion Express and his top management who are broadening kinship from the real to the metaphorical, and investing all who work in the factory with this defining characteristic of the 'firm as family'. The workforce is equally engaged in a parallel process, extending the sense of 'kin' within the factory walls from formal networks of blood relatives, to informal networks including other 'real life families' who have shared common experiences of *hijra* exile, or who now share home bases in the provinces from which workers are recruited. The result is to draw both workers and management into a shared sense of community within the 'firm as family', a sense referred to by the workers as *taraabut* (togetherness, solidarity), and regularly invoked when discussing or contesting workplace relationships elsewhere. The ties of *taraabut* strengthen the discourse of metaphorical kinship to give the community of the workplace, in its separate labour units, its imagined sense of distinct identity.

To the workforce of Fashion Express, the feeling of 'collective belonging' associated with *taraabut* is more important than wages and material benefits. This is stated explicitly by members of the workforce, often by contrasting the conditions they have encountered during temporary stints in other factories in the Zone. Thus in the words of Hasina – a machinist in Leitex:

> The folk here are good. If you don't feel too well, they give you a lighter load. When you're away for a few days, they ask after you, welcome you back with faces that genuinely look pleased to see you. There is *taraabut* and it's enough for me that I'm comfortable with the people here. Outside it's not like this. They may pay you more, and on time – but they give you orders, they think they are superior as if you were not educated and don't know a thing. It's work and a work relationship and nothing else. Here *il-nas ma' ba'ad* (we're in it together).

The most visible manifestation of *taraabut* is in the factory's ways of meeting material needs that result from unstable pay conditions, or from unexpected circumstances (such as a sudden need to pay high hospital bills) that hit individual workers. In instances of family crisis that require instant cash, workers rely on donations and loans from co-workers in the workplace. Family and kinship networks are said to be less reliable avenues for securing such financial assistance – either because kin members who do not work in the factory are often in financial difficulties themselves, or because even relatives have become more utilitarian in their relationships with each other. The metaphorical family of the workplace is thus identified as the preferred alternative network from which to secure loans and donations, with many stories told of how the 'firm as family' rallies round to help a member in distress, in effect substituting for the vital role previously played by the 'real life' family.

Another means by which the workers internalise metaphorical kinship in the 'firm as family', and articulate it as *taraabut*, is through the way in which they respond to management's key control mechanism of constant surveillance. Workers do not avoid, or resist, *'eyun il-sherka*, or the network of *gawasis* through which information is collected and conveyed to management. Instead, they take an active part in the system of surveillance by finding ways to turn management's gaze back on itself, and bend it to their own purposes. I have described earlier in this chapter how the physical landscape of the factory is arranged to maximise the visibility of production and the workforce to management's gaze. This open landscape however also allows a parallel system to be put into operation – one in which the bulk of the workforce is itself actively engaged in establishing and sustaining its own system of surveillance. Different vantage points in the production layout are close to exits and entry points, staircases, toilets and form strategic junctures that allow individual workers in different labour units stationed in close proximity to these points to get access to events unfolding within their immediate surroundings. Familiarity with the production scene on a day-to-day basis, the repetitive nature of the tasks performed, and an awareness of the physical positioning of the workforce on the production map enables workers to discern with relative ease any signs of the unusual. These items of information are hungrily absorbed and converted into meaningful episodes of shop floor speculation and narratives, which are then rapidly circulated through the same grapevines originally established by management for its own control purposes.

Entag workers also exploit employees who have been commissioned as management *gawasis* (i.e. to report shop floor developments to management) to in turn 'report back' on developments in the various management suites and offices. Moles whose duties involve reporting face-to-face to top management have special importance when compared to those who report by other means such as the telephone. The face-to-face mole conveys back to the shop floor what it is that his or her own eyes and ears have relayed to top management, supplemented by other relevant information they have gleaned when reporting in the spatially segregated offices of top management. These sets of impressions are reported to the shop floor as the 'behind the scene' scenarios of the family members running the firm. They include issues potentially affecting the full and timely payment of wages, such as pressing debts and other financial difficulties that appear to be troubling the firm; the steps being taken to solve the seemingly never-ending cash crisis; or the expected timing of a new production order, and who the subcontractor is likely to be. The grapevine of surveillance becomes a complex porous system that circulates information in both directions – not only from bottom to top, but also from top to bottom. The workplace becomes, in the telling formulation used by Khadija from Cutting, a *masna' malush asrar* (a factory without secrets).

The sense of togetherness inherent in *taraabut* is particularly evident when it comes to potentially contentious issues of religion. In the wider sociocultural environment outside the factory, as in much of the rest of Egypt and the Middle East, religious issues can often be the subject of increasingly strident public debate (Eickelman 1996; Schielke and Debevec 2012). Yet on the Fashion Express shop floor there seemed to be a widespread acceptance of Islamic religious discourse as encompassing a corpus of religious material sufficiently broad to defend or refute any of the conflicting viewpoints flying around the factory. This echoes Scott's more recent (2010) account of how different factions within Egypt's rising wave of Islamisation likewise base their claims to legitimacy on competing, alternative interpretations of the foundational texts of Islam, which all agree to be the Koran and the *hadith* (records of actions and sayings attributed to the Prophet). Religious discussions within the working environment of the factory might take place over, for example, recently issued *fatawi* (religious opinions issued by clerics) on a particular issue, with contrasts being drawn between the published views of a tolerant *sheikh* and those of a more extreme preacher. These often have the effect of reducing the significance, within the workplace, of the issue under discussion. Another commonly deployed means of responding to an extreme religious position would be by quoting a *hadith* to give another angle on the issue under discussion. These religious sources are actively exploited to develop an inclusive social critique of the factory's hierarchical and class landscape. For example, *edara* would justify its attitude towards *entag* by invoking a strict interpretation of the Islamic ordering of society into *tabaqaat* (classes), thus demanding acquiescence in a hierarchical arrangement of classes, and the social and economic differences between 'higher' and 'lower' orders. *Entag* would counter-attack by quoting a different *hadith*, which states that those who exhibit arrogance towards others less fortunate than themselves risk divine wrath, relishing the Prophet's warning of how on the Day of Judgement 'those insensitive creatures shall be crushed *like ants*' [spoken with spitting indignation]. More widespread were local proverbs that shared a strong resonance with Islamic tenets. Thus the proverb '*il-nafs il-hilwa liha il-gana*' ('the sweet soul gets to reach heaven') was often repeated when sharing bottles of iced water or edibles around the shop floor. And scrawled in chalk on the iron gate at the workers' entrance to the factory was the religious saying '*la tay'as min rahmit Allah*' ('Never despair of God's compassion'), indicating that those in difficulties – whether workers or owners – shall be saved, thereby reinforcing the *taraabut* spirit of the workplace.

This infusion of workplace *taraabut* with a quasi-religious quality provides the context for another distinctive feature of shop floor debate, namely its use of the concept of *haqq*. Often translated simply as 'rights', *haqq* is, as Rosen (1984), amongst others, has pointed out, central to the construction of social relations in Islamic society. In Rosen's view *haqq* is imbued with a range of meanings far richer than simply 'rights' – it also includes 'duty', 'truth', 'claim' and 'obligation', meanings that both describe and define the essentially relational quality associated with the concept. As he perceptively summarises it: 'To speak of *haqq* is, in short, to convey that sense of mutual obligation that binds men to men, and man to God … the web of indebtedness that links sentient beings to one another in a chain of obligations' (Rosen 1984: 62).

Haqq is a concept that has particular resonance in historical accounts of labour in Egypt and in petitions outlining workers' perceptions of justice and wrongdoing (Chalcraft 2007). I soon discovered that everybody in Fashion Express – from the owner right down to the cleaners – had their own conception of *haqq*, with everybody entitled to their just dues, although these differed according to their positions in the overall hierarchy (Scott 2010: 22). Thus the term was commonly deployed when protecting one's boundaries from exploitation or potential abuse, and could also be linked with maintaining one's dignity or stand. It was voiced in phrases such as '*Akhud haqqi*' ('I will take my *haqq*'), where it was used in the sense of a 'claim' and the right of an individual who feels wronged to fight back against the wrongdoer. In verbal skirmishes between supervisors, amongst workers, or between those lower in the hierarchy and others more senior in the professional ladder, a wronged individual has a *haqq* that needs to be retrieved. If this is not effected immediately, every incident from then onwards can be seen as an opportunity to retrieve *haqq*. If the wronged person is unable to achieve this by themselves, they will rely on others within their network who carry greater clout to retrieve it on their behalf.

On the shop floor, *haqq* provides a framework of understanding (based on justice according to one's position in the hierarchy, rather than any purported equality of human rights) within which retaliation may be expected to follow if exploitation or abuse of trust has taken place, or allegations been made, in personal relationships as much as work relationships. It implies rushing to the aid of a wronged person, taking sides in a fight until *haqq* is securely retrieved. An example would be when Zeinab objects that, at a time of peak production, the supervisor has reallocated her unit's workload to give Tamer, a male colleague, less work than she herself is required to get through by the pressing deadline. Picking the right moment, Zeinab, within earshot of her supervisor, soliloquises aloud:

A new system has been set up at my expense! I'm having to work more than Tamer, doing twelve sizes all by myself, though I didn't open my mouth at the time. I'm not a hired servant – let me make that clear! [She pauses for dramatic effect]. Have I said something out of order? My blood is boiling! I want my *haqq il-qadim* (my original *haqq*)! Now if *he* [talking of her supervisor] wants to gain extra merits in heaven, he is *not* to load me with yet more work this afternoon!

This sense of mutual obligation and shared entitlement can also extend from individual protest to collective workforce resistance to perceived exploitation by management. Previous scholars of the modern workplace have noted how the social contract between employer and worker often involves tacit expectations. Far from regarding them as simply market transactions, both employers and workers jointly devise rules forged in an agreement about what constitutes justice, as they draw on rhetorical strategies and shared values in their struggle over contractual terms and conditions of service (Golderg 1986; Fernandes 1997b; Collins 2003; Chalcraft 2007, 2008). Yet in Fashion Express the workforce went further than this, turning the very idioms deployed by management when making its demands for *ikhlaas* (loyalty), including religion, into instruments of shop floor protest and resistance.

The most regular occurrences of collective action, referred to as *film kul shahr* (action drama of the month), revolved around the vexed issue of late payment of wages. Workers were entitled to be paid on the first day of the month. It was when the delay stretched to a week that *entag* would take action. This could take one of two forms, depending on the stage reached in the production cycle. If the issue came to a head at a time when production was at its peak, with export deadlines looming, the workers were conscious of the increased bargaining power they held by virtue of being able to disrupt management's contractual obligations. My fieldnotes record how at such times word of mouth rapidly spreads that an *idrab* (strike) is to kick off at a specified time. Sewing machines grind to a halt, with silence observed by all workers. The resulting scene, despite its seeming lack of active protest, is dramatic in its effect. An eerie feeling seeps onto the shop floor, as groups of workers sit or stand immobile as if frozen in place, not lifting a pair of scissors or touching a single sewing machine or a garment. The Production Manager and workers lock eyes, as they pause to the call of a sarcastic comment from the shop floor, such as the *hadith* which says that a worker should be paid before the sweat dries on his forehead, or a simple call to God to be their witness. Other than these lone, loud utterances, a defiant silence is sustained as the clock ticks. The result of such a tense, confrontational atmosphere is to galvanise top management into action to find a way for payment of wages to be sorted out. Once an arrangement has been worked out, a spokesperson (frequently the Production Manager) is sent to spread word on the shop floor as to when workers are to be paid – an obligation that, once announced, needs to be honoured almost instantly for production to resume. As a rule of thumb, the cash appears within two hours of an *idrab* being staged.

This scenario is played out differently when *entag* is between production cycles – the lean phase of production. In these instances, a more aggressive mood prevails. Loud words are shouted as male workers attempt to invade top management's offices, and fights break out between Security and workers, and their mates who come to their aid. Male workers kick over the metal ironing tables, leaving ironing sets dangling from their sockets. Security dims the lights in the Assembly Halls, with the task of picking up the pieces and putting things back in their place left to the female supervisors on the shop floor. The workers refer to such expressions of pent-up anger through dramatic captions such as *youm il-'alami* (international day), *youm il-damir* (day of conscience), or *youm il-karama* (day of dignity). In each case, top management has to appease workers by sending intermediaries to give firm assurances of revised timelines for payment of wages.

In each such episode, the demands of the workers are not designed to renegotiate the terms of their employment, but to insist on the reinstatement of *haqq* being withheld or denied.[11] It is also instructive that, however confrontational such episodes appear to be on the face of things, both forms of shop floor protest are referred to by workers and management alike as periods of *qalaq*, a term whose use highlights the underlying commonality of mutual obligation and *taraabut*. *Qalaq* connotes a state of anomy, when 'something is not right', and whose advent is recognisable by the agitated behaviour of those who are involved or affected. Street demonstrations about political issues are, for example, frequently referred to as instances of *qalaq*. The use of the term *qalaq* within the context of labour disputes gains greater clarity, when, within Fashion Express, the explanation given is that delayed wages are not a result of a proprietor callously withholding the cash, but rather of a proprietor who is in the same boat as his workers – in debt, and unable to honour his obligations for reasons 'beyond his control'. In this case the state of anomie, 'what is not right', is the proprietor's inability to honour his side of the framework of mutual obligations that binds management and workers together within the *taraabut* of the workplace.[12] Yet this inability requires the workers to reaffirm through their endurance – a feature of working-class identity identified by Goldberg in his study in the textile industry (1986) – their commitment to the 'firm as family'.

The requirement for workforce endurance and resilience is made all the more poignant by the centrality of the father–offspring relationship within the discourse of metaphorical kinship around which the 'firm as family' is constructed. It is as if this metaphorical articulation of the employer–employee relationship has to be put into practice, particularly towards a proprietor who needs at that critical moment the support of 'his children', not their condemnation. Such a deployment of the metaphoric kinship is explicit in the account given by a member of *edara* of one such occasion, on which they had to resort to seeing the proprietor in person:

> *Baba* is a first-class politician! When he saw us, he knew what we were about to say. Before allowing us to speak he rose from his chair, his worry beads in his right hand. In a fatherly voice, he asked us to bear with him. He nodded his head saying *'arif, 'arif* (I know). He repeated it several times, looking pained and frail. The outcome? We stood there with nothing left to say. It shamed us to bring up the subject of money. Who doesn't have a father who has not been in a similar position, crippled by his feelings of impotence to provide for his children?

As a result, episodes of *qalaq* were usually projected as familiar scenes in any family situation, reminiscent of the sort of bad atmosphere that commonly erupts in a home, and that needs to be resolved through a dramatic fight that clears the air. Once aired, the whole family can pull its forces together again, and the firm be left to get on with 'business as usual'. And indeed, this is what usually took place following each *qalaq* incident. Within a few days, after the anger had subsided, workers and supervisors would join hands to give their units of labour on the shop floor a thorough spring clean – women workers and supervisors swabbing the floors with broomsticks, the boys filling and carrying heavy buckets of water, and the cleaning brigade mopping up the puddles of dirty water. With the grievance aired, and the anomie underpinning the instance of *qalaq* resolved, the *taraabut* of the 'firm as family' can be restored.

One of the most powerful articulations of entitlement and shared community was the phenomenon of 'raids' on the factory's workforce by other firms in the Zone, and how these were resolved within the Fashion Express 'firm as family'. Organised poaching of workers by fiercely competing firms was regarded as an inescapable fact of life in the Export Processing Zone. Fashion Express' management referred to it as *tasarub 'emala* (the disappearance, in the sense of melting away, of the workforce). In many cases the competing firms were blatant in their attempts to woo skilled workers away from Fashion Express.

An example recorded in my field notes involves the new factory being opened next door by Madame S (the female proprietor earlier described as having disturbed the male-dominated meeting of EPZ investors). Its preparations are staged with great ostentation, ensuring that the Fashion Express workers enjoying their mid-day break in the alley between the two factories have a front-row view of the deliveries of supplies of fresh paint for the walls, brand new sewing machines for the Assembly Hall, and new, bright red chairs for the machinists. The intentions of Madame S are obvious to all. As Amina, a machinist in Leitex, says as she admires the red chairs stacked up in the street: 'Why don't they just build a corridor, so we can move backwards and forwards between the two factories? And if these chairs had wheels on them, like *edara*'s office chairs, they could push us in splendour from one shop floor to the other!'

The prime actors in episodes of *tasarub 'emala* were not only the predatory owners of competing firms, but also the absconding workers themselves. Resistance to perceived management malpractice (such as late payment of wages, or personal disputes with supervisors) could be expressed dramatically by abruptly decamping to the establishment of a competitor. The first indication that a *tasarub 'emala* has taken place could, therefore, often come as a nasty shock to the factory on the losing end.

Thus one morning in May, after a period when Fashion Express wages have once again been delayed, Horeya (the female foreman of Leitex) arrives to find that a high ratio of absenteeism has hit her *sala*, providing evidence of a new round of *tasarub 'emala*. The buses transporting migrant workers to the Zone have also arrived late, adding to the tension and suspense of a shop floor gripped by circulating rumours. Standing at the far end of the *sala*, Horeya monitors the late arrivals pouring in through the back gate, and by interrogating individuals identifies from which *baladiyyat* (home villages or areas) the culprits come. The missing workforce is this time identified as the Manzala group, who have used the firm's buses as free transportation to reach the Zone and then disappeared to other factories. In this case it is suspected that the Manzala bus drivers have acted as the competitor firms' agents in masterminding the 'raid', thus bypassing the direct surveillance system of Fashion Express. Horeya's reaction to the sudden depopulation of her area of the shop floor is immediate. Surrounded by the other supervisors in her *sala*, she lashes out:

> It's one particular group of rebels who cut me up, tear me to pieces and throw me across the walls of this *sala*: the *beida* (inexperienced) workers whom I have nurtured. Those who began in this very *sala* as unskilled ancillary workers, and over the months I turned them into machinists. I've no tears to shed over the worker who arrives here already laden with credentials. If I have to face this every single day, production can rot in hell!

It can be seen that her rhetoric is an articulation of disloyalty, the negation of *ikhlaas* as a principle deployed in the training of skills. The absconding workers have not simply left her with a management problem; they have betrayed her in a more personal, immediate sense.

Edara however appears to take a more matter-of-fact approach to the sudden loss of a large chunk of its workforce. Within an hour, the Production Manager has compiled a list of runaway workers to be included in a formal letter of complaint to the Zone's Labour Office, which is nominally responsible for policing such infractions of the Zone's regulations. Sawsan Etrebi, upstairs in her Workers Affairs office, doubts whether such official sanctions, or assurances of forthcoming work in Fashion Express, will have much effect:

> Workers need concrete facts to stay put in one place: wages on time at the start of every month, and the security of knowing work is flowing in – cloth delivered, clients of subcontracting orders walking about, containers leaving factory premises. Words are not enough. In the past, *Baba* could leave them to work elsewhere for a while, until the new subcontracting order would come in. Then he'd call the other factories owners to tell them his *'iyal* (children) have been *birayaho* (having a rest) but now he needs them back to do some work. Today, pulling this off is not so straightforward. Factories need workforce numbers, and rely heavily on the internal problems of other enterprises to survive. It's a civil war!

Horeya's anger subsides once management's enquiries uncover more details about the three factories that have suborned the bus drivers. Surveillance reveals that they have recruitment policies that do not favour a migrant workforce and that the absconding workers had probably not been truthful about their 'status'. Moreover, the absconding *'iyal* will no longer be able to use the Fashion Express buses for their daily commute to the Zone, and the increase in their wages of LE50 (another detail surveillance has established) will not go far if they have to use public transportation at LE5 a day. Workers in the offending firms are also alleged to have spat at their supervisors, threatening to beat them up after work – shop floor 'incidents' of verbal and physical violence unheard of in Fashion Express's workplace environment. It is accordingly decided that retrieving the workers need not involve asking Zone officials to call up the offending factories, or Qasim Bey to intervene personally. Implicit within these negotiations in Fashion Express is the assumption that, one way or the other, in due course the absconding workers will return of their own accord.

And, within three days of the incident, junior workers from the Manzala team do indeed begin to send word to their supervisors expressing a willingness to return. Through these verbal channels (a face-saving mechanism for both absconding workers and management alike) the 'raided' workers can gauge the severity of the wrath against them, and their likely chances of clemency on return. The supervisors of the *salat* remain eager to retrieve their skilled workforce. As Nidal Hassan affirms, 'I've sweated to train them, not for others to receive them ready-made!' All parties involved, from the Production Manager to unit and assembly line supervisors, agree that they cannot afford to turn away skilled workers who have been trained on their shop floors, even if they have been gullible enough to be swayed by lucrative promises from other firms also in need of skilled workers. Within a week the wanderers have returned to the fold.

A central feature of the entire *tasarub 'emala* experience thus appears to be the unspoken assumption, shared by both management and workers alike, that the 'raided' workers' absence will only be temporary. The process can therefore be interpreted within the discourse of metaphorical kinship around which the 'firm as family' is structured. The aggrieved 'children' punish their errant 'father', who has failed in his duty of care towards them, by decamping to the establishment of a competitor and rival – though from the outset both sides share an assumption that this state of affairs is never intended to be permanent. And the granting of clemency to the aggrieved 'children' within the process of conflict resolution strengthens even deeper the metaphorical power of the firm-as-family with the patriarch at its head.

Entikhbo Qasim Fahmy! – the workers endorse their *kebir*

A powerful public demonstration of *taraabut* within the 'firm as family' was provided during the elections held in May 2004 for the Shura Council, or Upper House of the Egyptian Parliament, in which Qasim Bey stood as a candidate for the ruling NDP party. It provided a vivid expression of the continuing political aspirations of the Fahmy *'aila*, and the ways in which these ambitions were advanced through the active mobilisation of the metaphorical *beit* (household) which his economic enterprise, Fashion Express, represented.

Qasim Bey's candidature in this hotly contested election provided an interesting case-study of the mix of social, economic and political interests competing to dominate the local landscape in Port Said (Kienle 2001; Kassem 2004). At the start of the election, his prospects did not appear to be promising, despite the distinguished political heritage attached to the Fahmy name. A minimum of 5,000 votes would be needed to secure a seat – but in view of its current financial constraints, the Fahmy family lacked the cash to buy votes in the way other more recent arrivals on the political scene were reportedly doing. Support was however forthcoming from the group of EPZ local investors, who recognised that they had a vested interest in assisting one of their members to hold the *Shura* seat, since there was apprehension that Port Said would otherwise lose its competitive advantage in bidding for inclusion in the Government's new QIZ programme.

Their support was furnished through organised mass voting by the employees of their own firms. The owners confirmed their allegiance to send their workers on factory buses to vote 'the correct way'. Some were even rumoured to have locked their workers' voting cards securely in their office safes, to help ensure that all went according to plan. They also showed active support by hanging banners at the gates of the *istithmar* and in key areas of town, declaring how 'Firm X, and leading garment investor Mr Y celebrate the nomination of Qasim Fahmy to the *Shura* seat', the resulting carnival of election banners living up to the town's reputation as *balad il-yufat* (the town of banners).

The election campaign lasted a month, and involved the mobilisation of the entire workforce of Fashion Express, providing an explicit example of how the workforce of each firm actively constitutes the public image of its proprietor. In the factory, production came to a standstill as the literate employees were assigned to track down the names of potential voters in the electoral register, so that *edara* could contact them personally to lobby for their favoured candidate. Teams of male workers from *entag* were assigned, under the strict eye of Security, the task of pasting up posters of Qasim Fahmy in key areas of Port Said. Smaller flyers with his picture on one side also carried a Koranic verse printed on the other, in order to, in the words of Tewfik Saleh (responsible for the candidate's PR), 'deter voters from throwing the Fahmy name in the bin'. The cleaners in the firm were deputed to attend campaign rallies, and came back with glowing reports of the status of Qasim Bey in the community. 'They carried him on their shoulders after he finished his speech. The applause was a storm! At one moment, I thought they would catapult the car with him in it!' is the way Om Makram describes one such event to her captive audience in Security.

On the morning of the election the entire female workforce is organised to turn out en masse in factory buses, each adorned with several large posters of their employer and chosen candidate, scheduled to take them to the polling booths by noon. Migrant workers ineligible to vote in Port Said join the procession of buses to chant slogans supporting Qasim Bey. The exercise soon escalates into a fierce competition over which bus has improvised the best slogan and is creating the biggest electoral din. '*Ism Allah 'aleh! Hami rayetna! Entikhbo Qasim Fahmy!*' ('The name of God be upon him! He is the protector of our flag! Vote for Qasim Fahmy!') is agreed to be the winner. In the afternoon the buses travel from one polling station to another (mainly located in local schools), circling the town several times with the girls screaming their heads off and waving their arms wildly from the open windows. Their performance is spectacular enough to catch the eye of the local press – although one photograph, printed two days later in an opposition paper, deliberately misrepresents them as an 'angry mob'.

The success of their proprietor in securing election was widely interpreted by the workforce as an achievement which would help the factory survive its crisis, and so rebound to their benefit. His having won a seat in the *Shura* Council was considered sufficient for him to maintain his position of prominence within the local community: and this enhanced external reputation would, in turn, positively cement his image and presence within Fashion Express. By enthusiastically supporting their *kebir*, the *'iyal* had actively demonstrated the loyalty expected of them as well as ties of *taraabut* that bind them as members of the metaphorical *beit Fahmy* – thereby also improving their own economic prospects, as well as securing the future of the workplace environment.

This community of multiple and overlapping interests provides the foundation for my next chapter, in which I explore the extent to which the workforce negotiates with management's strategies for different purposes related to their wider aspirations in the external environment outside the factory walls.

Notes

1. www.portsaidtp.gov.eg: quotations are from screen prints taken in June 2008.
2. The programme had initially been launched in Jordan, with eleven QIZs established whose profits had reportedly risen from $100 million in 1998 to $800 million in 2005. The programme became increasingly attractive following the expiry in 2005 of the Multi-Fibre Agreement quota system. In Egypt three industrial zones were initially to be selected for designation as QIZs, as a preliminary phase in the implementation of the programme. Despite the economic benefits expected, reservations were expressed both at the seminar and in the media over the ethical and political implications of the benefits provided by this new U.S.–Egypt trade agreement for *ibn 'amina* (our paternal uncle's sons, i.e. our cousins the Israelis, our fellow 'children of Abraham').
3. The Chinese film director Zhang Wei's 2014 film *Dagong Laoban* ('Factory Boss' – see www.zhangweimovie.net) provides a compelling fictional portrait of a proprietor-manager of a toy factory in southern China who finds himself in similar financial straits, caught between an international client ruthlessly determined to squeeze costs and an increasingly restive workforce whose demands for fair wages he cannot, as a result, satisfy. It is relevant that, before turning to film making, Zhang Wei was himself a successful entrepreneur in China's initial drive for economic reform, making millions from a factory he founded in Shenzhen to make video intercom doorbells for export (Makinen 2014).
4. The phrase has been taken into everyday Arabic to imply the person in charge.
5. Springborg (1982) has made extensive use of the term *shilla* to highlight the power of informal male networking in his study of Sayed Marei.
6. See Beth Baron's (2005: 86–88) account of the development of *il-taswir il-shamsi* (pictures from the sun, i.e. photography) and its growing importance in Egyptian political circles in the 30s for providing markers of class and political aspirations.

7. The political term *marakiz il-quwa* has its origins in the dominance of the army in the 1960s, and to the growth of cliques connected to circles of power. The term was later used by Nasser when in 1968 he made specific reference to 'a military class that believed it was the legitimate heir of the government of this land' (Ayubi 1980: 398).
8. A local mosque in Port Said, renowned for the generosity of its charitable handouts.
9. A working-class drug, classified as category B.
10. The gendered nature of this fear is a theme which has been specifically highlighted in the earlier literature (Hammam 1980; Ibrahim 1985; Joekes 1985).
11. This echoes the observation in Posusney's seminal work on ostensibly unionised public sector factories in the *infitah* era, where the goal of collective action is 'not to negotiate or redefine the terms of exploitation, but to reinstate them after they have been abandoned' (1994: 213).
12. The factory portrayed in the Chinese film 'Factory Boss' (see Note 3 above), based on the real-life experiences of a self-made entrepreneur factory owner, shows a contrasting culture of individualism even within the collective demands the workforce make of their proprietor. Without any culture of *taraabut*, they show no understanding of the proprietor-manager's financial difficulties, striking and taking legal action which eventually results in him closing the toy factory where the story is located.

Chapter 3

SHOP FLOOR AS MARKETPLACE
– LOVE AND CONSUMPTION

One day I noticed, scratched on the surface of one of the cast iron quality control tables with a pair of sharp scissors, the messages *enta ghirhum* (you are not like the others) and *ana lek* (I am yours). The ceaseless vigilance by the guardians of *ihtiram* was evidently not without cause. Yet when first stepping into *entag*, it was not immediately apparent that the shop floor, with its team of veiled *mushrifat* (female supervisors) and soberly attired *mushrefin* (male supervisors) watching over a sea of women workers in *hijab*, might nevertheless be a sexually charged space.

Other hidden clues however soon started to surface. One day, as I joined the workforce for the midday break, I spotted, pinned to the back gate of the factory, a wedding announcement penned by a calligrapher on a poster. At its centre were entwined the names of Hashem and Nagla, around which a Koranic verse spelled out the meeting of souls. The date and place of the wedding were specified, to serve as an announcement and a public invitation. Over the ensuing fortnight the poster became covered in good wishes, as individual workers wrote their congratulations on it in a flourish of signatures, romantic doodles of hearts and arrows, and witty quotations from famous love songs. Closer to the appointed day, the poster was taken away, to be framed and later given to the happy couple as a memento of the *taraabut* of the workplace in which they had found love. Not long afterwards, I was invited to a *khutuba* (engagement party) bringing together workers across different units of labour – the boys dressed to kill in tight jeans and T-shirts; the girls in discreetly elegant attire, but in *hijab* styles very different from their everyday work clothes; and the prospective bride in a glittering evening gown hired for the occasion, her face covered in glamorous makeup and her hair proudly displayed, without *hijab*, in a celebrity-style cascade of black tresses modelled on the elaborate coiffeurs favoured by film and TV stars.

In this chapter I explore ways in which the workforce appropriates management's chosen control strategies within the 'firm as family', to convert the workplace into an arena for the realisation of their hopes and dreams for both romantic and material fulfilment. The shop floor is transformed into a landscape where personal aspirations of love marriages and financial security are made real, reinforcing further the environment of *taraabut* described in the previous chapter.

Central to these aspirations is the search for love and its fulfilment in marriage, as the social and commercial opportunities of the desegregated workplace give greater acceptability to love-marriages (as opposed to traditional arranged marriages). The ideal trajectory sees the lovers winning out through an arduous struggle. The workplace provides the arena where young men and women have the opportunity to attract each other's attention, and I explore the stratagems they deploy in terms of dress code and flirtatious behaviour. I also describe the formalised shop floor 'bride and groom' games which the workplace enjoy during lulls in production, exploring how they both draw on, and at the same time mock, a rich blend of class, gender and romantic stereotypes. All takes place under the watchful eyes of the *mushrifat* (female supervisors), who take an essentially empathetic attitude – if anything, focusing mainly on protecting young, innocent male workers from the wiles of more experienced females.

Alongside the endless interest in each other's romantic entanglements, workers also turn the shop floor into a hive of commercial activity – transforming it from a zone of production into one of consumption. I describe how class and status aspirations, associated with ideas of social mobility, are reflected in the contents of many of the mail order catalogues circulating endlessly on the shop floor, and the services which workers set themselves up to provide to their fellow employees. A particular focus of this commercial activity concerns the accumulation by young, single female workers of *gihaaz* (trousseau) items for furnishing the potential matrimonial home, ranging from toiletries to glassware to large items of furniture. Earning wages in the factory provides many of the young female employees with their first ever opportunity to earn money for themselves, an experience opening the doors to a world of consumer glamour and social status. But under the guidance of the older female *mushrifat*, their perspective is turned towards *il-nazra il-mustaqbaliyya* (the long-term view), as they are guided in the purchase and arrangement of domestic items, and mentored in the sexual mysteries and pleasures to be permitted in the marital bedchamber that awaits them.

I conclude the chapter with a description of the distinctive Port Said nuptial celebrations in which I was invited to participate, known as *tangid* (fluffing the quilt) parties. As far as I am aware this is the first time these have been recorded in the ethnographic literature of the area.

Sexualising the workspace – the struggle for love

Flirtation and flirtatious behaviour appears woven into the texture of workplace relations. I was first alerted to these dynamics when one of *edara*'s male monitors berated Madame Nermin, Head of Workers Affairs, on her choice of new female recruits:

> I like to feel refreshed as I walk down the assembly lines. I need to sense a buzz as I feast my eyes on those surrounding me. This latest batch is an eyesore! Three additions have been made. Two of them I would charge with life imprisonment and the third, she heads straight for the guillotine!

Once alerted to the phenomenon of expressed sexual interest, other signs started to catch my attention on the shop floor. It soon became evident to me that falling in and out of love is a pursuit in which single workers seemed to be engaged almost all hours of the working day. If not themselves at either stage, they appeared consumed by how others were faring in the entry/exit stages of emotional entanglements. These experiences formed a pervasive part of their world of *asrar* (secrets), constituting another layer of lively shop floor *aflam* (tales).

As I was increasingly exposed to the ferment of love entanglements on the shop floor, and their developments over weeks and months, I had a hunch. It was related to sensing a silent unspoken fear among single girls of an *'aris* (groom) failing to turn up – and of such a predicament forcing them to lead single lives. The next day Nura (a nineteen-year-old Port Saidian) confirmed this. Springing out of her normally contemplative mood, she described to me how remaining single for the rest of one's life is a fear which clouds the thought horizons of families with daughters, as they anxiously wait and watch for emerging signs of a serious commitment enabling marriage plans to be set in motion:

> Families living in our neighbourhood harbour the hidden anxiety of a daughter not getting married. It's like the nightmare of examinations. By the time I left school at eighteen, several of my classmates were at the stage of *katb*

il-kitab (formal signing of the legal marriage contract), some from as early as their *'edadiyya* (preparatory certificate, usually sat at fifteen). In single-sex schools, these arrangements take place between families that know each other. If such opportunities are non-existent then there is the university or college environment. In my case, as in others, the work environment does not expose us to the same range of better choices available in higher education. It creates a worse anxiety. For this reason, our mothers make it clear to the neighbourhood that they are in a process of starting to put together a lavish *gihaaz* (trousseau) which they actively bring together from when we are in primary school. Talking publicly of the *gihaaz* is a way of sending word around that there are families ready to make a commitment if the right person comes along.

For migrant workers in the factory, the anxiety is even more severe. Abeer, engaged to Hassan, whom she met through the factory pool, stops for a brief moment handling the garment she is checking as she reflects:

Single girls live through a phase of *qalaq*[1] that can make them physically ill. Getting engaged and married is contingent on being asked, and waiting for the step to be taken by the other party. Imagine in your mind's eye a family with, let's say, seven daughters – which is quite common in our rural areas. In the village way of thinking, our mentality is the mentality of *il-ghayatin* (those who till the soil) and malicious talk instigated by hidden rivalries is an inescapable part of community life. The constant state of *qalaq* is provoked because there are malicious tongues in villages. To be labelled *'ansa* (spinster) is hard to bear in the closed village community where every family's affairs is everybody else's business. *'Ansa* is a stigma one cannot carry around with grace. It means that you have no future apart from the family home in which you've been raised. It's the place where you were born, grew up in from childhood, and there is nowhere else to go – a complete dead end. In Salheya today, because of the heavy financial commitments demanded by local custom, single males prefer to seek brides from outside the community. It has become a fashionable trend, a way of not conforming strictly to local financial expectations – and of carrying a lighter financial burden when producing the *shabka* (jewellery given by the man to his fiancé on the occasion of their formal engagement). It means forking out two thousand Pounds rather than five thousand as required in Salheya. What would the fate of the family with seven daughters be? Their *qalaq* is an excruciating helplessness.

These two views from both urban and rural female workers readily find resonances in other ethnographic studies (Rugh 1984; Ibrahim 1985; Macleod 1991; Davies 1993; Early 1993b; Singerman 1995, 2011; el Kholy 2002; Kholoussy 2010b).[2] Homa Hoodfar (1997a) in her seminal ethnography on the lives of lower-income families in Cairo in the 1990s, succinctly captured the reasons behind the silent anxiety of singlehood:

Marriage is probably the most important social event in the lives of Middle Eastern men and women. It is through marriage and having children that adulthood and self-realisation are achieved ... The idea of remaining single by choice is beyond the imagination of almost everybody in the neighbourhoods – young and old, male or female. (1997a: 52).

It appears that the anxiety of remaining unmarried can be just as strong for single men. So when Hamza, from a village in Manzala described as a place 'where nothing much happens', confides one day to his co-worker Mahmud his concerns that he will never meet someone he likes enough to marry, the proverb he is quoted in reply encourages him to keep trying: '*el bir bilif wi yilif – lahad may laki ghata* ('the barrel turns and turns – until it finds its missing lid')'.

When, however, events develop as hoped, the traditional route for couples moving towards marriage involves a complex trajectory. Outlining it will provide an important context for the subsequent discussion of workplace romances in Fashion Express. The entire process is initiated when a woman's family is sent word by the father, or male guardian, of a man (whom she may not know) to say that he and his son, or ward, would like to call on them. A meeting, usually referred to as *il-ziyara* (literally simply 'the visit' – but universally understood to be specially for 'viewing the bride'), is accordingly arranged by her parents, with the actual suitor a silent, almost unnoticed member of the visiting party. The discussions between the two families centre on the financial assets of the man. If these prove satisfactory, the two male guardians shake hands and together read the first verse of the Koran. This critical stage, known as the *fatha* (the name of the opening verse of the Koran) represents the formal engagement of the couple. Families may refrain from reading the *fatha* if they have reservations, and the visit then ends with no commitment made. The resulting awkwardness is masked by polite expressions made of giving the bride's family further time to consider the offer – a face-saving way of acknowledging that the suit has in reality failed.

If the financial prospects appear suitable, then the *khutuba*, the public celebration of the engagement, usually follows soon after, during the course of which the man gives his fiancée the *shabka*, namely a gift of gold. Meanwhile, in the background, intensive negotiations will have been continuing over the financial settlement involved in the marriage, and in particular the *ayma*, or list of possessions, which forms a civil (not a religious) contract between the two parties. In Fashion Express numerous stories are told about the long drawn-out, tortuous path such *ayma* negotiations can follow: in many instances the couple and their families battle it out over title to every last item in the matrimonial home, down to the spoons in the kitchen drawer. The reason is that, whatever may happen in the future, everything listed on the signed *ayma* remains the property of the woman (el-Kholy 2002). By contrast the *shabka* remains the property of the man, and he can reclaim it, for example to sell so that he can settle an outstanding debt. This contrasts with the general position, commonly described in the ethnographic literature, that the *shabka*, once given, becomes the property of the woman.

Completion of the negotiations can take up to a year, during which time the engaged couple are also expected to get to know each other. Once all has been settled, the *katb il-kitab* takes place, in which the man and woman, and their guardians, sign the marriage contract, and the man alone affixes his signature to the *ayma*. Even though the *katb il-kitab* signing involves no celebration, from this point on the couple are formally and officially married, from both legal and religious perspectives, and the marriage can only be terminated through formal divorce proceedings. The period between the *katb il-kitab* and the celebratory wedding night, or *dukhla*, is thus characterised by a commitment which has not been consummated. For male workers in the factory, there are advantages to prolonging this stage. One is the mutual freedom the couple are given in the eyes of their families and communities, with no reservations publicly expressed over the hours the groom may spend with his bride. An added economic advantage for Port Said locals is that the marriage contract is an essential document for putting one's name on the waiting list for a flat under the local government's scheme to assist those with *mahdudi il-dakhl* (limited income).[3] The length of time it takes to obtain the flat can therefore be used, by both parties, to gather together their respective agreed contributions to the marriage *gihaaz* (the collection of worldly goods – furniture, electrical goods, soft furnishings, cutlery and crockery) that will provide the couple with their material foundation for married life.

Eventually the Big Night arrives, and the *dukhla* wedding celebration is staged. A large crowd of family and friends is assembled, after which the bride and groom arrive together, with the former resplendent in a white Western-style wedding dress hired for the occasion, and the latter in a suit and tie. After a long evening of entertainment in a public park or their street, the couple retire to their new flat, their pristine *gihaaz* and their new life together as a married couple.

I found workers in Fashion Express to be fascinated with every stage of the long-drawn out marriage process, in particular the circumstances through which the man and the woman first meet. Traditional arranged marriages, in which the parents make the match and the bride and groom have little involvement until the proceedings are well underway, were referred to as *hub il-bab* (love by the front door), the Port Said equivalent of the middle-class Cairene term *gawaz il-salunat* (drawing-room marriages) (Aspden 2016: 42). And many of the *entag* workers described *hub il-bab* marriages as having at least two major problems. The first problem is that the woman has no say in the choice of suitor. An example is the case of Asmaa, a machinist, whose first suitor saw her in the factory where she first worked and then approached her parents for an engagement. Of this experience, Asmaa comments:

> I'm not sure why he was in such a tearing hurry! He saw me briefly and before I even so much as glimpsed him he went to my parents to read the *fatha* – while I was still slaving at work. I returned home early evening to find the whole arrangement had been settled. There was a strange feeling to this whole exercise. It was as if I was reduced to *hetit haga* (a something, an object).

The second problem, explicitly articulated, is that such arrangements lack the essential component of love – they are loveless. Asmaa goes on:

> He made a habit of calling me every Monday and Thursday. We had some peculiar conversations on the phone. How am I supposed to act out a love scenario when my emotions are dead? In one conversation, he confessed 'he missed me' to which I replied 'and what do you expect me to say to that?' His answer was 'nothing' and so I said well, then 'nothing' is my answer as well!

Asmaa eventually broke off the engagement, as she explains:

> A few months afterwards, he was falling short of his initial promises of providing a flat, saying that his financial circumstances were tight. The only option on the cards was for me to live with his family in a two-bedroom apartment. I seized this as my chance to bring this joyless relationship to an end. I made my parents see the engagement as a waste of time. It was called off quickly. The *shabka* of gold was paid back, along with LE 100 in cash to compensate for the box of sweets he bought me for *mulid il-nabi* (the Prophet's birthday), even though this only cost him LE 20 in the first place.

Asmaa's experience is not unusual and fits in with the accounts of other girls who have had a series of broken engagements. Hamida Ali has twice been engaged to suitors whom she did not love, even though they had greater material assets to meet their side of the financial requirements than does her present fiancé Nasir – with whom it was a case of 'love at first sight'. Two broken engagements could have been expected to leave a single girl approaching her late twenties feeling insecure about her future marriage prospects, with the hint of personal problems that might prevent her from sailing smoothly in her relationships with the opposite sex. Indeed, being nicknamed among her three sisters as *awiyya* (the strong one), Hamida Ali is adamant that she was right to hold out for love:

> It's difficult in relationships with someone you do not love to say *hader* (yes) and to take on the small and big challenges of any marriage. Besides, the

thought of physical contact is abhorrent. Sex usually ends up being like some sort of duty that you just have to get through. I know of a friend who married for the financial security her husband was able to provide. Her life can be summed up in four words: food, drink, sleep – *wi bas* (and that's it).

Workers in *entag* emphatically prefer an alternative trajectory to marriage, which they refer to as *hub il-shibak* (love through the window). A man and a woman meet, are attracted (*ingizab*) and develop a liking (*'egab*) for each other. This blossoms into the full state of 'falling in true love' which provides, in their view, the most valid basis for a formal proposal being made to the family. The critical difference between *hub il-bab* and *hub il-shibak* can thus be seen to lie in the additional initial stages (*ingizab*, *'egab* and *hub* – attraction, liking and true love) that the latter involves, and which provide the essential prologue to the formal sequence of negotiations and celebrations outlined earlier.

The importance of such an idealised vision of love is illustrated in the account given by Hassan (a machinist) of how he met his wife on the daily bus, commuting to and from Salheya. His *'egab* for Hind began by his observing the girl's manner and way of speech as *kalam yigi 'ala hawaya* (words to my liking). He noticed for instance that she did not join the other girls in excessive *tahrig* (joking around) and was more restrained in her behaviour. He goes on:

> There was a kind of *tawafuk rohi* (compatibility of souls) between us. For a long time at the beginning of our relationship, we thought we were living the version of love in the cinemas – *Ahmad Mazhar wi Suad Hosny* (a famous couple in the black and white films of the 60's)!

Yet it was also noteworthy that the ideal *hub il-shibak* scenario was frequently referred to as a *rehlit kifah* (a journey of bitter struggle), with true love being found and consummated through enduring commitment on the part of the lovers in the face of repeated difficulties. The prime example given was that of Essam (another machinist), who despite being extremely conservative in his religious outlook had nevertheless decided to go for a love marriage. As he tells his story:

> You can say we were raised in a certain way. As three boys growing up in a strictly traditional family, we avoided women who were not family members. If we had to address them, it was with respect and some distance. In our environment, this was a mark of proper breeding, irrespective of money or social class. So none of us was your average kind of young man who knew how to walk behind a girl in the street and flirt with her, or chat her up on a mobile. As men we didn't have that kind of *gara'a* (courage, audacity – used in the colloquial sense of 'balls').

Before I met my wife, for four years I was deeply in love with a girl who lived in our neighbourhood. I used to see her walk by our street practically every day. Every morning, I'd tell myself 'this is the day I'll *zabat nafsi* ('sharpen up') and summon the strength to talk to her'. But the day I finally plucked up the courage to do it, my stupid foot kicked an empty packet of cigarettes in her way. When she turned to look at me, I found myself walking straight on – all my bravery had vanished! After that her journeys down our alley came to a stop. When I next saw her a year later, she was expecting a child. Believe me, I was deeply happy for her.

Then my friends urged me to join them on a day trip to Cairo, which is where I first met Nabila. I found her easy to talk to, and something between us clicked. She was shy and self-conscious. Whenever she wanted to address me, she'd turn to my friend and tell him what she wanted to say to me. It was a love story from then on, and when I was drafted into the army for three years we began to exchange love letters. One day her mother discovered the letters and demanded an explanation. There were only six months left to my release, and I didn't yet have a *ta'rifa* (half a piaster) to my name. So I made up my mind to meet her father immediately on my release. I found an intimidating figure! But I was honest from the start, telling him that at that stage of my life I had no money, while also setting out my financial potential. That's just my way, so that there's always light at the end of the tunnel. I then took three jobs to amass the cash I needed: a factory job that took me till the afternoon, a *warsha* (workshop) job till the evening, and then from midnight a security job as a night guard.

There are easier ways to get married! The arranged way is the most common. I once had a female cousin vetted for that role in my life, but I wasn't comfortable with the arrangement. I have three brothers and a sister, and with both our parents gone, if I'd brought her to live in the family home she'd be like a common law wife to my brothers, doing the household chores for all of us. She wouldn't be mine, except in the bedroom. This would constitute *zulm* (injustice – here used in the moral/religious sense) – for her as much as for me. So it wasn't right.

For Nabila, I needed five thousand pounds to go for a good *shabka*, so all my wages from all three jobs were tied up in *gam'iyyat* (informal savings clubs). But her mother was a good woman. She found someone in her social network who could also lend me part of the cash. So I managed to get together a *shabka* that fits *shakli ka ragil* (colloquial for 'my idea of a real man'). For our *khutuba* I provided, all expenses paid, for Nabila's entire appearance – her dress, the hairdresser, her accessories – so that she was shining *zay il-badr* (like the moon, implying stunningly beautiful). After all, I considered that she'd gone through a lot herself, putting up with my difficulties. And I've kept all our love letters from when I was doing my military service. They are precious mementos, tied in ribbons, and still kept in the cardboard box in which I bought Nabila her engagement shoes.

Yet as the opening episode in Essam's account illustrates, not all *hub il-shibak* stories have the much anticipated happy ending. Male and female protagonists come to terms with such disappointment in different ways. The men are expected to display stoical 'manly' behaviour, but are permitted, even expected, to verbalise their feelings in openly emotional language. Frequently such expressions emphasise the finality of the break, as in *'shedid bas khalaas'* ('it was strong – but it's over'); while others use words such as *'te'ebet wi gali daght'* ('I was ill with high blood pressure') to highlight the devastating effect on the disappointed lover. And through most such recollections runs a strong sense of lasting loss and regret: *'kan sa'ab ansaha'* ('it was difficult to forget her'), and *'bandam aleha lahad dilwaki – kanit kwayisa wi betesma' il-kalam'* ('I regret losing her till this very day – she was good and treated me as a somebody'). With the girls the position is reversed. They appear to have behavioural license to engage in dramatic 'female' histrionics, such as staging fainting fits – but they are restricted to expressing their feelings verbally in purely formulaic terms. Thus one afternoon I heard Sabah quietly singing to herself, as she worked at folding repaired garments, the words of a song describing her sense of loss and disappointment:

min nar 'azabi afalt babi
a-ul adari dam'i
khuft il-awazil yiban ala 'enay
garh il-ahiba malush 'atab
wili garahni aa'az habayyib

From the flames of my torture I closed my front door
I said to hide my tears
I feared the streams of tears would show in my eyes
The pain of the loved ones has no cure
The one to pain me is the one I loved the most

Yet for a couple even to have the option of embarking on the *rehlit kifah*, they must in the first place have the opportunity to meet, and to see if *ingizab* (attraction) will develop into *'egab* and *hub*. However even in an urban setting such as Port Said, children usually go to single-sex schools and, from puberty at least, therefore have little opportunity for interaction with the opposite sex, except within specific social contexts such as family gatherings at weddings. So the factory workspace, as described in the previous chapter, throws together, usually for the first time in their lives, large numbers of single men and women in their late teens and twenties, providing opportunities for male–female interaction that are proscribed in the world outside, and through which meeting a potential spouse is made possible.

'Love in a world ruled by money (*il-hub fi zaman il-felus*)'[4]

The initial step in the *ingizab-'egab* process is first of all simply to get noticed in amongst the crowd. In pursuit of this end both young men and women can be seen to be actively engaged in complex projections of self through both dress and behaviour. In this respect, women workers can be considered as having an inherent advantage, one deriving from the innate seductiveness with which the Islamic sexual code considers all women to be imbued. As Mernissi has summarised it: 'the Muslim woman is endowed with a fatal attraction which erodes the male's will to resist her and reduces him to a passive acquiescent role. He has no choice; he can only give in to her attraction' (1987: 41). Strictly speaking, therefore, the female worker does not need to dress attractively in order to get noticed – she simply has to 'be' at work. Yet matters were by no means as simple as that. Zeinab, a *tarqim* worker, summed it up when one day she said reflectively:

> What is *lebs* (dress)? Dress is about *mustawa* (standards), *style* [the same word used in Arabic], *shakl* (appearance). It's about [she pauses for a moment's silence before continuing dramatically] *'eish hayatak il-awil* (living your own life first – in the sense of doing yourself justice before attending to wider responsibilities).'

The need to dress well was universally accepted and acted on by women *entag* workers. At the very least, new recruits to the shop floor shared an understanding of the need to avoid any display of *lebs wihish*, a term which carried a dual meaning implying no sense of style, and also dire economic circumstances (such as holes in the material, or ill-fitting clothes). With increased experience of the workplace, girls came to develop a heightened awareness of how best to project positive aspects of feminine beauty and mystique. The dress practices and codes they adopted not only reflected continually changing waves of Islamic fashion, but also conveyed signals and messages about either their social origin and standing, or their sexual availability as *mish murtabita* (emotionally unattached). Yet women workers were also cautious not to turn up in expensive-looking garments which could provoke suspicions of additional earnings from other sources (notably prostitution, a thought never far below the horizon, given the widespread attribution of loose morality to *istithmar* girls and the economic reality that prostitution is one of the quickest ways of making instant cash). Others found the shop floor not to be a place in which to wear their best, because of the damage done to their clothes. Their more exclusive wardrobe was accordingly saved for outings such as going to the cinema, or attending engagements and weddings.

The one common item of dress worn by every woman in the factory was the *hijab*. This is partly because of the reassurance that wearing the *hijab* transmits about the intentions of a woman who goes against the Islamic sexual code by going out to work. As Hoodfar has perceptively noted:

> A veiled woman indicates that despite her unconventional economic activity she respects traditional values and behaviour ... Veiling has become an instrument through which women publicly dissociate themselves from some of the culturally disapproved traits and characteristics attributed to the stereotype of the modern woman. At the same time, veiling enables these women to safeguard their traditional rights. (1997b: 324, 321)

Yet at the same time the *hijab* remains the most affordable accessory through which a girl can easily make a statement of her sense of dress and style on the shop floor. When artfully worn, it shows off the beauty of the girl, especially the shape of her face, accentuating features such as eyes and complexion. While the *hijab* in theory constrains the expression of full femininity, in practice the diversity of styles worn on shop floor sent careful messages (Sandikci and Ger: 2005; Secor 2005; Whitlock 2007; Chakravarti forthcoming;). Thus, single workers wore long skirts, with a simple, short headscarf covering their heads by way of *hijab*. A newly engaged or married female would, however, often 'up-grade' her style of headscarf and dress, for example by putting on the *khumar* (head and shoulders veil), or would prefer an Arabian-style *'abaya* (long gown with buttons down the front) as a more formal attire. Each was selected, as far as means would allow, according to the latest fashion trends and colours circulating on the shop floor and in the urban markets of Port Said. Each style of headscarf came with its own pins and set of accessories, to hold them in place and make a statement of other personal touches of femininity (White 1999; Herrera 2001; Navaro-Yasin 2002; Sandikci and Ger 2005; Stratton 2006).

The universal prevalence of the *hijab* on the shop floor did not, however, seem to cramp male interest in the appearance of their colleagues. It instead appeared to incite enhanced curiosity over what was being concealed (Saadawi 1980; Zakaria 1988; Husain 2007). Expressions such as *'udha gamil* (her body is shapely), *muza* (a sexy figure), *sehna* (ugly), *sarukh* (a head-turner), *gamda* (hot), *wiz-wiz* (cute) and *tinka* (stylish but stand-offish) were common male remarks passed on female bodies in the workplace. The position seemed to be even more exaggerated when it came to the minority of girls who chose to don the full-face-and-body *niqab*. Rather than deflect male attention, they attracted it even more intensely, as was summed up by Horeya, when speaking pointedly of one of her assembly workers:

She's in a *niqab* and firmly supported by the *shari'a* (Islamic law). But have you seen her *niqab* opening for the eyes, which she's deliberately made bigger. And what would you say if you saw what her eyes are saying? *Hagat ketir* ('many things' – said with the final syllable dragged out suggestively, implying dangerously hot messages). And how about the way she moves her hips? The walk of the *niqab* ought to be like a man's – not swaying right and left and *betit-raqas fil sala* (dancing around in the *sala*). The boys in the lines can hardly ignore her black stiletto slippers with their tireless *trak trak* sound. Their ears are glued to her footsteps. We've called her type *il-kasiyyat il-'ariyyat* (the veiled nudes).

The *hijab*, however, constitutes but a single item in the entire female outfit. Talking to girls on the shop floor suggests their ideal wardrobe is assembled as a mix-and-match *taqm* (ensemble) that is worn for the maximum effect. Dressing well means paying acute attention to colour coordination, and to recognising the importance of disclosing variety in one's wardrobe. Nuances of dress are closely scrutinised, as Zeinab describes:

> My skirt and veil may not be new, but if I buy a printed blouse in a colour that is this combination of yellow and orange, I know it will draw attention. Everyone will notice I have something new on, and that I stand out. I have picked up the skills of dressing well by watching others carefully and developing an eye for the colours that match best and set each other off.

Zeinab is also vigilant in keeping an eye on what's new on the shop floor, from slippers, to dangling fake costume jewellery, to the latest colours of veils to hit the markets of Port Said. She has a sharp sense of the price tag attached to each item, and the code each *taqm* transmits about the social origins of its wearer. As she puts it, looking at the girls in Leitex:

> I can distinguish the migrants easily! See this one over there – the colours don't match. How can you ever be in your right mind and match a black and white polka dot headscarf with a green printed blouse and a navy blue skirt? It's all wrong. It's the taste of a *fellaha* (peasant woman). It's difficult for these girls to accept constructive advice. They see it as a personal criticism levelled at their provinces. But it is the only way to change. Unless they have the determination to change, they seldom do.

Young male workers express an explicit need to work harder at projecting their desired self-image through a dress style known as *shabaab riwish* (cool youth), a look modelled on popular pop and movie stars (see Illustration 3.1). When out of factory premises their clothes are characterised by *budihat* (tightly clinging lycra T-shirts) and *bantalon nedif* (trendy trousers). These styles follow the fashion trends worn by the male stars seen in video clips on local TV. Currently all the rage are hot-red, shiny trousers and ripped jeans (*bantalon meqata*'). The clothes are not bought singly, but as a set sold in Port Said's local market that specialises in male garments 'as advertised on TV'. Each ensemble is sold for LE 300 or 400 (equivalent to almost a full monthly wage for most young workers) and so must often be paid for in instalments. Trendy hairstyles emulating Egyptian footballers or film stars are the most affordable way of advertising the cool *shabaab riwish* look, using the latest wet-look lotions (sold at LE 3 a bottle). These hairstyles included the *caborya* (marine cut), the *sbike* (spiked hairbrush look), the *Douglas* look (a goatee) and *il-zero* (completely shaven-headed). At work in the factory, the cool look is maintained primarily by the hairstyle and other work clothing such as *fanilat* (sleeveless T-shirts), *bantalon training* (training gear), tight-fitting jeans, thick studded leather belts and baseball caps worn back to front.

Illustration 3.1 *Shabaab riwish* ('cool youth'): pop star Amr Diab

Simply looking cool does not, however, suffice: *shabaab riwish* also need to 'act cool', most typically through demonstrating their skill in a form of banter with the girls, referred to by both sides of the sexual divide as *mu'aksat* (flirtation). *Mu'aksat* is understood to be an acceptable, even desirable, form of flirtation – albeit one which is strictly *yilaghi* (verbal), in contrast to the *wasakha* (dirt) associated with *yimed ido* (to touch, in the sense of sexual harassment – something which, as far as I was aware, was non-existent in the workplace). *Mu'aksat* is a way of communicating a suggestive compliment of a sexual nature, through light hints that 'grab the moment' to create a *mawqif* (situation) which acknowledges that a woman has succeeded in attracting a man's sexual interest. It is to be taken as nothing more than a compliment paid to the woman, whether single or married, who has conjured this reaction in the passing and 'unsuspecting' male.

For men to excel in *mu'aksat* without running the risk of appearing objectionable, the art consists in delivering a compliment that is seen to come effortlessly, and with sufficient delicacy and wit so as not to be construed as having the sort of *elet adab* (sexual connotations) which could prejudice a man's good reputation. Thus, it is often expressed through remarks on the style and colour of a woman's attire, or the reason why perhaps today of all days she appears *mehliwa* (radiant, glowing inwardly) rather than simply *gamila* (pretty, but with reference to a woman's external physical characteristics). If the woman is married, the originator of the *mu'aksa* often playfully hints that the cause lies with her husband (such as in exclaiming 'may God preserve your husband!'), on the widely shared assumption that sex and sperm give women an inner glow of health (Brandes 1981); if she is single, it may be surmised that the cause relates to some current love interest in her life.

Another feature of *mu'aksat* is that the man often plays to an audience to evoke the image of his own masculinity, which he is just as eager to display. Thus spotting a girl looking for someone may induce a worker, seated among a sea of other male workers, to raise his hand in the air to catch her eye and ask if she is 'looking for me?'. Most preferable is to establish such an image among the largest number of girls possible. Thus one day Ali, a monitor, catches me standing at a quality control table chatting with six girls as we finish taking count of the garments. In a deft performance of *mu'aksa* he says, 'Look! Amira is madly in love with me but she won't admit it!' The girls duly collapse into giggles. 'See', he goes on, 'she's shaking her head! Let's lock eyes and see who's in the wrong'. Amira refuses to meet his gaze. Ali pauses for an awkward moment, then concludes with a flourish: 'Well, let's put it another way. She *used* to be madly in love with me!' Regardless of the accuracy or otherwise of its content, the *mu'aksa* has succeeded in projecting the desired image of his masculinity before a sizeable female audience.

In many instances the intended audience for the performance of masculinity can also be a group of other men, most commonly the *shilla* (peer group) of the man delivering the *mu'asksa*. Thus speaking of a couple of young men vying for the attention of Kawakib, a new *tarqim* worker, Zizi, a supervisor in Cutting, says:

> You need to see their relationship in a broader context. Boys in work teams often make up *shillet il-subyan* (boys' peer-groups). The relations between them go some time back, not simply the few months you've seen them hanging around in this factory. It's probably through one of them that the whole mob was dragged into the factory. There is a struggle between the boys within the *shilla*, each of them vying to appear in her eyes an *asad* (lion) through the strength of the jokes they crack. They make bets with each other over who can woo her quickest and most effortlessly, or has more light-hearted wit, or has made her smile, blush and respond in predicted and unpredicted ways.

A common example of such male 'joshing' involves boasting to each other over the size of the *rasid* (savings account) they have built up through making their mark with a series of girls. And since the girls are expected to appear publicly unresponsive to the *mu'aksat* they receive, delivering each one is, in principle, risk-free for the male. If it fails to have the intended effect on the girl, nobody will have cause to notice the potential dent in his masculinity. Repeated failure in the performance of *mu'aksa* can, however, on occasion lead to a form of social emasculation, as I saw in the case of Ahmed. Desperate to score a hit with the girls in the assembly lines, but failing miserably in his attempts, he found himself nicknamed Kamanana (after the socially inept film star Il-limbi, the Egyptian equivalent of Mr Bean) and told repeatedly to *ghur ba'aa'* ('get lost!').

From comments the girls make when in solely female company, it is clear that they actively enjoy the *mu'aksat* they arouse, taking them as recognition that their sexuality as women has not gone unnoticed. As Nidal Hassan remarks:

> I'd return home in a foul mood if I hadn't received a single *mu'aksa* during the day! The best one I received was when I got engaged, and a man down our street who had the hots for me clapped his hands in despair several times and loudly said for the entire street to hear *la hawla wala quwat ila billah* (a phrase uttered on hearing news of a death: in the *mu'aksa* it implies that his sense of loss on hearing of her engagement is as if grieving over a death).

Azima Mohamed, senior supervisor, goes on to describe the extent to which girls on the shop floor, far from being merely passive recipients of male gallantry, are usually actively – and mutually competitively – involved in snaring boys who have particularly caught their fancy:

> Girls get up to all sort of underhanded push and shove tactics. Their sights are set on the task of *tikalfito* (ensnaring him). They have hidden ways of producing *riq hilw* (sweet breath – implying promising signs) with the intent of inviting the boy to make friends. It turns into a competition between them, about who is declared the prettiest, the most popular, the social butterfly or the type all boys will fall for. It's how they gain inner confidence in the act of *tikalfito wi teashemo* (leading him to have hope) and most importantly without looking as if they're expert at it.

For each *mu'aksat*, the moment is fleeting – and the *mawaqif* (situations) can in an instant be reverted to what the shop floor calls the 'stand by' position (the same words are used in Arabic). Here almost instantly all the flirtation ceases as the interaction takes on a serious note and appears above board, though 'who is stupid enough not to *see* what's *really* going on?' as Tewfik Saleh, Head of Security, comments one day. *Mu'aksat* are a never-ending scenario, with no clear winner or loser, that can be evoked whenever the moment 'feels right'. In this way, the flow of *mu'aksat* becomes a constant part of the stream of daily social interaction between almost everybody around on the shop floor. The constant flow of *mu'asksa* provides a prime driver generating the sexually charged atmosphere of the workplace. In the *salat* of *entag,* against a background of deafening levels of noise, the flow also takes the form of a constant buzz of mobile 'missed call' rings (with coded meanings – 3 rings for 'hi', 5 for 'miss you', 7 for 'see you later') and frequent beeps announcing the arrival of texted love messages (sent out to more than one person). Female supervisors who have watched the *entag* scene for a long time have their own thoughts to add about the mixed interaction within their units. In public, Horeya's sharp voice is heard on the shop floor addressing two workers during production hours: 'What I see is that you (the woman) are seated – and he is glued to your sewing machine'. In the *ishraf* common room, in the company of her fellow supervisors, Horeya says quietly:

> We notice the *ingizab* (attraction) as it happens and as we speak. It's obvious to all of us who monitor production. We know where everybody is supposed to be and what they've expected to be doing. So no matter how discreetly the interaction is carried out to make it look nothing out of the ordinary, we sense a whiff of something else. We see the boy hanging round a girl's sewing machine, and then he lingers a bit longer until the expressed interest is set to develop into a relationship. When we press them with questions and explanations, the excuses come flowing – all credible reasons. He is asking to

borrow her scissors, or checking the serial number on the cloth, or saying that her sewing machine is giving her trouble and he is just helping out.

Although single girls are not permitted to initiate *mu'aksat*, they are given license to take a proactive role in an alternative form of initiating *ingizab*. This involves the spontaneous organisation and performance of a shop floor game referred to as *'aris wi 'arusa* (bride and groom), in which the sexes engage in improvised role-play around the relationship between a husband and wife.[5] There appears to be no set signal for such a game to begin. Instead, often during lulls between work orders, the dynamic between members of a work unit will suddenly shift, as one of the girls announces that she and a male worker (one who is single in real life) are now *ma' ba'ad* (together). The chosen partner seems to have no option but to join in and play his allotted role in acting out a standard scenario in which the couple encounter increasing turbulence in their 'marriage', performed through a series of increasingly dramatic and ludicrous quarrels and conflicts. Everyone's enjoyment of it comes from the imagination and energy that go into generating the 'marital rows' which make up the core narrative of the game.

In these *'aris wi 'arusa* games, the workers draw on, and simultaneously mock, a rich blend of gender and class stereotypes in the scenes they construct. Thus Khadija in *Qas*, the eldest married woman in the team, takes the matchmaker lead in announcing that Zeinab has been paired with Antonio (Ahmed's nickname) and Nura with Beckham (Ayman's nickname). Zeinab's response is immediately to assume the role of a 'posh madame' by altering her manner of speech to cover her rustic, croaky voice – a posture she maintains for a few days on the shop floor as she walks around telling her colleagues that '*rehitkom gibna rumi*' ('you all stink of Rumi' – a pungent local cheese) and working hard at pronouncing 'croissant'. Nura meanwhile sticks the white *tarqim* stickers onto her finger nails, pretending that they are long and sexy 'French nails', waving them around coyly when calling her *'aris* over, and defending his manhood when comparisons are made between the virility of Antonio and Beckham. The class dimension soon surfaces when, for example, Beckham is assumed to be unable to live up to Nura's requirements of a life of *rafahiyya* (affluence). When he offers her a handful of *khulul* (a snack of cockles commonly sold along the Port Said waterfront) during the course of the working day, she responds by saying sniffily that '*rihto wihsha*' ('it stinks'); and when his offering is some *ta'miyya* (Egypt's most enduringly popular snack) she loftily asks '*akulha izay?*' ('how am I supposed to eat this?'), as it is then established for a fact that Nura's food comes from take–away outlets (associated with the affluent classes' lifestyles).

In everyone's favourite episode, resumed repeatedly after break-time over a number of days, the *'aris* and *'arusa* return to the *tarqim* table and are assumed to be in an expensive restaurant. A male cutter, Hatim, takes on the role of the waiter. The couples, actively encouraged and egged on by the group, load Hatim with extravagant orders of special dishes such as *kaware' bil khal* (knuckles cooked in vinegar), roast duck (a Port Said delicacy, traditionally enjoyed on the first day of Ramadan), four slices of *gateau* each (a food item reserved for celebrations only, since it is expensive to purchase from bakeries), several bottles of Stella beer, and eventually the *shisha* (hubble bubble) for the girls which Nura specifies has to be *bil tifah* (apple-flavoured), along with several *laffat* (joints) for the boys. Khadija provides toothpicks to indicate that the meal which the newly married couples are about to consume is both rich and expensive, with money no object. To spin out everyone's enjoyment of the game – involving a complex mix of fantasy on the one hand, and mockery of the unattainable on the other – the 'waiter' deliberately acts out a performance of surly unhelpfulness, repeatedly declaring that the dishes that have been ordered are 'off', or that the menu has changed. The alternative selections he is given are carefully selected to be increasingly *haraaq* (hot and spicy), connoting the other items on the agenda of the newly married couple for *ba'din* (afters). To make the playful scenario more real, other 'waiters' may be called to take additional orders which the demanding, increasingly aroused couples and their guests have thought of on the spur of the moment, while other 'waiters' in the team are required to sing pop songs that have a *tish* (beat) implicitly indicating that the eating establishment is a posh nightclub.

The dynamic established is one of a succession of scenes in which marital tensions are exacerbated by the 'unreasonable demands of the wife', counter-pointed by 'the male temper' described as *wahsh il-wihush* (the fiercest of the fierce). The female role is to generate a set of increasingly intense marital conflicts, while the male role is to 'hold out' for as long as possible. This builds up to the point where the marriage teeters on the brink of divorce, and the wider group has considerable fun joining in various attempts to reconcile the 'couple'. Eventually a general understanding is reached that the 'marriage' has run its course, and the episode is brought to its conclusion. Then, after an interval, the whole cycle repeats itself, so that a sequence of 'serial marriages' is acted out between different members of the work unit.

In a world of make-believe, the collective effort of each unit is channelled towards the art of mastering improvisation, with everyone expected to come up with outrageous suggestions with which to challenge taken-for-granted gendered assumptions – while simultaneously keeping each pair 'in character' by egging them further on into the strengthening brew of seductive tensions of intimate moments. Humour is used not only to subvert gendered stereotypes, unmasking some of the glaring unresolved clichés of films and TV, but also to reaffirm performances of different styles of 'masculine action'.

Parallelling their real-life struggles to find love, these games disclose the power of money in scenes of seduction, power and domination, where getting out of sticky situations is contingent on living by one's wits. Competition evolves effortlessly between the different rounds of flirtatious *'aris* and *'arusa* games, with the winners voted for according to the imagination and style of their performances, and the level of wit each deploys to overpower their partner and 'opponent'.

Hub il-shibak – love matches

Mu'aksat and *'aris wi 'arusa* role-play games are ways in which both sexes use the mixed-gender shop floor as an arena for getting noticed and initiating relations which can develop into *e'gab* (liking) and *hub* (love). Yet a distinct gender differentiation can be discerned in the male and female views of the preferred dynamic for these initial stages of the *hub il-shibak* trajectory. In the initial stages of *hub il-shibak*, single women workers seem keen to move matters back into the formal marriage trajectory of formalising their engagement through the *fatha*; while single men seem to want to spin out the informal pre-*fatha* stages of the relationship for as long as possible.

The strong female preference for moving quickly from *ingizab*, *e'gab* and *hub* through to formal engagement (and then marriage) is readily explained in terms of the depth and prevalence of the fear of singlehood, and of becoming the object of male mockery. The young women workers on the shop floor have come to the factory to earn wages to finance the accumulation of the *gihaaz*, which will enable them to complete their side of the contractual negotiations that form the backbone of the formal marriage process. This latter imperative, which I will discuss in greater detail in the next section of this chapter, is captured in the comments made by Wafaa, a QC worker in Egytex:

> It is no longer considered a shame for a girl to work in order to set herself up in life. Most of us come from modest families. The truth we face today is that once in the labour market, we cannot rely on our families to provide for our *gihaaz*. A family that is not well off will only be able to provide a modest *gihaaz*. Once we are able to ascend above what our family can do for us financially, then we have made strides in what we want to achieve for ourselves. For this reason, many of us are determined to get the best *gihaaz* possible so that our parents don't look small in the eyes of the community. There is little respect for the bride whose *gihaaz* appears pathetic.[6]

With a male worker, however, the position is more complex. He tends not to be driven by a single over-riding imperative, such as the fear of singlehood prevalent amongst his female colleagues, but rather by having to earn money for a combination of three pressing priorities: for his personal expenses, to support his family, and to finance his marriage. This mixture is often spoken of as bringing together the *saa'b* (difficult) and the *mustahil* (impossible). For university graduates, the overwhelmingly preferred avenue for tackling this challenge is to secure a *wazifa* job in the civil service. This avenue provides security of tenure, assurance of regular payment of wages, fringe benefits that increase regularly with years of service, and also an unspoken promise of not having to do anything very much by way of hard work in return. The factory, by contrast, is characterised as a zone of uncertain payment of wages and minimal fringe benefits. Non-graduates also share the general preference for non-manual labour which I have described earlier. Male workers thus often speak of their work in the factory as a temporary measure, an opportunity to '*akawin nafsi* (set myself up)' through an initial step into the labour market.

Akawin nafsi is a phrase that binds all men in their teams on the shop floor. Working, whatever the skill area or wages offered, is part of the male image of declaring financial independence to avoid *amid idi li-had* (holding out my hand to others – like a beggar). In the factory, all *mawaqif* (work situations) allow any man on the labour landscape to become *insan ma'ruf* (a well-regarded person). Such a worker could be called *gada' ma' il-gada' wi bi ra'i damiro fil shughl* (macho among machos, throwing his heart into his work), or a *mukafih* (fighter), especially if his efforts are geared towards meeting his family's needs as well as his own projects, including marriage. If he is also able to help out workmates who are in financial difficulties (a common enough occurrence, for example if they fall behind on hire-purchase instalments, with the potential risk of imprisonment) then he is also praised for demonstrating *gad'ana* (machismo) (Goldberg 1986; Elchayar 2006; Ghannam 2013). A man's reputation and character in respect of this quality of *waqfit ragil* (male reliability and steadfastness) is often enquired after by female workers, drawing on their kin dispersed around the shop floor.

Added to this is the fact that a formal engagement, which can be subsequently broken off, constitutes a greater financial loss for the man than it does for the woman. Often it is only the *shabka* that the man can retrieve from the ruins of a failed engagement. Nadia, a machinist, tells of the case of her brother, who is the only son in the family. His engagement to a cousin required a concerted family effort to pull the cash together to go through the engagement and purchase the *shabka*. Nadia sighs as she recalls the problems of the engagement:

> There was no *nasib* (it was not fated). Our family had by then spent a fortune on an engagement party, the *shabka* and other personal gifts and expenses. Because she was a relative, it seemed improper to demand the return of the gifts

or retrieve part of the expenses paid in these long and elaborate arrangements. We regard the cash spent as a terrible waste. Now it's more the case that young men don't make a formal approach until everything is ready – the flat, and most of the cash. This is done to shorten the engagement period, and prevent the risk of endless conflicts and complications leading to second thoughts and cancellations.

The preferred male trajectory for drawing out the pre-*fatha* stages of *ingizab* and *e'gab* takes advantage of the relative freedom found in the factory, both during work and after hours, which allows mixed interaction to push the boundaries of relationships much further than is permitted within the strict environment of the home. The advantage is seized through the opportunities offered for an activity referred to on the shop floor as *yimsho ma'baad* (going, or stepping, out together), the sense of which is best captured in the American-English usage of 'dating'. 'Because they can't marry fast, *biyimsho ma'baad* (they date)' explains Khadija. Given the financial constraints, 'dating' does not involve spending large amounts of money. Couples who are interested in getting to know each other instead take long walks down Port Said's Mediterranean *corniche*, sitting on the public benches facing the water and the waves, with the boy buying paper bags of pumpkin seeds for a few pounds, and engage in an activity known on the shop floor as *yakul widn il-bint* (nibbling the girl's ear, implying whispering sweet nothings). Sometimes the pair are on their own, while at other times *yimsho ma'baad* becomes a social group activity.

Men initiating dating need to be skilled in deploying *il-rasm* (strategy) for different ways of attracting girls. It is a game that calls for expertise and experience, and one in which, ideally, skilled action needs to be able to pass itself off as effortless. In mixed-gender work units, the girls are acutely aware of the dating experience of their male colleagues, which are often discussed at length among them as a team. Thus, Mustafa from Cutting, nicknamed 'Dollar' in recognition of his repeatedly declared aspiration to get rich some day, also revels in his title of *ustaz il-tazbitat* ('Master of the dating game')[7] – a subject he is happy to talk about at length. Seated on his high stool, and banging the white, numbered *tarqim* stickers onto the cloth rolled out across the long table, he elaborates at length on his dating experience, even though being formally engaged to Nora from the factory next door. Mustafa describes his distinct style of *il-rasm* as:

'...*armi il-shabaka wi adawar il-istiwana* ('casting the fishing net, and then spinning hit records' – slang implying 'hooking them then chatting them up'). So I usually begin with a few questions to express my interest, such as 'your face looks familiar, do I know you?' – and if the response is positive, I take the matter forward. Later, when the girl turns up having claimed she made a confession to her mother about seeing me, then the game's reached a dead end. It's at this point that *a'adim isteqalti* ('I tender my resignation' – standard bureaucratic jargon). I've learnt the trick of quitting by getting her to first give up on me. I furnish a range of excuses in great detail, saying, for example, that it looks likely that the engagement period will have to last for as long as five years; or that my father is not able to give me financial support; or that my wages have been heavily deducted – so that I look pretty hopeless as a package, and not worth the chase. At other times, after succeeding in getting a girl to go out with me on several dates, my initial interest in the chase is lost. I'm then quite likely to leave her waiting for forty-five minutes before I turn up for the next one, and she gets the message. Of course, if the girl's from within the factory, then I'm immediately on my guard. It's quite likely she'll have a relative here who will make *shawshara* (gossip which gets you into trouble), and that's not a headache I want to put up with.

Mustafa divides his experiences of courtship into two broad types of dating:

> There is the serious relationship, the 'fair game' variety, where the girl in question is the one 'meant to be', and the other is just for the heck of it – the *tazbita* (date).

This point is later picked up by Zizi, a supervisor in Cutting who has a long experience of watching relations develop, as one afternoon she articulates her own views on courtship in the factory environment:

> There are two kinds of love in the courtship you see around in the factory, the first is *hub il-'azaar* (love by excuses) and the second is *il-hub il-salim* (sound, healthy love). The first type rests on a solid body of excuses the *shabaab* are experts at spinning out, such as '*baba misafir* (my Dad's not around right now)', or '*mafish felus* (I'm flat broke at the moment)', and the list grows with other, more ludicrous excuses of this nature. This is *il-hub il-fashil* (failed love). It's quite common around here because it thrives on wasting time, and spending it stringing the girl along, but without taking any concrete steps. The second type is more serious, with a commitment honoured and a formal approach eventually made to the family. In that sense, I see nothing wrong in dating. So often, a great many things can go wrong in a relationship before it reaches the front door.

The relative freedom that the workplace provides for mixed interaction outside the formal relationship of engagement is in reality a two-edged sword – since it also holds out considerable potential peril for the reputations of those who take advantage of the opportunities on offer. This is recognised by Nadia, a machinist in Egytex:

The perception of the *shabaab* (youth) these days is what's partly responsible for the double standards and tensions found in love relations between them. There is still the conservative view that a girl who is willing to date, and to linger in knowing a man for longer than is necessary, is not to be regarded as trustworthy. She may stand accused of being susceptible to acts of infidelity later on. She is consequently seen as not worthy of carrying the man's name and bearing his children. These views are the hardest to challenge, however much you might believe and declare that love is important.

The apprehension surrounding the concept of female modesty in the light of excessive male attention is not a straightforward matter (Harris 2006). With it comes the potential of endangering one's reputation – a situation any single girl can ill afford if she wants to continue to project herself as *kwayisa* (good) and be considered an eligible candidate for other single men in the *entag* pool. The pressures come from within labour units on the shop floor, with minds and tongues busy identifying developing love relations, however discreetly they are managed – eyes watching, speculations whispered and suspicions confirmed, until news of a nuptial event is announced. As not all love relations are destined to have happy endings, instances of a break-up are as intriguing as the relations themselves. In cases of a break-up, questions are pursued with persistence: 'Is she still in love with him or has she forgotten him?' Eyes focus on the couple emerging from a break-up in the attempt to detect signs of yearning for the lost beloved. 'Did her eyes soften when she caught a glimpse of him walking down the hall? Did she blush?' Or for the man, 'Was his speech coherent when he saw her? Did he appear composed, or on the verge of falling apart and disappearing between the cracks in the shop floor?'

The dangers of appearing an easy catch for young men addicted to *il-rasm* (trying it on) are graphically described by Zeinab as she whispers about the risks being run by Kawakib, a new *tarqim* worker:

> Look at Kawakib. She is related to Sheikh Yassin, and supposedly engaged. But because of her response to all the male attention she's getting *il-kalam yetla' 'aleha* (the gossip will come back to bite her). Her willingness to chat up the boys, and wear tight trousers along with this thin eye-liner which she uses, will all lead them to get the wrong idea. There are already bets between Tamer and Hatim over her. It will be said that she is *sahla* (easy) and *khafifa* (light – implying too weak to resist temptation). We've tried to warn her – but does she listen?'

These apprehensions are confirmed by Habiba, a quality control worker in Egytex, as she recalls her early days in *entag*:

Boys will flirt when you are new to the place, and still timid from the sheltered home environment. If a girl does not learn how to put the brakes on unnecessary flirtation, their audacity gets worse. Working in an environment where words can be misconstrued, and sent flying in all directions, is one of the first lessons of the shop floor. When I started I had to consciously give thought to the reputation associated with my name. It meant taking care of what I was saying, and more importantly to whom I was saying it. It took one situation after a few weeks to make me firm, and from then on I was fearless. But I'm not sure these are desirable qualities expected in an unmarried woman.

Supervisors watching and monitoring the production scene are strict in keeping an eye on moral standards on the shop floor, even though they take an understanding view of romantic interests between workers. Horeya explains quietly:

We can't judge them harshly when they are caught in that age group. People misinterpret the religion when they class everything as *haram* (forbidden). The term is badly misused in my opinion. *Haram* ought to be restricted to the *kaba'er* (major sins) such as not praying, or stealing – not applied to every single small, insignificant act. I'm certain that religion judges you differently if at fifty a man behaves like a twenty-year-old. Can and should they both be judged equally? In the *sala*, the boys are *utat mighamada* (newly born kittens whose eyes haven't yet opened – implying sexually uninitiated). We feel responsible for them. The girls are different – they are addicted to *tamsiliyat* (dramas). This is how life is lived.

The *aflam* (tales) on the shop floor of female *tamsiliyat* remain a theme that lies at the centre of the regulation of gender politics on the shop floor, highlighting the extent to which gender norms change as workplaces become more sexually integrated. The *mushrifat*'s gaze on the *aflam* of love entanglements revolves around uncovering girls' tactics, and protecting the men – however much a man may make public claims of being *lafif wi dari* ('been around and knowing what's what') and an *asad* (a lion), and however bent a girl may be on appearing *mu'adaba* (the polite, docile type). This is confirmed when, during the course of the working day, *mushrifat* receive calls from anxious parents of young male workers, specifically asking them to restrain the dangerous influences of the women on the shop floor.

Complaints about love triangles are taken particularly seriously. A vivid instance is provided by a phone call from the mother of Hashem, a *makwa* (ironing) worker who was expected to marry his cousin, but has reputedly been sidetracked by Fatima, a machinist in Horeya's assembling unit. Hashem is said to be having second thoughts about the arrangement, and rows have broken out in the family. Over the phone Hashem's mother specifically requests Horeya to intervene and put an end to the dangerous influence of Fatima, by dissuading the *khatafa* (snatcher of men) from derailing Hashem's marriage plans. As other parts of the story emerge, it turns out that this is not the first time Hashem has broken an engagement with a relative on account of a love relationship in the factory. He is described as 'having a light star' (implying that he is easily swayed from his course), and his family is fearful that a second cancellation will endanger their word in the village community of Kanater.

The *mushrifat* entrust Kifah Mansur, known for her more humane side, with the mission of having a private word with Fatima, whom they agree to be 'sick with love' and, at this point, as needing nothing more than a few stern words invoking religion to underline the moral implications of getting involved in a love triangle. Kifah fulfils her mission, reporting back that Fatima's tears of repentance were 'flowing like buckets', convincing her that her religious talk had got the temptress to think twice, and that some headway has been made in putting sense into Fatima's vision 'blurred and blinded by the mirror of love'. Some of the older *mushrifat* are however unimpressed at seeing Fatima crying her eyes out in the *sala*, advising her to '*ayati ziyada 'ashan temsahi demu' il-zenub* (keep on crying, so that your tears can wash away your sins)'. It soon transpires that Kifah's religious advice has not, in fact, done the trick. As she reports to the *mushrifat*, gathered around the table in their room nibbling pickled carrots:

> She sees herself fully justified in pursuing Hashem. This morning she told me that she'd followed my advice and said the *istikhara* prayer [the accepted channel for asking God 'to lead the way', leaving matters to take their course and believing that whatever happens is 'for the best'] – after which she saw Hashem's face beaming at her in all her dreams for seven nights. Shouldn't this be telling us something?

Another of the *mushrifat* suspects that the religious advice that has been given in good faith to Fatima is now being used to mock them indirectly. 'What kind of *istikhara* did she do? We *never* [uttered categorically] "see faces" in the *istikhara*. She's just making it all up.'

Within a few days, Fatima is seized by a fainting fit on the shop floor, surrounded by girls fanning her and searching for smelling salts. News of this quickly gets back to the *mushrifat*, who are unsympathetic. 'Keep slapping her till she recovers', says Maymuna to Kifah Mansur, recalling the robust technique a hired nurse had previously used to restore fainting workers to active production duty. 'And if she doesn't recover, drag her to the gates of the factory and throw her in the street! She'll recover soon enough'. Kifah returns twenty minutes later with an even more incredulous announcement. 'You won't believe this. The ambulance has arrived! *Who* called the ambulance? Should we fine security?'

The episode comes to an end with Fatima's dramatic statement of her emotional turmoil, regarded by the shop floor as the latest *film* (tale), in which the arrival of an ambulance provides concrete proof that severe ill health can be a side effect of love. Among the single girls, however, Fatima receives little sympathy. Zeinab's thoughts centre on the *haqq* (rights) of the potentially wronged fiancée:

> Fatima ought to have spared a thought for the feelings of the other girl in the village, locked like herself in trying to get a life. A derailed engagement could easily be misconstrued as Hashem deserting his cousin because of some fault in her – not because Fatima is playing her tricks. Taking what belongs to others, just because she's found an easy catch, is not right.

The reaction of others is more concerned with issues of *ihtiram* in the factory. 'This sort of behaviour is unbecoming, hardly acceptable in a workplace', comments one supervisor to Zizi. 'Had Hakim even heard of what she was up to, he'd have taken her out of the factory like he did with what's-her-name and instructed her to weep outside. Tears bring *il-faqr* (poverty) to the factory. Not that we need more of it!' Zizi's response is pragmatic: 'It's not worth getting dragged down into these squabbles. Their lives are *matahat* (mazes) and often the reasons are unbelievably trivial. It's their age: they're *too* young'.

Commodifying the shop floor – trading in dreams

In this section I explore a further dimension of *taraabut*, where the workforce appropriate the workplace for the purposes of a vigorous commercial trade in goods and services, thus subverting the primary purpose of the shop floor as a zone of production and converting it instead into an area of consumption. The shop floor's commercial activities expose a rigorous consumer market sustained through a wide range of goods and services. This enables unmarried girls to transform their hard-earned wages into concrete commodities which can then be stored away, safe not only from the risk of squandering hard-earned cash on short-term temptations, but also from exploitation by their families.

This last issue is one which loomed large in workers' perceptions. A constant preoccupation was protecting their earnings from being forcibly diverted to meet their family's financial requirements. The problem could be exacerbated if siblings and other family members also happened to be working on the shop floor, and able to provide information on their financial inflows. It was interesting that girls found the erratic pattern according to which wages were regularly paid to be a positive help in this respect, since it made it easier for them not to declare their full wages to their families – claiming instead that pay was again late, or exaggerating the amount which had been deducted as fines. And once their wages had been securely converted into commodities, the commodities were often hidden away, safe from the prying eyes of their families. I also found virtually all commercial activity by young female workers to be geared towards a specific end, namely the accumulation of *gihaaz* – the contribution which the female partner in a prospective marriage is required to make to the material circumstances of her new home. This turned out to be a process focused on the construction of gendered strategies for transforming workers' private dreams of wedding nights and subsequent married life into concrete, 'bankable' reality.

The first manifestation of these commercial interactions involves the appearance on the shop floor, at the start of each month, of a wide range of mail-order catalogues, with 'Avon products' and 'My Way – the social ladder to business success' the two most popular. Thus one day Habiba, a QC worker in Egytex, producing the latest edition of the 'My Way' catalogue from her synthetic handbag, tells me that:

> When I first began this small line of business my thinking was that *akl il-'eish mihtag il-khifiyya* (in this life one needs to grab every chance going). But I now realise it's more about *nafa' wi-istanfa'* (benefiting others whilst benefiting oneself).'

Her 'My Way' catalogue circulates amongst teams of workers until all units of *entag* have viewed the offers in that month's issue. Items include styling cream, two-in-one shampoo/conditioner, skin whitening cream (at a special 30 per cent discount), 'Active Man' eau de toilette, tooth freshener, two-in-one blush, mascara, a variety of lipsticks (in 'summer and winter colours'), His-and-Hers eau de toilette, Body Mist and shower gel, as well as disinfectants, detergents and washing powder.

Catalogue vendors focus their social and marketing skills on convincing single women workers that their products are good value for money, comparable with *markat 'alamiyya* (international brands), often emphasising the packaging and branding of the goods they are offering. Workers however also exert 'trade description' consumer rights normally unavailable to them in external markets, in demanding that the product lives up to its billing. Only once a product has been tried by the initial purchaser, and passed off as successful, do larger orders follow from other workers. Failure of a test specimen to live up to consumer satisfaction often leads to its being boycotted, as happened in the case of a rose shower gel that was initially thought to be an attractive bargain at LE 15 for a family-sized bottle, but once tested, was declared to be 'just bubbles in water'. It was instantly discontinued and replaced by the vendor with another item at the same price.

Other popular catalogues include food items, such as packets of pre-mixed herbs for use in lentil soup and other Egyptian staple dishes such as *kishk* (a yoghurt and chicken dish), *bashamil* (a savoury white sauce), and *bamya* (okra in tomato sauce). Instant pudding mixes include custards, chocolate rice pudding, orange cake-mix and jellies. It is noticeable that, far from being exotic, each dish represents the sort of food which an ordinary working-class Egyptian family would expect to see served on an everyday basis, so that the traditional flavour of these culinary products, as its vendors stress, is still retained. Yet it is equally evident that in each case the implicit marketing message transmitted is that these products are convenience foods, pre-packaged ingredients for 'busy working women', whose lifestyle leaves them with no time for the laborious business of shopping for fresh ingredients, and then preparing each dish from scratch in the kitchen. Instead their preparation requires the possession and use of kitchen appliances such as refrigerators, food mixers and ovens, i.e. *gihaaz* items signifying social mobility and a different order of 'class' aspirations.

A similar class aspiration can be seen to operate in the shop floor's interest in bartering staple foods obtained through the Egyptian Government's ration card system. This was one of the few remaining survivals of the Nasserist vision of all-providing state socialism (Singerman and Hoodfar 1996). Through it, citizens could have access to rationed quantities of basic food items at subsidised prices below those available in the open market. Long considered to be of material significance only to those declared to have *mahdudi il-dakhl* (low-income, i.e. the poor and marginalised), in the early summer of 2004 ration cards seemed to be making something of a social comeback in Port Said. The occasion was the inclusion in the programme by the Port Said Governorate of a number of food items previously available only in the exclusive military stores reserved for the use of officers and their families. These included items such as rice, sugar, ghee, palm oil, lentils and powdered soap. The prices of the additional items now made available through the civilian ration card were in fact only slightly lower than those on offer in public shops; and their quality was generally considered to be inferior to those available on the open market – as was confirmed when one of the workers passed supplies of home-baked biscuits using the ghee around the shop floor, only to have them sniffed at as *mayetakilsh* ('uneatable' – with the disparaging reference aimed at the ingredient, not the worker's culinary skills). Yet migrant workers in whose home provinces these additional items were not available on the ration card were eager to barter them for the more mundane rationed staples to which they did have access (such as tea and sugar), supplies of which they brought into work for this purpose.

The driver for this seemed to be a social aspiration to be associated with a group who had access to special privileges, i.e. the *zubbat* (officers in the military or police force). This was even more clearly demonstrated in the case of workers who exerted their right, as Port Said residents, to acquire a civilian ration card for the first time. As Hasanat Amin, one of the married supervisors, explained as she folded her new card (something she had not previously bothered with) into the plastic case she had specially bought for its safe-keeping:

> For a long time, we lived believing that these are privileges associated with the *zubbat*, who have their own cooperatives, clubs and special status. To have a ration card now is a way of partaking in these privileges, even if today nothing that is sold in the *zubbat* cooperatives is scarce any longer. The whole local market is saturated with these goods, and we know that a housewife's resourcefulness in making a small amount of cash go a long way is far removed from simply saving a few piastres over what can be gained from a ration card.

This interpretation is confirmed by the way in which even the *bizniz* women of the mail-order catalogues are obsessed with their ration cards. Thus Nadia, a successful mail-order catalogue vendor, takes the view that her newly acquired ration card enhances her social status as someone associated with privileged social networks, as well as reinforcing her image as a self-confident cook, organised mother and thrifty housewife, which in turn strengthens the foundation for her business dealings through the sale of other goods in the catalogue.

Through all these efforts, the workplace landscape is energised by an incessant stream of commercial activity, as workers place catalogue orders to mark events round the calendar such as the *Eid*, or seize the occasion of a new school term or the festive month of Ramadan to indulge in the entrepreneurial spirit at large on the shop floor. Each day at least one new product makes a discreet appearance, be it a line of cosmetics such as a new brand of shampoo, perfume or shower gel; or a bag of colourful eyeliners; or a new line in party toys; or plastic 'made in China' wrist watches for children; or socks for men. Each *sala* has its own individual *bizniz* women who compete assiduously for clients. Cheaper and better bargains are much sought after, and workers are keen to scan and exchange information on what is new, what is on offer, and who is the supplier. The varying prices and terms of payment, often for identical goods, that are available from different vendors are points of much shop floor debate. Free monthly gifts are offered to those who spend more than a certain amount, with the items changing from month to month, and different products added to sustain consumer interest.

Male workers are also active in shop floor commerce, frequently establishing their 'niche' through the provision of services rather than, as female workers do, trading in goods. Thus Osama, from Quality Control, seems to have established a distinct service niche in the hiring out of his personal mobile phone for use by others, both to make and to receive calls. By charging a small extra fee for each call, he provides workers with accessibility of his service and its confidentiality, since he prides himself on his reputation for strict discretion over love squabbles and the much awaited kiss-and-make-up calls. Using the service niche as a basis, Osama has also expanded his business into the direct selling of goods. Every fortnight, his dark-blue synthetic suitcase of specimens makes its appearance on the shop floor and a variety of goods appear. These include photo frames for LE 25 ('made to order', with personal 4x6 photographs of engaged couples, sprinkled with glittery gold dust and embellished with romantic phrases in – sometimes wrongly spelled – English, of the 'I love you forever and ever' variety), fluffy toys, mugs with romantic phrases inscribed on them, small vases, deodorants, soaps, edibles such as nuts and packets of jellies, herbal concoctions for losing (or putting on) weight with diet sheets to accompany them, and *wasfat* (prescriptions) for a variety of ailments. Osama's entrepreneurial skills have become celebrated in Egytex, to the point where his corner in the *sala* is popularly referred to as 'supermarket Osama'. Even *edara* joins in, as Sawsan Etrebi comments admiringly:

> He never misses an opportunity to make a quick sale: he's a real *uradati* (wheeler-dealer). If he could bottle the oxygen we breathe and sell it to us, I promise you the containers would be lining his suitcase every morning. He's a natural at that sort of thing – even *Baba* could learn a few tricks from him!

Given the temptation to consume, it is not surprising to find girls recalling their excitement over their first experience of *amsik felus* ('getting hold of some money' – implying receiving their first wage packages), and how they spent their first earnings on things they had long wanted, whether small luxuries available in the factory or personal purchases from the city's shops of dainty wristwatches, gold necklaces or cassette players. Yet it is also remarkable how these initial self-indulgent spending sprees switch to what is commonly known as *il-nazra il-mustaqbaliyya*, or the long-term gaze that 'looks towards the future'. This development involves the female worker converting her wages into more durable and valuable goods, most specifically in the pursuit of the *gihaaz* she will need to make to finalise marriage arrangements.

Ethnographic studies confirm that in traditional Egyptian society the costs of a couple's marriage were customarily met by the groom's family elders (Singerman 1995, 1996; Amin and Al-Bassusi 2003, 2004). With the advent of the more consumerist modern era, and the accompanying inexorable rise in the costs of marriage, it has become progressively necessary for contributions to be made by the bride's family, and, most recently, by the groom and bride themselves. During the long period of engagement, the couple collaborate in, or sometimes break up over, efforts to furnish and decorate their new home in ways that meet the status norms of particular classes, communities and regions (Singerman and Ibrahim 2003), while at the same time hiding them away from the prying eyes of jealous siblings or competitive relatives.

This is reflected in the notion, widely prevalent on the Fashion Express shop floor, that the dream of every woman (single and married) is *il-beit il-hilw* (the beautiful home) and the task of assembling a bride-to-be's *gihaaz* represents the first step in realising this dream. This is not, however, the end of the dream, for in another fifteen years, the *beit il-hilw* will be refurbished and given a new look known as *il-beit yetwadab* (the tidied-up home, in the sense of having a facelift). This second phase represents a further rite of passage for the family as a unit. The transition process of *'amra* (pruning) is considered to prevent the family home from becoming *beit gayif* (an adjective connoting tatty) and involves a second major expenditure of cash, one the parental couple carry out with the likelihood of receiving anticipated suitors for their children very much in mind. For these reasons, issues to do with *gihaaz* accumulation command sustained interest among all women workers on the shop floor, including the few older ones who are already married.

More recently, a distinctively competitive dimension has evolved in the process of *gihaaz* accumulation among single women (Ghosh 2002; Ghannam 2002, 2006; Chalcraft 2007). Thus one female worker, who was married the previous year, spoke of the way her cousins made 'surprise' visits to her home to 'check' that none of the items were 'borrowed', while another, from the provinces, described how she had to physically hide her *gihaaz* items from the eyes of prying siblings to whom 'the luxuries of the past have become today's necessities'.

Accumulation of *gihaaz* on the shop floor tends to begin with small items such as a set of sherbet glasses, fluffy toys, a set of bed sheets, a set of china and items of kitchen cutlery. The most popular purchases remain toiletries such as perfume, although women workers do not to wear perfume at work due to a religious observance that it has a sexually exciting effect on men, and is therefore only appropriate in the privacy of their homes. With perfume, the main driver of consumer popularity appears to be the shape of the bottle and whether or not it will look fetching amidst the array of other *gihaaz* items to be displayed on the dressing table in the matrimonial bedroom.

Girls whose fiancés work in the factory are at an inherent advantage, since the women workers doing perfume *bizniz* encourage the men to 'allow' the girls to pick the bottles they like, agreeing to pay for them later.

An added sales benefit offered to single women by married vendors involves the passing on of important tips on feminine hygiene, such as how to 'smell *zay il-ful* (like jasmine)' in bed. These tips form part of the sexual education passed on to single girls, who in general are preoccupied with notions of how, once safely married, they can shed their inhibitions and transform themselves into sex divas in the bedroom. While they were all circumcised by custom, it was noted that not all methods were the 'same'. Fear of female frigidity and male impotency could thus easily create anxiety on their part, especially within the context of a relationship that can only be consummated after the public *dukhla* ceremony.

This association of particular *gihaaz* purchases with free, one-woman-to-another sexual advice finds its most extreme expression in the case of lingerie purchases (vom Bruck 1997, Halasu and Salam 2007). In contrast to the different styles of *hijab* and the messages they convey about a woman's public persona, lingerie items were perceived as markers of a woman's persona in the privacy of the home. The purchase of lingerie continues well after marriage,[8] since it is generally accepted that while it is a woman's *bara'a* (sexual innocence and purity) that initially seduces a man in the *ingizab* stage of a relationship, her skill in keeping the flame of his love alive lies in her power to seduce him in private by creating many nights of *mufaga'at* (surprises). A bride-to-be's wardrobe would accordingly be expected to be dedicated to a range of this type of clothing, including the most recent trend for even including an elaborate belly-dancing costume.

Lulls in production and delays over the payment of wages are compensated for through the appearance on the shop floor of lingerie catalogues, together with samples of some of the racier items on offer (far beyond the bounds of suitability for public display in the garment stores of the *souk*). The latest designs have distinctive names such as *il-kontesa* ('The Countess'), a nylon gown that is over-the-shoulder on one side, with a long, fishnet lycra sleeve on the other, together with a single, matching fish-net glove to give it a purported look of aristocratic glamour. Each garment is examined with a view to establishing how much female flesh it reveals, what sort of addition it might make to an already existing wardrobe and, ultimately, its price. The views and experience of married women are sought, as they advise younger colleagues about which particular styles and colours can be relied on to *bishid il-ragil* (literally 'pull the man' – implying excite him sexually). At slack times the factory's toilets are turned into dressing rooms for trying out the samples, amidst a hubbub of racy comments. Thus Zizi, who prides herself on her understanding of the male psyche, declares with authority:

We are *sharqeyyin* (Middle Eastern women). It is improper for us to ask a man for sex directly. We are not like the West. Our kind of man pines for a woman who can dazzle him, through making him feel strong and protective. Her need for him is communicated through a glance, a little word here and there, or a hug, or [pointing at one item in the catalogue which she was thinking of buying] *kida* (like that). That is how his masculinity is ignited. Otherwise we would hear him complain he is living with a *ghaffar* (watchman – implying a masculine woman) and we may as well sit back and compare notes on a stream of *talakik azwag* (husbands' excuses). This does not mean we say *hader* (yes in the subordinate sense) to everything all the time: just a *slight* nudge to give a man *brestijuh* (his prestige). These garments allow us to communicate messages of this nature. No woman that I know of wants to live with a man who's just an *insan ma'dum* (wimp).

In all the commercial activity, it is noticeable that workers give shop floor trading priority over business ventures outside the factory gates, it being taken for granted that the shop floor provides advantages not found elsewhere. Even workers who have left the factory continue to enrich their *gihaaz* accumulation through the factory-based networks they maintain. The shop floor system operates on trust, with the goods ordered being produced within a day or two, without the need for formal signing of orders or payment forms. Terms of payment are also more flexible, with instalment plans (albeit with an additional price premium) available to workers who are short of cash, as they often are as a result of the factory's erratic wage-payment schedules. The benefits are also social, as workers do additional favours for each other and share in common actions, the spirit of encouragement generating a shopping experience that is both communal and personalised. This is evident not only in material dimensions (e.g. workers helping each other out financially) but also in non-material ones (e.g. in the way girls working in teams often purchase the same product so they can be *zay ba'ad* (all the same – implying a togetherness of equals). This important dimension to the busy pattern of shop floor commerce, and its relation to Rosen's eloquent formulation of 'the circle of *kheir* (beneficence)' (Rosen 2002: 12, 13), is on vivid display one day when Zizi, who bought her *gihaaz* items through shop floor purchases and networking, declares:

> The factory may have its own share of troubles but no one around here can deny that it is also a place with a lot of *kheir* (goodness – in the sense of 'the blessings of providence'). Where would I be if I had worked elsewhere and relied on my own resources? The assistance I received from my *shilla* in making the cash available when I needed it, in helping me arrange ways of paying off my debts, and their active assistance in transporting the furniture and giving the new place a thorough spring clean, all leads me to suspect that if it hadn't

been for this place, I would never have got married. I don't believe that my siblings would have been able to help me succeed in achieving everything I have done here.

Also being constructed through the process of shop floor *gihaaz* accumulation by the female worker is an enhancement of the social status that she, as a result, acquires in her home community outside the factory. It is a distinctive form of respectability that can best be described as 'material *ihtiram*' (to distinguish it from the social and moral forms of *ihtiram* which I have previously described and discussed) since it is calibrated according to the quantity, quality and cost of the goods amassed. And central to the concept of material *ihtiram* is the requirement that the young woman should have acquired the goods in question through her own efforts, not by the grace of her father, brothers, fiancé or any other male. Zizi explains this, taking herself as an example:

> This factory attracts the type of girl who finds her *shakhsiyya* (identity) through her labour. She is not the type with parents who lavish her with cash. She perseveres and stands on her own two feet. She gains *ihtiram* in the eyes of others because of what she has achieved for herself. It is not the same with working in retail shops, which relies on different skills such as looking glamorous and chatting up the customers to buy and keep coming back. There you have to spend the cash you earn on your own appearance, which is deadly tedious. The factory girl ends up knowing her own mind, so the employer fights tooth and nail to keep her. It says a lot for our kind of *mohtaram* (respectable) and *nidif* (proper) environment.

Horeya, emphasising the dimension of self-reliance, elaborates on the change in workers after they have spent some time in the factory:

> They arrive here looking a mess! After one year they have become *mutfatehin* (broad-minded), and their skills are much in demand. Their experience of work is not different from that of their male siblings who, a decade ago, were working in the Gulf and earning hard currency. Our factory jobs are the equivalent, except that at the end of the day the girls return home to sleep.

There even appeared to be evidence that on occasion this form of self-help driven material *ihtiram* could, within the wider sociocultural environment, carry greater weight than social or moral *ihtiram*. This was illustrated by the story of two sisters, Kimo and Nura, who came from Isma'iliyya and worked as machinists in the factory. For different reasons both had ended up unmarried, and spoke of pooling the cash they were saving in a spirit of sisterly *taraabut* (i.e. without having to call on their married male siblings) in order to build an extension to their house, in which they planned to retire and look after their aging mother. They thus appeared confident that the material *ihtiram* they would, as a result, be accorded by their home village would outweigh the social stigma of their unmarried status.

Celebrating dreams – a picture says a thousand words

A similar spirit of *taraabut* underpins and infuses workers' nuptial ceremonies. These are staged as events bringing the workers together in a consumer vision, crafting a distinctive Port Saidian image of the ideal glamorous bride and good-looking groom, which is widely shared across the shop floor. The shared vision is constructed through the circulation of commemorative albums of photographs of the most recent *khutuba* (engagement) or *dukhla* (wedding consummation) celebrations to have taken place. These large, ornate albums provide brightly coloured illustrations of the latest consumerist trends, which are expected to be on extravagant display during the nights of celebration. These include having the most fashionable DJ to preside; colourful discotheque lighting; billows of dry ice illuminated by yellow, red and blue beams of lights across a darkened dance floor; and a hired car to transport the bride and groom to the venue. Much attention is given to the cosmetician making up the bride, and the special effects he is able to conjure up in transforming her into an unrecognisable person, with a *new look* (the same words are used in Arabic). The distinctively Port Saidian character of this vision is provided through the greater and more modern range the local market is able to offer by way of new ideas in fashion and accessories – a range not found in neighbouring and less cosmopolitan provinces.

These nuptial celebrations were widely attended by almost everybody in *entag*, who saw their participation as vital in livening up the party atmosphere, and not leaving the bride and groom simply reliant on family members and neighbours to create the appropriate mood. They spoke of the importance of ensuring that the party provided a boisterous event, something that in their view distinguished the emotional life of their class from that of the *nas il-metnashena* ('stiff people' implying management and higher classes). The most memorable event, which was the talk of the shop floor for weeks before and after it took place, was Azima Mohamed's *dukhla*. It entailed hiring two buses to transport the workers to Gamaliyya (a traditional district of Cairo) for what was described as a street wedding out of *Alf leila wi leila* (*The Thousand and One Nights*). As her husband had a second job acting as a *kumbars* (tough-guy) in Arabic films, the celebration was organised to emulate the details of a *farah baladi* (street wedding) in a film in which he had recently had a part. No expense had been spared in the provision of all sorts of drugs (*bango*, pills and the like – handed out straight from the groom's pockets), a plentiful supply of beer and the hire of a belly dancer in a clinging leotard, with the workforce thoroughly enjoying themselves until the dawn call to prayer and a journey that would take them straight back to the shop floor.

The 'affirmation through performance' of *taraabut* lies at the heart of an additional, distinctively local Port Saidian nuptial ceremony. Known as the *haflit il-tangid*, it is staged after the accumulation of the *gihaaz* has been completed, and usually about a week before the *dukhla* ceremony. Ethnographic accounts of Middle Eastern Islamic marriage ceremonies have not, as far as I am aware, included descriptions of this particular event. I therefore conclude this chapter with a description of the *tangid*, as it integrates several themes around the social and commercial opportunities made possible on the shop floor and the broader changing expectations of more consumerist trends in society.

Tangid is the traditional trade of fluffing up raw cotton and then stuffing and sewing it into mattresses, quilts, pillows, cushions and other soft household furnishings. As its name suggests, the *haflit il-tangid* celebration centres around calling on a *minagid* (one who performs *tangid*) to bring in the tools of his distinctive trade, along with his team of three or four male workers (see Illustration 3.2), to prepare and assemble the soft furnishings for the newly-weds' bedroom into a fetching and prestigious ensemble. The costs of purchasing the sacks of raw cotton and paying for the services of the *minagid* and his team fall on the bride's family.

Originally the *haflit il-tangid* seems to have involved little more than family and close friends. Today's *tangid* party has however developed into

Illustration 3.2 The *minagid* (quilt fluffer) at work

a more elaborate event of much longer duration. The event usually begins in the early afternoon. As many guests are invited, the hospitality on offer is restricted to soft drinks. Much of the emphasis focuses on arranging as elaborate a display as possible of the soft furnishings that make up the *gihaaz* of the celebrating couple. The newly made mattresses are piled in a corner, surrounded by displays of other *gihaaz* items for the bedroom and kitchen, such as fluffy toys, dolls, jars, lampshades, kitchen electricals – and more cushions. The prime purpose of the occasion seems to be a public display of the couple's conspicuous consumption, as the guests are obliged to view the range and quality of the *gihaaz* items which have been accumulated in preparation for the newly-weds' married life together. Older workers tend to find the younger generation's displays to be decidedly vulgar, as when Fatma (a supervisor in her thirties) remarks at one of the *tangid* parties:

> Why is there such a burning desire to show all those intimate belongings in public? At this rate it will reach a point where the bride's racy knickers will be hung out, next to the duvet she's about to cover herself with to sleep! I don't recall having the inclination to make such a public display in my *tangid*. Today it's a show of what money can buy.

Guests are provided with an incentive to stay on, thus giving them longer to admire the display, by laying on a DJ whose sound system blares out a sequence of popular hits for guests to dance to (see Illustration 3.3). The dancing can take a particularly interactive form when the piled mattresses are laid out as an impromptu dance floor on which guests dance, further

Illustration 3.3 A *tangid* (quilt fluffing) party getting into gear

softening up the bridal bedding, and flinging a banknote or two (typically one or five pound notes) to contribute their personal blessings to the union to be consummated on it.

The success of a *tangid* is measured by the number of girls attending the event. Sohair's *tangid* has brought two dozen girls from the *istithmar* – from Fashion Express and her sister's factory. It is also dependent on the skill of the DJ at conjuring up a party atmosphere in his capacity as Master of Ceremonies, the choice and variety of *aghani shababiyya* (pop hits) he plays, and the quality of the dancing on display. Among the girls, showing off one's skills in *raqs sharqi* (Egyptian dancing) is an important way of demonstrating that one's duty to, and ties of friendship with, the bride-to-be have been publicly honoured. The DJ joins in with equal zeal and professionalism, excelling the women in his theatrical hip and arm movements. A good number of lads from the shop floor have also turned up, joining in the *raqs sharqi* dancing, uninhibitedly mimicking the excessive and exaggerated hip movements. Others show their prowess at the male dance moves that have become fashionable through videos of *shaabi*[9] songs as ways of showing masculine mastery and cool. Examples of the latter include a rather self-consciously *riwish* (cool) young male tapping the knuckles of one hand on his forehead, while at the same time keeping the beat by tapping the heels of his shoes with a pair of metal spoons.

As the event draws to an end, the guests help load the entire display – mattresses, quilts, fluffy toys, cushions and *gihaaz* goods – onto vehicles, for transporting to the new residence of the bride and groom. This can in itself provide another index of conspicuous consumption, especially if the collection is too big to fit onto one vehicle, when the success of the event is measured by how many vehicles are needed to transport the goods.

In Sohair's *tangid*, both the amount of *gihaaz* and the party mood are such that extra transportation is needed for both the goods and guests who want to accompany their transfer (along with children of both family and neighbours). Once the *tangid* convoy of goods and guests has moved to the new residence, the goods are unloaded and taken in, and the task of assembling the home begins. The process takes place over several days. It resembles a doll's house game, in which family members and a selected number of guests are invited to join in turning the rooms, empty of everything save furniture, into a home. It involves filling the cupboards in the kitchen with utensils, stocking the fridge with food and soft drinks, laying out towels and toiletries in the bathroom and bedroom, organising the display cabinet so that the treasures are properly on show (and ready to use), and generally ensuring that every *gihaaz* item has its proper place, right down to the slippers placed next to the bed.

Some *tangid* parties can be sufficiently elaborate to substitute for a separate *dukhla* celebration. In such instances, the convoy of vehicles will take longer to transfer the *gihaaz* goods – and the bride and groom – to their new residence. Much honking and cheering is an essential part of the journey, indicating that a *zaffa* (marriage procession) of suitable style is being performed. In such cases the actual night of consummation of the marriage is still marked by the couple dressing up in formal *dukhla* attire and having their official wedding photographs taken, before formally moving into their new house to begin their married life together. Though unable to have marked the transition with a traditional wedding, their family would still have hosted a *tangid* that celebrated valued aspirations, resulting in a new album of glossy photographs that would circulate the shop floor within a few weeks.

Conclusion

In this chapter I have explored how workers move beyond straightforward resistance to management's control strategies, and instead turn them back on themselves, in order to appropriate the workplace and transform it into an arena for the realisation of personal aspirations. A complex set of practices operate as vehicles to convert the shop floor into their own space, ranging from the stratagems young workers (men as much as women) employ in order to exploit the opportunities offered – and sanctioned – by the desegregated workplace for attracting the attention of the opposite sex, to material practices that enable girls to exploit the shop floor as a market for goods and services.

The older females, who play a key role in monitoring and overseeing the romantic activities in play on the shop floor include the *mushrifat* (female supervisors). There are many additional ways in which the *mushrifat* serve as the linchpins of the entire edifice of the 'firm as family', making them a distinctive subgroup within the workforce. In the next chapter I develop this theme by turning the focus of my enquiry to this group in particular.

Notes

1. This is the individualised instance of the concept of *qalaq*, described in its collective form in the previous chapter. In this instance 'what is not right' is the failure of a male suitor to appear as 'in the nature of things' he should. Abeer is explicit about the personal emotional state of anxiety denoted by the term.
2. *Abdel Aal* (2010) is the English publication resulting from a well-known blog *'Ayiza 'Atgawiz* (I want to get married) started in 2006 by a 27-year-old living in Mahalla, which attracted a huge following of around half a million readers, recounting a fictional Egyptian woman's search for marriage. Kholoussy (2010b) provides valuable contextualisation and

commentary on the original Arabic blog's serious underlying messages around the social reality of spinsterhood, and how these were commercialised and watered down in the subsequent (and wildly popular) Egyptian TV series, as well as the presentation and commercial positioning of the published English translation.
3. Flats purchased through this scheme were registered in both names of the couple and not solely in the name of the man, as the case would be if he were to purchase the flat without the assistance of the spouse. Married women workers in *entag* who had consummated their relationship often took advantage of fluctuating hours of the factory to take up residence in shanty accommodation to receive the official inspectors who assessed each applicant's case. They projected the image of poverty and destitution, declaring themselves unemployed, while their *gihaaz* was stored in rented accommodation for which they continued to pay rent until they succeeded in obtaining a flat under this scheme.
4. *Il-hub fi zaman il-felus* – a line of graffiti scratched on a QC work station.
5. The game has been mentioned in Ammar's (1954) village study. There it is played out in single-sex groups with different rules. It also resonates with Korczynski's more recent (2014) study of the role of popular music in shop floor resistance in a UK factory.
6. The ethnographies of Hoodfar (1997a) and el-Kholy (2002), amongst others, have supported this viewpoint. The assumption is that enhanced respect and a stronger bargaining position can be secured through the size of *gihaaz*.
7. The word *tazbitat*, used originally to refer to work arrangements (as in *tazbitat il-shughl* – see chapter 1), is here wittily purloined to refer to other 'arrangements', with the girl in question given the slang appellation of *tazbita* (equivalent to 'chick').
8. M. Halasu, 'What Lies Beneath', *New Statesman*, 5 June 2006.
9. *Shaabi* (literally 'the people's') music is a comparatively recent development in Egyptian popular music. Some European commentators seem keen to discern subversive political undercurrents in the songs of *shaabi* musicians such as Shabaan Abdel Rahim, Adaweya and Oka w Ortega.

Chapter 4

DAUGHTERS OF THE FACTORY
– DISCIPLINE AND NURTURE

లు⊚•⊚౨

In this chapter I explore the critical role of the *kawadir*[1] on the shop floor, beginning with their immediate, distinctive physical presence amidst the surrounding hubbub, and the self-conscious theatricality with which they impose their authority on the workers under their control. This deliberately overbearing, aggressive style of discipline, linked to the spatial and hierarchical structuring of the firm, generates its own shop floor games. These give work the qualities of play and reinforce structures and hierarchies on the shop floor, so that workplace politics can frequently be explained almost entirely in terms of the labour process itself (Burawoy 1979; Edwards 1979).

Supervisors vie with each other to be seen to be performing heroic feats of production, sometimes resorting to tricks of the trade to appear to be efficient and purposive in the eyes of senior management. This is primarily motivated by their constant fear of being 'reduced to the ranks', an action tantamount to dismissal. It also derives from the status which management bestows on long-serving supervisors, who have been with the firm through thick and thin, of *abna' wi banat il-masna'* (sons and daughters of the factory). The title provides a vivid illustration of the 'firm as family' in action.

By shifting focus to the way labour practice produces gendered subjects and differentiated gendered performances, the exigencies of the supervisory role place special burdens on the female supervisors, requiring them to adopt behaviours (such as shouting loudly, and maintaining an 'in your face' physical presence) which are generally regarded as distinctively masculine. Their response is to craft a gendered labour identity which I describe as 'tomcat femininity' – combining the territoriality and aggression of a male street cat with the essentially feminine traits of caring for and nurturing the workers in their charge. This distinctive femininity provokes a particular response in the other women in positions of authority in the firm, namely the administrators of *edara*, whose calculated strategy is to distance themselves 'as women' through cultivating an exaggerated class-differentiating religiosity (which is itself the subject of much shop floor mockery). The supervisors lead the workforce in defending the shop floor's tradition of tolerance of a range of religious viewpoints. Male supervisors also produce gendered responses, invoking and reinforcing external constructions of 'pious masculinity'.

I also show the measures which the tomcat supervisors deploy to remain ahead of the game, including ensuring that male supervisors are publicly recognised as protégés whom they have nurtured. In this way I use the distinctive position of the *kawadir* to highlight not only the gendering processes of the factory that sustain the power relations of hierarchical space and its internal politics, but also the ways in which local discourses of class, gender and religion are articulated in specific contexts to contest the politics of production, which are, in turn, defended through similar discourses.

Discipline as performance

Within the organisational pyramid of the firm, the rank of *kawadir* is used to denote the thin strata of foremen and supervisors who are sandwiched between the wide base of *entag* (production) and the much narrower layer of *edara* (administration) beneath the apex of top management. *Kader* (plural *kawadir*) is an Arabicisation of 'cadre', and is deliberately borrowed from the Egyptian civil service in order to evoke not only its reputation for clear lines of ordered seniority, but also its wider occupational prestige. Each of the Fashion Express *kawadir* is in charge of a specific *takhassus* (specialisation) or unit, as shown in the diagram provided in Figure 4.1.

The first characteristic that strikes one about the *kawadir* is their distinctive, highly individualised physical presence on the shop floor. Individual supervisors maintain control of their areas through a public, highly dramatic performance of their duties. They are not passive, distanced observers of the labour scene like *edara* upstairs; on the contrary, they maintain a loud, active, hands-on involvement in their workers' – and each others' – performance of their labour duties. A key component of this performance requires the maintenance of vigorous, visible movement. This involves incessant patrolling up, down and around their area, in stark contrast to the largely stationary workforce. Supervisors seldom sit during the entire working day, except during designated breaks.

In the open-plan layout, this is combined with constant observation of, and intrusive interaction with, not only the workers under their supervision, but also each other. When I joined the assembly lines on a quality control stand, I found myself dazzled by the 'in your face' performance of the *kawadir*: the volume and unremitting intensity of their voice and body language. Yet with more time on the shop floor, I began to see how their actions moved up and down a scale of interactive performance, the skill being not only in the accomplished performance of each degree of interaction, but also in the selection of which particular note to strike, and which particular register to adopt, for any given shop floor *mawqif* (situation).

A basic strategy is to proactively 'find faults' in the half-finished garment to which a worker is adding his or her particular component of the assembly process. This is frequently supplemented by verbal assaults on the worker (not simply his or her work), through the use of insults, such as *ghabiya* (thick, stupid), *gazma* (a shoe – implying thick and stubborn), or *gamusa* (a buffalo – taken to mean slow, lazy, wallowing), progressing to even more personal remarks such as commenting that the worker 'smells bad', or adopting in a sarcastic tone the honorific titles of *bahawat* and *bashawat* (Beys and Pashas) when addressing the team and decrying them as a *ziriba* (penful of animals) picked up and 'dumped in this factory'. This fierce style of discipline and control is not unknown in other authoritarian institutions in Egypt. In a study conducted in a public school in Alexandria, Naguib explored the use of 'beating, ridiculing, degrading, and belittling students' as means of 'enforcing the hegemony of the master slave principle in the classroom' (Naguib 2006: 70).

On the shop floors of the Assembly Halls, Horeya and her team of *mushrifat* (female supervisors) have a well-rehearsed litany of such expressions of humiliation, which are delivered in a loud, theatrical voice and manner, making a point of ensuring that as many others as possible see and hear everything that's going on. For the workers, it is a battle of endurance – and not all are passive in accepting the criticisms. Many are vigorous in responding to the supervisor's intrusion, and banter can easily grow heated as arguments break out between supervisors and workers. In the course of such verbal exchanges, whether initiated by the worker or the supervisor, and irrespective of its content, great importance is attached to the ability to answer back, to beat the interlocutor through the arguments that are being raised. Inherent in the banter is a determination not to be put down, using an array of expressions and verbal techniques which workers know annoy their supervisors. These range from cool indifference, to maintaining silent eye contact for as long as possible, to verbal threats to submit an *istiqala maktuba*

142 • Made in Egypt

	LEITEX (Salat Leith) Sala Foreman: Horeya (F35s)			EGYTEX (Salat Qasim) Sala Foreman: Zaim (M28s)		
	Assembly Line 1 (Khat Hanadi Amin)	Assembly Line 2 (Khat Mamduh Khalifa)	Assembly Line 3 (Khat Kawsar Morsi)	Assembly line (Khat Zaim)		Cutting
Darga Tanya (seconds) Ex-Supervisors: Maymuna (F30m) Fatma (F30m)	Line Supervisor: Hanadi Amin (F30m) Jr Supervisors: Sharihan (F30e) Kifah Mansur (F30s)	Line Supervisor: Mamduh Khalifa (M30s) Jr Supervisors: Lamya Faruk (F30s) Enayat (F30s)	Line Supervisor: Kawsar Morsi (F35s) Jr Supervisors: Olfat Anwar (F20s) Abeer Mohamed (F20s)	(Only 1 Line = no Line Supervisor under Zaim) Jr Supervisors: Mohamed Fadel (M20m) Akram (M20s) Naguib (M30s)		Supervisors: Mohsen (M45m) Zizi (F40m)
Packing Supervisor: Sabri (M40m)	Internal (Sala) Quality Control Line Supervisor: Azima Mohamed (F30s) Junior Supervisors: Shadya (F30s) Morad (M30m) Khairi (M25m)			Internal (Sala) Quality Control Line Supervisor: Hamida Ali (F35e)		KEY: M40m = male, forties, married F30s = female, thirties, single F35e = female, mid-30s, engaged
Central Quality Control Line Supervisor: Nidal Hassan (F23m) Jr Supervisors: none						
Laundry/Ironing Supervisor: Ali El Masri (M40m)						

Figure 4.1 Schematic location of *kawadir* (supervisory cadres)

(written resignation) carried out with animation, as the worker dramatically demands that 'paper and pen' be brought down from *edara*.

With machines roaring amid the general shop floor din, each female supervisor takes a turn at yelling at her team, her interventions prompted by the problems erupting among the workers on the line. It can easily escalate into a competition between female supervisors as each gets carried away with her stylised rhetoric. The *sala* is subject to a pandemonium of raised female voices, as personal power is projected on the shop floor by the volume of each individual voice. The *mushrifat* are explicit that their *islub* (style) is defined as *isti'raad bil sawt* (demonstrating one's abilities through the voice) – which workers refer to in shop floor slang as *fatih zor* (opening your throat) or, less politely, simply as *il-ga'ura* (slang for vulgar hawking and spitting). Zizi, a supervisor in Assembly, is explicit on this point when she describes her *islub*:

> My voice is my *damgha* [the ubiquitous 'Eagle Stamp' which makes a government document official]. How else do I *a'alim makani* (mark my territory)? Otherwise a passing visitor could easily draw the conclusion that this group has no *mudira* (superior).'

Yelling at workers and turning later to yell at one another, each *mushrifa* develops her own individual shop floor *islub* of use of voice and theatrical bodily movement. Thus Sharihan wrings both her hands in exaggerated despair, brings them to her face and, bending her torso forward, lets them fall with a dramatic thud on the sewing machine of a worker. Azima Mohamed, a broad woman, walks around with arms akimbo under her waist-length chiffon veil, dramatically uncoiling a hand from under it to jab a finger as she points out a worker's mistakes in a loud voice. Hanadi Amin is shouting at another with similar gusto, but without any of the accompanying arm movements since her arms are clutching a stack of garments to move along to the next station. Nidal Hassan has her team stand in a semi-circle as she reads out her rules in a commanding voice, enumerating them one by one on her raised fingers. Lamya Faruk walks about, wearing the facial expression of *hagib fuq wi hagib taht* ('one eyebrow up, the other down' – implying a sour, displeased look). After a particularly ringing dismissal of a worker as being 'totally hopeless, he broke the whole sewing machine', Kawsar Morsi walks off in disgust waving one hand in a dismissive manner, while clutching in the other some pumpkin seeds which she continues to crack noisily between her teeth as she shuffles towards the quality control stand at the end of her assembly line. The effect, implicitly putting work disputes into everyday proportion, is enough to lighten the mood, which quickly changes to one of laughter among the *mushrifat*.

Throughout it all Horeya (foreman of both assembly halls, and Head of Leitex *sala*) is the most mobile of all, pacing back and forth across her shop floor domain. Horeya's voice announces her presence before she makes an appearance. It is distinctive mainly because of a certain croakiness in the way vowels are stressed, and the way sounds die off at the end of the sentences. Her yelling is an incessant cycle of sound that ceases periodically, and then begins again. After a while her voice mingles with the sound of sewing machines, as both noises become equally constant features of the *sala* workplace environment. Horeya is aware that her 'words carry power', including the power to irritate and vex, and she takes pride in making her point without resorting to sugar-coated words. After a visit to Egytex she sums things up with a ringing assertion that, 'I have nothing to fear in this place. My work and employment record is all that anybody needs to know'. Horeya, however, firmly believes that her style of yelling is taken by the workforce in the spirit in which she intends it:

> They know I have their interests at heart. It's in their interest that they get yelled at. They have to learn that they need to *earn* their skills. If they get upset and walk out, it means they aren't dedicated: they can't take the heat in the kitchen, it's that simple.

The established pattern of domination and mutual dependency is summed up by a proverb popular among long-serving workers on the assembly lines: '*il-ott bihib khanaqo*' (a set phrase, meaning 'a cat loves the one who grabs it by the scruff of its neck').

Gender stereotypes and expectations also come into play, as women workers seem more explicit in accepting being shouted at by male supervisors – or by some of them, at least. Thus Awatef, a machinist down one assembly line, says of two of her *mushrefin* (male supervisors):

> It's not a huge crime if a supervisor under the pressures of work screams at me when I make mistakes. There are quotas that make us rush, and they are pushing us to work faster. Islam often does that, widening his eyeballs in disbelief at our sloppy ways. I might even get a *giza* (fine) if his temper gets the better of him. At the end of the day, though, he will come over to make it up, and this counts as a sort of apology: it settles the matter, and no hard feelings are stored. But as for Akram – conceit has made him hateful.

The *giza* to which Awatef is referring is a fine which a supervisor can impose on a worker, to be paid through deductions from their wages organised by the Workers' Affairs unit. The fine can be from one to three days' wages, a significant amount of money given the tight financial circumstances of the workers. Fines are mainly given for disciplinary offences, such as unruly behaviour at one's workstation or loitering in the toilets (or, for male workers, smoking in them).

The process of issuing a *giza* constitutes a key stage in the escalation of the *kawadir*'s performance of shop floor power. The opening gambit is invariably to issue a loud, theatrical threat to fine the offending worker – who either remains silent or, quite often, volubly answers back, protesting his or her innocence. The heated arguments to which this gives rise can come to a head with a dramatic demand from the supervisor for another worker to run upstairs and fetch *waraqit giza* (an official form) from *edara*. Sometimes, by the time the runner returns, the conflict has quietened down, with no further action called for. Often, however, the argument is still in full flow, giving the supervisor the chance to seize the *waraqit giza*, produce a biro with a flourish, and then virtually stab the paper with it, covering it with rapid Arabic handwriting, all the time declaiming aloud the contents of the report being made, and the size of the *giza* being imposed.

Such incidents usually end with the supervisor ostentatiously pocketing the completed *waraqit giza*, for subsequent submission to Workers' Affairs. In practice, not all supervisors get around to formally submitting the *giza*, since they are conscious not only of the workers' financial constraints, but also of their own need to keep up motivation and commitment within their units. The initial threat, and the subsequent drama of completing the form, are often considered to constitute sufficient admonition for the errant worker, and even if submitted to Workers Affairs, can be later withdrawn. Indeed, all the prior shouting is often intended as a way of not having actually to enforce the fines, since supervisors are acutely aware that their bargaining power on the shop floor is weakened by the current conditions of the firm. Horeya is quite explicit on this point:

> Today with the lack of clients and no regular work orders coming in, I am forced to yell and shout. I don't want to be cornered into having to enforce *giza*. When wages are seldom paid on time, and with the *'iyal* asking me every other day when the wages are likely to get paid, how can a worker get their pay both late and with penalties deducted? As it is, it's difficult to push them to *want* to work. Even when they produce only four hundred pieces a day, rather than the thousand they're supposed to, I'm forced to keep my mouth shut. I have no room for manoeuvre.

Sometimes the heated arguments can spill out of control. Kawsar Morsi, for example, is notorious for once having broken a chair by attempting to throw it at a male worker, and for getting herself into an actual fistfight with another after she had thrown a plastic waste-bin at his head. These instances created genuine shock on the shop floor. This is partly because physical fighting of this kind violates deep-rooted social conventions governing the performance of public disputes in Egypt. In all social situations, including most commonly the numerous minor traffic collisions that take place on crowded roads, everyone takes great pains to ensure that, however self-consciously theatrical and dramatic the verbal arguments which ensue, they are not allowed to degenerate into any form of actual physical violence. In Kawsar's case, there were also major risks of violation of gender and religious boundaries: had she not given thought to what would have happened had the worker slapped her back – or if, even inadvertently, he had pulled off her headscarf? The widespread and extreme disquiet to which these episodes gave rise resulted, in each case, in top management intervening to issue Kawsar with a formal reprimand and *giza* of her own – though with the effect depersonalised by the General Manager calling the entire team of supervisors into his office for a lecture on the need to maintain production quotas and the 'reputation of the firm'.

Such instances of physical violence breaking out are, however, rare. In most cases where it looks as if things might be threatening to spin out of control, the worker involved will remove himself or herself from the scene of the dispute by storming off the shop floor in a dramatic display of righteous self-restraint. Since they are not allowed to leave the factory premises until the end of the shift, they are left in Security, where a well-rehearsed routine sees them provided with a chair while they cool down. Other supervisors who have been watching the skirmish then rush after the worker with soothing words aimed at bringing about reconciliation, something which follows after a suitable period of time. This behaviour is framed as conforming to the religious 'good deed' of *solh* (reconciliation). But it also demonstrates self-interest on the part of the supervisors concerned since, with all the problems of production besetting their units, one of the last things they can afford is a further reduction in the number of skilled workers simply in reaction to the temperament or mood of a supervisor.

Short of having a worker dismissed, the heaviest sanction a supervisor can impose is to 'freeze out' the worker by moving to ostracise them completely. Overt ostracism has the effect of denying the shop floor worker their personality as an individual, their essential humanity, and reducing them to an anonymous cog in a faceless process. From this point on, the supervisor's dramatic performance is re-orientated to demonstrate, again with ostentatious theatricality, that the offending worker has ceased to exist in their eyes. Workers find this even harder to take than being yelled at or issued with a *giza*. They require the human interaction in which their supervisors' performances involve them. Hatim in Cutting explains:

> *Il-ishraf 'amaliyyit ta'amul mish edara* (supervision is a matter of interacting as human beings, not of bureaucratic administration) … at the core of the

relationship between supervisor and worker are *'amaliyyit seluk* (issues of human ethics).

Episodes of dramatic ostracism tend not to be prolonged, as in most cases some reminder of putting things in perspective is all that is needed for the mood on the shop floor and its units to lighten, and for communication and interaction to be restored. These may include someone voicing the latest *nukta* (joke) or the circulation of a new product for sale.

If everything fails, and the position of the worker becomes entirely untenable, then the supervisor moves to the final sanction, which is to write a letter of *'adam salahiyya* (lack of suitability) which officially declares the worker to be unsuitable for employment – not only in the factory, but also in any other enterprise in the Zone. These letters are formal reports, rather after the manner of school reports, giving concrete examples of why the worker has been found wanting. They are formalised by Workers' Affairs, who dismiss the worker and register the letter with the Labour Office in the Zone, so as to prevent the individual concerned from obtaining employment elsewhere. In practice, however, the acute shortage of skilled labour in the Zone means that qualified workers tend to be rapidly snapped up by other factories, regardless of the circumstances of their dismissal. Similar factors militate against the issuing of dismissal notices for skilled employees, however acrimonious the disputes and arguments into which they may have sunk. *Ishraf* (supervision) on the Fashion Express shop floor can thus be seen to incorporate the 'fragile balance between control and consent' that Michael Burawoy has highlighted as a common feature of the shop floor environment (Burawoy 1985: 11). It also illustrates a feature highlighted in Melissa Wright's analysis of north Mexican factories, where a supervisor who demonstrates personality through strength generates staunch support on the shop floor (Wright 1997).

One of the main effects of these powerful, differentiated performances of *ishraf* is to personalise the disciplinary style of each individual *mushref* or *mushrifa*. So completely and vividly do they dominate their zones of responsibility that the spaces concerned become theirs in an intensely personal sense. The effect is seen most explicitly in the convention within Fashion Express that each labour unit is referred to not by its *takhassus* (specialisation) or area (e.g. a *sala*), but instead by the name of the individual supervisor who presides over it. This is not the case in other factory shop floors, where assembly lines are typically given names of Islamic battles (such as *il-Qadisiyya* or *Badr*) or Islamic sites (such as *il-Safa* and *il-Marwa*) according to a convention which is also used in the naming of government school sports teams (Herrera 2006). Within Fashion Express the effect produced has something in common with the individualised demarcation of offices in the top management suite at the front of the factory, where *Baba's* office is plainly his alone, as is the General Manager's. The position is in sharp contrast to that found in *edara*, where the different offices are known by their departmental title, and not after the head of the department.

Using the personal names of supervisors to demarcate the different labour *takhassusat* and units helps give the factory its air of 'firm as family' cohesiveness and *taraabut*. It also has the effect of making each supervisor personally and individually accountable for the unit's production and reputation, and for the workforce within it. As a result, supervisors develop a vested interest in cultivating images of productivity that are carefully constructed through the labour resources and workforce under their control. Their individualised visibility on the shop floor, coupled with this intensely personal accountability for their stage of production, transforms the physical landscape into one of contrasting visual images of efficient labour across the spectrum of each production cycle.

Performing efficiency

Each individual supervisor's credibility is dependent on their overcoming, on a daily basis, a host of unpredictable production problems and difficulties such as absenteeism, workers' buses breaking down en route to the factory, finding that the wrong accessories (buttons, zips, etc.) have been dispatched, machinery breaking down, and the other issues that seem continually to go wrong on the shop floor, on a daily – hourly, almost – basis. They respond with a variety of strategies, all informed by a knowledge of the individual skills and potential of each worker, and the different configurations that can be arranged on the shop floor to produce optimum results.

On a good day when things are going well, a common strategy is for a supervisor to deliberately organise production above the specified quota – but without declaring the excess to *edara*, so as to have *il-rasid* (reserves) on which to draw on in combating unexpected production shortfalls in subsequent days. Generating *il-rasid* can easily turn into a game which is intensely competitive between different units, yet at the same time facilitates bonding within each team and its own supervisors.[2] Thus one day the unit supervisors down the assembly line of *Khat Zaim* find that the assembly of a local order of children's shorts is proceeding well enough for them to organise a competition between their sub-teams (each typically of six machinists) to produce extra garments above the quota top management expect to see. As the game gets going, each unit supervisor uses a separate piece of paper to keep close count of garments their machinists are rushing to produce, and all in the space of a few hours. The frenzy causes a pile-up towards the end of the line, and as the tallies begin to rise to thirty extra garments, then fifty, then seventy, so that the unit supervisors and Zaim himself, caught up in the fever of production, leave their posts and take a turn on the line, deploying their multi-skilled capabilities to increase the bumper crop of *il-rasid*. When production is finally completed, the excess harvest is carefully hidden away in the plastic bins normally used to hold *daraga tanya* (garments with faults – seconds) and needing to be sent for repair. Biscotta, as the worker at the end of the line is nicknamed on account of his sweet tooth, proudly shows me two such 'reserve' bins and, invoking the Islamic Day of Judgement's concept of a recording angel, jokingly tells me, 'This one holds the *hasanat* (deeds of merit – implying garments that have passed quality control), and this one the *sayyi'at* (sins – implying garments requiring further work)'.

Throughout this process, and endemic to the wider politics of the shop floor, is the importance to each supervisor of building, though a record of successive production feats, an image of appearing as *il-montasir* (the triumphant one). Male and female *kawadir* are adept at this game, though their individual tactics can differ. Thus Mohsen, the foreman of the initial stages of the Cutting Unit, devises a strategy to keep the tables in his unit 'looking busy', even at times when work is slack. His solution is to insist that the *faradin* (workers who unroll the bales of cloth) spread the material across both the long cutting tables in his section – even if the material could easily be unrolled onto a single table without exceeding the maximum number of layers the cutters can slice through. This does not impress his workers. Two of the cutters – Mido (nicknamed after the Egyptian footballer playing in the English Premier League) and Dollar (nicknamed for his reputed financial prospects) – complain that these strategies are wasteful and not time-efficient. Mohsen's intended audience is, however, not the workers under his charge, but rather Top Management as it comes by on one of its surprise visits to the shop floor. It is in their eyes that he needs to be seen as a paragon of efficient production, whatever his workers may think about the tactics to which he resorts for this purpose.

In most such instances, however, workers play along in creating a visual impression of efficient productivity, since they have an equal vested interest in being seen as 'diligent'. Thus when Mohsen learns through the internal surveillance system that the General Manager is on his way, he produces from the storeroom a pile of jackets produced under an ancient contract from an overseas client, ostensibly for *tashtib* (tidying up the seams). The girls on the *tarqim* (marking) table look at the denim jackets, with orange Donald Duck patterns, dumped in front of them and exclaim: 'They've been in the storeroom for over two years! They keep making regular guest appearances on this table whenever Mohsen is in one of his moods. Soon they'll go back to where they belong – and then later be out again'. A young worker nicknamed Gorilla is watching the exits, and whispers '*Kalbuz*' ('the fat one' – the unit's codename for the General Manager) as Imam Azmi appears on the shop floor with a visiting client. The unfolding drama leads Zeinab, a *tarqim* worker, to quickly grab a jacket and, with an expression of studious concentration, proceed to examine its stitching, skilfully moving her hand round the seams. The performance appears wholly convincing on the surface – even though it is a complete pantomime, since it is performed without scissors, the essential tool of garment inspection.

In other units supervisors take differing measures to construct a visual image of efficient production, according to the requirements of their posts. Within in-line assembly QC work, garments disappear at the same speed with which they appear (regardless of how carefully they have been checked), since a pile-up could be construed as a supervisor being unable to organise her team effectively. By contrast, the stands in *Gawda Nihai* (Final Quality Control) appear visually as being inundated with masses of garments, providing vivid testimony of the productive efficiency of the assembly lines, as the checkers rely on the incessant sound of their scissors, noisily clicking away, to create their own image of labour efficiency. Seeing these 'games' in operation, I came to understand why in other factories in the Zone, management continually rotate supervisors around different shop floor units, in order to prevent the formation of the bonds of mutual complicity that sustain such performances.

Underpinning the *kawadir*'s drive to maintain, at all costs, their *il-montasir* image of efficient labour is a deep-seated fear of the danger, through top management decisions, of losing their status and being reduced to the ranks as mere workers. The *mushrifat* seemed particularly prone to these anxieties and insecurities, even when their visible shop floor presence appeared at its most powerful and secure. These fears are brought about because they themselves had originally seized and secured their promotions from the shop floor through stratagems known among the *kawadir* as *'asfura wi hidaya* ('sparrow and crow') tactics. These included, for example, seeking support from other members of the *kawadir* to grab an opportunity to step into the shoes of a *mushrifa* on maternity leave, in order to *tizhar min il-mawqif* (be spotted in the situation) by top management, or actively undercutting competitors on the shop floor. *Mushrifat* are therefore acutely aware that among the assembly lines there are other female workers who are capable of emulating their distinctive shop floor roles, and who are equally ambitious to rise to power on the shop floor by masterminding even greater, as yet unheard of, feats of production. This insecurity is so pervasive that during my entire time at Fashion Express absenteeism among *mushrifat* was virtually non-existent. As Nidal Hassan puts it:

From the simple worker to any *mushref* or *mushrifa* of my standing – each has the power and clout to push me off the cliff with each production order that passes this unit. They can put a stop to an order, or trick me into thinking all is moving smoothly until, at the eleventh hour, hair-raising problems suddenly turn up. It's not difficult for top management to find a replacement (*badil*) and who cares what standards the *badil* will flaunt when the words *ma'il salama* (goodbye) have been uttered, and you've been shown the door. I can ill-afford this in a job and rank I have sweated hard and long to achieve. I protect myself by being *mifataha* (alert).

In the *kawadir*'s eyes, being reduced to the ranks is tantamount to being branded *'awila* (dependent – implying useless, a term to which female workers were particularly averse) and, in effect, to being dismissed. Axing staff directly is not Fashion Express's style for terminating its *kawadir* employment contracts. For top management to directly declare someone of *kawadir* status to be redundant would be tantamount to an act of *qat' 'eish had* (taking bread from someone else's mouth). It would also risk evoking powerful connotations of tearing apart the metaphorical family, of which the *kawadir* are close and important members, and so destroying the entire edifice which sustains the operations of the factory. So instead, top management prefers to take indirect measures, by proffering alternative, less prestigious job-offers to any *kader* who may be under a cloud, in the calculated knowledge that the response will almost certainly be a self-initiated resignation. These subtle demotions in rank are considered to be so fundamentally undermining to the individual's position that they are known among the *mushrifat* as *taghir gensiyya* (a change of citizenship – implying a demotion in both status and identity).

Anxieties on this score were voiced many times during my fieldwork. Ominous warnings from the past were vivid in the oral memory of workers and supervisors alike. Supervisors who had left the firm were spoken of as figures of shop floor power for whom *iga waqtaha* ('her hour has come'), who had 'run their course' in the unstable conditions of production within the struggling firm. The most recent story told was the case of Sakina, *il-haqiqa il-taeha* (the 'lost truth' as she was commonly known) who was eventually manoeuvred into leaving of her own accord. Interestingly, her fault was described in terms of violating the principle of *ihtiram* (respectability), rather than any failings in terms of lax production.

As disciplinarians of shop floor morality, the *mushrifat* are expected to be beyond *shubuhaat* (suspicions related to sexually inappropriate behaviour). Thus, they give their dress a formality appropriate to their rank and visibility, whilst also appearing to adhere to a relatively formal Islamic dress. This 'professional presentation' is intended to cement the formal character of the workplace and its 'firm-as-family' ethic. Married *mushrifat* usually wear *abayas* (long-sleeved, ankle-length gowns) and headscarves, while single *mushrifat* typically dress in long-sleeved blouses and skirts, their upper bodies draped in *khumars* (head-and-shoulders veils). A few go for the full *sidal* (a more austere religious form of dress, covering the body from the head downwards in a single, billowing garment). Against this sober, formal dress-code, Sakina is remembered for her excessive make-up; for how her veil was just a flimsy scarf tied high round her head exposing her neck and blouse buttons; for her tight, ankle-length skirts; and for legs 'that any woman would kill for'. Her figure was the talk of the entire factory, especially as her employment in the upstairs *sala* (then in full production, but since closed and disused) meant that she went up and down the staircase all hours of the working day. Her power was seen in her claims that she had standing permission to walk into Qasim Bey's office *manghir moqadimat* (without any preliminaries – such as having to make an appointment). Her dressed-to-kill appearance, and her reputation for being able to 'get whatever she wanted', displayed a shop floor personality laying claim to undisputed power as an *ism* (a 'name' – implying a big shot player in the factory). Flaunting a workplace personality that rested on sex appeal had the effect of creating jealousy, and considerable workplace hostility to an individual prepared to emphasise sexuality as a tool of advancement – and Sakina's success proved to be short-lived. Her reputation earned her neither the respect nor the sympathy of her fellow *mushrifat*. She had, as Horeya saw it, 'offered them the chance to call her *mish shaghala* (unprofessional).'

Sakina left on three months' maternity leave only to find, on returning, that her supervisory position had been given to another *mushrifa*. This was understood to be top management's way of indirectly hinting that she was a problematic case. Sakina was left hanging around repairing *daraga tanya* (seconds) – an activity for which there were more pairs of hands than available work. Her attempts to clarify her position by requesting a meeting with the General Manager led to repeated rescheduling of promised appointments. Eventually Sakina was offered a post as a *khayata* (machinist) with 'set hours', a clear demotion in status with loss of face scripted into the offer. It was seen as unacceptable by other *mushrifat*, not only because *khayata* work is physically harder and requires greater stamina, but also because it would entail being supervised by another *mushrifa*, who, although gaining more *solta* (power), could well be younger in age. Sakina rejected the offer, and continued to hang around the *daraga tanya* workroom. The consequence was that a second, even worse, offer followed, of a job in Security. Joining Security entails being physically moved off the shop floor and dumped 'by the door' in a post that strips the person of prestige, most especially in the case of a person whose one time *ism* had radiated *shohra* (fame) and *solta* (power). Sakina was no fool, and not a newcomer to how the game is played out like acts in a play. As the offers rolled in, and their implicit messages became clearer, she handed in her resignation.

The story of Sakina's departure does not create controversy on the shop floor or in *edara*. As Horeya and Azima explain:

> In this culture redundancy schemes appear harsh measures. They never ask you to leave in a straightforward manner. It reflects negatively on their reputation as a firm. It may require them to pay indemnities if you're on their insurance books. They may be called to account if the case goes through *tahqiq* (an appeal to the Labour Court). Instead, the *zoq* (civil) way is to propose a job transfer which, depending on what is being offered, will determine the fate the person has cooked up for themselves in the first place – resignation. This is what happened to Sakina.

Most of the *kawadir* have however continued in employment with the firm for long periods of time – in some cases up to twenty years. This is a striking feature, since other factories in the Zone complain of extremely rapid rates of labour turnover. Another distinctive feature of Fashion Express is that their *kawadir* have risen through the ranks, starting work as machinists and skilled workers on the shop floor, and then progressing to the position of section-supervisor, line-supervisor and foreman. In other factories in the Zone, supervisory positions are often held by contracted foreign management – preferably from Muslim countries such as Bangladesh. When such posts are held by locals, they have usually been recruited directly into their supervisory positions (often from neighbouring factories), and have seldom worked their way up from the shop floor.

Within Fashion Express the long-serving *kawadir* have been given a title by the proprietor Qasim Bey, who when addressing the *mushrifat* individually calls each of them *bint il-masna'* (daughter of the factory) or, in the case of the male supervisors *ibn il-masna'* (son of the factory). By doing so he is referring not only to their loyalty to the firm, but also to his own personal investment in, and commitment to, them – both as employer, and as the *kebir* of the metaphorical family. Once the appellation has been bestowed by the patriarch, its use by other members of top management provides a means of visibly legitimising the power of the *kawadir* on the shop floor, most especially in terms of their relationship with middle management. The position within Fashion Express can be seen to mirror that observed by Samer Shehata in public sector textile factories in Alexandria, where employees 'within one firm occupied positions of superiority and subordination simultaneously' resulting in a complex web of power relationships that 'make up the bricks and mortar – the architecture – of authority relations' (2003: 106). *Edara* are nominally superior to anybody 'downstairs' in *entag*, including the most senior of the *kawadir*. Yet the legitimacy established by the metaphorical kin titles cements the undisputed positions of authority the *kawadir* have secured on the shop floor. Thus Azima Mohamed is clear that her status on the shop floor and within the hierarchical order derives from the respect she is awarded *min foq* (from above), so that, as she puts it, '*illi taht* (those below) can see that you are not someone they can chew up for breakfast and spit out before lunch'.

There is universal agreement on the shop floor as to which *kawadir* are recognised as having been granted the status of *bint* or *ibn il-masna'*. They are widely recognised to have sprung from within the ranks of *entag,* and so to have been crowned as committed model workers, members of the old guard identified with the growth over the years of the factory as an enterprise. Asmahan, a machinist, articulates this clearly:

> *Bint il-masna* is exemplified in Horeya. She is someone who has been with the firm for a long time, and has grown over the years in rank and wages. You would not find her actively rushing after *felus ziyada* (extra cash – implying by seeking more lucrative work elsewhere). Work has consumed most of her life so that she has *ahmalit fi nafsaha* (neglected herself). She is someone who looks out for the welfare of the firm, and if something is not right, she reports to top management. She is *mukhlisa* (loyal[3]).

Among males, the exemplar most frequently pointed to is Sabri, the *rayis* (boss) of the Packaging Department. This is the final stage in the production process, critical to meeting contract deadlines, and Sabri is renowned for getting every work order packed and despatched on time, regardless of the delays and disruptions that might have beset production at earlier stages. All firms are required to meet strict deadlines, with punishing financial penalties for missing them (including, if necessary, having to air-freight the finished garments back to the client rather than loading them onto the waiting ships). Sabri's professional reputation is one of rock-solid reliability at work, where he maintains tight control of his all-male work unit. He enjoys this despite being, in his private life, linked with a range of rumoured shady goings-on, including habitually using all sorts of drugs. Yet these personal peccadilloes are invariably excused on account of his years and loyalty to the firm.

Qasim Bey's view is that loyalty of the workforce comes from their *asl* (roots) as much as the hierarchical structure of the firm. As he tells me one day:

> In today's increasing materialism, *akhlaq il-forsan* (the ethics of chivalry) is a delusion. Search for the *asl*. It is a quality that has stood the test of time, in all my years. The workforce has borne with my difficulties. My achievement is that they feel this factory is their place – they have made it theirs. This is not a minor achievement, regardless of the difficulties of the firm.

Pride in their *asl* is reflected in the self-image of *bint il-masna* expressed by Kifah when she defines the relationship between the firm and its employees: '*Il-shirka homa ili khalefuna* (It's the firm that gave birth to us)'. We will only know it is time for us to go elsewhere the day they hand us the keys, and order us to lock up the factory forever'. The bond between the firm and its loyal workers likewise shines through the account Horeya gives of her own employment history with the firm. One day, during a lull in production, she takes the time to look back into her own past in the firm. Her voice covers a range of emotions, from nostalgia to pride, as she recounts her working years with the firm:

> I was with Qasim Fahmy and Imam Azmi from the days of *il-Asher* [the 10th of Ramadan City, where the factory first started up]. In those days I was a *khayata* (machinist) on a single-needle sewing machine. We were young then, and I was hugely ambitious. I was fuelled by a determination to succeed. I so badly wanted to excel that if anybody beat me to finishing my quota, I'd cry tears of *qahr* (frustration). I was competing with myself, encouraging others to speed up, not to be defeated. I knew then I had the qualities of *qiyada* (leadership). To this day, I deeply believe that *roh il-khat* (the spirit of the assembly line) is the teacher of all the skills needed to be a success.
>
> The day I decided to follow the work to the *istithmar*, where I knew the pay is better, I took an oath to myself never to allow *il-ersh* (a piaster – i.e. money matters) to humiliate me, or make me compromise my principles. Because of sheer hard work, I was happy with the cash I made and the way I spent it. I dressed well, I went on vacations with friends. I refused to do what others I have seen do – play the *maskana* (one who fakes poverty and need) to climb the professional ladder of the firm. We've come across cases of that variety.
>
> When the factory closed with the previous *naksa* (setback), I stayed at home. Tahani, a supervisor in a competitor factory, sent for me. But I didn't like her very much, and didn't want to stand accused of not being solid enough to withstand the difficulties we were facing at the time. It would show lack of strength and *asala* (authenticity in the sense of being true to one's roots). So I waited until the day Qasim Bey called us back. When we returned, there were twenty of us, and only seven machinists. Not everybody could leave their employment and join us right away. We began again from scratch, and slowly gathered our workforce once more. The girls were not all skilled. Some had never seen a sewing machine! There was no *gawda* (quality control). Each *entag* team in this *sala* had to monitor its own work. The first pair of trousers to appear resulted in a *mahragan* (carnival) in this *sala*. The *zagharid* (ululation sounds made at weddings) echoed, and we went wild with exhilaration. We'd crossed the critical line and production began once again.

The titles of *bint* and *ibn il-masna* crown committed and loyal workers as members of the firm-as-family. In their own eyes, as in the eyes of their workers and top managers, the *kawadir* are the force that holds the firm as family together, in good times and in bad.

Mishmish alley cats – distinctive femininities

The *kawadir* personalise their workplace through the type of dramatic, intrusive, visible performance described above. With time, I came to identify a strongly gendered basis to how these performances are perceived by others in the factory. In the case of a male supervisor (for example, Zaim in Egytex), yelling and issuing *gizaat* is seen as a natural extension of male authority – his behaviour accepted as uncontroversial, because of the assertive quality expected of male public behaviour. This however poses a problem with respect to the female *kawadir* – in engaging in such masculine behaviour, are they not in some senses ceasing to be women? And furthermore, what are the implications of such a performance for challenging deep, socioreligious demarcations of gender boundaries in a mixed-gender setting? Even in modernist Islamic interpretations that concede gender equality in such matters as belief, reason and judgement, the crossing of behavioural gender boundaries remains proscribed. As one perceptive commentator has summarised this view:

> Those men who mimic women and those women who mimic men transgress gender boundaries, and for that reason they were damned by God ... In this demand for (behavioural) equality with men, women transgress divinely sanctioned gender boundaries and deserve God's wrath and damnation. Men who transgress these boundaries by imitating women – a euphemistic reference to homosexual identities – were also damned. (Hatem 1998: 93)

The ambivalence created by gendered workplace identities is expressed by one of the girls working on a quality control stand when she unexpectedly exclaims:

> The male machinists in the *sala* are not men – they are women. Look at them! At the end of the working day: they have little energy left in them. They are *na'min* (soft – generally used to describe docile, deferential women). You see the reverse pattern with the *mushrifat*, like Horeya. Horeya *mistargila* (Horeya is masculinised): *heya bint ragil* (she is a girl who's like a man). This is what's been demanded of her to work herself up to the position she's now in, and to make *il-shughl yegri* (the work move forward). The price is that *unusetha 'odwiyya* (her femininity is now merely physiological).

This equation of production with masculinity recalls Joan Scott's historical analysis of the ambiguity generated by women's changing economic position in the European workforce and how workplaces are gendered by the cultural interpretations of given types of work (Scott 1988: 64–66). Top management's views on the matter imply no such ambivalence. As well as calling the female supervisors *shatra* (smart, clever), top management use other adjectives of greater force, such as *sharisa* (fierce – as of warriors: the European equivalent would be Amazons); *asad fil masna'* (a lion in the factory – with the use of the masculine form of the noun 'lion' having the effect of conjuring up a fierce and territorial image, whereas using the feminine 'lioness' would have the derogatory implication of a sexually aroused woman); and most explicitly, *zay il-ragil* (like a man), or *zay mit ragil* (like a hundred men). Far from there being any suggestion of criticism and condemnation in the terms used, they are expressions of discreet admiration of female strength, and the quality of the leadership found in the firm for running its shop floor production. Authorised by top management as a style 'that works', these masculinised roles for women supervisors are specific to the firm's boundaries and gendering processes, a product of its organisational structure and of the expectations of managerial views of its production landscape.

For a long time I struggled to find an appropriate term for the distinctive behavioural styles which the female *kawadir* had constructed within the factory. Simply labelling it 'masculinised femininity' or 'butch femininity' posed difficulties by evoking alternative associations from recent and current debates in gender and gay/lesbian literature (Halberstam 1998). A solution to the conundrum suggested itself one day when, after witnessing a particularly forceful performance by Nidal Hassan, I saw her come over to me and, in a self-congratulatory spirit, triumphantly declare: '*Shufti?* (Did you see that?) *Mish ay ott teolo ya mishmish!* (It's not just any old cat whom you can call *mishmish*!). *Mishmish* literally means apricot-coloured, but within this particular context the word evokes in the listener's mind the image of an alley cat who is tough, individual, forceful, who stands out from the crowd, knowing what it wants and how to get it.

Nidal's figure of speech serves the purpose of showing how, like others who lack resources in the established social order, she is compelled to survive on her wits – and takes personal pride in battling on single-handedly so as to triumph over adverse circumstances. Her use of metaphor is located firmly within the well-established Egyptian tradition of *fahlawi* (a colloquial nonce-word which has no equivalent in standard – much less classical – Arabic) personality, behaviour and parlance (El-Messiri 1978; Barakat 1993; Rejwan 2009). Long associated with the powerless and their survival tactics, such as their skilled ways of using humour in the face of adversity, *fahlawi* behaviour is characterised by tongue-in-cheek reactions, resorted to as part of a person's engagement with the complexities of their daily lives, and the creativity brought to attempts to dodge or side-step *hard-i-luck* (the same words are used in colloquial Arabic) situations. This form of individual resourcefulness calls for charm and wit, great adaptability, and a repertoire of acts that merge idealism with self-assertion. Reaching one's goals by the smartest, shortest route, and with the minimum of effort, remains a prime objective. This typically generates amused – and if anything predominantly admiring – scepticism over *fahlawi* claims to superhuman powers to overcome impossible odds, such as the power to 'get all the ants crawling about to walk in a straight line', or, rather like 'Supermarket Osama' (see page 128), to 'sell anything to anybody'. Mindful of how the term *fahlawi* is only ever used in its masculine form (the never-heard feminine form would be *fahlawiyya*), this rich background has led me to the view that the most appropriate term for the *mushrifat*'s distinctive gendered performance would be '*mishmish* femininity'. And if a single English analogue is required then, following the feline theme, the closest might be 'tomcat femininity'.[4]

The *mushrifat* are uninhibited about recognising the 'tomcat' aspects of their crafted workplace personality. In the newly configured context of a differently gendered hierarchy, women aspire to achieve more pronounced and multifaceted roles and there are contradictions in how to merge this trend with other facets of their lives. Thus Azima Mohamed, expecting a marriage proposal at the advanced age of thirty-six, reflects on her unease about being expected to act out the role of the blushing bride and her own changing, perhaps contradictory, subjectivity:

> The shop floor environment is bound to change any woman here – the girls like us who have been here for a long time. Production is a daily concrete performance of labour, where you find yourself in the push and shove of quotas and deadlines. It turns any woman placed in a supervisory role into a *shakhsiya matluba* (high profile figure). For all of us, our first selves when we first started work – that's gone now. We have ceased to recognise that part of ourselves. It's been fourteen years for me now.

Azima Mohamed's comments show that she has internalised the changes involved. Others, however, compartmentalise them within public performances which nevertheless disappear in their private dealings, as Fatma describes:

> It is as if we live in two separate worlds: at work, where we are tough and demanding – and at home, where a gentler self is present. Horeya's voice on the phone has a softer tone. Men at work fail to see the other, more private side and assume we are like that all the time.

These stances resonate with the tensions and ironies identified in Freeman's work (2002) in Barbados's high-tech 'informatics' enterprises, showing how

Afro-Caribbean women workers redefine corporate profiles of the 'ideal worker' and craft new 'pink collar' working identities which are in sharp contrast to those of their earlier work experiences, and, to some extent, their class base. Kondo's (1990) work on gender relations in a Japanese factory similarly demonstrates how the effects of such transformations are never complete, since the 'matrices of power and meaning are open-ended, with room for play, subversion and change' (1990: 224).

In contrast to the supportive position adopted by both top management and shop floor workers, the *mushrifat's* tomcat femininity comes in for direct and vehement criticism from the middle managers in *edara* 'upstairs', most particularly from the female administrators. Female *edara* administrators' attacks on the *mushrifat* are often explicitly class-based. To them, *taht fil-entag* ('down below', in *entag*) is *bia mish muhazaba* (an uncivilised environment), a world of *il-sawt il-'ali* (loud voices), *waqaha wi tahziq* (uncouth and loutish insults), and *talwin kalam* (excessive innuendo). *Edara* sees female *kawadir* in Leitex as *shakhsiyat mish sawiya* (distorted personalities, implying dysfunctional). As Sawsan Etrebi in Production Studies put it to me one day, effortlessly sliding from class to religion:

> What is left in the end, when your sense of self-respect as a woman is shattered? They are responsible for bringing this state of affairs onto themselves. I have seen women in other factories conduct the shop floor quite differently. Women can be tough supervisors without resorting to these outrageous acts! In Islam, this type of loud, loutish and piercing voice is *haram* (forbidden). But you have seen for yourself, it is applauded as the style that goes undisputed.

Edara even link these criticisms to their observations on the single status of many of the older *mushrifat*. In point of fact, about half the female supervisors were married – but *edara*'s stereotyped profiles (as when they stigmatised Leitex as a terrain where 'spinsterhood reigns with a vengeance') imposed a dominant image of spinsterhood being the shop floor norm. This echoes Singerman's analysis of the political economy of delayed marriage in Egypt, where 'waithood' – her eloquent reformulation of 'spinsterhood' – attracts social criticism because of its potential threat to the religious, moral and economic order (Singerman 2011: 74). In *edara*'s view the *mushrifat's* preference for 'waithood' over marriage offers confirmation that their desire to shine at all costs and cultivate a following reflects deep-rooted disturbances of a *nafsi* (psychological) nature, providing sufficient evidence to reinforce labelling them as deviant. For this reason, the unmarried *mushrifat's* personal lives are scrutinised for additional evidence to support these claims. Disapproval is expressed even of their recreational pursuits, for example the novels of Sonallah Ibrahim (a well known leftist writer) which Fatma reads during break-time, or the martial arts championship trophies won (despite her conservative background) by Kifah Mansur in Isma'iliyya. None of these are considered 'normal', much less conventional, feminine pursuits. These views however remain whispered criticisms which *edara* women are careful not to share with male colleagues, lest it hint at persistent, hidden female jealousies. Male *edara* personnel tend to share top management's assessment, primarily because their reputation in doing their job relies on the commitment of the *kawadir* in undertaking 'tough jobs' on the shop floor.

The *mushrifat*'s line of defence is to dismiss the women of *edara* as not having proper jobs to do – indeed, of not having anything very much to do on any given day. 'Upstairs, the day hardly moves', declares Zizi. The *mushrifat* share the view that in *edara* the day is taken up gossiping, pen pushing and little else. In a cutting image, which rapidly takes root on the entire shop floor, the women in *edara* are cruelly characterised as *shillet il-ons* (a term from *The Thousand And One Nights*, referring to the ladies of leisure and pleasure in the Sultan's harem). The class antagonism is further captured in the *mushrifat*'s and *entag*'s view that '*homa gherna khaalis* (they're completely 'other'), *shayfin nafsuhum!* (utterly self-regarding)!'

The religious dimension to *edara*'s criticism is also explicitly contested. As well as being reputed to have nothing to do all day, *edara* is known to display an exaggerated performance of public piety. This is evident in the way female administrators believe their dress exemplifies *il-mazhar il-la'eq* ('proper appearance' – capturing in the single phrase both the class and religious dimensions) which by implication *entag* lacks, or their tendency to bring in portable electronic gear and play CDs of sermons by popular preachers such as Amr Khaled, 'the Arab Billy Graham',[5] whose TV shows, cassettes and CDs are celebrated for guiding modern youth in finding the path of religion (Hardaker 2006; Stratton 2006; Bayat 2011, 2013). The *mushrifat* retaliate by drawing on the shop floor's more pragmatic recognition that there are limits to how much religion any individual can perform, arguing that the spirit of the faith is more important than individual interpretations or specific behaviours. Thus one afternoon Azima Mohamed (a senior quality control supervisor) and Zaim (a male foreman in Egytex) are discussing a current hot topic of religious debate, a preacher's recently published views on the impropriety of males and females who are not *mehrem* (relatives) sharing the same workplace. Azima laughs at both religious inconsistency and her own naivety when she was younger as she recalls that:

> When I first started work in the EPZ, I used to turn up to work all dressed up. That was during my three years stint in Transnational. I then returned home one evening to be told that the *Mufti il-azhar wil diyar il-misriyya* (the Supreme Head of el Azhar and the Egyptian lands) had broadcast a *fatwa* on the radio

prohibiting women from wearing trousers or using lip-stick at work. So the next day I turned up at work in an austere outfit, and ignored my male colleagues. Overnight, the *Mufti* was quickly replaced by another, who instantly reversed the *fatwa*, arguing that every working woman's wages were *halal* (approved of – in line with religious teaching), including even the belly dancer's!'

Zaim agrees and, as he examines a garment, proceeds to justify the apparent contradiction in the *Mufti*'s final point: 'After all, even a belly dancer sweats for her living!' Azima laughs loudly and dismisses both *fatawi* as irrelevant to current realities on the shop floor as she reinforces the bond between them by saying: 'Anyway I'm sure that by now you count as my *mehrem*. We've known each other for seven long years, and [looking at him with a theatrical coyness] you've just devoured one of my home-baked cookies!'

Given its tolerant approach to religious issues, *entag* is quick to expose fake religiosity amongst its own ranks as another shop floor game in its own right. Any such pretentiousness on the part of *edara* is likewise rapidly challenged. This is illustrated by the story told about Rasmeya, an unmarried monitor in Planning, who took to wearing the *hijab* a few months after her arrival, with her religious behaviour growing ever more extreme thereafter. She became the butt of shop floor gossip when she was seen repeatedly taking a small mirror out of her handbag and obsessively rearranging any errant strands of hair that might have slipped out from under her elaborate *tabaqat* (multi-layered) headscarf, or overheard claiming that the thin layer of lip gloss she wore was lip balm 'strictly for medicinal purposes'. She took to attending religious lessons in the mosque, with the results broadcast the following day as she handed colour-printed tracts out in the *edara* offices, or ostentatiously hung them on the walls. She began uttering long strings of religious phrases whenever she walked into, or left, an office, and insisting on taking the leading role of *imam* for the women's prayers in *edara*. *Entag*'s reservations began to be openly voiced when Rasmeya was heard issuing verbal *fatawi* (religious pronouncements) criticising the girls in *entag*, condemning and classifying their social behaviour as *haram* (prohibited) or *makruh* (not desirable). She made it known that her own religious activities, by contrast, included *mustahab* (commendable) practices such as extracting regular monthly donations from *edara*'s pay packages for the mosque's *kafalit il-yatim* (programmes for orphans).

This newly acquired, self-proclaimed image, even as she herself insisted on being called Rubi (after a pop star known for her explicitly sexy performances on TV), soon earned her the mocking nickname of *Rab'aa il-'Adawiyya* (a revered female Muslim saint from the tenth century who became devout after having previously led a less-than-savoury life). Far from being convinced that this public display reflected a deep or genuine transformation of a spiritual nature, the shop floor dismissed her behaviour as feminine wiles, aimed at attracting the attention of the single, religious-minded manager on whom, it was alleged, she had *ashimit nafsaha* (set her heart). The truth of such speculation was taken to be confirmed when, having enticed him into a formal engagement, she immediately afterwards started to tone down much of her ostentatiously religious strictures.

Conflicting religious opinions become more acrimonious when they infiltrate the shop floor in the form of radical or extreme ideologies that threaten the *kawadir*'s authority. The *kawadir* are well aware of the growing trend towards Islamisation in the wider social world outside the factory walls, and fluctuating workforce numbers bring onto the shop floor diverse '*aqliyyat* (mentalities), the term used by *kawadir* to describe social and economic disparities among the *'iyal*. They however defend their territory and their authority with zeal, invoking the more tolerant traditions of the workplace.

Thus on one occasion I observed, a group of machinists hired by *edara* were immediately identifiable on the shop floor for their extreme Salafist religious dress and appearance. The length of their beards, white gowns and skull caps complemented the black or dark brown *niqab* dress style of their wives. The *mushrifat* rapidly labelled the group as 'our latest wave of *sheyukh* (clerics)'. Rather than dispersing them around the shop floor, as management's policy would have required, they arranged for them all (men and women alike) to sit together in one corner of a *sala*, in order to keep them under close shop floor surveillance. Soon critical comments started to be made, for example about how the men's faces were 'sour', habitually held in a stern *kushur* (frown). The covered faces of the women machinists provided a further focus for the *mushrifat*'s irritation, as it was impossible to tell, without access to facial expressions, whether instructions had been understood or followed. As Kifah Mansur explained one afternoon as she walked into the supervisors' common room:

> When I point out something in the work, I have no clue whether they've understood my instructions. I can't see their facial expressions, or hear their reactions: I have to keep reminding them to nod their heads. It's a 'presence that is absent' – a bit like talking to someone on the telephone.

The increasing frequency with which the *sheyukh* were creating dissension through the expression of their religious opinions rapidly became evident. Hostilities began with criticism of the *mushrifat*'s style of supervision, in particular by comparing their raised voices to *'awra* (shameful female parts). It led Hanadi Amin, a robust *mushrifa*, to publicly invoke the Islamic concept of *niya* (intent)[6] when responding that she was not using her voice to 'titillate men' or seduce them, but rather 'to push you lot to pay more attention to your work'. The situation grew more acrimonious when the *sheyukh* were heard repeating a *fatwa* condemning women's work as *haram* (prohibited).⁷ Their own wives, it however transpired in the course of this vigorous exchange, had license to work since they were accompanied by their *mehrem* (religiously sanctioned relatives). Many girls on the shop floor took personal offence at these remarks, which sought to shame them for not being sufficiently upright. Defending her right to earn wages, Rahma, at her QC stand, whispered to me with restrained rage as she went on examining a pile of garments, 'I'd never stand on my own two feet if I follow this advice. It's absolutely ridiculous'.

Religious tapes began to make a discreet appearance on the shop floor, provoking more vigorous debates. These were examples of the new market in *il-Islam il-sowti* ('voiced Islam') which since relaxation of censorship in the the 70s had grown to rival 'print Islam' and thus – despite its many contradictions and failure to address current socioeconomic problems, especially of the country's youth – to challenge the state's monopoloy on religion (Eickleman 1996). One such cassette urged all women to wear the *niqab,* an injunction which contradicted the unspoken consensus on the shop floor that single women should be exempted, because of their need to expose their faces in order to increase their chances of getting married. This was followed by another that attacked women as 'the source of evil' on the grounds that watching TV had led them to aspire to new consumer habits, thus showing their men up as poor providers. This was likewise met with resistance, as articulated by Sima who, bent over a pile of garments she was working on, and referring to the current craze for getting one of the factory electricians to set up an illegal feed from a neighbour who had installed a satellite TV dish (paying an illegal LE 20 fee for the privilege), whispered:

> These excessively religious Sunnis are never such a great catch. We have some neighbours just like them – they live on another planet. I can't live without *il-dish* 'satellite TV', and I love my musical doorbell. So what if my thoughts are on life's luxuries – it's I who am earning the cash, right?

The argument grew even more intense when it focused on other shop floor consumer activities, as when the *sheyukh* were heard condemning as *haram* the rose-scented candles and aromatherapy kits purchased through circulating mail order catalogues. Many workers took part in these debates, the majority disapproving of the oppressive attitudes and sexist discrimination of the *sheyukh* who, because they had been the prime providers of these cassettes, also sought to set themselves up as expert Islamic jurists. Young female workers, in particular, grew increasingly vocal in their protests that their daily personal experience as women could not possibly live up to the religious strictures being expressed.

The ensuing disruption on the shop floor, and the direct challenge to the *mushrifat*'s authority, eventually led to collective retribution. A couple of the shop floor girls were put up to test whether the *sheyukh* could be tempted to flirt – with the result that two of them immediately fell for the bait. One afternoon, Maymuna summed up to me the results of the ensuing shop floor surveillance:

> For all their sermons about women, they seized the moment as soon as a chance to chat up a girl came their way. Then when they caught us watching them, their behaviour suddenly changed as if God had made an appearance. These days everybody is a pontiff when it comes to religion. It's used to serve their interests, and has nothing whatever to do with Islam.

As rumours rapidly spread about their religious hypocrisy, the *sheyukh* came under even closer observation. Shop floor surveillance soon revealed additional intelligence, as the *sheyukh* were caught using shop floor time, machinery and thread to sew wallets which they then sold for personal gain. The *sheyukh* had thus provided a breach in their religious defences, and the *mushrifat* took it into their hands to orchestrate the removal of the religious regiment in a way that was *bil zoq* (civilised) but nevertheless exploited the anti-union labour laws of the Zone. Maymuna described to me how, at a time strategically chosen to coincide with a slump in production and when there was no pressure to maintain workforce numbers:

> Horeya deliberately provoked a work-related disagreement with the *ras il-af'a* (the cobra-head – implying the ringleader) over some trivial matter, and refused to back down. The result was that at his command all the *sheyukh* stood up, left their machines, and walked out in a single file – the men in front, and the women behind them.

Nurturing and performing male power

The episode of the *sheyukh* versus the *mushrifat* (which the latter won hands down) demonstrates how the shop floor provides the arena for a clash between the gendering process of the firm and gendered meanings constructed within the wider external environment. The contest takes on the nature of a power struggle to resist or reinforce the hierarchical order of labour processes within *entag*, a struggle which is both bounded, and exacerbated by, the fluctuating nature of the production cycle. This is also evident in the behaviour of newly appointed male *kawadir* within the mixed-gender units, especially in assembling work, the lifeline of the factory.

The reintroduction of male supervision in assembly line work was, however, a relatively recent development. Leitex's experience with a male line supervisor was exemplified by Mamduh Khalifa, who had been brought in a few years previously from the rival Export Processing Zone in nearby Isma'iliyya. Horeya had then assigned him to an assembly line manned by some of the weakest workers, who were one step away from being shown the door, so that *Khat Mamduh* (Mamduh's line) did not take long to become known among the *sala* workforce as '*islah wi tahzib*' ('reform and rehabilitation' – an official remedy for people with addictions or other social disorders). This placed him in a situation where, as supervisor, he needed to work ever harder to produce his quota.

During my time on the shop floor Leitex's oral memory was rife with episodes when Mamduh had been shrieked at by Horeya, and how he had always been at a complete loss as to how best to respond. To yell back ran the risk, in his own words, of 'appearing like the *niswan* (colloquial for women)' – but to remain silent meant accepting the crippling public humiliation of being *tisagharo* (transformed into looking small), with all the connotations of emasculation and loss of face among the workers down his line and in the *sala*. Mamduh was advised by *edara*'s female personnel that his only option was to confront Horeya in the presence of the Production Manager, though the latter seldom seemed to be around at moments when the time was right for Mamduh to stage a suitably theatrical confrontation. Within a short period of time Mamduh left the factory on sabbatical, on the grounds that he needed a break from the stress of Leitex's working environment, and it was two months before he returned.

The power of Horeya and the female *mushrifat* over the male *mushreffin* stemmed in part from their control over the opportunities available to male workers to rise through the ranks of *entag*. All male machinists start out as operators of single-needle sewing machines. In theory any one of them can, under the guidance of their direct *mushrifa*, move to becoming multi-skilled in a range of additional assembly-line positions, and so attain the status of *joker* (a term for someone who can perform many roles in a variety of positions – used across a range of professions including, for example, in TV football commentaries). And any *joker* can, in principle, be eligible for promotion to the ranks of *kawadir* at a time of top management's choosing. In practice, however, this progression does not occur except with the implicit approval of the *mushrifat*, who play an active, if behind-the-scenes, role in spotting opportunities for their preferred candidates, and then for seizing the right moment within the changing circumstances of production to assist them in being catapulted up the hierarchical structure of *entag*.

Beginning with their subjective assessment of a particular *joker* as suitable for promotion, they seek to manipulate circumstances so that the candidate grows in prominence in top management's eyes and favour. Tactics include covering up for any mistakes the *joker* may have made, ensuring that there is no occasion for giving the impression of *shakl wihish* (a negative image) – for example by clearing up any mess created around his work station – and praising the potential of the candidate whenever top management is on the shop floor. As Kifah Mansur comments, 'A *mushrifa* has the discretion either to assist a worker, or to withdraw, leaving the worker unsupported'. The *mushrifat* were conscious of their power in this respect, which they regarded as an application of their innate feminine skill at cultivating talent within the workforce, thereby embodying the nurturing potential and power of the factory.

The subtlety of the gender dynamic driving this process of nurturing became evident in the story of Zaim, *rayis* of Egytex, the formal equivalent of Horeya's position in Leitex. Twenty-nine years of age, Zaim was a university graduate who, while holding out for the much sought-after *wazifa* (civil service) post to which this entitled him, was nevertheless prepared to undertake factory work for its comparatively lucrative wages. Ambitious from the start, and eager to undertake the training required for promotion, he soon found himself benefiting from the active preferment of the *mushrifat* on his line, and most particularly of Horeya, the *rayis sala*, who took to him at an early stage. Within a short space of time he had progressed from a simple machinist in Leitex (where all the factory's production was conducted at the time) to the status of *joker*. A major new work order from an Italian client then required that a new production line be opened, and the only space available was adjacent to Leitex, in the area in front of the smoked-glass doors to the top management offices. Zaim was favoured as the *mushrifat*'s candidate for the post of line supervisor of the new assembly line, and through their assistance he secured the position. And since the line was in a separate 'hall' of its own, Zaim also attained the title and status of *Rayis Sala* (even though his wages remained much lower than Horeya's).

Zaim's first move to craft a distinctive, personalised image of productive labour, and establish his own distinct male *islub* (style) in *ishraf* (supervision) was to masculinise his territory through the use of language. Thus he began to refer to his days of training as *ayyam il-shaqaa'* (days of torture), a practice which was soon taken up by other male supervisors in Egytex. He also imported into the workplace patriarchal expressions in use in the external sociocultural environment, for example by deliberately changing the term female *kawadir* use when talking of the workforce under their charge from *il-'iyal* (the children) to *il-nas ili 'andi* (my people). This is a *shaabi* (working-class) term commonly used by conservative men to refer to their dependents in *il-beit* (the private sphere of the home), the actual names of their wives and children never being mentioned (al-Aswany 2002). Zaim's appropriation of the phrase thus had the effect of masculinising his relationship with the workers under his charge, whilst at the same time remaining within the discourse of metaphorical kinship around which the factory is structured.

His next move involved modifying his appearance and behaviour to establish an image of male *ihtiram* (respectability), a particular requirement for the male *rayis* of a mixed labour force which included more women workers than men, and was also more rural than urban. Thus shortly after his appointment Zaim, while continuing to wear the stylish jeans, leather-studded belts and trendy accessories (such as silver key rings, or leather mobile phone holsters) worn by other workers, adopted a well-trimmed beard typical of the *multazim* (consistent with Muslim principles) style then being popularised among educated bourgeoisie keen to demonstrate their piety, but without associating themselves with more extreme Sunni displays of religiosity such as a long, unkempt beards (Ouzgane 2006; Husain 2007). He also refrained from smoking, making a distinctive break with a social practice widespread among factory males of all ranks. He took up other *multazim* behaviour, such as not shaking hands with women, being more respectful and formal, avoiding flirtatious behaviour or excessive *tahrig* (joking around, joshing), and appearing knowledgeable in religious matters such as the categories of *haram* (forbidden) and *halal* (permitted). Within the *multazim* viewpoint, these *selukiyyat* (behavioural practises) are deemed important in cultivating within a mixed-gender workplace an atmosphere of *ihtiram mutabadil* (mutual respect), which enables the sexes to engage with one another without personal apprehension or fear of malicious gossip. In the factory, it was widely recognised that for a man to adopt this image of 'pious masculinity', as I came to label it, was similar to a woman adopting the *hijab*: once adopted, it became exceedingly difficult to remove.

Precisely because it differed from the styles and behaviour preferred by the *shabaab riwish* (cool youth) in the workplace, who generally wore trendy clothes and hairstyles designed to attract feminine attention, Zaim's adopted image of piety strengthened his moral authority as a *kader*. He reinforced this through a subtle balance between coercion and consent in getting his workers to increase their *entagiyya* (production), a balance which was itself reliant on his distinctively gendered view of the differences between male and female workers. Thus he described his approach towards the young and single women workers under his charge as *il-shedid il-hunayin* ('the firm and the tender'), while towards his male workers he relied on the strategy of *bil siyasa wil fahlawa* ('politics and games'). One result was that Egytex became a much quieter labour zone than Leitex, with much less yelling of insults and hurling of expletives. Other expressions reflecting traditional values came into circulation instead, as when female workers slacking in their work would be 'firmly but tenderly' reminded that they were *rabit beit* (housewives and homemakers) of the future, who accordingly needed to show more commitment to their duties, a greater willingness to endure more and complain less, and to view the skills they were acquiring as part of their education 'as women'. Zaim's articulation of traditional views provides a reminder of what Butler describes as 'regulatory fictions' of gender identity, whereby women's unpaid labour in the home becomes a 'prime duty', and women's waged work is situated discursively by the sharp distinctions made between out-of-the-house work and housework. The girls on the shop floor soon learned to play along with these developments, and it was widely remarked how increasing numbers of single rural women began turning up on Zaim's shop floor in more rigorous styles of *hijab*, in the hope of catching the attention of their *rayis*.

It was however in the tone and style of his engagement with top management that Zaim most dramatically demonstrated the more traditionally masculine *'anif* (fierce) and *'asabi* (temperamental) aspects of his crafted labour image. I saw several incidents when Zaim's temper escalated on the Egytex shop floor to outdo even the performative dramas of Leitex. Each episode would start with a minor work-related issue between Zaim and the Planning Manager, which would then grow in intensity and volume until the Production Manager had to be called to the shop floor. The skirmish would then develop into a shouting match between Zaim and the Production Manager, who, aware of the watching workforce, would insist that the discussion be continued in the Design Unit's room to one side of the *sala*. For the next hour both men could be seen, through the glass partition, shouting furiously at each other. The episode would reach its climax with Zaim emerging loudly threatening to hand in his resignation, then dramatically walking out of the factory whilst, in a loud voice – and flinging his arms right, left and centre – summoning his workforce, who had stopped production, to leave their shop floor positions and follow him out into the streets of the *istithmar*. The street would then become the setting for a highly emotionally charged scene as Egytex girls standing by the gates of the factory, in their austere *hijabs*, would plead with him not to desert them and declare themselves 'willing to follow him', while Zaim, emotively fighting back tears, would insist that they return to Egytex. On other occasions the Egytex workforce, rather than follow him into the street, would stage a two-hour shop floor strike, requiring top management to get involved, by phoning him on his mobile to request his return to his *sala*. It was also known that, on occasion, the personal intervention of Qasim Bey himself had been required for a satisfactory conclusion to be reached and for Zaim to resume control of his domain. These *aflam* (drama episodes) were peculiar to Egytex, and seemed to occur regularly after several production cycles.

Horeya and the other female *kawadir* were, however, not hesitant in devising and implementing their own strategies of resistance towards Zaim's manoeuvres for carving out a distinctively masculinised zone of power within the factory, and presuming to a *rayis sala* position of power equal to Horeya's (rather than modestly accepting his formal position as simply one line supervisor amongst others). At the time I gained access to the shop floor, it was clear that Horeya's female colleagues were eager to create every opportunity to support the retrieval of her *haqq* for what was considered to be a serious breach of the basic rules of *ikhlaas* (loyalty). Interestingly, their first recourse appeared also to be to the deliberate use of distinctive language. Thus my field notes show how Horeya repeatedly adds the prefix *ibnina* ('our son') whenever Zaim's name is mentioned, re-emphasising not only his junior status, but also the debt he owes her and the *mushrifat* who have nurtured him through the process of skills acquisition necessary for gaining promotion. Frequently the discourse is developed along the lines of 'ungrateful and disloyal son' as when one day Maymuna explicitly expresses her contempt:

> Zaim's tune has changed. Gratitude has been brushed under the rug. It's become 'I have reached this status because I am exceptional' – forgetting that Horeya is the one who made him what he is. What kind of man does that make him?

Criticism of Zaim's interactions with his female workers soon follows, notably of how the young rural girls under his charge are showing every sign of developing a crush on him. 'This situation is not right', says Hamida Ali, an Egytex supervisor, as she watches the shop floor:

> These girls come from sheltered environments, are vulnerable when in their first workplace, and they badly crave the attention they think he is personally showering them with. He manipulates one group against the other: one day it is Manzala, the next Salheya. It looks as if it's a trick to get them to work harder and become more committed – but all it really does is serve his ego.

Eventually it turns out to be the fluctuating conditions of production which resolve the power dynamic between Zaim and the *mushrifat*. In September, as client work-orders dwindle to a trickle, I witness how dwindling production orders result in Egytex being closed, and Zaim's assembly line subsumed into Leitex. Top management declares a new policy of 'One Factory, One *Sala*' so his title of *Rayis Sala* is withdrawn. Both Horeya and Zaim have now become top line supervisors within the same *sala*, each watching developments in the other's assembly line. Three of Zaim's male line supervisors soon leave, forcing him to find replacements from within the remaining female *jokers* down his line. By this time, however, Zaim has finally secured the long-sought *wazifa* appointment in the civil service, as a mathematics teacher in a government school in Port Fuad. His teaching schedule means he can only get to the factory by noon, so he has to rely on his moles on the assembly line to call him on his mobile with news of shop floor developments. The *mushrifat* do not, however, seem to see the position as necessarily representing a triumph for their side of the dynamic. As Maymuna watches the shop floor, she announces with disgust: 'This has the hallmarks of a Jewish plot! Horeya will be in the limelight, all the *'iyal* can see her. But if there are problems in Zaim's line then she will be the one who has to sort them out. So the question is – will she get the recognition she deserves?'

The contest of power between the *kawadir* appears set to continue in the new work environment, showing again how the unstable conditions of production continually shape the changing gendered dynamics of shop floor politics. As Nidal Hassan exclaims to me from her quality control table: 'It will be theatre at its most spectacular. And we have the best seats in the *sala*! – just stick around. I've even swiped two fans from Egytex for my *'iyal*. We're going to need them as things hot up!'

Conclusion

In this chapter I have explored the pivotal role within the 'firm as family' of the 'sons and daughters of the factory', the *kawadir* who form the linchpin of the entire operation. Their distinctive physical presence, their self-consciously theatrical performance of discipline and productive efficiency, and the gendered labour identities crafted by both female and male supervisors, provide explicit instances of ways in which discourses of gender, class and religion are deployed to constitute as well as contest the power-struggles and politics of the shop floor in the unstable conditions of production that shape its labour landscape.

In the final thematic chapter I describe an abrupt change in this labour landscape, caused by the sudden introduction of a foreign management firm whose self-declared aim was to drag Fashion Express into the twenty-first century, by abolishing the old 'firm as family' structures and principles and replacing them with modern methods of production and labour control. The response of the Fashion Express 'family members', from the most junior to the most senior, provides a case study in contesting a parody of modernity

– one which throws into sharp relief the deep-rooted nature of the principles and issues I have been highlighting in the preceding thematic chapters.

Notes

1. The term was introduced during the modernisation of the Egyptian civil service in the early twentieth century along lines of the French model (Ayubi 1980: 307).
2. This provides a vivid instance of Burawoy's (1979) analysis of the role games play in establishing team spirit and hierarchies on the shop floor.
3. See the discussion provided in chapter 2 of *ikhlaas* (loyalty), a key principle according to which the narrative of metaphorical kinship in the 'firm as family' is structured.
4. I am indebted to Professor Deniz Kandiyoti for this creative suggestion.
5. D. Hardaker, 'Islam's Billy Graham: More Popular than Oprah Winfrey, the World's First Islamic Television Evangelist Commands an Army of Millions of Followers', *The Independent*, 4 January 2006; see also Aspden (2016) and L. White, 'The Antidote to Terror; Lesley White meets "the Arab Billy Graham"', *The Sunday Times Magazine*, 13 May 2007, 42–51.
6. Rosen (1984: 49–50) specifies *niya* as having a particular significance in religion. Intent is not separate from action, and there is a close link between interior mental state and overt forms of behaviour. To act with *niya* implies to do so in good faith, and invokes a multiplicity of positive connotation around purpose, plan, will, desire and volition.
7. Hatem (1998: 94–95) explains the religious context as follows: 'While Islam did not forbid women to work, it required those who did to be motivated by necessity. Aspiring to a better living standard than that provided by the husband's income did not qualify as necessity. Devout women were those who accepted their husband's income as a basis for their lifestyle. They should not pressure their husbands to provide them with this alternative way of life, and they should not abandon their roles as wives and mothers in search of that goal. If they think they could perform this difficult juggling act (of being wife, mother and working woman), they could take on public work provided it was framed by Islamic principles.'

Chapter 5

GLOBALISED TAKEOVER
– PERFORMANCE AND RESISTANCE

☙•❧

The change in management regime was as swift as it was unexpected. My field notes record how, on a Monday afternoon in September, *edara* and *entag* are told to gather in Leitex for an important announcement. At 3.30 p.m. Qasim Bey descends to the shop floor to address the workforce. He is accompanied by a team of Egyptian men dressed in business suits who have not previously been seen on the premises. Using the shop floor microphone, he announces that he is placing day-to-day management of the factory in the hands of 'a British firm', which is being brought in to assist the factory in its crisis by modernising the workplace. In his usual warm and paternal tone he calls for everybody's cooperation in helping the *edara agnabiyya* (foreign management) undertake this critical task.

Towards the end of his speech his voice falters, and in a distinctly more emotional tone he goes on to promise that the new era will allow every worker to know that the factory is truly their place. He ends his announcement to polite applause as he hands the microphone to one of the new faces on the scene. Ismail Tukhi, deliberately calling himself 'Mister' (using the English title), introduces himself as the local agent of the British firm, which I shall call BGB. Shifting to a more brisk and business-like mode of address, he lists the benefits BGB is about to bring by introducing a new, modern manufacturing system and securing contracts from well-known British clients. In this way the factory's fortunes will be revived, and Fashion Express will re-join the globalised world of transnational manufacturing. As a result workers' wages will increase, flats will be given to diligent workers, and, he assures everyone, there will be no redundancies ('we are patient and intend to train'). Crucial to the success of a scheme designed to move with the times will be the issue of *wala lil-masna*, i.e. loyalty (in the sense of allegiance to an institutional power)[1] to the factory as a workplace and not, as in the past, to 'certain individuals'.

Refashioning the labour landscape

After the announcement the shop floor was soon agog with rumours. The factory had been leased or sold to a British firm, and the British partner would be arriving in three months to take up command of the factory. Until then, the task of the local agents of the British firm was to prepare the ground, both physically and psychologically, for the coming change. The day following the announcement, a number of visible changes were carried out in almost military fashion. The guards at the doors of the factory were replaced by uniformed employees of a professional security company. The Fahmy family members who had previously occupied the Top Management suite abruptly disappeared from the scene, their offices occupied by BGB managers in business suits and ties, with individualised name badges in English and lapel buttons displaying BGB's red and white striped logo. The black-and-white portrait of Qasim Bey's father, crucial to the family's image and social standing, was summarily taken down, to be replaced by a bigger plaque sporting the BGB logo. Khadija in Cutting, spotting its removal through the double doors, was quick to grasp the symbolism of the moment: 'Did you see that? His father's portrait has been flung onto the floor! *Mat il-malik, 'ash il-malik!* (the King is dead, long live the King! – used as a euphemism for fickle loyalties).'

The first major change to the established routine of the factory came with the organisation by the new BGB management of a series of daily open *igtimaa't* (meetings). These were held from 1 P.M. to 4 P.M. on the dot, with the names of the particular *edara* and *entag* employees required to attend each day published in an advance timetable.

These encounters were carefully choreographed. One of the middle-management offices was set aside especially for the *igtimaa't* and given the name of *ghurfit il-'amaliyyat* (military terminology for Operations HQ). It was furnished with a long rectangular table on which were placed three small Union Jacks and three similarly sized flags displaying BGB's logo, boxes of tissues, and supplies of biscuits, fruit juice and mineral water. Before each *igtima'* began, the day's group of nominated participants had a group photograph taken, with the process repeated at the end of the session causing much amusement among the teams of happily smiling employees. Deliberate prominence was also given to a video camera, used to film selected proceedings of each *igtima'*.

Once the group had settled, BGB management would appear promptly at 1 P.M., looking well prepared and organised with neat folders holding lists of the day's participants, the names printed out on paper headed with BGB's logo. Charts and layout plans of the factory were produced and spread on the long table, with PowerPoint presentations to clarify points of the *sharh* (explanation) given by BGB's principal representative. The setting and the organisational skills transmitted an instant air of professionalism which, especially by contrast to how things were previously done, embodied the new 'foreign' and 'modern' aspirations underpinning the promised changes.

The vision of the future presented was invariably referred to as *il-manshud*, an Arabic term for an aspirational goal (rather than an immediate, lower-level target). BGB's clear message was that they had arrived to introduce a *nizam gadid* (new system) which they identified as *hadith, 'elmi wi britani* (modern, scientific and British). State-of-the-art, hi-tech equipment was to be installed in the factory, which would be reorganised according to a new, scientifically designed layout. The workforce was to be increased from three hundred and fifty to a thousand, and the working day divided into two shifts. A new system of *edara ingliziyya, edara gadida* (British management, new management) was to be established. This would be decentralised and flexible – terms much used in the Mubarak neoliberalist wave of privatisation of state industries (Ayubi 1996) – but remain *maska il-nas* (firmly in control of the workforce), in contrast to the previously prevalent *tasayyub* (laxity). Workers would clock on and off using newly issued electronic time cards. A new system of production was to be introduced, in which every step would go like clockwork, with no delays for breakdowns to machines or absenteeism amongst workers. CCTV cameras would be installed throughout the factory, with a monitoring screen in Qasim Bey's office showing 'production moving steadily at the push of a button'. In this way a steady volume of production orders would be delivered for the new British clients, generating a high level of profits that would enable the factory to systematically pay off its debts.

It was underlined that, in order for this system to work, employees would, as emphasised in the inaugural speech, be expected to cultivate and display *wala lil-masna'* (institutional loyalty to the factory). In return, the workforce would receive a package of benefits on par with *il-mustawa il-britani* (British standards) and those of *il-'alam il-mutahadir* (the modern/civilised world). Working conditions in the factory, including the workers' refreshment facilities and toilets, would be improved beyond recognition. Workers were promised new rights and benefits, including improved health and social security schemes, generous bonuses, recognition of individual efforts through monthly ballots of the entire workforce to elect the best worker, and a joint committee of elected representatives of the workers and management to voice the opinions of the workforce. Suggestion boxes were to be installed to collect the views of the workforce, and to provide feedback for the new management. Educational and recreational activities were also to be part of the new order, including *'eraf baladak* ('know your country') staff excursions, with comfortable buses equipped with TV screens broadcasting educational material and light entertainment. Diligent workers and their supervisors could look forward to short training visits, sponsored and paid for by the firm, to garment factories in the U.K. and Italy. Bank cards (invariably spoken of as linked to the electronic time-cards) would be issued to workers so that they could immediately access their wages once these had been automatically calculated and transferred directly into their accounts, without any of the delays and hiccups that were the cause of such difficulties under the previous regime.

'Is it true? Is it really happening?' Excited questions reverberated along the assembly lines where workers were busy assembling a local order of colourful summer slacks. Rumours embellished the changes as ever more glamorous, as the shop floor buzzed with excited talk of new toilets being refurbished to five star hotel standards, complete with flowers and towels; of new, refrigerated water fountains with disposable plastic cups; and of sparkling new sewing machines and state-of-the-art technology to be installed on the assembly lines. Some left their meetings with BGB voicing their hopes and dreams, exemplified by the Planning Manager's comments: 'Is my *shabah* (local slang for a Mercedes) waiting for me at the factory door? Are my parents residing in Marina?[2] Is my bank balance bordering a million pounds? Not yet! But that's how I'm feeling after the meeting'. Others articulated their feelings in terms of their entitlement, as when a machinist from Leitex summarised the general sense of optimism: 'We want to live the good life! We've made this place, and it's our *haqq* (right)[3] to reap the benefits of this new change, not leave it for others to grab'.

'*Dakhalna il-alfeya il-gadida*' ('We've entered the new millennium') became the catch-phrase that captured the spirit of the change, especially when BGB began to organise 'internal elections' to nominate 'model workers', and encouraged workers to write down their vision of the ideal workplace. Yet underlying this was a shared understanding that while moving forward, the factory was, in many ways, reverting to the prosperity it had once enjoyed in the past. For although it was not known to BGB, as they strove to pass themselves off as an authentic British firm, working with Britain was not in fact a new experience for the factory. It was already present in the collective memory, owing to past contracts during the factory's heyday, for producing garments for leading British brands. On account of this vividly remembered experience, Britain already stood in the minds of many as 'strict', 'stiff' and 'efficient', particularly over its standards of quality control, with every single garment having to be an exact replica of the original template. Thus for many workers the future that was waiting to happen was echoing the experiences of a prosperous past.

The first actual changes seen in the factory focussed on making Fashion Express 'look British'. The existing security staff, typically dressed in studded leather jackets and dark sunshades, were replaced by smartly uniformed guards from a newly contracted commercial security company. Soon afterwards another change was noticed in the Top Management suite. Om Makram found herself confined to her kitchen, as her role of serving tea in the top management offices was taken over by a newly appointed butler, wearing a white shirt and a large black bow tie with a starched white tea towel hanging from his arm. These changes were part of a *ru'yya* (vision), which, Mr Ismail Tukhi explained to me, was 'in order to help British clients feel at home'. It was for the same reason, he continued, that he was thinking about refurbishing one of the offices as a Christian chapel, complete with altar and candles – a plan he celebrated as 'the first in a workplace in Egypt'. He was explicit that his intention was not merely to add a few British touches to Fashion Express, but rather 'to re-create Britain as an environment within this small garment factory in Port Said'. This change of environment would allow any British client walking through the front door of the factory to recognise the place as home territory – an essential element of BGB's plan to secure work orders from Britain and restore the reputation of a factory in crisis.

The much-heralded British client never, in fact, materialised during my time at the factory. The closest BGB got to delivering on their promise was a visit by the British Managing Director of their own company, to review and approve the changes that the advance team had been putting in place. Yet Mr Ismail and his team were seen always to maintain a studied opacity over the precise status of the imminent British visitor, allowing the anticipation to grow that his arrival would let the workforce of Fashion Express see for themselves that the British client did indeed exist in the flesh. Two weeks in advance of the visit, preparations were well underway, with the BGB team keen to present the factory looking its best. Preparations were made for a meeting between the distinguished British visitor and leading figures of the firm, including preparation of a further PowerPoint demonstration of the firm's production capabilities, and displays of samples of their garments, ready to be taken to the United Kingdom to trigger orders.

On arrival, the distinguished visitor was ushered into a meeting room where a hand-picked group of managers and supervisors had been gathered to view a new specially prepared PowerPoint presentation. To a soundtrack of soothing music, a sequence of scanned postcard images of the Pyramids, the Suez Canal and the like appeared, declaring Egypt to be 'the mother of invention' and Port Said to be 'the gateway of Egypt'. These were followed by images of the Houses of Parliament and other British landmarks, establishing the connection that had been forged between these two great civilisations. As the slideshow proceeded, it showed the faces of the new members of the BGB team scrolling down one after another, with highlights of each person's CV. These were followed by images of the state-of-the-art sewing machines to be installed in the factory. The visual impact of the presentation was to transport the factory into the twenty-first century, a stark departure from what it had been like even a few weeks previously. The effect on the audience of *edara* managers and *kawader* was not, however, exactly what had been intended. Some came away under the impression that plasterboard replicas of Big Ben and the Houses of Parliament were about to be fixed to the frontage of the factory premises in a few months' time, as part of the refurbishment plans. Others were more worried by the technological capacities of the new sewing machines, with one supervisor heard to whisper loudly in some alarm, 'At this rate the factory will come down to ten workers! Shall we send Hamid [an autistic worker given the simple job of pushing a trolley] packing?'

After the formal presentation, the VIP visitor was taken on a tour of the premises, with Mr Ismail escorting him at a fast walk. For the shop floor this was the highlight of the visit, for which the whole of *entag* had been waiting. The *mushrifat* had ensured that there was no clutter or debris, that everything sparkled, and everybody was looking their best, in clothes reserved for special occasions – it was the day the factory could begin to look forward to better days to come. The sight of the 'British client' on the shop floor created a buzz of excitement, confirming the change as a *fait accompli*. Qasim Bey walked a few paces behind the BGB team escorting the VIP visitor, giving a tangible reality to one supervisor's comment that it was as if *zamanu rah* (his era had passed). I nevertheless became aware that this was not the way he himself was reading these developments, when he quietly expressed to me the view that: 'Two captains cannot sail a single boat. I'd rather give them a fair chance to get on with the job and see what results turn up. If it doesn't work, I have the option to pull out from the arrangement'.

After the changes to the visual environment of the workplace, the next innovations to catch the eye of the workforce centred on the new management team's recruitment policies. These effects were most immediately seen in *edara*, with a number of new BGB faces crowding their first-floor offices. Among the new arrivals on the scene was at least one old familiar face, in the person of Marzuk Salama, a quality control manager who had been released from Fashion Express for lacking professional credibility and for allegedly bearing a personal grudge against the Fahmy family in general, and against the person of the proprietor in particular. The reasons for bringing him back were related to his recent employment experience in another garment firm, Factory S. Through its successful management practices in securing overseas orders from the U.K. market, Factory S was considered by BGB to offer a blueprint of the future also to be realised in Fashion Express within three months.

It was not long before the effects of the new *edara* arrivals began to be felt on the shop floor, beginning at the supervisory level. When a new post of Senior Quality Control Supervisor (in charge of the entire QC work of the Leitex assembly *sala*) was announced, Zizi, who had been working as a supervisor in the Cutting unit, approached Marzuk Salama in an attempt to persuade him to reinstate her in *khutut* (assembly), an area of work she described as 'her space'. Marzuk Salama listened to Zizi's request, but proceeded to ignore her. Zizi and the *mushrifat* began to sense rejection in his dismissive attitude, especially when the new post was given to somebody else. This turned out to be Hamida Ali, a QC supervisor previously in charge of a single assembly line, but someone whom Marzuk Salama had personally introduced to the factory during his previous spell at Fashion Express. The choice of candidate was illuminating, providing a strong hint that the new management – for all its fashionable rhetoric of decentralisation, flexibility and efficiency – was showing signs of rekindling past factional divisions, and sustaining favouritism built once again on personal *ikhlaas* to individuals, rather than institutional *wala'* to the firm.

Shortly afterwards, following a similar pattern, the established practice of only filling supervisor posts through promotions from the ranks of *entag* was abandoned, and two entirely new recruits, freshly graduated from university, were placed directly into supervisory positions. The two young women in *hijab* arrived, escorted by two BGB men, perfumed and in suits, and ascended the staircase to the first-floor *edara* offices. This time, though, they did not proceed, as had routinely been the case with previous applicants, to the office of Workers Affairs to be screened for suitability, but instead were ushered straight to Marzuk Salama's new glass-walled office. In the supervisors' common room, where I was at the time, the *mushrifat* were just receiving the news. Maymuna spoke her thoughts aloud, envisaging the two new entrants seated in Marzuk's office *rigl 'ala rigl* (cross-egged – implying class pretentiousness), drinking tea *bi-fatla* (from tea bags) in fancy cups with saucers, something which previously had only been offered to distinguished visitors by top management. Zizi quietly warned that this *dakhla* (slang for 'way in' – implying via the back door) directly through a senior manager's office was clearly intended to bestow the newly recruited supervisors with extra leverage on the shop floor.

New, 'scientific' criteria were also announced for new recruits to positions on the shop floor, representing a radical departure from the established recruitment system in which 'suitability' had always been a feature negotiated by both *edara* and *entag*. Mr Ismail also announced a prohibition on the return to the factory of 'floating' workers who had been tacitly allowed to leave Fashion Express for a few months during the factory's lean spells, so that they could earn some money in other, better provided, factories in the Zone. In stern tones he declared:

> This is a time for *ne'ish il-hilw wil mor ma'baad* (living together, in sweetness and in bitterness alike). The loyalty is to be to the factory – not because someone is here or there. There is a difference between *ili yikamil wili maykamilsh* (those who continue to the finishing line, and others who falter). The rule is simple. We are going to be strict in implementing the new policy.

It also became increasingly clear to the workforce that, underlying the new recruitment criteria and systems, there appeared to be a deliberate policy on the part of the new BGB management to shed the migrant workers who were bussed in daily from neighbouring provinces, and thereby transform Fashion Express into an all Port-Saidian workforce. As the formal recruitment process of *bab il-ta'inat* was declared open, new criteria for employment were introduced, waiving skill, sex and age and requiring instead that the applicant be a local resident of the town. Stories meanwhile became more widespread of increasing congestion, delays and cancellations to the daily bus runs to neighbouring provinces (by then considered by migrant workers to be an important part of their benefits package).

A similar degree of stringency, and controversy, soon attached itself to BGB's new policies and systems for training workers. The provision of training was high on the agenda of the new management – as had been emphasised in the inaugural meetings. However, as the new policy became clearer, it was also increasingly apparent that the training of new entrants was viewed by BGB as a prime means for re-shaping the labour landscape. The promised training schemes, for example, were to be restricted to new recruits from Port Said, in strict preference to other locations. BGB's most vital project for implementing this new, scientific strategy was to be an entirely new training school. A dedicated BGB unit was set up in a first-floor *edara* office, charged with the administrative arrangements involved in setting up the training school, proudly announced to be named as the *Madrasat tadrib il-khiyata li-sharikat Qasim Fahmy* ('The sewing training school for the Qasim Fahmy group of companies'). Its purpose was to provide Fashion Express with the skilled workers needed for the planned increase in its workforce from three hundred and fifty to one thousand. New applicants were told that the *madrasat tadrib il-khiyata* would produce a qualified and skilled worker in six weeks, qualifying them for a *shahada mu'tamada* (authentic certificate) which fulfilled the requirements of *il-edara il-ingilizeya* (the British management).

However the deployment of the first cohort of six trained recruits led to a considerable amount of disagreement, as the supervisors of the units to which they had been assigned rapidly accused them of having *ashkal tikhawif* (unsavoury appearances), and not blending in with others on the shop floor. The BGB team responded by accusing the supervisors of seeking to protect the privileges they had previously enjoyed under the well-established '*edara* recruits, *entag* trains' regime, and for a time there was a complete face-off. This was eventually resolved through an accommodation under which it was agreed that, in the future, on every third day of their six-week training programme newly recruited trainees were to be sent downstairs to the shop floor, to immerse themselves in the work and 'accustom their eyes to those already hired by the firm' – a process which had always been seen, on the shop floor at least, as an education in itself.

Along with their new recruitment and training policies, the BGB team also began to introduce a series of rules and regulations to implement their modern, scientific policy of greater firmness in control of the workforce, under the slogan '*kul wahid fi makanuh, kul wahid yesbit nafsu!*' ('Everyone in their proper station, everyone proving their worth!'). The new rules were introduced in stages in order to allow the workforce to gradually become accustomed to the new disciplinarian order. First to make itself felt was an increased emphasis on punctuality, with the strict requirement that all workers report at 8 A.M. sharp, and remain at their work stations until a break period. The bathrooms and prayer rooms were locked, and only opened during lunch breaks. Distractions were no longer permitted on the shop floor. Workers were told to leave their personal items in lockers or with Security, and collect them during breaks. Even chewing gum and the other small edible treats (such as pumpkin seeds and salted cockles), which workers had previously shared around, were confiscated.

These regulations had the additional effect of applying a stringent clampdown on the busy shop-floor trade in goods and services, an activity dear to the hearts of many in the workforce. The clampdown was felt especially intensely since the timing of the ban coincided with the start of the new school year in October. This was a peak period in the seasonal pattern of trade on the shop floor, where immense personal and emotional value was invested in the children or younger siblings of the workforce being in formal education. Although the wages of the workforce were primarily directed at big projects like *gihaaz*, smaller special treats were also expected to be handed out to their young ones going to school. Thus the entire shop floor was looking forward to the range of seasonal goods expected to arrive at that time of year, particularly the fluorescent pink Barbie pencil cases, Mickey Mouse erasers, school notebooks that came with colourful plastic folders, fancy textbook labels with famous Disney characters, and bars of *il-Nabulsi* olive-oil soap (not readily available in local markets, and favoured because of its special potency for giving the young ones a good scrub on the evening before their first day at school). Also brought to a halt was the supervisors' habit, at this time of year, of turning a blind eye to diversion of attention from production to the adjustment of school uniforms or, for the poorest workers such as the cleaners, the sewing of new uniforms using factory cloth, which were then ironed and wrapped in cellophane, as if bought from a regular retail outlet. The shop-floor service sector also suffered as much as did its trade in goods. The time-honoured factory system of despatching junior male assistants to pay school fees and return with receipts, to transfer an application from one school to another, or to take care of miscellaneous chores such as having a pair of school shoes re-soled at the cobblers was brought to an end.

BGB management's new policy of firmness was also evident in the requirement that, at the end of each shift, workers leave the shop floor in a single file, with the shortest at the front and the tallest at the rear. Mr Ismail elaborated on the theme when I asked him why this almost military-looking marching order was being introduced:

> We want a new image to *sharikat Fahmy* (the Fahmy group of companies). We actually have two different uniforms in mind. One is for the workers to wear during their eight hour shift, and the second is for when they leave the premises and head home. When they are walking to their buses, we want them to be visible, to stand out, as 'workers of the Fahmy factory'. We don't want the workers looking the way they do now. I mean look at those beards some of the men are wearing! Why not shave, and put a light eau de toilette that smells enticing, something like *talat khamsat* ('three fives' – the local way of referring to a popular brand whose mark was a distinctive '555')?[4] We want them to be seen to be *mutahaderin* (civilised individuals). We are embarking on a process – but how to change the mentality here? It's a key question. They always talk about nothing but money, ask about nothing but wages. Is money everything?

Retrieving the firm as family

The shop floor reaction to the proposal to put workers in uniform was one of ambivalence. For the girls and women, a sense of dress formed an integral part of expressing their individuality and status. As a result they were not enthusiastic about wearing a uniform and 'all looking the same'. As Wafaa, a quality control worker, put it: 'It's so embarrassing – we will end up looking like nurses! I once worked in a factory that had a uniform. But I'm no longer prepared to walk down the street to catch my five-thirty ride looking like a clown'. A potential compromise was eventually formulated: if the uniform was to be white, then the choice of *hijab* should be left for each girl to decide which style suited her best. Others had more practical concerns, such as how the entire procedure of 'getting changed' could, if modesty was to be preserved, risk unnecessary delays and compromise 'production time'.

The emphasis on feminine propriety extended to other new *tahakumat ghilsa* (irksome rules). The policy of locking the bathrooms during working hours was criticised on the grounds that girls needed to use them more frequently when menstruating; but the female supervisors did not consider it proper to raise this with BGB's all-male management team. The closure of the prayer rooms, except during breaks, raised a similar pressing concern, though not on the religious grounds that might have been expected. The issue highlighted instead was that these spaces also served as a rest room for girls who needed to take short recuperation breaks during working hours.

As the weeks passed, it became evident to the workforce that the disciplinary components of the 'modern, scientific and British' features of BGB's vision were becoming part of their daily reality – but that the compensating benefits and rights, also promised as integral elements of *il-manshud*, were not. Nor were there any concrete signs of the promised British work orders. The initial effect was a noticeable rise in critical questioning of the changes being brought about by the new regime, and a steadily more strident criticism of the new BGB management.

A telling incident occurred when the *mushrifat* arrived one morning to find that their common room had been ransacked overnight, with their prized kettle overturned, the knife they used for slicing bread and fruit flung on the floor, and the tea leaves normally kept in an old marmalade jar lying scattered all over. Fatma was the first to voice her thoughts about the implicit message: '*They* want us to use the room solely for work'. Other supervisors were called in to witness the damage. As Zizi began to clear the tea leaves scattered on the floor, she declared with authority:

> It's the way that, as a rule, newcomers behave. Their prime objective is to *yisbit shakhsiyyitu* (to assert their presence). They're just flexing their muscles. It's all *harakat wi awamir* (bogus displays of power), *yimil shida* (acting tough). The new *'ameed* (colonel[5]) is just another *ragil show* (showman)'.

Voicing their thoughts explicitly in this way seemed to help the *mushrifat* take the intimidation in their stride. As they settled down, having restored their familiar surroundings to order, Fatma produced from her large vinyl handbag a supply of *fino* bread, so that preparations for their customary morning snack could begin as normal.

Eventually criticism of BGB was voiced in a way that became public and unashamedly critical, with the shop floor using their customary unrestrained humour to deliver a sarcastic commentary on developments. Workers developed a new game called *Tom wi Jerry* (Tom and Jerry). This involved mimicking the familiar cartoon characters' cat-and-mouse actions, in particular when seated workers deliberately synchronised exaggerated, swivelling movements of their heads to follow the BGB managers' business-like progression around the shop floor. When Mr Ismail was seen walking into the male toilets in *entag*, the time was carefully noted on the *sala* clock, as was the time he emerged (after, it was hoped, measuring up the place for its promised refurbishment). This led to much ribald comment about how he was able to spend no less than seventeen carefully counted minutes in a toilet whose stench was reputed to 'kill anyone within six minutes flat'. As he emerged 'Am Naguib – the elderly cleaner – resumed his task of sweeping the floor with exaggerated gestures and energy, to a mocking male workers' chorus of the BGB slogan *kul wahid fi makanuh, kul wahid yesbit nafsu!* ('Everyone in their proper station, everyone proving their worth!').

These displays of overtly critical and hostile behaviour bore strong similarities to earlier episodes of what both management and workers referred to by the term *qalaq* (as described in chapter 2). This time the anomie (what was not right) related to the disruption of pre-existing chains of command within the factory, including *entag*'s hierarchical structure. The *mushrifat* had not been slow to sense the threat to their positions on the shop floor, with Horeya, for example, voicing her concerns explicitly:

> We don't have confidence *they* know very much about the expertise needed in the technical side of garment production. I'd like them to know they ought to leave this part to us. Just bring us the orders, is my message – and then collect them up at the end of the day. How we execute them, how we *squeeze* labour out of the workforce, is our task on the shop floor.

Others were more concerned that their personal relationship with Top Management had changed, without an appropriate alternative to replace the previous levels of face-to-face interaction. As Fatma put it one day:

> *Il-islub itghayar* (the style has changed). In the past we could walk into their offices and talk. They listened to us, we listened to them. All problems could be solved by discussion. Now we have no idea what is stewing in BGB's pots. It's hardly reassuring to others. What are all these decisions? Their wages come

from overseas, unlike us. I've come to the conclusion that as a team they simply *mish behibo il-nas* (don't like people).

The most vivid demonstration of an outbreak of *qalaq* came in response to BGB's new rule prohibiting the use of strong language on the shop floor. At the peak of production, Kawsar Morsi found herself getting into a fight with Sawsan Etrebi from *edara*, who had allegedly moved one of the sewing machines from her line without notification. By itself, this constituted a serious breach of shop floor codes, not only because of the direct interference of *edara* in shop floor organisation, but also because past cases of premeditated foul play between supervisors (bent on slowing down the production quotas of their rivals) had involved resorting to tactics such as moving vital sewing machines, and hiding them with other mothballed equipment. Kawsar Morsi, a single woman in her early thirties and widely considered to be somewhat *ghariba* (strange), was already well known for her violent temper. However, her acknowledged competence in meeting deadlines, and the fact that there was a tacit tolerance in the familial management regime towards 'single women who behave strangely' had meant that she had kept her job and rank, and continued to be held in some esteem and fear.

The incident of the sewing machine led her to stand up for herself by hurling abuse at Sawsan Etrebi. In this she found herself supported by other workers across many shop floor units, as having a valid case for retrieving her *haqq*. Nevertheless the Production Manager, shocked by her language and mindful of the new prohibition against it, wrote up a *giza* (fine) and, to humiliate her further, had it publicly pinned to the front door of the factory. Kawsar Morsi's *mushrifat* colleagues were outraged, and Kifah Mansur dramatically tore it down and ripped it to shreds. Sawsan's *edara* colleagues also took sides, and the incident rapidly degenerated into a state of all-out confrontation between *edara* and *entag*. *Edara* insisted that Kawsar Morsi should step down as a supervisor and revert to becoming a machinist, while *entag* criticised Sawsan Etrebi for behaving in a high-handed *edara* manner and, they alleged, deliberately orchestrating the whole incident. Even the Production Manager, despite having been the one who issued the *giza*, stood firmly behind Kawsar Morsi in her quest to retrieve her *haqq*, 'defending her with a strange ferocity', as Mr Ismail described it.

The manner in which the crisis was eventually resolved proved to be instructive, as it involved the new management reverting to old-style ways of bringing about reconciliation between feuding members of the 'firm as family'. Within forty-eight hours Mr Ismail arranged for the warring parties to be gathered in the Top Management office he had moved into, with, as customary, a cake wheeled in for all to share as an act of mutual good will and conciliation. The recourse by the new BGB management to traditional 'family' methods for resolving workplace disputes suggested that the state of anomie underlying this particularly intense, agitated episode of *qalaq* could well have been related to issues deeper and more fundamental than simply disrupted or muddled chains of command. It instead seemed to involve violation of other deep-seated principles, closely allied to notions of support and tolerance in the workplace, according to which the firm-as-family had been constructed by managers and workers alike.

The enduring importance of kinship ties within Fashion Express was also vividly captured by the reaction of the workforce to the eviction of the Fahmy family members who had previously occupied top management positions. The evicted managers' own responses were initially ones of shock, as exemplified by Tewfik Saleh, who, the first time we met after BGB's arrival, said to me:

> I don't get the point of removing us. What harm can we do to the firm or cause to Qasim? We are the family, his close kin. It's easy for youngsters like Ismail Tukhi to come along with bags of cash, playing at improving the firm. As kin, we did the harder work. We managed with peanuts for over ten years.

To the workforce, the Fahmy family members' exclusion from the scene was just as difficult to come to terms with – to them it was almost inconceivable. Across both *edara* and *entag* it was anathema, within the ethics of a workplace that had been struggling for years, to see family members distanced, especially familiar and loved figures whose personalised style of family management had shaped the labour and power relationships of the firm and were part of *il-ayyam il-hilwa* (the happy days). Their removal was viewed as an act of *qat' 'eish* (taking the bread from someone's mouth) which, as one machinist in the assembly line said 'is never nice to see'. It was particularly abhorrent when reinforced by the religious precept of honouring kin, a principle respected and deployed in the composition of the factory from its top echelons down to the workforce. And although the exiled senior managers were known to have other means of subsistence, the factory was still perceived as their, as much as everybody else's, bread and butter. As Qasim Bey had often in the past had occasion to remind both workers and family members, *'kulina binakol min tabaq wahid'* ('we all eat from the same cooking pot')'.

The reassertion of the 'firm as family' was further reinforced by the manner in which members of the workforce continued to demonstrate their *ikhlaas* (personal loyalty) to former senior family managers, even after they had been banned from the premises. This was a contentious issue, which the new BGB management tried hard to counter, since depersonalising management relations had been one of their initial motives for replacing the top managers. The tenacity of *ikhlaas* was manifested by the persistence, even under the new circumstances, of the grapevine of internal surveillance based on individual loyalty, as members of the workforce continued to feed the deposed family members information on a daily, if not hourly, basis. Even though they were separated from the factory, it was, for the former members of top management, almost business as usual, as the information poured in relaying the details of a normal production day. Even greater detail was provided over the changes BGB was initiating, for example by some family *gawasis* (moles) who surreptitiously left their mobile phones switched on all through BGB's introductory *igtimaa't* briefings, transmitting the entire proceedings to the absent family managers. The exiled family managers also continued to be consulted by the workforce for news of their *kebir*, and about a wide range of issues, such as the new paperwork BGB was bringing in, or how relationships were being maintained with other local investors, whose continued subcontracting work was known to be vital to keeping the factory running until such time as the promised British work orders materialised. In these ways, the family management's internal surveillance continued to infiltrate the workplace, as they maintained a cohesive entity continuing to watch over, albeit from a distance, the interests of the firm. It gave them much-desired personal reassurance that they still commanded the loyalty and commitment of their workforce 'family', in whose eyes they continued to be seen as the legitimate guardians of the firm.

The central importance of kinship was also confirmed by workforce reactions to BGB's new 'scientific' recruitment procedures, systems and policies. Previously (as described in chapter 2) the workforce was able to exercise a degree of control over their environment through the freedom they were given to bring their kin into the workplace. BGB's recruitment policies actively disrupted these arrangements, and proved to be a turning point in causing many to see the new management to be far more controlling than had initially been apparent.

This new understanding led to the first real demonstration of active resistance, both overt and covert, by the workforce. It was noticed that, following the announcement of the new recruitment policies, more than a week passed without a single new recruit being delivered to the new training school – even though a steady stream of applicants had been seen ascending and descending the staircase to the *edara* offices. The girls in *tarqim* eventually let it be known that this was because Madame Nermin, in Workers' Affairs, had put all the potential recruits off by emphasising the social insurance and related benefits BGB planned to introduce – signing up for these would have the effect of disqualifying them from later applying for posts in the civil service. As Khadija said quietly:

She told them about the new social insurance policies for the workplace, reading them out as if they were non-negotiable, and new work benefits for our *edara*. To tell the truth, she was doing her job. The whole Zone is curious about our *edara inglizia* (British system), who wouldn't be with all the rumours flying about? She must have known that just whispering this clause would be enough to send them packing.

Khadija's analysis was confirmed when Mr Ismail and Marzuk Salama discovered the ploy and, furious over such obstruction from middle management, re-channelled future applicants away from 'the inflexible' Madame Nermin and directly towards BGB staff members instead.

Shop floor workers' resistance grew even more overt in the month of Ramadan, when, in order to complete a subcontracting order for fifteen thousand garments, the new BGB management required workers to stay on late for several days in a row (instead of, as usual, clocking off in time to break their fast with the traditional sunset *iftar* meal). Dire warnings were issued that non-compliance would be punished by heavy fines. One of the quality control *mushrifat*, Nidal Hassan, prevented under the new rules from using her customary strong language to push workers in her unit to deliver results, declared herself defeated. She locked herself in the bathroom sobbing, and lashing out angrily against the *kus om il-shirka* (a crude expletive used against the BGB team) responsible for the new regime:

> It doesn't work the way they want it. We can't keep fining the *'iyal*. They sweat to get the peanuts they earn, and are lucky if they get even that on time. Right now the *'iyal* are dead on their feet, and I have no *entagiyya* (production figures) worth talking about.

Her anger at the new BGB management was compounded by her frustration with the lack of professionalism she saw in their failure to notify her of precise delivery times, or to provide required supplies of cleaning detergent. In the tradition of shop floor politics, she spotted an opportunity to shame the new management and expose its vision as a sham. She did this by seizing on the *iftar* meal which BGB had contracted a local supermarket to provide for her *'iyal* on enforced overtime, declaring the quality to be unacceptable. For five working evenings in a row the meal, presented as the symbol of new management's commitment to change, was minutely scrutinised for flaws. It arrived late; it was cold and unappetising; the servings were *wagbit tifl* (kids' portions), a *tasbira* (snack), or even *taflita* (left-overs); it didn't even include a bottle of fruit juice or *haga saka'a* (a cold drink). Declaring that it had given some of her *'iyal* food poisoning, she ordered the new security guards to call the ambulance four times in a single evening to ferry her sick workers to hospital – to the point where the ambulance drivers informed Security they would be rejecting any more emergency calls from 'this address'.

On account of its sustained length over five full working days, and the quantity and vividness of the details she and her team furnished each day in critically examining their new entitlements, Nidal Hassan's campaign constituted one of the most powerful acts of overt resistance to have been staged on the shop floor. It not only threw doubt on BGB's ability to live up to their promises of change, but also showed them to be deeply inexperienced in organising a matter even as mundane as a hot meal. As Tewfik Saleh commented when news of the event reached him through the grapevine:

> Giving each worker LE 5 to buy what they felt like having, and saving a pound or two, would have sorted out this mess without the need for these dramatics. It would have cost Qasim far less than the LE 15,000 he is now having to pay the supermarket. BGB are not experienced. I keep finding more reasons every day for thinking that way.

Reassertion of the principle of *ihtiram* (respectability) as a central feature of the firm-as-family also found expression in critical comments voiced about BGB's new standards for employees, as when Hanadi Amin, a Leitex supervisor, said:

> We're now spectators in a game intended to shame us. We are treated like *baqar* (cattle), as if we're uneducated and uncouth. We may not all have university degrees, but I have machinists down my assembly lines who are taking their entitlement of three-weeks paid leave to get *il-bakalorioz wil lisanz* (baccalaureates and licenses, i.e. university qualifications). We are far removed from the image they are seeking to project onto us.

The reassertion of this principle also found expression in the reaction of the workforce to some of the new employees BGB introduced to the firm. Thus two female graduates who had been placed directly into supervisory positions were explicitly described as *mish mohtaramin* (not respectable) on account of their chosen dress styles involving *Bermuda* (knee-length shorts) and '*il-cut*', (a low-necked, clinging, lycra T-shirt). As the two newcomers appeared in the *sala*, a female voice along one assembly line was heard calling loudly to their BGB escort, '*Ya Handasa' da mish laye'laha* (Hey 'Mr Engineering'! [a deliberately derogatory variation on the polite honorific *Bashmuhandis*] those clothes don't look good on her)'. This in turn provoked boisterous catcalls and whistles from other male machinists down the assembly lines. The cry of *'ersa!* (ferret – an animal considered disgusting) reverberated particularly loudly, not simply because the choice of epithet was aggressive, but because such initial shop floor appellations often had a way of cementing themselves into permanent factory nicknames.

The newcomers' seemingly unrespectable demeanour also reflected negatively on Marzuk Salama, with crude comments made about where he might have found his 'specimens' (meaning recruits). The news got back to him, causing him to realise that his own reputation was on the line and that he had at most a working day to be seen to handle matters professionally, and thus save the situation from growing profoundly more embarrassing. Thus later in the afternoon the two girls were taken to Production Studies for a quiet word from Sawsan Etrebi. Referring to herself as 'elder sister', she reminded them that dressing properly was an important part of the image of the factory because, as she stressed several times over, 'this place has *she'ur* (sensibilities)'. Disapproval of the newcomers' failure to fit in with workplace demonstrations of *ihtiram* nevertheless continued to make itself felt on the shop floor, as verbal skirmishes with supervisors followed each other in rapid succession. The two newcomers accused Leitex supervisors of giving them blunt scissors and asking them 'to pull out pieces of thread from garments for hours on end'. One of them burst into tears, and both complained to BGB that the factory workspace was 'an inhospitable nest of vipers'. In response *edara* and *entag* rapidly closed ranks to provide BGB with a shared professional assessment that the two entrants were 'inexperienced' in shop floor work. The upshot was that both left within a week.

The pulling together of *edara* and *entag* in the face of management change offered a demonstration of *taraabut* (solidarity), albeit in a different direction from the way it had usually been expressed and exercised under the previous managerial regime. BGB was widely criticised for seeking to deliberately break up the carefully nurtured familial ethos. As one supervisor, Hamida Ali commented: 'They seem keen to separate us from what we've been used to in the past. It's as clear as sunlight. They want to break our spirit. They want us divided'.

The figure of the *kebir* was expressly invoked in this reassertion of *taraabut*. Much sympathy was expressed that, over the twenty years it had taken Qasim Bey to build his business, he had never properly received his due *haqq* in terms of the prosperity that other investors in the Zone had reaped. His willingness to countenance the management changes being introduced was explained and excused in terms of his having had no other option in the face of mounting debts and other financial difficulties. There was apprehension that he might have been hoodwinked by a *shirka mashbuha* (dodgy company) passing itself off as professional, and aiming to steal the firm from him by first setting up new management structures deliberately designed to isolate the *kebir* from his trusted 'family' (his real kin in management, and his metaphorical kin the workforce). One evening Tewfik Saleh expressed his exasperation at not being able to find anything about BGB on the Internet, and shared his suspicions with me that the company was a fraudulent sham:

It's not difficult today with all the technological advances in software and hardware to transport your Queen of England to the Zone, and show her receiving red carpet treatment. A faked photograph can show her shaking hands with Qasim and kissing the *'iyal* – here, right here!

The shop floor's protective stance towards their *kebir* extended to defending his patrician reputation as *mohtaram* (respectable). The much-heralded CCTV cameras provided a case in point, as workers on the shop floor discussed among themselves how installing a monitoring screen in the office of Qasim Bey, a point raised in Mr Ismail's inaugural address, would be a case of *manzarha mish sah* ('not looking proper'). Far from being a hi-tech gadget symbolising BGB's vaunted image of a modern, scientific managerial system, it ran the risk of reducing their *kebir* to looking like a security guard in a shopping arcade, an image conjured up by male shop floor workers whose second jobs as night time security guards in local banks involved precisely the activity of sitting in front of a console switching CCTV images 'at the push of a button'.

The confrontation between two contrasting systems of management, and workforce resistance to most aspects of the change, was summarised by Zizi when one afternoon she reflected with bitterness on the high hopes she had shared a few months earlier about the innovations which were set to change the course of the factory's fortunes. Yet now all the beguiling promises of the *igtimaa'at* had been exposed as *il-madina il-fadila* (utopia). Her views captured succinctly the general mood of the 'firm as family' workforce:

> What concerns me most are *asrar il-masna'* (the secrets of the factory). They are bent on manipulating us into showing ourselves to be *mish mukhlessin* (disloyal) in a manner which I find quite unpalatable. It's got to the point where I've ceased to feel this factory is ours any longer. Now it's as if suddenly *ehna gudad il masna'* (we're the ones who are the newbies around here).

The end of the road?

This remained the position as I left it when, in early 2005, the time came for me to conclude my fieldwork and return to London. Leaving the factory carried more profound meanings than the simple physical act of moving out of a research site (Buchanan et al 1988). I felt that my departure from Port Said had left things abruptly suspended in mid-sentence. One day I was at the heart of intrigue on the Fashion Express shop floor – the next I was back in Cairo to collect notes and belongings, struggling to cope with my feelings of loss and separation. I had been told at the beginning of my struggles to find a research site that factories and their workforce were an *'alaam khaas* (separate world) – and, true to this description, the workplace's unique *mu'aysha* (shared lived experience) was captured by the Production Manager's final words to me as he said goodbye: 'We have lived *ayyam hilwa* (good days) together'. The future of Fashion Express and its community of *taraabut* weighed on my mind. Despite the best efforts of many, the future of the enterprise was hanging in the balance.

Phone calls to some of the workers indicated that restlessness began to invade the shop floor by February, when the subcontracting orders secured by the *ancien regime* of family management ran out, yet there were still no signs of either new orders or of wages. During the six months BGB had been in the firm, the workforce had received only two months' dues, even less than they had previously been used to. It led the *mushrifat* to dismiss the managerial changes as purely cosmetic. As Horeya put it, 'It can all be summed up in two words: polishing the copper nameplates, and covering things with a thick crust of sweet-coated words'. BGB were pointing to the costly refurbishments they were undertaking in order to justify their inability to pay wages, but their excuses were read as a smokescreen. Khadija was adamant: 'That's bullshit. They've got the cash hidden somewhere. They're deliberately trying to cheat us'.

She also reported that other rumours were circulating that the much touted 'British client' was a hoax and did not exist. The 'internal elections' for model workers were starting to be interpreted as 'attempts to derail us'. I was told that strikes and protests were being dealt with in a heavy-handed way, with instigators and workers harassed or even fired, rather than as before simply being fined. At the same time, migrant workers were told not to report to work – a policy interpreted as aimed at saving costs, but in reality leading many to fear the firm had lost its sense of direction. There were dark hints that, despite the efforts of BGB to control internal surveillance, workers were beginning to piece together the politics behind BGB's managerial style.

Some members of the exiled group of family top management whom I rang also shared their consternation over developments at the factory. Imam Azmi, the General Manager, expressed deep dismay at the fractious mood that had taken hold, and the deterioration in the firm's position within the Zone:

> They have taken us back ten years. All the hard work of building bridges has been ruined. They accuse us of having created *shulaliyya* (factions) in the workforce. I admit this happened, but it was in personal relations, not on the professional scene. *Ehna masna' wahid wi 'aila wahda* (We are one firm and one family): this spirit has been badly punctured.

Enquiries made by family members were also giving cause for suspicion that BGB had a history of past involvement in several unsuccessful contracts of this kind elsewhere in Egypt, and were now pinning their hopes on the Fahmy family name to secure a foothold in a city they claimed was 'rich with hidden resources'. Such enquiries had also revealed several individual BGB members' clandestine connections to the *mukhabarat* (secret police) and the Egyptian air force.

Since I had only known the BGB managers for a few months, after I left Port Said I was not expecting to have much further contact with them. It turned out, however, that I ended up hearing as much from their side as from any other, as Ismail Tukhi sent me regular e-mails, in English, and often with large PowerPoint and multimedia attachments. Initially he reported progress, though 'some people fight me and my vision'. Soon, however, his upbeat tone changed, as he described increased levels of shop floor resistance. He told me that he was aware that I was still in contact with 'some girls' in the factory and 'so you may have some news' – but he was anxious that I should not be misled by the 'battle' between his plans and 'people who maybe could not see my vision'. He also hinted darkly at 'some unprofessional act, maybe from family sources, as if it was better not to have this order. I work in very difficult weather, only a small number of people understand me'. The last e-mail I ever got from him was the shortest of them all: 'I would just like to inform you of the unhappy news that we left the factory, based on unprofessional activities of Fahmy and his unprofessional people outside and inside the factory, which caused some problems in our work. The story will be mentioned to you later'. But it never was – from his side, at least.

According to the workers, the story behind BGB's abrupt ejection from the firm began when rumours started to circulate that a major decision was going to be announced by the proprietor on the final day of April. It was immediately evident that BGB management had been tipped off, since it was only their junior staff who had come to work on that day: there was no sign of BGB's top management team. Instead, reinstalled in their old offices, were the familiar faces of the former Top Management family members, a clear sign of Qasim Bey's direct intervention. In a later phone call he confirmed to me that his suspicions about BGB's ability to deliver the promised British clients had steadily hardened, and he had been looking for ways of edging them out before their six-month contract was up: 'It was all a pack of lies and deceit'.

Subsequent news from the factory was not, however, encouraging. As May turned into June, the workers continued to report the complete absence of orders, and the continuing non-payment of wages, despite the restoration of the old 'firm as family' regime. By early July, it was declared that the firm had fallen upon its third *naksa* (catastrophe). Workers began leaving in droves, as shop floor numbers shrank day by day from 350 to 200 to 150 to 80. When departing, each worker left their contact details with the General Manager as a sign of their continuing personal commitment to the firm, and in the expectation that one day Fashion Express' fortunes would be reversed and they would be 'summoned home'. But the call never came, and eventually Top Management and Security were the only people left on the premises. Finally in August 2005, Qasim Bey ordered the factory to be vacated and its gates locked.

Soon after, I heard that most of the Fashion Express workers seemed to have had little difficulty in finding employment elsewhere, as other proprietors in the Zone stepped in to help them find alternative work. Rumours however had it that many were not in stable jobs, but had become permanent 'floaters' in the labour market of the Zone, working in one factory until its orders had been finished, before moving on to another. I still ask myself if it is merely wishful thinking to wonder whether they are still waiting for the doors of Fashion Express to re-open. I remember how, the day after the workforce had left, Imam Azmi told me defiantly over the phone, 'When we get back on track only the *mukhlis* (loyal) workers will fill our production lines'. And I recall the comment the Director General of the Zone made during our final phone conversation:

> We helped the workers find their feet elsewhere. Other factories were lining up to recruit them. Mind you, there are endless complaints about the *'iyal*. The proprietors say that they are an undisciplined lot compared to their other workers. They outdo them not in terms of delivering higher quotas, but by collecting more fines! But these other firms are not *family* [same word used in Arabic] in the way Qasim had been. The girls complain bitterly to me every time they see me, even though their wages have tripled. Whereas at one time we thought Qasim was spoiling them, we now see that he had nurtured a family.

Notes

1. In contrast to *ikhlaas*, which is loyalty in the sense of devotion to a person.
2. A beach resort on the north coast where influential and wealthy people have villas.
3. See the analysis of the concept of *haqq* provided in chapter 3.
4. A cheap eau de cologne available widely in the shops, but resisted, especially in *entag*, because of its reputed use in the washing of corpses being prepared for Islamic burial.
5. The post of Head of Security, previously held by Tewfik Saleh (a relative of Qasim Bey), had been given to a retired colonel who was now made responsible for discipline.

Chapter 6

DOMINATION AND RESISTANCE

This has been an ethnography of the public and visible economic activities of women in an institutional workplace in Port Said. It both builds on, and moves on from, previous studies that have focused on the domestic, home-based and informal sectors of the economy. It has examined how gender relations, as well as discourses of religion and class, operate and intersect within the setting of a garment assembly factory subject to the exigencies of the globalised supply chain. The specific questions (set out in chapter 1) on which I initially sought to focus my exploration of issues of gender, class and religion on the globalised shop floor related to: (a) ways in which globalised economic forces and local factors interact to determine the distinctive environment of the factory; (b) whether, and if so how, management invokes or manipulates notions of class, gender and religion in order to recruit, retain and control the workforce required for meeting exacting contractual deadlines, quality standards and cost ceilings; and (c) the extent to which workers resist or contest these management control strategies, and to what effect.

In this concluding chapter I begin by revisiting the first question, summarising how the Fashion Express shop floor becomes the nexus of myriad interacting global and local economic forces, whose interplay creates a distinctive workplace environment for the ensuing exploration of issues of gender, class and religion. I then revisit the second and third questions together, since it is the interactions between management and workers within this setting that define the factory's distinctive articulations of these categories. I show how the various management–labour power structures, discourses and dynamics in play reveal the 'firm-as-family' as operating within a symbiotic framework of what I call 'mutual co-optation', which both invokes and turns back on itself the corporatist model of 'coercion and consent' which has, to varying degrees, characterised Egypt's national polity from the early years of Nasser's state socialism. Finally I return to the theme with which I opened my first chapter, namely the part played by successive waves of labour unrest and protest in the years leading up to Egypt's Arab Spring uprising of February 2011. I ask what, if any, pointers my 2004 fieldwork (conducted in the year in which these protests first spiked) might – if only with the benefit of hindsight – be seen to offer for the momentous events surrounding the deposing of President Mubarak and all that came after: the political victory, and then defeat, of the Muslim Brotherhood, and the arrival of the latest in modern Egypt's line of supposed military strongmen, Field Marshall Abd El Fatah el Sisi.

Globalisation and localisation

In the introductory chapter to this ethnography I summarised how Port Said – created in the 1860s on previously empty desert, at the mouth of a newly dug arterial maritime canal linking East and West, North and South – has ever since its original foundation been at the centre of a complex nexus of global and local economic and political currents. Throughout this ethnography I have also highlighted how the city's distinctive heritage remains very much part of its current day-to-day life.

The time I was working in the factory (2003–2005) is now recognised as the heyday of late Mubarak neoliberalism. Its measures, building on Sadat's earlier *infitah* policies, were designed with the explicit intention of displaying a highly filtered form of economic openness in which market-led reforms and unrestricted foreign investment were to demonstrate Egypt's engagement with IMF-prescribed policies of domestic privatisation and increased exports. These trajectories were pinned on a newly established mercantile bourgeoisie, expected to deliver specific economic gains (such as increases in hard currency revenues) and, most importantly, to create employment opportunities, especially for young graduates, in the face of the simultaneous downsizing and privatisation of many of Egypt's mammoth public sector enterprises. Thus from the start the EPZ projected itself as distinct and separate from existing state-owned enterprises, designed to give visibility to modern, dynamic, efficient models of economic enterprise. Yet the realities underlying the Zone's operations, as I soon discovered, tended if anything to confirm the persistence of the influence of the Nasserist corporatist model of state–society relations, and the enduring importance of local factors such as social, economic and political constraints and imperatives. This model has been well defined by Ayubi (1995) as aiming to achieve the state's hegemony and control over its citizens through co-optation, achieved by a balance of mechanisms of coercion (heavy domestic surveillance and security) and instruments of consent (entitlements to free education and subsidised housing, fuel and staple foodstuffs).

A prime example of this type of corporatism within the Zone involved the measures applied for the definition and protection of workers' rights. In the public sector, these were the sole preserve of the government-sponsored Egyptian Trades Union Federations (ETUF) which – as I pointed out in chapter 1 – operated in effect as an arm of the centralised security state, co-opting all employees through a mixture of coercion and benefits. The ETUF's statutory remit did not extend to the private enterprise area of the Zone, where independent trade unions were also non-existent. Workers' rights were instead looked after by the Civil Association of Investors in Port Said, which defined its purpose as incorporating the mutual interests of capital and labour, investors and workers, in a single holistic framework. Thus the Civil Association maintained strict records of worker registration and mobility (a mechanism of coercion, designed to prevent workers from freely changing their place of employment), and at the same time was ready to exercise its independent status as an autonomous body to settle work disputes at an early enough stage to ensure that they did not escalate into collective action (an instrument for securing consent through deploying incentives and benefits).

Similarly it was the Civil Association which took the lead in assisting firms to adopt 'the language of fair trade and labour', so that they could come through their periodic inspections by foreign clients and campaigners seeking to assure themselves that appropriate labour standards were being met in the fashion and garment industry. This involved ensuring that the Zone was free of child labour, that health and safety systems were in place in all factories, that workers were not physically or verbally abused, and that they were fairly remunerated for overtime. On the face of it, such 'importers' wishes' requirements – as they were referred to in the factories – evoked a vocabulary that contested local practice in favour of the workers, and at the owners' expense. Yet obtaining a certificate of compliance with these requirements was also of vital interest to the investors, since it was an important condition for securing a much-coveted export license. The Civil Association accordingly absorbed and sought to balance these competing requirements within its corporatist framework, so that the local interests of both workers and investors could continue to be served, even if at a largely cosmetic level, and without the necessity for any radical, deep-rooted change.

The official image the Zone sought to project to local and international clients (and likewise to the Egyptian Government) was one of a modern, ethical, integrated, smoothly humming machine, the efficiency (and therefore profitability) of whose operations was unimpaired by internal friction or conflict of any kind. My data demonstrates the extent to which this was a façade, masking much more contested relationships between capital and labour (topics to which I return below). And even at the level of relations between the different investors themselves, the aura of bland unity and homogeneity proclaimed by the Civil Association sought to disguise deep-rooted hostilities, and cut-throat competition between the personality-driven management styles of the owners and managers of the different firms which made up its membership. The same applied, if anything with even greater force, to competition between Egypt's nine EPZs, as they fought each other for market share and orders from clients.

After completing my fieldwork, I was able to keep in touch with developments on the ground through regular follow-up visits to Port Said. And since 2011, the Public Free Zone (as the old EPZ was rebranded) has appeared markedly different from how I had first known it. The drab, gated community of seventeen working firms which I knew has been transformed into a manufacturing landscape of conspicuous affluence, with an increased number of operational factories crowding within its walls. Many premises now sport imposing facades (some self-consciously 'commercial' in their use of glass, brick and steel, others fancifully modelled after French *palaix* or American ranch houses) deliberately remodelled to project their new self-image as 'fashion houses' rather than mere 'garment assembly plants'. Some firms have set up their own websites and Facebook pages, with photographs of the modern equipment on offer, and of samples of the fashion items they have produced, as well as the 'Workers' rights' and 'Health and Safety' training courses they have organised to demonstrate the Zone's commitment to fair-trade standards. Patterns of ownership have also changed dramatically since my day, with an influx of new, cash-rich Egyptian investors, alongside foreign owners from the Gulf States, and the withdrawal of many of the representatives of the city's prominent *shurafa* (honourable) families who had dominated the scene during my time there.

Two external developments dating back to 2005 were the main drivers for these dramatic changes to the Zone's economic profile and status. One, a direct consequence of globalisation, involved the ending of the 'quota system' protection that had been provided to Egypt's garment sector under the 1974 Multi Fibre Arrangement. With this move all the garment assembly factories in the Zone, and indeed elsewhere in Egypt, abruptly found themselves exposed to full-blown international competition from alternative suppliers around the globe. In the same year Port Said succeeded in its aggressive campaign to lobby the Egyptian Government to select it for designation as one of the country's Qualified Industrial Zones (QIZ) promoted by the U.S. Government. This programme was aimed at increasing trade and economic relations between Israel and other Middle Eastern countries. This second development, linked to international/bilateral (rather than full-blown globalisation) drivers, proved to be the dominant factor of the two, and the one which underpinned the enhanced prosperity and greatly changed ownership structure of the EPZ which I saw taking place between 2005 and 2011.

Even during my time in the factory I had heard reservations being expressed – by managers and workers alike – about how the new QIZ programme was evidently aimed primarily at serving the interests of Israel (see chapter 2). And many of these doubts and reservations had, indeed, come back to haunt the Zone in the years following Port Said's success in obtaining QIZ status. Initially, the 'cash up front' purchase costs involved in the scheme's requirement that 11.7 per cent of any garment's components be sourced from Israeli accessory manufacturers proved to be beyond the capacity of many of the EPZ's cash-strapped, debt-ridden proprietors, who could only operate on the established 'Cut and Make' basis under which the client is required to provide all the raw materials and components to the assembly factory (see chapter 1). After considerable pressure from the Zone, the Egyptian Government negotiated a reduction in the required percentage to 8 per cent. Yet even this compromise was seen as punitive, in effect replacing 'Cut and Make' with the alternative contractual framework of FOB ('Free on Board'), under which the contractor is required to purchase all materials and components in advance, and only recoups these outlays once the client has paid for the finished garments. The result was that many of the Zone's established local investors began to identify hidden risks and dangers which threatened to change the face and fortunes of Port Said. The only prosperity they could see was for cash-laden, noveau riche investors from outside the city (not simply from other parts of Egypt, but more prominently from the Gulf and other Arab states) giving their industrial zone a harsher, more discriminatory character. The general disillusionment with the QIZ programme and its effects were summarised in an interview I conducted in 2010 with one of the Zone's leading local investors:

> As a businessman, I started out building my small fortune in a very contained and secure way. I started with two vans, and the only cost I had to carry was for a single electric bulb for a secure garage in which to park them. Money was flowing in from sales, and I did not need to fear what tomorrow would bring. Things were of course different when I grew my business so I could join the Zone – and since then QIZ has changed the entire network of business relations inside it. Now profits are nothing close to what we were led to expect. Even before the tenth of each month, pressures start building about how to

pay wages and meet my other month-end financial obligations. Before QIZ it was only the odd month in which these thoughts gathered like dark clouds – but now it's almost constant. And it's the same for my colleagues, our health has been affected. To save face we don't talk about it – but look how, in our meetings, there are tablets for migraines, high blood pressure, diabetes and anti-depressants laid out alongside the usual refreshments on offer.

Faced with all these exigencies of globalisation, compounded by a range of additional local pressures and difficulties, and with the entire mix exacerbated by the bottom falling out of the international garment market as a result of the crash of 2008, one of the first of the 'old guard' *shurafa* investors to throw in his hand and close his EPZ factory was Qasim Fahmy. In retrospect, the most intriguing question perhaps is how he was able to keep Fashion Express in business for as long as he did. This brings me to the second and third of my initial research questions concerning Fashion Express management's articulation and manipulation of categories of class, gender and religion – and the workforce's responses in terms of resistance or compliance. It is to these that I now turn.

Co-optation and appropriation

This ethnography has shown how the proprietor of Fashion Express and his top-management colleagues, in pursuit of their interests, articulate notions of class, gender and religion which are then woven together and deployed within a crafted discourse of 'firm as family' – and how the workforce, in pursuit of its own objectives, appropriates and turns this discourse back on itself. This tussle provides confirmation of Foucault's observation that discourse is not a passive, theoretical construct of intellectual interest only, but instead is actively central to real life definitions and assertions of, and struggles for, power: 'Discourse does not simply express struggles or systems of domination – it is for it, and by it, that one struggles. It is itself the power to be seized' (1971: 12). In order to focus more closely on the dynamics of the power struggles taking place within the factory, it will accordingly be useful to start by exploring the parties' differing interests, motivations and aspirations.

The motives of the proprietor of Fashion Express in establishing and protecting the interests of the firm were clearly very different from those generally attributed to a capitalist entrepreneur, who makes a financial investment primarily in order to secure a financial return. My ethnography shows that, by contrast, Qasim Bey was focused just as much on using Fashion Express to generate Bourdieu's (1977) 'symbolic capital' (as distinct from 'economic capital') amongst his peers in the Port Said elite, and amongst the electorate to whom he planned to submit his candidature for a seat in the Upper House of the Egyptian Parliament.

The context for this was his family's reputation within the Port Said community (as I have described earlier in chapter 2) as one of the city's *shurafa* (honourables), an informal title commanding recognition and respect. The *shurafa* class, though numerically small, had always been associated with the patrician 'old ways' of a nationalistic era when scions of prominent families were usually leading members of the old school professional circles, who were duty-bound to serve the country; and this remained significant in contemporary Port Said. The continued involvement in the politics of the community of such respected figures, grounded in the politics of former eras, assured continuity in the face of marked social fragmentation in a city badly damaged by recent wars as well as eight years of enforced evacuation, and therefore in need of economic reinvigoration. Such nationalistic overtones resonated powerfully in a community that continued to feel that it had single-handedly borne the brunt of Egypt's recent wars, and which looked to its *shurafa* 'elders' to step forward at times of dislocation to restore stability and continuity to the social, political and economic scene. The emphasis had become all the more powerful at a time of rapid flux in the composition of the city's elites, with the *infitah* influx of out-of-towners seeking a quick buck, and the increasing prominence within the city's upper echelons of a network of nouveau riche contractor-supplier '*Mubarak biznis*-men' making common cause with former government bureaucrats and ex-military and security services officers (Khalidi 1988; Springborg 1989, 2003).

Qasim Fahmy, however, had been brought up outside Port Said, and therefore had a special need to re-establish his local credentials and provide substantive proof of his family's commitment to the *shurafa* title. So although Fashion Express was a business venture for his family, the simple fact of its continuing existence *as a local venture* – irrespective of whether it was profitable or going through a rough patch – is what signified status, and also enhanced his networking powers with other members of the local community. And because of Port Said's history of involvement with the international garment trade, and the special cachet accordingly attached to foreign fashion, the fact that it was an export-orientated fashion garment-making venture further increased its significance in this respect. The motivational bottom line for Qasim Fahmy was not, therefore, to make a profit from his factory and firm – it was instead *simply to keep Fashion Express going as an operating venture*, even when it was not making visible profits or, indeed, was incurring further losses.

The motivations driving his workers proved to be of a different order, reflecting both their sense of collective citizenship (within the Egyptian state) and of personal identity (within the world economic order). Under Nasser's

1950s corporatist model of state socialism, citizens were seen (both by the state and by themselves) as social actors in their own right, exerting their entitlement to public benefits as their 'moral economy' (Posusney 1997) emoluments for consenting and contributing to state power, policy and programmes. In Sadat's 1970s *infitah* reforms this was subtly morphed into a view of citizens as passive recipients of such largesse as the bountiful state/ruler might, in his generosity, see fit to bestow on them – and active only in their new roles as consumers within the emerging areas of market economy. By the time of Mubarak's 1990s neoliberal reforms, the role of 'citizen as consumer' had swollen to cover the entire spectrum of services and products, from such vestigial state benefits as still remained (principally the country's overstretched and deteriorating public health and education facilities) to the ever-burgeoning privatised and marketised sectors of the Egyptian economy (Wickham 2013).

The predominantly young workforce of Fashion Express articulated this full-blown 'citizen as consumer' stance in ways that revealed the extent to which the *shabaab* (youth) had also begun to internalise the materialist lifestyle-and-choice aspirations of the twenty-first century globalised economy (Albrecht 2013). It could be seen, for example, in their choice of shop floor nicknames such as 'Dollar' and 'Beckham'; their emphasis on personal workplace fashion styles; how local economic pressures were behind subtle but important changes in gender norms, as workplaces became sexually integrated; and in the displays of materialist consumption, success and 'hopes and dreams' aspirations which workers wove into their public engagement, *tangid* (pre-nuptial) and *dukhla* (wedding consummation) celebrations.

In coming to work for the factory, the workers were distancing themselves from their traditional, often rural, backgrounds, and instead building their new chosen identities as participants in the wider, modern world of consumerist affluence. It was in focused pursuit of these ambitions that the workers appropriated management's 'firm-as-family' discourse, and turned it back on itself to transform the factory from a landscape of production to one of consumption, a free-wheeling market in goods and services directly channelled to fulfil the needs of a youthful workforce facing the financial and personal challenges implicit in their dreams of securing greater stability in marrriages of their choice, and their hopes for material and financial security linked with enhanced social mobility.

The landscape of such a workspace – transformed from what Bourdieu has referred to as a 'production habitus' (1977) into what we might call by contrast a 'consumption habitus' – offers far greater material and lifestyle opportunities than the more limited economic and social options on offer in the bleaker socioeconomic environment outside the factory's gates. So even though the workforce's motivations and aspirations were evidently of a different order from those of the proprietor and his top management, the *means* through which they sought to achieve these common ends meant that they shared an equal vested interest in *simply keeping Fashion Express going as an operating venture*. Having transformed their workspace into a social and economic space for the realisation of their personal projects, one of their prime objectives became the need to sustain its continued availability as their 'arena of opportunity'.

How does this square with the inherently (and necessarily) adversarial relationship which forms the backbone of a more classical Marxist reading of management–labour class consciousness and conflict? A useful connection is provided by Lockman's insight that:

> Working class formation (in fact, all class formation) is as much a *discursive* as a *material* process. In Egypt, as elsewhere, the working class as an entity and 'worker' as a form of subjectivity can be usefully conceptualized as products, as *effects*, not only of certain material practices ... but also of a particular discourse that, by providing categories of worker and class identity, gives people a (never unambiguous) language with which to organize their experience, to make several different and possibly conflicting kinds of sense of the world and their own places and possibilities within it. (1994b: 158–59)

That classic, adversarial management–labour conflict existed within the walls of Fashion Express is manifestly clear, since individual, group and collective instances of conflict were a regular feature of daily life on the shop floor. The workers regularly provided active demonstrations of de Certeau's analysis (1984) of how subjects of domination can be almost endlessly creative in finding opportune moments, and subtle ways, to 'trick the order of things' and subvert the control frameworks being applied; and also of Scott's concept (1990) of 'hidden transcripts' of resistance which are to be found within public performances of deference (by the powerless) to displays of power. They also staged collective acts of protest – sometimes formally, as in the silent *idrab* ('down tools' strikes) and noisy protest demonstrations; and sometimes informally, as in the 'melting of the workforce' episodes of 'raids' (as described in chapter 2).

Yet the particular forms these manifestations of labour conflict (both informal and formal) took, and their means of resolution, made it clear that, throughout, the workers recognised that, just as the *kebir* was dependent on them for the continued operation of the enterprise through which he was seeking to build *il-wagha il-igtima'iyya* (social capital), they were in turn dependent on him for continued employment in the 'firm as family' which provided them not only with their salaries, but also with the workplace arena which they had transformed into a zone of *taraabut* and opportunity for both material and non-material gains. Here I wish to be clear that I am not claiming that management and workers were 'natural allies', that they shared identical interests, or that they had negotiated a mutually satisfactory trade-off between adversarial interests of equal power. Rather I am arguing that, through the crafting by management of a discourse of 'firm as family', and the accommodation and appropriation of this discourse by the workforce for the pursuit of their wider objectives, they had forged a mutuality of interest in the continuing operation of the firm.

If we return to the governing framework of co-optation through which the Nasserist corporatist state held power, and the ways in which this model (with its delicate balance between mechanisms of coercion and instruments of consent) was adapted within the EPZ, it seems that within Fashion Express itself the labour–management power dynamic can usefully be characterised as being one of what I will call 'mutual co-optation'. On the one hand, the management co-opts the workforce to its purpose (survival and continuation of the firm) – while on the other the workers themselves 'co-opt' their bosses and proprietor to their own specific purposes.

An instance of the balance of mechanisms of coercion and instruments of consent through which this mutual co-optation was effected was the creation by management of the 'second stratum' (Binder 1978) of female supervisors, the *mushrifat* whom I have discussed in chapter 4. In the past, when the firm was near to economic collapse, and a scarcity of skilled labour continued to characterise the local employment market, the proprietor fell back on the longest-serving female shop floor workers, who had stood by the firm through thick and thin and through all its moves around various industrial zones in Egypt. He took the radical step of promoting them into the supervisory ranks that had, up until then, been an exclusively male preserve. Given the title of *Banat il-Masna* (Daughters of the Factory), the *mushrifat* rapidly consolidated a key role as, in Binder's telling formulation, the second stratum 'that does not rule – but without which the rulers cannot rule' (1978: 26). Developing and performing their distinctive brand of *mishmish* (alley cat) 'masculinised femininity', the *mushrifat* deployed a highly gendered performance of female *qiyada* (guidance, leadership) – securing new pools of labour by tapping their informal social networks in search of new recruits, until the firm had sufficient numbers with which to resume operations in its new base in Port Said; organising the workforce under their charge into viable units which could work, both separately and together, to meet exacting contractual deadlines; acting as prime arbiters of everyday shop floor concessions and compromise with individual workers; providing a channel through which workforce demands could be revealed to management without appearing as acts of overt resistance, where compromises could be negotiated within the 'firm as family' framework and without uncalled for public scrutiny;

keeping close tabs on the *iyal* to ensure standards of *ihtiram* (respectability) and morality were maintained in the mixed gender workforce; monitoring and facilitating (or, where called for, discouraging and disrupting) the development of love marriage interests between young men and women, a prime workforce objective; and supporting and even funding shop floor workers through times of personal need or difficulty, including late payment of wages or the costs of significant social events (from informal shopping outings and picnics to more formal occasions such as *tangid*, engagement or wedding celebrations). In all of these the *mushrifat* were aware of their corporatist, dual responsibilities, not only to drive the workforce to ever greater feats of production in the face of formidable financial constraints, but also at the same time ensure that workers were assured that their individual needs and aspirations were being respected and nurtured alongside those of the management.

Such a 'pulling together' of the ostensibly opposed class-interests of management and workers is a phenomenon that has been noted elsewhere in the literature as being a direct consequence of the forces of globalisation summarised earlier, and in particular the deeply precarious nature of the global supply chain. Cairoli (1999), Lee (1995, 1997) and Collins (2003), among others, have noted how garment assembly plants supplying labour within the globalised contracting chain are acutely vulnerable to this effect – and, as a result, are particularly prominent in displaying an affinity between the interests of proprietor and workforce, united in their common vulnerability to the whims of fickle international capital and clients. This reinforces Burawoy's formulation of 'hegemonic despotism' in which 'capital flight' has become a dominant form of labour control affecting plant-owners and workers alike, creating a situation where: 'the rational tyranny of capital mobility over the collective worker ... [is such that] ... the fear of being fired is replaced by the fear of capital flight, plant closure, transfer of operations and plant disinvestment.' (1985: 150)

If, under the threat of capital flight, Marxist class-conflict becomes, in the words of Roberto Saviano (2011) ' as soft as a soggy cookie', then were does this leave another important dimension for the contestation of entrenched power, namely the feminist struggle for gender equality? As a female Egyptian anthropologist 'doing fieldwork at home', I feel a profoundly personal resonance with many of the issues around gender, patriarchy, domination, exploitation, resistance and defiance raised by feminist scholars and ethnographers of the Middle East (as summarised in my opening chapter), resonances which inform the ways in which my ethnography relates to these debates. My first observation is that, although current theoretical frameworks have largely discredited early accounts suggesting links between the feminisation of labour and the discourse of 'nimble-fingered docility' in order to explain the institutional forces behind hiring women in paid manufacturing jobs, it can be seen that an association of female garment-assembling labour with an ostensible attribute of 'feminine dexterity' evidently retained its local currency in the Zone, even with the visible growth of male labour. It is also apparent that modulations within the ways in which gendered work was stereotyped, and their adaptation to the differing specificities of each firm's production landscape, provided small but important economic openings which encouraged women to take up more challenging roles on the shop floor, and contest hegemonic interpretations of gender roles. At the same time, subtle cultural pressures from the wider community to reproduce gender segregation on the shop floor also influenced the different layers of politics at play within the formation of each institution's gendering processes.

My study also provides ethnographic material that not only shows the active role women can play as economic protagonists, but also how workplace processes can give multiple, contextually variable meanings to their gendered roles. Far from being 'passive' and 'docile', the women workers of Fashion Express were actively involved in labour affairs in their public workplace. Indeed, the female supervisors were explicit in rejecting *ne'uma* (docility) – ascribed to women workers by male supervisors who felt their positions under threat – as an inherently 'female trait'. As I experienced first-hand, the *mushrifat* immediately seized on any display of feminine docility within their work areas as a strategy employed by lazy female workers to trick both them and the system. Explicit forms of active involvement by women in the work of the factory included the 'nurturing' roles they played in introducing new workers (males as well as females), training them in the specific skills required for different positions on the shop floor, monitoring and supervising the process of production, and engaging on occasion in overt resistance to management's attempts at workforce control. They also played significant roles in creating the factory's distinctive workplace environment, one which appropriated the structures of 'firm as family' – initially introduced as a management control stratagem – to create a shared sense of community within which workers could realise 'both meaningful and manageable gains' (Bayat 1997a: 160). These gains carried a very *personal* sense of purpose, as it was the workers themselves, rather than management or some remote government agency, who were influencing the agendas and the outcomes. Throughout these interventions they performed a flexible array of gendered roles, with multiple meanings generated through the different aspects of the labour and production processes in play.

Yet there remain stark limitations to the practices through which they defined, negotiated and defended their gains as women. Even workplace practices which challenged prevalent negative associations with manual labour, verified by the material accumulation which a working woman was able to generate, must be seen as achievements which themselves remained anchored in norms that valorise women's social and sexual roles – since the ultimate purpose of the accumulation of *gihaz* remains, after all, the marriage contract on which it is focused. A similar reinforcement is to be found in the way in which unmarried female workers were invariably referred to by the traditionally derogatory term *'anis* (old maid, spinster), rather than the more contemporary and value-neutral *mish mitgawwiza* (not married). And by presenting itself as the defender of 'family values', the firm endorsed these traditional characterisations still further, especially since its distinctive articulation of the familial bond was what gives the 'firm as family' its organisational definition. So although workers crafted distinctive shop floor discourses which informed 'appropriate' gendered behaviour in the processes (often personalised rather than collective) of bargaining and negotiation – processes which led to real life material consequences that were often favourable to the interests of women workers – it remains the case that I did not observe any instances (collective or individual) of critical interrogation of deep-rooted notions with a view to producing long-term change to existing gender ideologies.

So with respect to power/resistance debates as to whether women workers manipulate, oppose or resist their oppressive conditions (e.g. Bibars 2001), my ethnographic data supports Deniz Kandiyoti's (1988) theoretical framework of 'bargaining with patriarchy' in which 'resistance itself is framed by the terms of an already existing contract rather than with reference to some future utopian arrangement' (1998: 141). The women workers of Fashion Express evidently contested, accommodated and appropriated the patriarchal discourse of the firm's management to their own advantage, generating often significant rewards of material benefit and status: yet the 'existing contract', within and outside the factory walls, was not itself subjected to fundamental challenge. And it is not only the results of the gendered struggles within the factory that were ambiguous – so were the struggles themselves, which, to quote Kandiyoti's eloquent formulation, were 'not only over resources and labour but also over socially constructed meanings and definitions which are often multiple, contradictory, fluid and contested' (1998: 137). The ethnographic data supports Kandiyoti's subsequent reassessment of her own 'bargaining with patriarchy' explanatory framework, in which she reflects with hindsight that:

> The concepts we employ to designate the workings of power and domination never seem to fully capture the specificity of their manifestations ... Gender appears to resist an unproblematic incorporation into frameworks which are meant to explicate the reproduction and maintenance of other forms of social hierarchy such as those based on race and class ... This may be another way of

saying that the messiness of social reality has always exceeded the explanatory power of our conceptual frameworks and that this is all the more so in the area of gender. (1998: 145, 147)

In reflecting, on this basis, on my own positionality within the body of feminist scholarship and struggle which has been one of my fundamental inspirations throughout my research, I have tried consciously and scrupulously to maintain the perspective which Cynthia Enloe (2004) has succinctly articulated as that of 'curious feminism'. This is one which questions the workings of gendered meanings by paying attention to issues that are conventionally treated as either 'natural' or, failing that, dismissed as 'trivial' and without explanatory significance. In this sense, I have continually sought to ask 'where is the gendering power here?' and 'how is it working?', not as an end in itself, but in order to reveal the subtle, as much as the more blatant, forms that processes of gendering can take in one location. For as Enloe persuasively puts it:

> Seeing patriarchy, even misogyny, is not enough. In each instance, we need to know exactly how it works and whether, even if continuing, it has been contested. At a gross level of analysis the patriarchal outcomes may seem to be more of the same, but discovering what is producing them may come as a surprise. (2004: 18)

The revolution that wasn't

Discussions about Egypt focusing on issues around domination and resistance, and struggles against hegemony (economic, political and patriarchal) inevitably lead one to reflect on all that has happened in the years since I was a worker in Fashion Express. These are perhaps best summarised in the title of Hugh Roberts' 2013 *London Review of Books* review article, 'The revolution that wasn't'. I accordingly bring my work to a close by considering what pointers, if any, my ethnography can be seen as having provided (however unaware of them I may have been at the time) for the upheavals which came after.

The unseating of President Mubarak in early 2011, however momentous, is probably still too recent an event for any definitive analysis to be attempted of the various currents which ended his long rule. It does, however, seem to me that, even at this early stage, it is possible to identify three principal waves of resistance and protest, which waxed and waned with different profiles over prior decades, then eventually built to a head in early 2011, simultaneously crashing with sufficient pent up power to sweep away what had up until then seemed an immovable obstacle. The first of these is the wave of unauthorised labour protests which I charted in my introductory chapter (see Figure 1.1). Perhaps the most critical moment in the development of this waveform came when, in 2007, the striking workers of Mahalla turned their anger outward from the mismanagement of their own company and against the government's neoliberal policy in general, a progression picked up in subsequent labour disputes elsewhere. As Joel Beinin has put it, 'By challenging the economic policies of the Mubarak regime, they undermined its political legitimacy' (2012a: 101). The workers of Fashion Express, however, expressed no clear political opposition to the regime – and were, indeed, forthcoming in support of the proprietor's adoption as an election candidate for Mubarak's National Democratic Party. Yet with the benefit of hindsight I can now also see that the incessant labour incidents on the Fashion Express shop floor were taking place simultaneously with, and thus at the very least need to be understood within the wider perspective of, the larger-scale labour disputes which peaked in 2004, the year of my fieldwork.

The second of the three waves I identify consisted of what we might call 'progressives' – a loose coalition of mainly urban, predominantly middle-class leftists, liberals, and social and human rights activists. This wave had reached an apex with the huge *Kifaya* demonstrations organised from 2004 to try to prevent Mubarak seeking re-election in the presidential election due in 2005 (in which he went on to win 88 per cent of the vote). After that the movement rapidly declined in profile and participation. However, it gained a new lease of energy when its activists, along with those from the net-based '6th April' group, joined forces with the striking workers of Mahalla and the other companies involved in large-scale labour unrest (Achcar 2013; Gunning and Baron 2013; Abdelrahman 2014). The reinvigorated 'progressive' surge was given a further boost by the Tunisian Arab Spring revolution of 2010, releasing a new level of energy in anti-Mubarak pro-democracy protests coordinated and publicised through social media (Facebook, Twitter, blogs, websites) which so caught the imagination of Western onlookers and reporters (Campbell 2011; Idle and Nunn 2011). Although none of the workers in my ethnography can be construed as 'People of the Square' (Friedman 2014 – see chapter 1), I do not consider it far-fetched to see in their rejection of their tradition-constrained class backgrounds, and the building of their new chosen identities as participants in the wider, modern world of consumerist choice and fulfilment, some early harbingers of the ambitions and expectations for personal space and opportunity which found voice in the run-up to February 2011.

The third wave I identify involves the long-standing political opposition of the Muslim Brotherhood. Their fortunes had waxed and waned as they were alternately suppressed (frequently with great brutality) or tolerated with differing degrees of laxity as a useful safety valve for Islamic-based opposition to the regimes of Nasser, Sadat and then Mubarak. Through the 90s and early years of the twenty-first century the Brotherhood had been forced to maintain a relatively low political profile, and had focused instead on building its networks and support base in Egypt's disadvantaged communities (both rural and urban) through the provision of medical and social services – the only alternatives available in the face of the removal by the government of most of Nasser's 'moral economy' social benefits (Wickham 2013). Their political breakthrough came with the parliamentary elections of 2005, in which the Brotherhood won an unprecedented eighty-eight seats. Although they had always had an ambivalent – and if anything predominantly probusiness – stance towards labour movements and protests, the politically strengthened Brotherhood was active in mobilising its support base for large-scale participation in the mass demonstrations against Mubarak in early 2011. They thus formed the third of the three waves that built to a head and peaked in the momentous events of February 2011. And it was, of course, the Brotherhood's wave which best sustained momentum in the turmoil which followed, culminating in Mohamed Morsi's narrow victory in the presidential election of 2013 (the first ever to be held in Egypt on anything resembling a genuinely open and democratic basis).

Morsi and the Brotherhood's constructions of Islam and its values were far removed from the more flexible, open, and inclusive articulations of religion that I had encountered in Fashion Express. So it is in Morsi's subsequent failure to deliver on the promise of his presidency, his enforced removal by the military in 2013, and the 2014 election of the military General (soon to be Field Marshall) who dismissed him, Abd el Fatah el Sisi, as the latest in line of Egypt's military strongmen, that I believe the strongest resonances can be found with my 2003–2005 fieldwork, and in particular the takeover by, failure of, and eventual removal from Fashion Express of the 'new wave' firm which I have called BGB (see chapter 5).

Morsi had assumed office promising the immediate replacement of the top-down Mubarak *dawlat rigal il-a'mmal* (rule/regime of businessmen) with a new era of inclusive (of women, Coptic Christians, the young, and the disadvantaged) participatory democracy, driven by the needs and choices articulated by engaged and active citizens rather than the narrow interests of the self-serving *Mubarak biznis* elite of crony capitalists, military/security officials and government bureaucrats. BGB had likewise swept into Fashion Express promising to transform the economic trajectory and prospects of the factory by dismantling the highly personalised 'firm as family' networks and alliances which had confined workers to the role of passive beneficiaries, and instead empower them as individual stakeholders actively engaged and involved in building the firm's bright new future within the global economy.

And the aspirations of change articulated by the revolutionaries of 2011 find a parallel in the Fashion Express workforce's 2004 sense of the enhanced power of labour, and their pride in the products which showcased a new order to the wider world. As Zizi, a supervisor with long years of work experience, once described to me: 'Each finished garment is the sum of our skills, and what we stand for. It is our firm's reputation on the world stage – and we (workers) are the ones who made it'. Engagement and participation were the drivers which underpinned BGB's emphasis, right from the start, on staging *igtima'at* (workforce meetings), and their repeated use of buzzwords such as *wala' lil-masna* (institutional loyalty to the factory) in place of *ikhlaas* (individualised loyalty) to the *kebir*. Yet in the highly stage-managed *igitim'aat* it always remained the case that the workers were nevertheless being told (rather than consulted) about the reforms from which they were to benefit – a stance which resonates with Andrea Cornwall's analyses of the tendency (in her case within international aid and development projects) towards 'the use of invited participation to rubber stamp and provide legitimacy for pre-conceived interventions' (2000: 34). Yet as she has effectively shown, 'participation' by itself does not get anyone very far – the critical issues are *who* participates, in *what*, and *how*. As a result: 'Participation emerges as a more complex terrain of contestation that is shaped by multiple influences, understandings, and processes. These stretch beyond the bounds of "the project" ' (2001: 50). It is also clear that, in their rush to bring about radical change, BGB were riding rough-shod over multiple pre-existing forms of nuanced participation, both individual and collective, by the workforce in the tacit social contract of 'mutual co-optation' already in operation in the 'firm as family', bound together through *taraabut*, and their resulting sense of empowerment and commitment. Suppressing established practices such as the use of personalised recruitment channels, or the vigorous shop floor trade in goods and services, in the name of business-like 'efficiency and effectiveness' had the effect of cutting off the workers' access to the benefits and advantages which these forms of existing participation were bringing them, choking off their role as active agents in shaping their evolving aspirations, and constricting their crafting of a new collective identity as participants in a modern, prosperous and shared future. BGB's tighter control and absence of transparency was instead seen to be deeply distrustful of the workforce as actors in their own right, aimed at neutralising their agency, and instead objectifying them as 'stakeholders' in the new operational model being unveiled to them.

As a result the workers soon understood that the new regime firmly intended there to be strict limits to their purported 'participation' and 'engagement' in what was rapidly being seen as a sham project – one designed to further the interests of the new dominant group in using Fashion Express as a pilot for their expansionist plans to secure further contracts with other struggling firms, not only in the Zone but across Egypt as a whole. The position echoed that described in Rosen's work on Morocco, where:

> Corruption is, in the Arabic idiom, 'to eat' the good things that should be shared with others. In this sense corruption is seen as interfering with 'the game', as getting in the way of the formation of negotiated ties of interdependency by which society is held together and by which individuals form the associations in terms of which they are themselves known. (Rosen 2002: 13)

And it is in this failure to secure meaningful workforce participation and engagement that I believe the most illuminating parallel emerges on the national scale with the subsequent conduct of the new Morsi government. For all its inclusive, participatory rhetoric, it was not long before virtually all Egyptians except members and supporters of the Muslim Brotherhood came to see it as pursuing its own interests in the name of revolutionary change. The consequence was the coming together of previously disparate interest groups (including principally the 'progressives' to whom I have referred to earlier, the military/security apparatus, and even ostensibly apolitical citizens wearied by the inefficiency, chaos and insecurity of daily life under the new government), in massive street protests which were invoked by General el-Sisi as his mandate to overthrow the elected president in 2013.

In the national polity of Egypt, as within the walls of Fashion Express in 2004, the *fulul* (literally 'remnants, leftovers') of the *ancien regime* were waiting in the wings to take advantage of the failure of the supposed new broom administration. The blogger with whose words I opened my first chapter, Hossam al-Hamalawy, had continued his 2011 exhortation 'to take Tahrir to the factories' with the explicit caution that:

> In every single institution in this country there is a mini-Mubarak who needs to be overthrown. In every institution there are figures from the old … regime … These guys are the counter-revolution.

I cannot, however, conclude my ethnography without reiterating the extreme degree of difference, as I see it, between the re-emerging sources and structures of power in post-uprising Egypt, and those which operated in Fashion Express in 2005. The data recorded in my ethnography speak for themselves regarding Qasim Fahmy's more corporatist approach of nurturing a 'firm-as-family', and the workforce's 'mutual co-optation' response, all of which is more redolent of the early Nasserist 'moral economy' than the raw neoliberal authoritarianism of Mubarak and his eventual successor. Yet in the end, I am mindful that the ultimate effect of the return of Fashion Express's *ancien regime* was the complete closure of the factory. And it is in that outcome, with all its implications for the precarious balance between hope and expectation, that perhaps lies the final relevance of my ethnography for the future of the country. Time will tell.

Appendix

THE FASHION EXPRESS WORKFORCE

Obtaining basic data on workforce statistics proved to be no easy matter. All the computers, files and records of *edara* seemed inadequate to answering my basic questions about the numbers of workers the factory employed, and the age, gender and skills profiles these presented. After persistent enquiry, Workers Affairs eventually provided me with data for two months, September and October 2004, as shown in Figure A1. The variation from month to month was itself revealing – workforce stability was not a characteristic of Fashion Express.

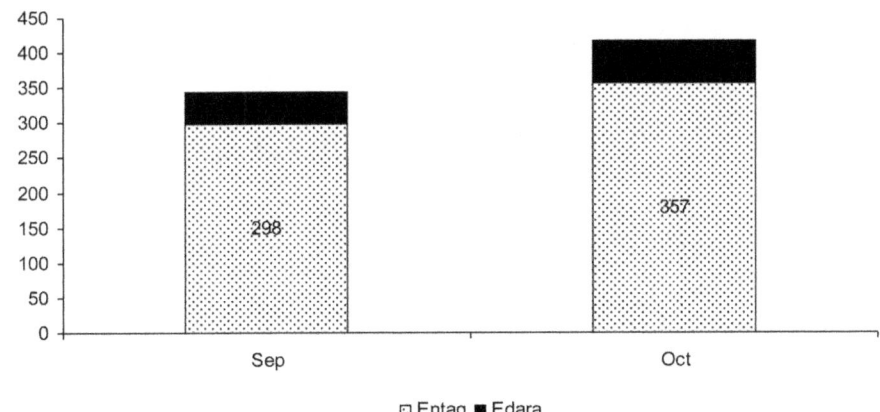

Figure A1 Monthly fluctuations in total workforce numbers

Originally the workforce had been almost entirely female (as described in chapter 1). The statistics provided to me by Workers Affairs demonstrated the extent to which the position had since changed, as shown in Figure A2 below, with men now accounting for over half the total workforce.

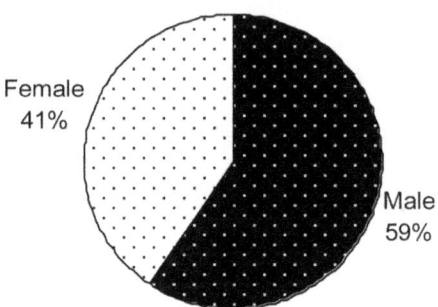

Figure A2 Gender mix of workforce

The statistics also revealed the age distribution of the workers, as shown in Figure A3.

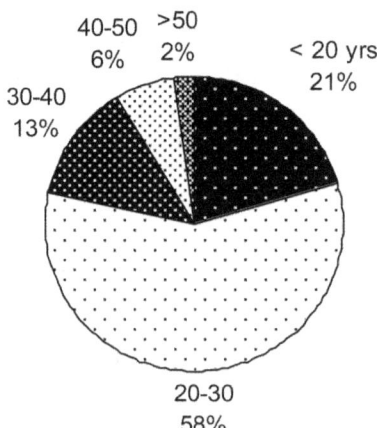

Figure A3 Age distribution of workforce

Evidently the workforce was (as summarised in chapter 1) overwhelmingly young, with a fifth still in their late teens, and less than a quarter over thirty years old. The numerical preponderance of men over women was most pronounced in the 20–30 age-group, as shown in Figure A4 below.

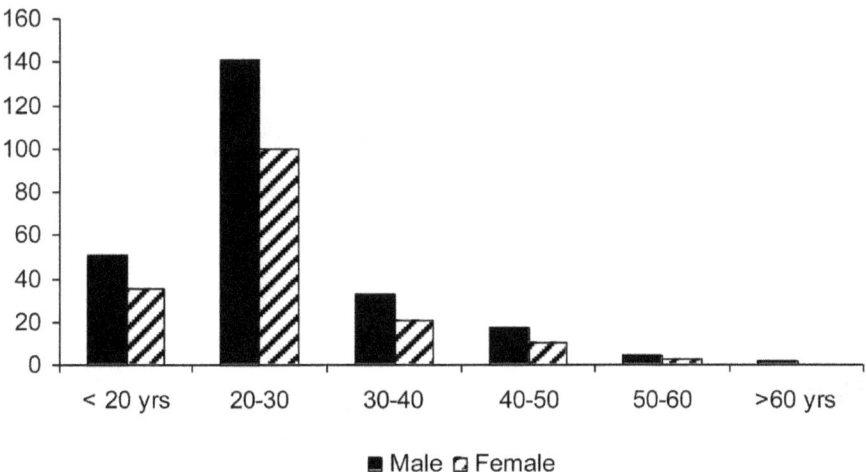

Figure A4 Number of workers by age and gender

The comparative age profiles of the male and female groups however presented a more uniform pattern, as shown in Figure A5, in which 78 per cent of men and 80 per cent of women can be seen to be under thirty years of age.

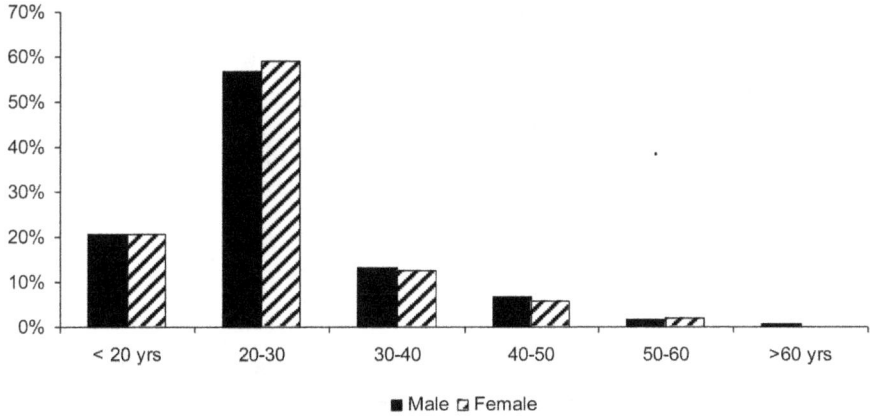

Figure A5 Proportion of males/female workers by age group

Data on education levels is charted in Figure A6. This shows a workforce of which only 26 per cent is unqualified, with 12 per cent having attended university.

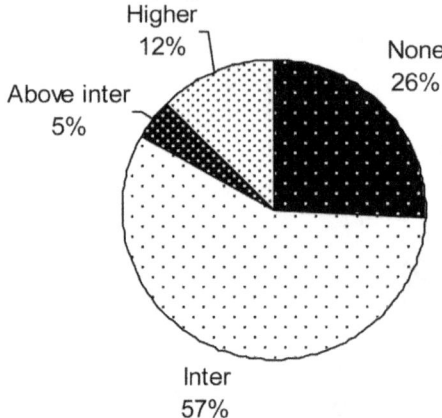

Figure A6 Education levels of workforce

Education levels do not vary significantly between male and female workers, as shown in Figure A7 below, though a higher proportion of male workers have graduated from university.

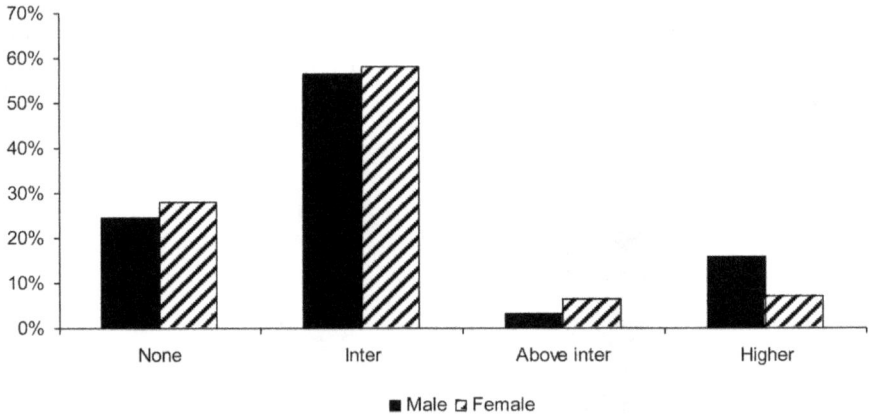

Figure A7 Proportion of male and female workers by educational level

I was unable to obtain figures for educational level by age as well as gender, but my clear impression from my time on the shop floor was that there were more young men with above-intermediate or university level qualification than there were young women.

Select Glossary

aflam	(lit: films) tales, gossip and rumours
'aila	family (in the sense of blood lineage), usually with a 'name'
akbar ras fil shirka	top head of the firm
'ansa	spinster
arayib	kin members of the family as a cohesive unit
'aris wi 'arusa	bride and groom
asrar	secrets
ayma	list of possessions which belong to the bride on marriage
bab il-ta'inat	(lit: door of appointments) official channel for recruitment
balad il-yufat	city of banners
bashmuhandis	engineer
beit	family (in the sense of household entity)
bint il-masna'	daughter of the factory
dukhla	celebration of the night when a marriage is consummated
edara	middle management
'egab	physical attraction, liking
entag	production area – the shop floor
entagiyya	production quotas
'esami	self-made person
'eyun il-shirka	'the eyes of the firm' – surveillance
fatha	the opening verse of the Koran
feduliyya	gossip, idle talk
gawasis (sing: *gusus*)	spies
gawda	quality control
gawdit khutut	in-line assembly quality control
gawda nihai	final quality control
gihaaz	purchases to furnish the future marital home

gid'an	chivalrous, macho
giza (pl: *gizaat*)	fine, financial penalty
hadith	reported sayings and doings of the Prophet
haqq	rights
haram	religiously proscribed, forbidden
hijab	woman's head-covering (headscarf style)
hub	love
ibn il-masna'	son of the factory
idrab	labour strike
ihtiram	respectability
ikhlaas	loyalty
ingizab	attraction (as in the chemistry of love)
il-sawhliyya	people of the coastal areas
infitah	Sadat's policy of economic 'opening'
irfa	spirit (in factory context, of a garment)
irsh	piaster (implying money issues)
ishraf	supervision
istithmar	export processing zone, investment zone
'iyal	(lit: children) the firm's workforce
katb il-kitab	marriage contract (post-engagement but pre-consummation)
kawader (sing: *kadr*)	(lit: cadres) foremen and supervisors
kayaan	structure and form in an entity (as in a family or firm)
kebir	the head of the household, the most powerful male authority
khat (pl: *khutut*)	assembly line
khumar	female veil covering the head and shoulders
khutuba	engagement celebration
kism (pl: *aksam*)	department, section
madinet il-tuggar	town of small shop-keepers
maghsala	laundry
Majlis il-Shura	Upper House of Parliament
makan muhtaram	respectable place
maktab (pl: *makatib*)	office with desk for paperwork
malabis gahaza	ready-made clothes
marakiz il-quwa	centres of power
mawakif (sing: *mawkif*)	situations
mehrem	relatives (consanguine or by marriage)
mu'aksat	flirtatious compliments
mu'aysha	joining in a common experience of life

multazim	(masculine) consistent with Islamic principles and practices
mulid	a feast, celebration
mushrifat	female supervisors
mushrefin	male supervisors
muwazaff	a civil servant
naksa	(lit: calamity) Egypt's crushing military defeat in 1967
nasab	ties of kinship claiming descent from a family tree
niqab	female dress covering the entire body and face (with eye slits)
qalaq	helplessness, anxiety, agitated behaviour, disturbance
qas	cutting
rab usrit il-masna'	head of the firm as family
rasid	reserves
rayis	President, leader, the boss, helmsman
rehlit kifah	a journey of bitter struggle
rizq	pre-ordained blessings
sahib il-'amal	the owner (and boss) of the business
sala (pl. *salat*)	garment assembly hall
sawabiq	ex-convicts, people with 'previous'
shabaab	youth
shabaab riwish	cool youth
shabka	the groom's gift to the bride of gold and jewellery
shahn (pl. *shuhna*)	a completed, packaged order ready for shipping
shakhsiyya	presence, personality (in the sense of 'having an attitude')
sharif (pl. *shurafa'*)	honourable
shilla	peer group determined by gender and age
shirka	firm or factory
sila	tie, relationship based on kin affiliation
silah	blade, weapon
solta	power
sura	verse or chapter of the Koran
ta'bi'a	packaging
tagnid	surplus labour sent to work elsewhere on the shop floor
taht	below, downstairs
takdiz	pile-ups (as in traffic jams, used for production)
takhassusat il-malabis il-gahza	specialisations of garment work

tangid	'fluffing the quilt' – a Port Saidian pre-nuptial ceremony
taraabut	togetherness, cohesiveness, solidarity
tarqim	marking (part of the cutting process)
tazbita (slang)	a date, a girlfriend
waraqit giza	official form used to deduct fines from wage packages
warsha	sweatshop (as in small-scale industrial outfits)
wazifa	civil service position
yesh-hetuh	Port Saidian slang: to discard, throw away, dismiss
zaffa	wedding procession
zulm	injustice

BIBLIOGRAPHY

Abdalla, A. 1985. *The Student Movement and National Politics in Egypt, 1923–1973.* London: Al Saqi Books.
―――― 2000. 'The Egyptian Generation of 1967: Reaction of the Young to National Defeat', in *Alienation or Integration of Arab Youth: Between Family, State and Street*, ed. R. Meijer, 71–81. London: Curzon Press.
Abdalla, N. 2012. 'Egypt's workers – from protest movement to organised labor', SWP Comments, October 2012 (http://www.swp-berlin.org/en/publications/swp-comments-en/swp-aktuelle-details/article/egypts_workers.html).
Abdel Aal, G. 2010. *I Want To Get Married!* Translated by N. Eltahawy. Austin, TX: Center for Middle Eastern Studies, University of Texas at Austin.
Abdel-Latif, A.M. 1993. 'The Nonprice Determinants of Export Success or Failure: The Egyptian Ready-made Garment Industry, 1975–1989', *World Development* 21(10): 1677–84.
'Abd al-Quddus, I. 1975. *Al-hazimah kana ismuha Fatimah: majmu'at qisas (And the defeat was named 'Fatimah': short stories).* Cairo: Dar al-Ma'arif.
Abdel Majeed, M. 2003. *Share'i masna' al-nasig (The street of the Textile Factory).* Cairo: Riwayat al-Hilal.
Abdelrahman, M. 2012. 'A Hierarchy of Struggles? The "Economic" and "Political" in Egypt's Revolution', *Review of African Political Economy* 29(134): 614–28.
―――― 2014. *Egypt's Long Revolution: Protest Movements and Uprisings.* London: Routledge.
Abisaab, M. 2006. 'Gendered Discourse and Labour among Lebanese Women', in *Geographies of Muslim Women. Gender, Religion, and Space*, ed. G. W. Falah and C. Nagel, 249–74. New York: The Guilford Press.
Aboud, M. 2004. *Al-ab'ad al-iktisadiyya lil mantiqa al-sinaiyya al-mu'ahala bayn masr wi al wilayyat al-mutahida al-amrikiyya (The Economic Dimensions to the Qualified Industrial Zones between Egypt and the United States of America).* EPZ unpublished manuscript, Port Said.
Aboul Wafa, A. 2005. 'Controversial Trade Agreement has Egyptians divided', *Middle East Times*, 15 January 2005.
Abu Hashish, S.A. and M.A. Peterson. 1999. 'Computer *Khatbas*: Databases and Marital Entrepreneurship in Modern Cairo' in *Anthropology Today* 15(6): 7–11.
Abu Lughod, L. 1988. 'Anthropology's Orient: The Boundaries of Theory on the Arab World', in *Theory, Politics and the Arab World. Critical Responses*, ed. H. Sharabi, 81–131. New York: Routledge.
―――― 2005. *Dramas of Nationhood: The Politics of Television in Egypt.* Chicago: University of Chicago Press.

Acar, F. and A. Ayata. 2002. 'Discipline, Success and Stability: The Reproduction of Gender and Class in Turkish Secondary Education', in *Fragments of Culture: The Everyday of Modern Turkey*, ed. D. Kandiyoti and A. Saktanber, 90–111. London: I.B. Tauris.

Achcar, G. 2013. *The People Want: A Radical Exploration of the Arab Uprising*, trans. G.M. Goshgarian. London: Saqi Books.

Acker, J. 1990. 'Hierarchies, Jobs, Bodies: A Theory of Gendered Organisations', *Gender and Society* 4: 139–58.

Adler, J. 1989. 'Travel as Performed Art', *American Journal of Sociology* 94: 1366–91.

Afkhami, M. and E. Friedl (eds). 1997. *Muslim Women and the Politics of Participation: Implementing the Beijing Platform*. Syracuse, NY: Syracuse University Press.

Afshar, H. (ed.) 1991. *Women, Development and Survival in the Third World*. London: Longman.

Agawaral, B. 1995. *A Field of One's Own: Gender and Land Rights in South Asia*. Cambridge: Cambridge University Press.

Ahmad, M.A. 1987. *Aris il-ahlam. Ayyam il-hub wi ayyam il-khutuba (The Groom of Dreams: Days of Love and Days of Engagement)*. Cairo: Nasr publications.

Akhavi, S. 1982. 'Egypt: Diffused Elite in a Bureaucratic Society', in *Political Elites in Arab North Africa: Morocco, Algeria, Tunisia, Libya, and Egypt*, I.W. Zartmaqn, M.A. Tessler, J.P. Entelis, R.A. Stone, R.A. Hinnebusch, S. Akavi, 223–65. New York: Longman.

Al Aswani, A. 2004. *The Yacoubian Building*. Trans, H. Davies. London: Fourth Estate.

Al-Batayneh, A.J.N. and Y. Al-Bakhit and Y.K.A. Al-Louizi, 2009. *Ten Years of Qualified Industrial Zones: Absolute Success or Relative Success*. Cairo: Royal Scientific Society and Friedrich Ebert Stiftung (http://library.fes.de/pdf-files/bueros/amman/06802.pdf).

Albrecht, H. 2013. *Raging Against the Machine: Political Opposition under Authoritarianism in Egypt*. Syracuse, NY: Syracuse University Press.

Alexander, C.E. 2002. '"One of the Boys": Black Masculinity and the Peer Group', in *Ethnographic Research: A Reader*, ed. S. Taylor, 91–113. London: Sage Publications, The Open University.

Alexander, M.J. and C.T. Mohanty (eds). 1997. *Feminist Genealogies, Colonial Legacies, Democratic Futures*. London: Routledge.

Al-Heeti, A.G. and C. Brock. 1997. 'Vocational Education and Development: Key Issues, with Special Reference to the Arab World', *International Journal of Educational Development* 17(4): 272–389.

Al-Nowaihi, M.M. 1999. 'Constructions of Masculinity in Two Egyptian Novels', in *Intimate Selving in Arab Families: Gender, Self and Identity*, ed. S. Joseph, 235–63. Syracuse, NY: Syracuse University Press.

Althusser, L. 1999. 'Ideology and Ideological State Apparatus (Notes towards an Investigation)', in *Visual Culture: The Reader*, ed. J. Evans and S. Hall, 317–23. London: Sage Publications.

Altorki, S. 1999. 'Patriarchy and Imperialism: Father–Son and British–Egyptian Relations in Najib Mahfuz's Trilogy', in *Intimate Selving in Arab Families: Gender, Self and Identity*, ed. S. Joseph, 214–35. Syracuse, NY: Syracuse University Press.

Ammar, H. 1954. *Growing up in an Egyptian Village: Silwa, Province of Aswan*. London: Routledge, Kegan and Paul.

Amin, M. 1974. *Sanah ula sijn (First Year in Prison)*. Cairo: Il-maktab il-misri il-hadith.

Amin, S. and N.H. Al-Bassusi. 2004. 'Wage Work and Marriage: Perspectives of Egyptian Working Women', Working Papers, Cairo: US Aid project.

——— 2004. 'Education, Wage Work and Marriage: Perspectives of Egyptian Working Women', *Journal of Marriage and Family* 66 (5) Special Issue: 1287–99.

Anderson, B. 1983. *Imagined Communities*. London: Verso.

Anderson, L. 1997. 'State Policy and Islamist Radicalism', in *Political Islam: Revolution, Radicalism, or Reform?* ed. J.L. Esposito, 17–32. Boulder, CO: Lynne Rienner.

Anker, R. and M. Anker. 1995. 'Measuring Female Labour Force with Emphasis on Egypt', in *Gender and Development in the Arab World: Women's Economic Participation: Patterns and Policies*, ed. N.F. Khoury and V.M. Moghadam, 148–76. London: Zed Books.

Appadurai, A. 1986. 'Introduction: Commodities and the Politics of Value', in *The Social Life of Things: Commodities in Cultural Perspective*, ed. A. Appadurai, 3–63. Cambridge: Cambridge University Press.

——— 1996. *Modernity at Large: Cultural Dimensions of Globalization*. Minneapolis: University of Minnesota Press.

Armbrust, W. 1996. *Mass Culture and Modernism in Egypt*. Cambridge: Cambridge University Press.

——— 1998. 'Sexuality and Film: Transgressing Patriarchy: Sex and Marriage in Egyptian Film', *Middle East Report* 206: 29–31.

——— 2000. 'Farid Shauqi: Tough Guy, Family Man, Cinema Star', in *Imagined Masculinities: Male Identity and Culture in the Modern Middle East*, ed. M. Ghoussoub and E. Sinclair-Webb, 199–226. London: Saqi Books.

——— 2007. 'Celebratory Ramadan and Hyperpiety in a Mexican Standoff: Counterhegemony in the Crossfire', in *Counterhegemony in the Colony and Postcolony*, ed. J. Chalcroft and Y. Noorani, 155–76. Basingstoke: Palgrave Macmillan.

'Ashur, E. 1972. *Sina'at wa tigarat il-aqmisha fi Misr – il-guz' il-awil (Textile manufacturing and commerce in Egypt – Part I)*. Cairo: Dar al-Ma'arif.

——— 1973. *Sina'at wa tigarat il-akmesha fi Misr – il-guz' il-thani (Textile manufacturing and commerce in Egypt– Part II)* Cairo: Dar al-Ma'arif.

Aslop, R., A. Fitzsimons and K. Lennon. 2002. *Theorizing Gender*. Cambridge: Polity.

Assaad, R.1996. 'Structural Adjustment and Labor Market Reform in Egypt', in *Economic Liberalization and Privatisation in Socialist Arab Countries: Algeria, Egypt, Syria and Yemen as Examples*, ed. H. Hopfinger, 91–119. Gotha: Justus Perthes Verlag.

——— 2003. 'Gender and Employment: Egypt in Comparative Perspective', in *Women and Globalization in the Arab Middle East*, ed. E. Abdella Doumato and M. Pripstein Posusney, 119–42. Boulder, CO: Lynne Rienner.

——— (ed). 2002. *The Egyptian Labor Market in an Era of Reform. An Economic Research Forum Edition*. Cairo: The American University in Cairo Press.

Aspden, R. 2016. *Generation Revolution: on the Front Line Between Tradition and Change in the Middle East*. London: Harvill Secker.

Assaad, R. and G. Barsoum. 2009. 'Rising Expectations and Diminishing Opportunities for Egypt's Young', in *Generation in Waiting. The Unfulfilled Promise of Young People in the Middle East*, ed. N. Dhillon and T.M. Youssef, 67–96. Washington, DC: Brookings Institution Press.

Ayubi, N. N. 1980. *Bureaucracy and Politics in Contemporary Egypt*. London: Ithaca Press.

——— 1995. *Overstating the Arab State: Politics and Society in the Middle East*. London: I.B. Tauris.

——— 1996. 'Perestroika at Last?! The Egyptian Political Economy from "Opening" to "Restructuring"', in *Economic Liberalisation and Privatisation in Socialist Arab Countries: Algeria, Egypt, Syria and Yemen as Examples*, ed. H. Hopfinger, 51–65. Gotha: Justus Perthes Verlag.

Azim, A.N. 1989. 'Egypt: The Origins and Development of a Neo-colonial State', in *Power and Stability in the Middle East*, ed. B. Berberoglu, 1–14. London: Zed Books.

Azruyil, F. al-Zahra. 2001. *Al-bagha'a aw il-gasad il-mustabah (Prostitution – or the Permitted Body)*. Morocco: Afrikia al-Sharq.
Azzam, M. 1996. 'Egypt: Islamists and the State Under Mubarak', in *Islamic Fundamentalism*, ed. A.S. Sidahmed and A. Ehteshami, 109–22. Boulder, CO: Westview.
Baker, R.W. 1978. *Egypt's Uncertain Revolution Under Nasser and Sadat*. Cambridge, MA: Harvard University Press.
Balfour-Paul, J. 1998. *Indigo*. London: British Museum Press.
Barakat, H. 1985. 'The Arab Family and the Challenge of Social Transformation', in *Women and the Family in the Middle East: New Voices of Change*, ed. E. Warnock Fernea, 27–48. Austin: University of Texas Press.
——— 1993. *The Arab World: Society, Culture and State*. Berkeley: University of California Press.
Baran, B. and S. Teegarden. 1987. 'Women's Labor in the Office of the Future: A Case Study of the Insurance Industry', in *Women, Households and the Economy*, ed. L. Beneria and C.R. Stimpson. Brunswick, NJ: Rutgers University Press.
Barbour, K.M. 1972. *The Growth, Location and Structure of Industry in Egypt*, Praeger Special Studies in International Economics and Development. New York; London: Praeger.
Baron, B. 2005. *Egypt as a Woman. Nationalism, Gender, and Politics*. Berkeley: University of California Press.
Barsoum, G.F. 2002. *The Employment Crisis of Female Graduates in Egypt. An Ethnographic Account*. Cairo Papers in Social Science, 25(3). Cairo: The American University Press.
Bayat, A. 1997a. *Street Politics. Poor People's Movements in Iran*. New York: Columbia University Press.
——— 1997b. 'Cairo's Poor: Dilemmas of Survival and Solidarity', *Middle East Report* 202: 2–12.
——— 2002. 'Activism and Social Development in the Middle East', *International Journal of Middle East Studies* 34: 1–28.
——— 2011. 'Reclaiming Youthfulness', in *Arab Youth. Social Mobilization in Times of Risk*, ed. S. Khalaf and R.S. Khalaf, 47–67. London: Saqi Books.
——— (ed.). 2013. *Post-Islamism: The Changing Faces of Political Islam*. Oxford: Oxford University Press.
Beinin, J. 1989. 'Labour, Capital, and the State in Nasserist Egypt, 1952–1961', *International Journal of Middle East Studies* 21: 71–90.
——— 2001. *Workers and Peasants in the Modern Middle East*. Cambridge: Cambridge University Press.
——— 2005. 'Popular Social Movements and the Future of Egyptian Politics', *Middle East Report Online* (Middle East Research and Information Project), 10 March (http://www.merip.org/mero/mero031005).
——— 2006. 'Egyptian Textile Workers in the Transition to a Neo-Liberal Order', *Historical Perspectives* 1(3): 16–18.
——— 2007. 'The Militancy of Mahalla al-Kubra', *Middle East Report Online* (Middle East Research and Information Project), 29 September (http://www.merip.org/mero/mero092907).
——— 2009. 'Workers' Protests in Egypt: Neo-liberalism and Class Struggle in the 21st Century', *Social Movement Studies* 8(4): 449–54.
——— 2010. *Justice for all: The Struggle for Worker Rights in Egypt: A Report by the Solidarity Centre*. New York: Solidarity Center (http://libcom.org/files/Egypt-workers-rights.pdf).

―――― 2012a. 'The Working Class and the Popular Movement in Egypt', in *The Journey to Tahrir: Revolution, Protest and Social Change in Egypt*, ed. J. Sowers and C. Toensing, 92–106. London: Verso.

―――― 2012b. *The Rise of Egypt's Workers*, The Carnegie Papers, June 2012. Washington DC: Carnegie Endowment for International Peace (http://carnegieendowment.org/files/egypt_labor.pdf).

―――― 2012c. 'Egyptian Workers and January 25th: S Social Movement in Historical Context', *Social Research* 79(2): 323–48.

Beinin J. and M. Duboc, 2015. 'The Egyptian Workers' Movement Before and After the 2011 Popular Uprising', *Socialist Register* Vol. 51: Transforming Classes (www.socialistregister.com)

Beinin, J. and H. el-Hamalawy. 2007a. 'Strikes in Egypt Spread from Center of Gravity', *Middle East Report Online* (Middle East Research and Information Project), 9 May (http://www.merip.org/mero/mero050907).

―――― 2007b. 'Egyptian Textile Workers Confront the New Economic Order', *Middle East Report Online* (Middle East Research and Information Project), 25 March (http://www.merip.org/mero/mero032507).

Benin, J. and Z. Lockman. 1987. *Workers on the Nile: Nationalism, Communism, Islam and the Egyptian Working Class, 1882–1954*. Princeton, NJ: Princeton University Press.

Berger, J. 1972. *Ways of Seeing*. London: Harmondsworth: BBC and Penguin Books.

Berik, G. and N. Cagatay. 1994. 'What has Export-Oriented Manufacturing Meant for Turkish Women?' In *Mortgaging Women's Lives: Feminist Critiques of Structural Adjustment*, ed. P. Sparr, 78–95. London: Zed Books.

Berneria, L. 2003. *Gender, Development and Globalization: Economics as if All People Mattered*. New York: Routledge.

Beynon, H. and R. Hudson. 1993. 'Place and Space in Contemporary Europe: Some Lessons and Reflections', *Antipode* 25(3): 177–190.

Bianchi, R. 1985. 'Businessmen's Association in Egypt and Turkey', *Annals of the American Academy of Political and Social Science* 482: 147–59.

―――― 1989. *Unruly Corporatism: Associational Life in Twentieth-Century Egypt*. Oxford: Oxford University Press.

Bibars, I. 2001. *Victims and Heroines: Women, Welfare and the Egyptian State*. London: Zed Books.

Bill, J.A. and R. Springborg. 1994. *Politics in the Middle East*, fourth edition. New York: Harper Collins.

Binder, L. 1978. *In A Moment of Enthusiasm: Political Power and the Second Stratum in Egypt*. Chicago: Chicago University Press.

Birks, J.S. and C.A. Sinclair. 1982. 'Employment and Development in Six Poor Arab States: Syria, Jordan, Sudan, South Yemen, Egypt and North Yemen', *International Journal of Middle East Studies* 14(1): 35–51.

Bolbol, A. 1999. 'Arab Trade and Free Trade: A Preliminary Analysis', *International Journal of Middle East Studies* 31(1): 3–17.

Bocchialini, C. and A. El Gazwy. 2012. *The Factory: A Glimpse into Life inside Egypt's Mahalla Textile Factory – A Cauldron of Revolt where Workers Inspired an Uprising*. Aljazeera TV documentary (http://www.aljazeera.com/programmes/revolutionthrougharabeyes/2012/01/201213013135991429.html)

Bolle, M.J., A.B. Prados and J.M. Sharp. 2006. 'Qualifying Industrial Zones in Jordan and Egypt'. Washington DC: Congressional Research Service, for the Library of Congress.

Borneman, J. 2009. 'Fieldwork Experience, Collaboration, and Interlocution: The "Metaphysics of Presence" in Encounters with the Syrian *Mukhabarat*', in *Being There: The Fieldwork Encounter and the Making of Truth*, ed. J. Borneman and A. Hammoudi, 237–59. Berkeley: University of California Press.

—— (ed.). 2005. *Death of the Father: An Anthropology of the End in Political Authority*. New York: Berghahn Books.

Boserup, E. 1989. *Woman's Role in Economic Development*. London: EarthScan.

Botman, S. 1999. *Engendering Citizenship in Egypt: The History and Society of the Modern Middle East*. New York: Columbia University Press.

Bourdieu, P. 1977. *Outline of a Theory of Practice*. Cambridge: Cambridge University Press.

Bowles, J. 2000. 'The Empire Has No Clothes: Raising Real Estate Prices and Declining City Support Threatens the Future of New York's Apparel Industry'. New York: Center for an Urban Future.

Brandes, S. 1981. 'Like Wounded Stags: Male Sexual Ideology in an Andalusian Town', in *Sexual Meanings: The Cultural Construction of Gender and Sexuality*, ed. S.B. Ortner and H. Whitehead, 216–39. Cambridge: Cambridge University Press.

Braverman, H. 1974. *Labor and Monopoly Capital: The Degradation of Work in the Twentieth Century*. New York: Monthly Review Press.

Breman, J. 1996. *Footloose Labour: Working in India's Internal Economy*. Cambridge: Cambridge University Press.

Brownlee, J. and J. Stacher. 2011. 'Change of Leader, Continuity of System: Nascent Liberalization in Post-Mubarak Egypt', *APSA Comparative Democratisation Newsletter* 9 (2): 1, 4–9.

Brumberg, D. 1995. 'Authoritarian Legacies and Reform Strategies in the Arab World', in *Political Liberalization and Democratization in the Arab World*, volume 1: *Theoretical Perspectives*, ed. H.J. Barkey. New York: St. Martin's Press.

Bryman, A. 2001. *Social Research Methods*. Oxford: Oxford University Press.

Buchanan, D., D. Boddy and J. McCalman. 1988. 'Getting in, Getting on, Getting out and Getting back', in *Doing Research in Organizations*, ed. A. Bryman, 53–67. London: Routledge.

Bulford, B. 1999. 'Sweat Is Good,' *The New Yorker* 75: 130–39.

Burawoy, M. 1979. *Manufacturing Consent: Changes in the Labour Process under Monopoly Capitalism*. Chicago: University of Chicago Press.

—— 1985. *The Politics of Production*. London: Verso.

—— 2000. 'Introduction', in *Global Ethnography: Forces, Connections and Imaginations in a Postmodern World*, 1–40. Berkeley: University of California Press.

Burgmann, M. 1980. 'Revolution and Machismo', in *Woman, Class and History*, ed. E. Windschuttle. Australia: Fontana.

Bush, R. 1999. *Economic Crisis and the Politics of Reform in Egypt*. Boulder, CO: Westview Press.

Butler, J. 1993. *Bodies that Matter: On the Discursive Limits of 'Sex'*. New York: Routledge.

—— 1997. *Excitable Speech: A Politics of the Performative*. New York: Routledge.

—— 2007. *Gender Trouble: Feminism and the Subversion of Identity*, second edition. New York: Routledge.

Cairoli, M.L. 1999. 'Garment Factory Workers in the City of Fez', *Middle East Journal* 53 (1): 28–43.

Campell, D.G. 2011. *Egypt Unshackled: Using Social Media to @#:) the System: How 140 Characters can Remove a Dictator in 18 Days*. Camarthenshire U.K.: Cambria Books.

Certeau, M. de. 1984. *The Practice of Everyday Life*. Berkeley: University of California Press.

Chakrabarty, D. 1989. *Rethinking Working-Class History: Bengal 1890–1940*. Princeton, NJ: Princeton University Press.
—— 1994. 'Labour History and the Politics of Theory: An Indian Angle on the Middle East', in *Workers and the Working Classes in the Middle East: Struggles, Histories, Historiographies*, ed. Z. Lockman, 321–35. Albany: State University of New York Press.
Chakravarti, L.Z. 2010. 'Denim: Production and Consumption on the Globalized Shop-Floor'. London: University College London, Global Denim Project (http://www.ucl.ac.uk/global-denim-project/lzc).
—— 2011. 'Material Worlds: Denim on the Globalized Shop-Floor', *Textile: The Journal of Cloth and Culture* 9(1): 62–75.
—— forthcoming. 'Veiled Prospects: Hijab Politics on the globalized Shop Floor'. Unpublished manuscript.
Chalcraft, J. 2007. 'Counterhegemonic Effects: Weighing, Measuring, Petitions and Bureaucracy in Nineteenth-century Egypt', in *Counterhegemony in the Colony and Postcolony*, ed. J. Chalcraft and Y. Noorani, 179–204. Basingstoke: Palgrave Macmillan.
—— 2008. 'Popular Protest, the Market and the State in Nineteenth and Early Twentieth-century Egypt', in *Subalterns and Social Protest: History from Below in the Middle East and North Africa*, ed. S. Cronin, 69–91. London: Routledge.
—— 2009. *The Invisible Cage: Syrian Migrant Workers in Lebanon*. Stanford, CA: Stanford University Press.
—— 2012. 'Horizontalism in the Egyptian Revolutionary Process'. *Middle East Report* 262 (Spring), pp. 6–11.
Chang, L.T. 2008. *Factory Girls: Voices from the Heart of Modern China*. London: Picador.
Chhachhi, A. and R. Pittin. 1996. 'Introduction', in *Confronting State, Capital and Patriarchy: Women Organizing in the Process of Industrialization*, ed. A. Chhachhi and R. Pittin, 1–31. Basingstoke: Palgrave MacMillan.
Chilsom, N., N. Kabeer, S. Mitter and S. Howard. 1986. *Linked by the Same Thread: The Multi-Fibre Arrangement and the Labour Movement*. London: Tower Hamlets International Solidarity and Tower Hamlets Trade Union Council.
Collins, J.L. 2003. *Threads: Gender, Labor, and Power in the Global Apparel Industry*. Chicago: University of Chicago Press.
Collombier, V. 2007. 'The Internal Stakes of the 2005 Elections: The Struggle to Influence in Egypt's National Democratic Party', *Middle East Journal* 61(1): 95–111.
Connell, R.W. 2002. *Gender*. Cambridge: Polity.
Cornwall, A. 2000. *Beneficiary, Consumer, Citizen: Perspectives on Participation for Poverty Reduction*. Stockholm: SIDA Studies.
Cornwall, A. and G. John. 2001. 'Bridging the Gap: Citizenship, Participation and Accountability', World Bank PLA Notes 40, February 2001 (http://siteresources.worldbank.org/INTPCENG/1143372-1116506145151/20511060/plan_04007.pdf).
Cornwall, A., E. Harrison and A. Whitehead (eds). 2007. *Feminisms: Contradictions, Contestations and Challenges in Development*. London: Zed Books.
Coyle, A. 1984. *Redundant Women*. London: Women's Press.
Davis, S.S. 1993. 'Changing Gender Relations in a Moroccan Town', in *Arab Women: Old Boundaries, New Frontiers*, ed. J.E. Tucker, 208–23. Bloomington: Indiana University Press.
Dauh, A. 1973. *Kifah al-shabaab al-jami'i ala al-Qanah* (The Resistance of University Youth in the Canal Zone). Kuwait: Dar al-Qalam.

Dedeoglu, S. 2004. 'Working for Family: The Role of Women's Informal Labour in the Survival of Family-Owned Garment Ateliers in Istanbul, Turkey'. Working Paper No. 281, May 2004. Southampton: Southampton University.

Dedeoglu, S. 2005. 'Hidden Hands – Invisible Workers: Women's Work in Istanbul's Garment Industry', PhD dissertation. London: School of Oriental and African Studies.

Deeb, L. 2006. *An Enchanted Modern: Gender and Public Piety in Shi'i Lebanon*. Princeton, NJ: Princeton University Press.

Donnell, A. (ed.). 1999. 'The Veil: Postcolonialism and the Politics of Dress', Special Issue, *Interventions: International Journal of Postcolonial Studies* 1(4): 489–499.

Douglas, M. and B. Isherwood. 1979. *The World of Goods: Towards an Anthropology of Consumption*. London: Routledge.

Douglas, A. and F. Multi-Douglas. 1994. *Arab Comic Strips: Politics of an Emerging Mass Culture*. Bloomington: Indiana University Press.

Doumato, E.A. and M. Pripstein Posusney (eds). 2002. *Women and Globalization in the Arab Middle East: Gender, Economy, and Society*. Boulder, CO: Lynne Rienner Publishers.

Dreyfus, H.L. and P. Rabinow. 1983. *Michel Foucault: Beyond Structuralism and Hermenuetics*. New York: Harvester Wheatsheaf.

Duboc, Marie. 2011. 'Egyptian Leftist Intellectual Activism from the Margins: Overcoming the Mobilization/Demobilization Dichotomy', in J. Beinin and F. Vairel (eds.), *Social Movements, Mobilization, and Contestation in the Middle East and North Africa*, 61–82. Stanford, CA: Stanford University Press.

Dunne, B. 1998. 'Power and Sexuality in the Middle East', *Middle East Report* 206: 8–11, 37.

Early, E.A. 1993a. 'Baladi Egyptian Businesswomen', in *Arab Women: Old Boundaries, New Frontiers*, ed. J.E. Tucker, 84–102. Bloomington: Indiana University Press.

―――― 1993b. *Baladi Women of Cairo: Playing with an Egg and a Stone*. Boulder, CO: Lynne Rienner Publishers.

Ecevit, Y. 1991. 'Shop-Floor Control: The Ideological Construction of Turkish Women Factory Workers', in *Working Women: International Perspectives on Labour and Gender Ideology*, ed. N. Redclift and M.T. Sinclair, 56–78. London: Routledge.

Edwards, R. 1979. *Contested Terrain: The Transformation of the Workplace in the Twentieth Century*. New York: Basic Books.

Eickelman, D.F. 1996. *Muslim Politics*. Princeton, NJ: Princeton University Press.

Elchayar, J. 2005. *Markets of Dispossession: NGOs, Economic Development, and the State in Cairo*. Durham, NC: Duke University Press.

Elgeziri, M. 2012. 'Marginalisation and Self-Marginalization: Commercial Education and Its Graduates', in *Marginality and Exclusion in Egypt*, ed. R. Bush and H. Ayeb, 191–219. London: Zed Books.

El-Kholy, H. 2002. *Defiance and Compliance: Negotiating Gender in Low-Income Cairo*. New York: Berghahn Books.

El-Ghonemy, M.R. 1998. *Affluence and Poverty in the Middle East*. London: Routledge.

El-Khasab, Karim. 'As Political as it Gets'. *Al-Ahram* weekly, 4-10 October 2007, Issue No. 865.

El-Kogali, S. and N.H. Al-Bassussi. 2001. *Youth Livelihood Opportunities in Egypt*. New York: Population Council.

El-Ghonemy, M. Riad. 1998. *Affluence and Poverty in the Middle East*. London and New York: Routledge.

El-Kilsh, K. 1997. *Arba'un Amman 'ala il-udwan Bur Said: Ayyam il-muqawama (Forty Years after the hostilities against Port Said: days of resistance)*. Cairo: Kitab al-ahali.

El Mahdi, R. 2012. 'Against Marginalization: Workers, Youth and Class in the 25 January Revolution', in *Marginality and Exclusion in Egypt*, ed. R. Bush and H. Ayeb, 133–48. London: Zed Books.

El Masri, Hoda. 2008. *Gil shahadat bila maharat (The generation with certificates but no skills)*. Cairo: *Roz El Youssef*. Special Edition on education. 8 March 2008, 64–66.

El-Messiri, S. 1978. *Ibn al-Balad: A Concept of Egyptian Identity (Social, Economic and Political Studies of the Middle East)*. Leiden: Brill.

Elson, D. 1992. 'From Survival Strategies to Transformation Strategies: Women's Needs and Structural Adjustment', in *Unequal Burden: Economic Crisis, Persistent Poverty and Women's Work*, ed. L. Berneria and S. Feldman, 26–49. Boulder, CO: Westview Press.

——— 1996. 'Appraising Recent Developments in the World Market for Nimble Fingers', in *Confronting State, Capital and Patriarchy: Women Organizing in the Process of Industrialization*, ed. A. Chhachhi and R. Pittin, 35–55. Basingstoke: Palgrave Macmillan.

Elson, D. and R. Pearson. 1981. 'The Subordination of Women and the Internationalization of Factory Production', in *Of Marriage and the Market: Women's Subordination in International Perspective*, ed. K. Young, C. Wolkowitz and R. McCullagh, 144–66. London: CSE Books.

Enloe, C. 1989. 'Blue Jeans and Bankers', in *Bananas, Beaches and Bases: Making Feminist Sense of International Politics*, 151–76. London: Pandora.

——— 2004. *The Curious Feminist: Searching for Women in a New Age of Empire*. Berkeley: University of California Press.

Esbenshade, J. 2004. *Monitoring Sweatshops: Workers, Consumers, and the Global Apparel Industry*. Philadelphia: Temple University Press.

Essam El-Din, G. 2000. A New Boost for Privatization. (http://www.ahram.org.eg/weekly/2000/511/ec5.htm)

Farnie, D.A. 1969. *East and West of Suez: The Suez Canal in History, 1854–1956*. Oxford: Clarendon Press.

Fawzi, S. and A. Galal (eds). 2002. *Globalization and Firm Competitiveness in the Middle East and North Africa*. Washington DC: The World Bank.

Feldman, S. 1992. 'Crisis, Islam, and Gender in Bangladesh: The Social Construction of a Female Labor Force', in *Unequal Burden: Economic Crises, Persistent Poverty, and Women's Work*, ed. L. Beneria and S. Feldman, 105–30. Boulder, CO: Westview Press.

Fernandes, L. 1997a. *Producing Workers: The Politics of Gender, Class, and Culture in the Calcutta Jute Mills*. Philadelphia: University of Pennsylvania Press.

——— 1997b. 'Beyond Public Spaces and Private Spheres: Gender, Family, and Working-Class Politics in India', *Feminist Studies* 23(3): 525–47.

Fernandez-Kelly, M.P. 1983. *For We Are Sold, I and My People: Women and Industry in Mexico's Frontier*. Albany: State University of New York Press.

——— 1997. 'Maquiladoras: The View From Inside', in *The Women, Gender and Development Reader*, ed. N. Visvanathan, L. Fuggan, L. Nisonoff and N. Wiegersma, 203–15. London: Zed Books.

Foucault, M. 1978. *The History of Sexuality, Volume 1: An Introduction*, trans. R. Hurley. Harmondsworth: Penguin.

——— 1979. *Discipline and Punish: The Birth of the Prison*. New York: Vintage Books.

——— 1982. 'The Subject and Power', in *Michel Foucault: Beyond Structuralism and Hermeneutics*, ed. H. Dreyfus and P. Rabinow, 208–26. Chicago: University of Chicago Press.

——— 1997a. 'Of Other Spaces: Utopias and Heterotopias', in *Rethinking Architecture: A Reader in Cultural Theory*, ed. N. Leach, 350–56. London: Routledge.

——— 1997b. 'Panopticism (extract)', in *Rethinking Architecture: A Reader in Cultural Theory*, ed. N. Leach, 356–67. London: Routledge.
Freeman, C. 2002. 'Designing Women: Corporate Discipline and Barbados's Off-shore Pink-collar Sector', in *The Anthropology of Globalization: A Reader*, ed. J.X. Inda and R. Rosaldo, 83–99. London: Blackwell.
Friedman, Thomas L. 2014. The Square People, Part 1. *(http://www.nytimes.com/2014/05/14/opinion/friedman-the-square-people-part-1.html)*
——— The Square People, Part 2. (http://www.nytimes.com/2014/05/18/opinion/sunday/friedman-the-square-people-part-2.html).
Frith, M. 2005. 'The Ethical Revolution Sweeping through the World's Sweatshops', *The Independent*, 16 April 2005.
Frobel, F., J. Heinrichs and O. Kreye. 1980. *The New International Division of Labor: Structural Unemployment in Industrialized Countries and Industrialization in Developing Countries*. Cambridge: Cambridge University Press.
Fuad, S.1980. *Laylit il-qabd ala Fatma (The Night Fatma was Arrested)*. Cairo: Kitab el-yom.
Fuentes, A. and B. Ehrenreich. 1983. *Women in the Global Factory*. Boston: South End Press.
Geertz, C. 1993. 'From the Native's Point of View: On the Nature of Anthropological Understanding', in *Local Knowledge: Further Essays in Interpretive Anthropology*, 55–70. New York: Basic Books.
Gell, A. 1998. *Art and Agency: An Anthropological Theory*. Oxford: Clarendon Press.
Gellner, N. and E. Hirsch (eds). 2001. *Inside Organizations: Anthropologists at Work*. Oxford: Berg.
Gereffi, G. and M. Korzeniewicz (eds). 1994. 'The Organisation of Buyer-Driven Global Commodity Chains', in *Commodity Chains and Global Capitalism*, 95–122. Westport, CT: Praeger.
Gerges, F. (ed.) 2014. *The New Middle East. Protest and Revolution in the Arab World*. Cambridge: Cambridge University Press.
Ghannam, F. 1997. 'Re-imagining the Global: Relocation and Local Identities in Cairo', in *Space, Culture and Power: New Identities in Globalizing Cities*, ed. A. Oncu and P. Weyland, 119–39. London: Zed Books.
——— 2002. *Remaking the Modern. Space, Relocation, and the Politics of Identity in a Global Cairo*. Berkeley: University of California Press.
——— 2006. 'Keeping Him Connected: Globalization and the Production of Locality in Urban Egypt', in *Cairo Cosmopolitan: Politics, Culture, and Urban Space in the New Globalized Middle East*, ed. D. Singerman and P. Amar, 251–66. Cairo: The American University in Cairo Press.
——— 2013. *Live and Die Like a Man: Gender Dynamics in Urban Egypt*. Stanford, CA: Stanford University Press.
Ghosh, A. 2008. *The Imam and the Indian*. New Delhi: Penguin Books.
Giddens, A. 2002. *Runaway World: How Globalization is Reshaping our Lives*. London: Profile Books.
Gilsenan, M. 1996. *Lords of the Lebanese Marches: Violence and Narrative in an Arab Society*. London: I.B. Tauris.
Glaister, D. 2006. 'Nice and Sleazy', *The Guardian*, 1 October 2006.
Glass, C. 2006. *The Tribes Triumphant: Return Journey to the Middle East*. London: Harper Perennial.
Goldberg, E.J. 1986. *Tinker, Tailor and Textile Worker: Class and Politics in Egypt, 1930–1952*. Berkeley: University of California Press.

——— 1994. 'Worker's Voice and Labor Productivity in Egypt', in *Workers and Working Classes in the Middle East*, ed. Z. Lockman, 111–33. Albany: State University of New York Press.

Gole, N. 1996. *The Forbidden Modern: Civilization and Veiling*. Ann Arbor: University of Michigan Press.

Goldstein, D. 2013. *Laughter out of Place: Race, Class, Violence and Sexuality in a Rio Shantytown*. Berkeley: University of California Press.

Green, N.L. 1996. 'Women and Immigrants in Sweatshop: Categories of Labour Segmentation Revisited', *Comparative Studies in Society and History* 38(3): 411–33.

——— 2002. 'Paris: A Historical View', in *Unravelling the Rag Trade: Immigrant Entrepreneurship in Seven World Cities*, ed. J. Rath. Oxford: Berg.

Guha, R. and J.P. Parry (eds). 1999. *Institutions and Inequalities: Essays in Honour of Andre Beteille*. New Delhi: Oxford University Press.

Gunning, J. and I.Z. Baron. 2013. *Why Occupy a Square? People, Protests and Movements in the Egyptian Revolution*. London: Hurst and Company.

Hakimian, H. and Z. Moshaver (eds). 2001. *The State and Global Change: The Political Economy of Transition in the Middle East and North Africa*. Richmond: Curzon.

Halberstam, J. 1998. *Female Masculinity*. Durham, NC: Duke University Press.

Halasu, M. and R. Salam. 2007. *The Secret Life of Syrian Lingerie: Intimacy and Design*. San Francisco: Chronicle Books.

Hale, A. and J. Wills (eds). 2005. *Threads of Labour: Garment Industry Supply Chains from the Workers' Perspective*. London: Wiley-Blackwell.

Hammam, M. 1980. 'Women and Industrial Work in Egypt: the *Chubra El-Kheima* Case,' *Arab Studies Quarterly* 2 (1980): 50–69.

Hammoudi, A. 1997. *Master and Disciple: The Cultural Foundations of Moroccan Authoritarianism*. Chicago: University of Chicago Press.

Hammersley, M. and P. Atkinson. 1983. *Ethnography: Principles in Practice*, second edition. London: Routledge.

Hamrush, A. 1970. *Asrar Ma'rakit Bur Said* (Secrets of the Battle of Port Said). (Pamphlet with no publisher)

Hamzawi, A. 2003. 'The Local Deconstruction of Global Events, News and Discourses: Case Studies from Egypt', in *Politics from Above, Politics from Below: The Middle East in the Age of Economic Reform*, ed. E. Kienle, 266–84. London: Saqi.

Handoussa, H. and G. Potter (eds). 1991. *Employment and Structural Adjustment: Egypt in the 1990s*. Cairo: The American University in Cairo Press.

Handoussa, H. and Z. Tzannatos (eds). 2002. *Employment Creation and Social Protection in the Middle East and North Africa: An Economic Research Forum Edition*. Cairo: The American University in Cairo Press.

Haney, L. and L. Pollard. 2003. 'Introduction: In a Family Way: Theorizing State and Familial Relations', in *Families of a New World: Gender, Politics, and State Development in a Global Context*, ed. L. Haney and L. Pollard, 1–14. New York: Routledge.

Hanieh, A. 2013. *Lineages of Revolt. Issues of Contemporary Capitalism in the Middle East*. Chicago: Haymarket Books.

Hansen, K.Y. 2000. *Salaula: The World of Second-hand Clothing and Zambia*. Chicago: University of Chicago Press.

Haraway, Donna. 1991. 'Situated Knowledges: The Science Question in Feminism and the Privilege of Partial Perspective', In *Simians, Cyborgs, and Women. The Reinvention of Nature*. London: Free Association Books.

Hardaker, David. 2006. 'Amr Khaled: Islam's Billy Graham'. London: *The Independent*, 4 January 2006. (http://www.independent.co.uk/news/world/middle-east/amr-khaled-islams-billy-graham-6112733.html).
Harik, I. and D.J. Sullivan (eds). 1992. *Privatization and Liberalization in the Middle East*. Bloomington: Indiana University Press.
Harders, C. 2003. 'The Informal Social Pact: The State and the Urban Poor in Cairo', in *Politics from Above, Politics from Below: The Middle East in the Age of Economic Reform*, ed. E. Kienle, 266–84. London: Saqi.
Harris, C. 2006. *Muslim Youth: Tensions and Transitions in Tajikistan*. Boulder, CO: Westview Press.
Harvey, D. 1989. *The Condition of Post-modernity*. Cambridge: Blackwell.
Hasso, F. 2010. *Consuming Desires: Family Crisis and the State in the Middle East*. Stanford, CA: Stanford University Press.
Hatem, M. 1994. 'Privatisation and the Demise of State Feminism in Egypt', in *Mortgaging Women's Lives: Feminist Critiques of Structural Adjustment*, ed. P. Sparr, 40–60. London: Zed Books.
——— 1998. 'Secularist and Islamist Discourses on Modernity in Egypt and the Evolution of the Postcolonial Nation-State', in *Islam, Gender and Social Change*, ed. Y.Y. Haddad and J.L. Esposito, 85–99. New York: Oxford University Press.
——— 1999. 'Modernization, the State and the Family in Middle East Women's Studies', in *A Social History of Women and Gender in the Modern Middle East*, ed. M.L. Meriwether and J.E. Tucker, 63–87. Boulder, CO: Westview Press.
Hatem, M.A.K. 1981. *Misr hata 'amm 2000. Sina'at il-ghazl wil nasig wil malabis il-gahza (Egypt until the Year 2000: The Textile and Ready Made Garment Industry)*. Cairo: Silsilat dirasat al-majalis al-kawmiyya al-mutakhasisa.
Hazbun, W. 2008. *Beaches, Ruins, Resorts: The Politics of Tourism in the Arab World*. Minneapolis: University of Minnesota Press.
Hearn, J. and W. Parkin. 1995. *'Sex at Work': The Power and Paradox of Organization Sexuality*. New York: St. Martin's Press.
Heikal, M. 1977. *Qissat al-Suwis: akhir al-ma'arik fi 'asr al-'amaliqah (The Story of Suez: The Last Battle of the Age of Giants)*. Beirut: Maktabal Unkal Sam.
——— 1983. *Autumn of Fury: The Assassination of Sadat*. London: Andre Deutsch.
——— 1986. *Cutting the Lion's Tail: Suez through Egyptian Eyes*. London: Andre Deutsch.
Hennessy, R. 1993. *Materialist Feminism and the Politics of Discourse*. New York: Routledge.
Henry, C.M. and R. Springborg. 2001. *Globalization and the Politics of Development in the Middle East*. Cambridge: Cambridge University Press.
Herrera, L. 2001. 'Downveiling: Gender and the Contest over Culture in Cairo', *Middle East Report* 219: 16–19.
——— 2006. 'Islamization and Education: Between Politics, Profit, and Pluralism', in *Cultures of Arab Schooling: Critical Ethnographies from Egypt*, ed. L. Herrera and C.A. Torres, 21–52. Albany: State University of New York Press.
——— 2014. *Wired Citizenship: Youth Learning and Activism in the Middle East*. London: Routledge.
Hewamanne, S. 2008. *Stitching Identities in a Free Trade Zone: Gender and Politics in Sri Lanka*. Philadelphia: University of Pennsylvania Press.
Hewedy, A. 1989. 'Nasser and the Crisis of 1956', in *Suez 1956: The Crisis and its Consequences*, ed. W.M.R. Louis and R. Owen, 161–72. Oxford: Clarendon Press.
Hey, V. 1997. *The Company She Keeps: An Ethnography of Girls' Friendship*. Buckingham: Open University Press.

Hijab, N. 2001. 'Women and Work in the Arab World', in *Women and Power in the Middle East*, ed. S. Joseph and S. Slyomovics, 41–51. Philadelphia: University of Pennsylvania Press.

Hill, E. 2003. 'Norms and Distribution Processes in Egypt's New Regime of Capitalist Accumulation', in *Politics from Above, Politics from Below: The Middle East in the Age of Economic Reform*, ed. E. Kienle, 77–98. London: Saqi Books.

Hinnebusch, R.A. 1990. 'Formation of the Contemporary Egyptian State from Nasser and Sadat to Mubarak', in *Political Economy of Contemporary Egypt*, ed. I.M. Oweiss, 188–209. Washington DC: Center of Contemporary Arab Studies, George Town University.

Hirst, D. and I. Beeson. 1981. *Sadat*. London: Faber and Faber.

Hobsbawn, E. 1983. *The Invention of Tradition*. Cambridge: Cambridge University Press.

Hoekman, B. and A. Galal (eds) 1997. *Regional Partners in Global Markets: Limits and Possibilities of the Euro-Med agreements*. Cairo: The Egyptian Center for Economic Studies.

Hopfinger, H. (ed.). 1996. *Economic Liberalization and Privatization in Socialist Arab Countries: Algeria, Egypt, Syria and Yemen as Examples*. Gotha: Justus Perthes Verlag.

Hoodfar, H. 1997a. *Between Marriage and the Market: Intimate Politics and Survival in Cairo*. Berkeley: University of California Press.

——— 1997b. 'Return to the Veil: Personal Strategy and Public Participation in Egypt', in *The Women, Gender and Development Reader*, ed. N. Nisvanathan, L. Duggan, L. Nisonoff and N. Wiegersma, 320–25. London: Zed Books.

Hopkins, N.S. 1988. 'Class and the State in Rural Arab Communities', in *Beyond Coercion: The Durability of the Arab State (Volume III)*, ed. A. Dawisha and I.W. Zartman, 239–59. London: Croom Helm.

——— (ed.). 2001. *The New Arab Family*. Cairo Papers in Social Science, Volume 24, Numbers 1/2. Cairo: The American University in Cairo Press.

Hourani, A. 1983. *Arabic Thought in the Liberal Age, 1798–1939*. Cambridge: Cambridge University Press.

Hsiung, P. C. 1996. *Living Rooms as Factories: Class, Gender and the Satellite Factory System in Taiwan*. Philadelphia, PA: Temple University Press.

Husain, E. 2007. *The Islamist*. London: Penguin Books.

Husayn, A. 1982. *Al-Iqtisad al-Misri min al-istiglal ila al-taba'iyah 1974–1979 (The Egyptian Economy from Independence to Dependence 1974–1979)*. Cairo: Dar al-Mustaqbal al-Arabi.

Ibrahim, B.L. 1985. 'Family Strategies: A Perspective on Women's Entry to the Labour Force in Egypt', in *Arab Society: Social Science Perspectives*, ed. S. Ibrahim and N. Hopkins, 257–68. Cairo: The American University in Cairo Press.

Ibrahim, B. and H. Wassef. 2000. 'Caught between Two Worlds: Youth in the Egyptian Hinterland', in *Alienation or Integration of Arab Youth: Between Family, State and Street*, ed. R. Meijer, 161–85. London: Curzon.

Ibrahim, B., B.S. Mensch, S.M. Lee and O. El-Gibal. 2003. 'Gender-role Attitudes among Egyptian Adolescents', *Studies in Family Planning* 34(1): 8–18.

Idle, N. and A. Nunns (eds). 2011. *Tweets from Tahrir*. OR Books (http://www.orbooks.com).

Ikram, K. 1980. *Egypt: Economic Management in a Period of Transition*. Baltimore, MD: John Hopkins University Press.

——— 2005. *The Egyptian Economy, 1952–2000: Performance, Policies, and Issues*. London: Routledge.

Ismail, S. 2006. *Political Life in Cairo's New Quarters: Encountering the Everyday State*. Minneapolis: University of Minnesota Press.

Issat, I. 1997. *Al-shakhsiyya al-misriyyah fi al-amthal al-sha'biyyah (Egyptian identity through popular expressions and sayings)*. Cairo: Dar al-Hilal.

Jackson, S. 1999. *Heterosexuality in Question*. London: Sage Publications.
Jin, J. 2007. 'There's the Rub. What's it like working in the kind of clothing factory that has come under fire this week.' London: *The Guardian Weekend*, July 21 2007 (http://www.theguardian.com/theguardian/2007/jul/21/weekend7.weekend2).
Joekes, S. 1985. 'Working for Lipstick? Male and Female Labor in the Clothing Industry in Morocco', in *Women, Work and Ideology in the Third World*, ed. H. Asfar, 183–213. London: Tavistock.
——— 1987. *Women in the World Economy*. Oxford: Oxford University Press.
Joseph, S. 1999a. 'Introduction: Theories and Dynamics of Gender, Self, and Identity in Arab Families', in *Intimate Selving in Arab Families: Gender, Self, and Identity*, ed. S. Joseph, 1–21. Syracuse, NY: Syracuse University Press.
——— 1999b. 'Searching for Baba', in *Intimate Selving in Arab Families: Gender, Self and Identity*, ed. S. Joseph, 53–77. Syracuse, NY: Syracuse University Press.
Joseph, S. and S. Slyomovics (eds). 2001. *Women and Power in the Middle East*. Philadelphia: University of Pennsylvania Press.
Kabeer, N. 2000. *The Power to Choose: Bangladeshi Women and Labour Market Decisions in London and Dhaka*. London: Verso.
Kandiyoti, D. 1988. 'Bargaining with Patriarchy', *Gender and Society* 2(3): 274–90.
——— 1991. *Women, Islam and the State*. Philadelphia, PA: Temple University Press.
——— 1996. 'Contemporary Feminist Scholarship and Middle East Studies', in *Gendering the Middle East: Emerging Perspectives*, ed. D. Kandiyoti, 1–28. London: I.B. Tauris.
——— 1997a. 'Beyond Beijing: Obstacles and Prospects for the Middle East', in *Muslim Women and the Politics of Participation: Implementing the Beijing Platform*, ed. M. Afkhami and E. Friedl, 3–10. Syracuse, NY: Syracuse University Press.
——— 1997b. 'Gendering the Modern: On Missing Dimensions in the Study of Turkish Modernity', in *Rethinking Modernity and National Identity in Turkey*, ed. S. Bozdogan and R. Kasaba, 113–32. Seattle: University of Washington Press.
——— 1998. 'Gender, Power and Contestation: Rethinking "Bargaining with Patriarchy"', in *Feminist Visions of Development: Gender Analysis and Policy*, ed. C. Jackson and R. Pearson, 135–51. London: Routledge.
——— 2001. 'The Politics of Gender and the Conundrums of Citizenship', in *Women and Power in the Middle East*, ed. S. Joseph and S. Slyomovics, 52–60. Philadelphia: University of Pennsylvania Press.
——— 2002. 'Introduction: Reading the Fragments', in *Fragments of Culture: The Everyday of Modern Turkey*, ed. D. Kandiyoti and A. Saktanber, 1–21. London: I.B. Tauris.
Karabell, Z. 2003. *Parting the Desert: The Creation of the Suez Canal*. London: John Murray.
Kassab, S. 1997. 'On Two Conceptions of Globalization: The Debate around the Reconstruction of Beirut', in *Space, Culture and Power: New Identities in Globalizing Cities*, ed. A. Oncu and P. Weyland, 42–55. London: Zed Books.
Kassem, M. 2004. *Egyptian politics: The Dynamics of Authoritarian Rule*. Boulder, CO: Lynne Rienner Publishers.
Keddie, N.R. 2007. *Women in the Middle East: Past and Present*. Princeton, NJ: Princeton University Press.
Kemp, T. 1983. *Industrialization in the Non-Western World*, second edition. London: Longman.
Kerr, M.H. 1965. 'Egypt', in *Education and Political Development*, ed. J.S. Coleman, 169–95. Princeton, NJ: Princeton University Press.
Kienle, E. 2001. *A Grand Delusion: Democracy and Economic Reform in Egypt*. London: I.B. Tauris.

——— 2003. 'Domesticating Economic Liberalisation: Controlled Market-building in Contemporary Egypt', in *Politics from Above, Politics from Below: The Middle East in the Age of Economic Reform* ed. E. Kienle, 144–56. London: Saqi Books.
King, A. (ed.) 1991. *Culture, Globalization and the World-System: Contemporary Conditions for the Representation of Identity.* Minneapolis: University of Minnesota
Khalaf, S. and J. Gagnon. 2006. *Sexuality in the Arab World.* London: Saqi Books.
Khalidi, R. 1988. 'Social Transformation and Political Power in the Radical Arab States', in *Beyond Coercion: The Durability of the Arab State (Volume III)*, ed. A. Dawisha and I.W. Zartman, 203–19. London: Croom Hill.
Kheir-El-Din, H. and H. El-Sayed. 1997. 'Potential Impact of a Free Trade Agreement with the EU on Egypt's Textile Industry', in *Regional Partners in Global Markets: Limits and Possibilities of the Euro-Med Agreements*, ed. A. Galal and B. Hoekman, 205–37. Cairo: The Egyptian Center for Economic Studies.
Kholoussy, H. 2010a. *For Better, For Worse: The Marriage Crisis That Made Modern Egypt.* Stanford, CA: Stanford University Press.
——— 2010b. 'The Fiction (and Non-Fiction) of Egypt's Marriage Crisis'. Middle East Research and Information Project. (http://www.merip.org/mero/interventions/fiction-non-fiction-egypts-marriage-crisis).
Klein, N. 1999. *No Logo: Taking Aim at the Brand Bullies.* New York: Picador.
Kondo, D. 1990. *Crafting Selves: Power, Gender, and Discourses of Identity in a Japanese Workplace.* Chicago: Chicago University Press.
Korczysnski, M. 2014. *Songs of the Factory. Pop Music, Culture, and Resistance.* Ithaca and London: Cornell University Press.
Kuchler, S. and D. Miller. 2005. *Clothing as Material Culture.* Oxford: Berg Publishers.
Kung, L. 1983. *Factory Women in Taiwan.* Ann Arbor: University of Michigan Press.
Kyle, K. 1991. *Suez: Britain's End of Empire in the Middle East.* London: I.B. Tauris.
Leacock, E. and H.I. Safa. 1986. *Women's Work: Development and the Division of Labor by Gender.* New York: Bergin & Garvey.
Lee, C.K. 1993. 'Familial Hegemony: Gender and Production Politics on Hong Kong's Electronic Shop Floors', *Gender and Society* 7(4): 529–47.
——— 1995. 'Engendering the Worlds of Labor: Women Workers, Labor Markets, and Production Politics in the South China Economic Miracle', *American Sociological Review* 60: 378–97.
——— 1997. 'Factory Regimes of Chinese Capitalism: Different Cultural Logics in Labor Control', in *Ungrounded Empires: The Cultural Politics of Modern Chinese Transnational*, ed. A. Ong and D.M. Nonini, 115–43. New York: Routledge.
Lefebvre, H. 1997. 'The Production of Space (Extracts)', in *Rethinking Anthropology: A Reader in Cultural Theory*, ed. N. Leach, 139–47. London: Routledge.
Lenczowski, G. 1975. 'Some Reflections on the Study of Elites', in *Political Elites in the Middle East*, ed. G. Lenczowski, 1–15. Washington, DC: American Enterprise Institute for Public Policy Research.
Lévi-Strauss, C. 1967. *The Scope of Anthropology.* London: Jonathan Cape.
Lim, L. 1983. 'Capitalism, Imperialism, and Patriarchy: The Dilemma of Third-World Women Workers in Multinational Factories', in *Women, Men and the International Division of Labor*, ed. J. Nash and M.P. Fernandez-Kelly, 70–91. Albany: State University of New York Press.
——— 1990. 'Women's Work in Export Factories: The Politics of a Cause', in *Persistent Inequalities*, ed. I. Tinker, 101–19. Oxford: Oxford University Press.

Lindisfarne, N. and A. Cornwall (eds). 1994. *Dislocating Masculinity: Comparative Ethnographies*. London: Routledge.

Lippert, J. 1977. 'Sexuality as Consumption', in *For Men Against Sexism*, ed. J. Snodgrass, 207–13. Albion, CA: Times Change Press.

Lockman, Z. 1994a. 'Imagining the Working Class: Culture, Nationalism, and Class Formation in Egypt, 1899–1914. *Poetics Today* 15(2): 157–90.

——— 1994b. '"Worker" and "Working Class" in pre-1914 Egypt: A Rereading', in *Workers and Working Classes in the Middle East: Struggles, Histories, Historiographies*, 71–109. Albany: State University of New York Press.

——— (ed.). 1994c. *Workers and Working Classes in the Middle East: Struggles, Histories, Historiographies*. Albany: State University of New York Press.

Loe, M. 1996. 'Working for Men – At the Intersection of Power, Gender, and Sexuality', *Sociological Inquiry* 66(4): 399–421.

Lukose, R.A. 2009. *Liberalisation's Children: Gender, Youth, and Consumer Citizenship in Globalizing India*. Durham: Duke University Press.

Mabro, R. 1974. *The Egyptian Economy 1952–1972*. Oxford: Clarendon Press.

Mabro, R. and S. Radwan. 1976. *The Industrialization of Egypt 1939–1973: Policy and Performance*. Oxford: Clarendon Press.

McDermott, A. 1988. *Egypt From Nasser to Mubarak: A Flawed Revolution*. London: Croom Helm.

Macleod, A.E. 1991. *Accommodating Protest: Working Women, the New Veiling, and Change in Cairo*. Cairo: The American University in Cairo Press.

——— 1996. 'Transforming Women's Identity: The Intersection of Household and Gender in Cairo', in *Development, Change and Gender in Cairo*, ed. D. Singerman and H. Hoodfar, 27–50. Indianapolis: Indiana University Press.

McNay, L. 1994. *Foucault: A Critical Introduction*. New York: Continuum.

Mahmood, S. 2005. *Politics of Piety: The Islamic Revival and the Feminist Subject*. Princeton, NJ: Princeton University Press.

Makinen, J. 2014. 'China Entrepreneur Turns to Film to Take on Social Issues. *Los Angeles Times*, 3 September 2014 (http://www.latimes.com/world/la-fg-c1-china-factory-boss-20140903-story.html).

Marei, S. 1980a. *Awraq Siyasiyya: min al-qaria ila il-islah (Political Papers: From Village to Reform)*. Cairo: Al-Maktab al-Misri al-Hadith.

——— 1980b. *Awraq Siyasiyya: min azmit maris ila il-naksa (Political Papers: From the March Reforms to the 'Naksa' (Calamity))*. Cairo: Al-Maktab al Misri al-Hadith.

Massey, D. 1993. 'Power, Geometry, and a Progressive Sense of Place', in *Mapping the Futures: Local cultures, Global change*, eds. J. Bird, B. Curtis, T.Putnam, G. Robertson and L. Tickner, 59–69. London: Routledge.

——— 1995. *Spatial Divisions of Labor: Social Structures and the Geography of Production*, second edition. New York: Routledge.

Mather, C. 1985. 'Rather than Make Trouble, It's Better Just to Leave', in *Women and Ideology in the Third World*, ed. H. Afshar, 153–77. London: Macmillan.

Meijer, R. 2000. 'Introduction', in *Alienation or Integration of Arab Youth: Between Family, State and Street*, ed. R. Meijer, 1–14. London: Curzon.

Mena Development Report. 2004. *Gender and Development in the Middle East and North Africa: Women in Public Space*. Washington, DC: The World Bank.

Mensch, B.S, B. Ibrahim, S. Lee and O. El-Gibali. 2006. 'Gender-role Attitudes among Egyptian Adolescents', *Studies in Family Planning* 34(1): 8–18.

Meriwether, M.L. and J.E. Tucker. 1999. 'Introduction', in *A Social History of Women and Gender in the Modern Middle East*, ed. M.L. Meriwether and J.E. Tucker, 1–24. Boulder, CO: Westview Press.

Mernissi, F. 1984. *Al-hubb fi hadaratuna al-Islamiyyah (Love in Islamic Civilisation)*. Beirut: al-Dar al-'Alamiyah lil-Tiba'ah wa-al Nashr wa al-Tawzi'.

―――― 1987. *Beyond the Veil: Male–Female Dynamics in Modern Muslim Society*, revised edition. Bloomington: Indiana University Press.

Messiri, N.N. al-. 1987. 'Family Relationships in a 'Harah' in Cairo', in *Arab Society: Social Sciences Perspectives*, ed. N.S. Hopkins and S.E. Ibrahim, 212–22. Cairo: The American University in Cairo Press.

Mies, M. 1986. *Patriarchy and Accumulation on a World Scale: Women in the International Division of Labour*. London: Zed Books.

Miller, D. (ed). 1995. *Worlds Apart: Modernity through the Prism of the Local*. London: Routledge.

Mills, M.B. 1999. *Thai Women in the Global Labour Force: Consuming Desires, Contested Bodies*. New Jersey: Rutgers University Press.

―――― 2001. 'Auditing for the Chorus Line: Gender, Rural Youth, and the Consumption of Modernity in Thailand', in *Gendered Modernities: Ethnographic Perspectives*, ed. D.L. Hodgson, 27–53. New York: Palgrave MacMillan US.

Mills, S. 2003. *Michel Foucault*. London: Routledge.

Mitchell, T. 1991. 'America's Egypt: Discourse of the Development Industry', *Middle East Report* 169: 18–34, 36. Washington, DC: MERIP Middle East Research and Information Project (http://www.merip.org/mer/mer169/americas-egypt).

―――― 1999. 'Dreamland: The Neoliberalism of Your Desires', *Middle East Report* 210: 28–33. Washington, DC: MERIP Middle East Research and Information Project (http://www.merip.org/mer/mer210/dreamland-neoliberalism-your-desires).

―――― 2002. *Rule of Experts: Egypt, Techno-politics, Modernity*. Berkeley: University of California Press.

Modelski, S. 2000. *Port Said Revisited*. Washington DC: Faros.

Moghadam, V.M. 1995a. *Manufacturing and Women in the Middle East and North Africa: A Case Study of the Textiles and Garments Industry*. Durham: University of Durham, Centre for Middle Eastern and Islamic Studies.

―――― 1995b. 'The Political Economy of Female Employment in the Arab Region', in *Gender and Development in the Arab World: Women's Economic Participation: Patterns and Policies*, ed. N.F. Khoury and V.M. Moghadam, 6–34. London: Zed Books.

―――― 2004. 'Population Growth, Urbanisation, and the Challenges of Unemployment', in *Understanding the Contemporary Middle East*, second edition, ed. D.J. Gerner, 239–61. Boulder, CO: Lynne Rienner Publishers.

Moghadam, F.E. 1994. 'Commoditization of Sexuality and Female Labor Participation in Islam: Implications for Iran, 1960–1990', in *In the Eye of the Storm: Women in post-revolutionary Iran*, ed. M. Afkhami and E. Friedl, 80–97. Syracuse, NY: Syracuse University Press.

Mohammadi, A. (ed). 2002. *Islam Encountering Globalization*. London: Routledge.

Mohanty, C.T. 1988. ' Under Western Eyes: Feminist Scholarship and Colonial Discourses', *Feminist Review* 30: 61–87.

―――― 1991. 'Cartographies of Struggle: Third World Women and the Politics of Feminism', in *Third World Women and the Politics of Feminism*, ed. C.T. Mohanty, A. Russo, and L. Torres, 1–50. Bloomington: Indiana University Press.

——— 2003. *Feminism without Borders: Decolonizing Theory, Practicing Solidarity*. Durham, NC: Duke University Press.
Morawetz, D. 1981. *Why the Emperor's New Clothes Are Not Made in Colombia*. New York: The World Bank / Oxford University Press.
Moss, D. 2005. 'Introduction: The Ethnography of Policy and Practice', in *Cultivating Development: An Ethnography of Aid Policy and Practice*, 1–20. London: Pluto Press.
Myntti, C. 2015. *Paris along the Nile – Architecture in Cairo from the Belle Epoque*. Cairo: The American University in Cairo Press.
Naguib, K. 2006. 'The Production and Reproduction of Culture in Egyptian Schools', in *Cultures of Arab Schooling: Critical Ethnographies from Egypt*, ed. L. Herrera and C.A. Torres, 53–81. Albany: State University of New York Press.
Najm, Z. 1987. *Bur Said: tarikhuha wa-tatawwuruha, mundhu nash-atiha 1859 hatta am 1882 (Port Said: its History and Development from its Foundation in 1859 to 1882)*. Cairo: al-Hay'ah al-Misriyah al-Ammah lil-Kitab.
Najmabadi, A. 2005. *Women with Mustaches and Men Without Beards: Gender and Sexual Anxieties of Iranian Modernity*. Berkeley: University of California Press.
Nash, J. and M.P. Fernandez-Kelly. 1983. *Women, Men and the International Division of Labor*. Albany: State University of New York Press.
Nashat, G. and J.E. Tucker. 1999. *Women in the Middle East and North Africa: Restoring Women to History*. Bloomington: Indiana University press.
Nasif, A. 1979. *Ayyam al-intisar: al-Jabhah al-Muttahidah lil-Muqawamah al-Sha'biyyah (The Days of Victory: The United Front of Civilian Resistance)*. Cairo: Dar el-Thakafah al-Jadidah.
Nassar, H. 2003. 'Egypt: Structural Adjustment and Women's Employment', in *Women and Globalization in the Arab Middle East: Gender, Economy and Society*, ed. E.A. Doumato and M.P. Posusney, 95–118. Boulder, CO: Lynne Rienner Publishers.
Nasser, G.A. 1959. *Khutab el-rayyis Gamal Abdel Nasser fi ihtifalat el-eid el-sabe' lil-thawra (Speeches of President Gamal Abdel Nasser on the 7th anniversary of the Revolution)*. Cairo: Dar il-Kahira lil teba'a.
Navaro-Yasin, Y. 1999. 'The Historical Construction of Local Culture: Gender and Identity in the Politics of Secularism versus Islam', in *Istanbul: Between the Global and Local* ed. C. Keyder, 59–75. Lanham, MD: Rowman and Littlefield.
——— 2002. 'The Market for Identities: Secularism, Islamism, Commodities', in *Fragments of Culture: The Everyday of Modern Turkey*, ed. D. Kandiyoti and A. Saktanber, 221–53. London: I.B. Tauris.
Nelson, C. and V. Olesen. 1977. 'Veil of Illusion: A Critique of the Concept of Equality in Western Thought', *Catalyst* 10(11): 8–36.
Noorani, Y. 2007. 'Redefnining Resistance: Counterhegemony, the Repressive Hypothesis and the Case of Arabic Modernism', in *Counterhegemony in the Colony and Postcolony*, ed. J. Chalcraft and Y. Noorani, 75–100. Basingstoke: Palgrave Macmillan.
Okely, J. 1996. *Own or Other Culture*. London: Routledge.
Ong, A. 1990. 'Japanese Factories, Malay Workers: Class and Sexual Metaphors in West Malaysia', in *Power and Difference: Gender in Island South East Asia*, ed. J.M. Atkinson and S. Errington, 385–422. Stanford, CA: Stanford University Press.
——— 1991. 'The Gender and Labor Politics of Postmodernity', *Annual Review of Anthropology* 20: 279–309.
Osella, F. and C. Osella. 2010. 'Muslim Entrepreneurs in Public Life between India and the Gulf: Making Good and Doing Good', in *Islam, Politics, Anthropology*, ed. F. Osella and B. Soares, 194–213. Oxford: Wiley-Blackwell / Royal Anthropological Institute.

Ossman, S. 2002. 'Fashioning Casablanca in the Beauty Salon', in *Everyday Life in the Muslim Middle East*, second edition, ed. D.L. Bowen and E.A. Early, 180–89. Bloomington: Indiana University Press.
Ortner, S. 1989. 'Gender Hegemonies', *Cultural Critique* 14: 35–80.
Ortner, S. and H.Whitehead. 1981. *Sexual Meanings: The Cultural Construction of Gender and Sexuality*. Cambridge: Cambridge University Press.
Oweiss, I.M. 1990. 'Egypt's Economy: The Pressing Issues', in *The Political Economy of Contemporary Egypt*, ed. I.M. Oweiss. Washington DC: Center for Contemporary Arab Studies, Georgetown University.
Owen, R. 1992. *State, Power and Politics in the Making of the Modern Middle East*, second edition. London: Routledge.
——— 1994. 'Socio-Economic Change and Political Mobilisation: The Case of Egypt', in *Democracy without Democrats: The Renewal of Politics in the Muslim World*, ed. G. Salame, 183–99. London: I.B. Tauris.
——— 1997. 'Modernizing Projects in Middle Eastern Perspectives', in *Rethinking Modernity and National Identity in Turkey*, ed S. Bozdogan and R. Kasaba, 245–51. Seattle: University of Washington Press.
——— 2003. 'What Constitutes Business Rationality in Egypt at the end of the Twentieth Century: A Political Economy Approach', in *Politics from Above, Politics from Below: The Middle East in the Age of Economic Reform*, ed. E. Kienle, 157–66. London: Saqi Books.
——— 2012. *The Rise and Fall of Arab Presidents for Life*. Cambridge, MA: Harvard University Press.
Ouzgane, L. (ed.) 2006. *Islamic Masculinities*. London: Zed Books.
Palmer, M. 1988. *The Egyptian Bureaucracy*. Syracuse, NY: Syracuse University Press.
Papps, I. 1993. 'Attitudes to Female Employment in Four Middle Eastern Countries', in *Women in the Middle East: Perceptions, Realities and Struggles for Liberation*, ed. H. Afshar, 96–116. London: Macmillan.
Parry, J.P. 1999. 'Two Cheers for Reservation: The Satnamis and the Steel Plant', in *Institutions and Inequalities: Essays in Honour of Andre Beteille*, ed. R. Guha and J.P. Parry, 128–70. Oxford: Oxford University Press.
Partima, P.-M. and S. Begum. 1997. *Upward Occupational Mobility Among Female Workers in the Garment Industry of Bangladesh*. Dhaka: Bangladesh Institute of Development Studies.
Pearson, R. 1998. '"Nimble Fingers" Revisited: Reflections on Women and Third World Industrialisation in the Late Twentieth Century', in *Feminist Visions of Development: Gender, Analysis and Policy*, ed. C. Jackson and R. Pearson, 171–88. London: Routledge.
——— 2007. 'Reassessing Paid Work and Women's Empowerment: Lessons from the Global Economy', in *Feminisms: Contradictions, Contestations and Challenges in Development*, ed. A. Cornwall, E. Harrison and A. Whitehead, 201–13. London: Zed Books.
Pfeifer, K. 1999. 'How Tunisia, Morocco, Jordan and Egypt became IMF "Success Stories" in the 1990s', *Middle East Report* 210: 23–27
Phizacklea, A. 1990. *Unpacking the Fashion Industry*. London: Routledge.
Piore, M. and C. Sabel. 1984. *The Second Industrial Divide: Possibilities for Prosperity*. New York: Basic Books.
Pollard, L. 2003. 'The Promise of Things to Come: The Image of the Modern Family in State-Building, Colonial Occupation, and Revolution in Egypt, 1805–1922', in *Families of a New World: Gender, Politics, and State Development in a Global Context*, ed. L. Haney and L. Pollard, 17–39. New York: Routledge.
Port Said Public Relations Office. 1993. *Gawharet Misr – Bur Said (Port Said – The Jewel of Egypt)*. Port Said: Idarit al-ilaqat il-amma.

Posusney, M.P. 1993. 'Irrational Workers: The Moral Economy of Labor Protest in Egypt', *World Politics* 46(1): 83–120.

——— 1996. 'Labour and Privatisation in Egypt: Recent Developments and Future Scenarios', in *Economic Liberalisation and Privatisation in Socialist Arab Countries: Algeria, Egypt, Syria and Yemen as Examples*, ed. H. Hopfinger, 67–89. Gotha: Justus Perthes Verlag.

——— 1997. *Labour and the State in Egypt: Workers, Unions and Economic Restructuring.* New York: Columbia University Press.

——— 1999. 'Egyptian Privatization: New Challenges for the Left', *Middle East Report* 210: 38–40.

Posusney, M.P. and M.P. Angrist. 2005. *Authoritarianism in the Middle East: Regimes and Resistance.* Boulder, CO: Lynne Rienner Publishers.

Posusney, M.P. and L.J. Cook (eds). 2002. *Privatisation and Labour: Responses and Consequences in Global Perspective.* Cheltenham: Edward Elgar.

Poya, M. 1999. *Women, Work and Islamism: Ideology and Resistance in Iran.* London: Zed Books.

Pratt, N.C. 1998. *The Legacy of the Corporatist State: Explaining Workers' Responses to Economic Liberalisation in Egypt.* Durham, NC: Centre for Middle Eastern and Islamic studies, University of Durham.

——— 2007. *Democracy and Authoritarianism in the Arab World.* Boulder, CO: Lynne Rienner.

Pringle, R. 1989. *Secretaries Talk.* London: Verso.

Rath, J. (ed.) 2002. *Unravelling the Rag Trade: Immigrant Entrepreneurship in Seven World Cities.* Oxford: Berg.

Reed-Danahay, D. 2005. *Locating Bourdieu.* Bloomington: Indiana University Press.

Rejwan, N. 2009. *Arabs in the Mirror: Images and Self-Images from Pre-Islamic to Modern Times.* Austin, TX: University of Texas Press.

Riad, T.F. 2000. 'The Legal Environment for Investment in Egypt in the New Millennium', *Arab Law Quarterly* 15(2): 115–17.

Richards, A. and J. Waterbury. 1998. *A Political Economy of the Middle East*, second edition. Boulder, CO: Westview Press.

Rizzo, H. 2014. *Masculinities in Egypt and the Arab World.* Cairo: American University in Cairo Press, Cairo Papers in Social Science, 33(1) (Spring 2010).

Roberts, Hugh. 2013. 'The Revolution that Wasn't'. *London Review of Books,* 21 March 2013 (http://www.lrb.co.uk/v35/n17/hugh-roberts/the-revolution-that-wasnt).

Rofel, L. 1997. 'Rethinking Modernity: Space and Factory Discipline in China', in *Culture, Power, Place: Explorations in Critical Anthropology*, ed. A. Gupta and J. Ferguson, 155–79. Durham, NC: Duke University Press.

——— 1999. *Other Modernities: Gendered Yearnings in China after Socialism.* Berkeley: University of California Press.

Rosen, L. 1984. *Bargaining for Reality: The Construction of Social Relations in a Muslim Community.* Chicago: University of Chicago Press.

——— 2002. *The Culture of Islam: Changing Aspects of Contemporary Muslim Life.* Chicago: University of Chicago Press.

Ross, A. (ed.). 1997. *No Sweat: Fashion, Free Trade, and the Rights of Garment Workers.* London: Verso.

Rugh, A.B. 1984. *Family in Contemporary Egypt.* Syracuse, NY: Syracuse University Press.

——— 1985. 'Women and Work: Strategies and Choices in a Lower-Class Quarter of Cairo', in *Women and the Family in the Middle East: New Voices of Change*, ed. E.W. Fernea, 273–88. Austin: University of Texas Press.

——— 1986. *Reveal and Conceal: Dress in Contemporary Egypt*. Syracuse, NY: Syracuse University Press.
Saad, R. 2000. 'War in the Social Memory of Egyptian Peasants', in *War, Institutions, and Social Change in the Middle East*, ed. S. Heydemann, 240–57. Berkeley: University of California Press.
Saadawi, N. el-. 1977. *Al-mara' wa il-sira' al-nafsi (Women and their Struggles)*. Beirut: Al-Muassasah al-Arabiyyah lil-Dirasat wa al-Nashr.
——— 1980. *The Hidden Face of Eve: Women in the Arab World*, trans. and ed. S. Hetata. London: Zed Books.
——— 1991. *Al-ragul wa il-gins (Men and Sex)*, fourth edition. Cairo: Dar wa-matabe' al-mostakbal.
Said, M., H.-J. Chang and K. Sakr. 1997. 'Industrial Policy and the Role of the State in Egypt: The Relevance of the East Asian Experience', in *Economic Transition in the Middle East: Global Challenges and Ajdustment Strategies*, ed. H. Handoussa, 220–63. Cairo: The American University in Cairo Press.
Safa, H.I. 1990. 'Women and Industrialization in the Caribbean', in *Women, Employment and the Family in the International Division of Labour*, ed. S. Parpart and J. Stitcher, 72–97. London: Macmillan.
——— 1995. *The Myth of the Male Breadwinner: Women and Industrialization in the Caribbean*. Boulder, CO: Westview Press.
St. John, R. 1960. *The Boss: The Story of Gamal Abdel Nasser*. New York: McGraw-Hill Book Company.
Salaff, J. 1990. 'Women, the Family and the State: Hong Kong, Taiwan and Singapore – Newly Industrialized Countries in Asia', in *Women, Employment and the Family in the International Division of Labour*, ed. J.L. Stritcher and S. Parpart, 93–136. London: Macmillan.
Salama, A. 1980. *Mashakil al-shabab al-Misri (Problems of Egyptian Youth)*. Cairo: Maktabat al-Anjlu al-Misriyyah.
Saliba, T., C. Allen and J.A. Howard (eds). 2002. *Gender, Politics, and Islam*. Chicago and London: The University of Chicago Press.
Salzinger, L. 1997. 'From High Heels to Swathed Bodies: Gender Meanings under Production in Mexico's Export-Processing Industry', *Feminist Studies* 23(3): 549–74.
——— 2002. 'Manufacturing Sexual Subjects: "Harassment", Desire and Discipline on a Maquiladora Shopfloor', in *Ethnographic Research: A Reader*, ed. S. Taylor, 115–37. London: Sage Publications.
——— 2003. *Genders in Production: Making Workers in Mexico's Global Factories*. Berkeley: University of California Press.
Sandikci, O. and G. Ger. 2005. 'Aesthetics, Ethics and Politics of the Turkish Headscarf', in *Clothing as Material Culture*, ed. S. Kuchler and D. Miller, 61–83. Oxford: Berg Publishers.
Sassen-Koob, S. 1984. 'Notes on the Incorporation of Third World Women into Wage-Labour Through Immigration and Off-Shore Production', *International Migration Review* 18(4): 1144–67.
Saviano, R. 2011. *Gomorrah: Italy's Other Mafia*. New York: Pan Media.
Sayyid, M.K. 1991. *Privatization: The Egyptian Debate*. Cairo: The American University in Cairo Press.
Schlumberger, O. 2007. *Debating Arab Authoritarianism: Dynamics and Durability in Non-Democratic Regimes*. Palo Alto, CA: Stanford University Press.
Schielke, S. and L. Devebec (eds) 2012. *Ordinary Lives and Grand Schemes: An Anthropology of Everyday Religion*. New York: Berghahn.

Scott, Joan. 1988. *Gender and the Politics of History*. New York: Columbia University Press.
Scott, James. 1990. *Domination and the Arts of Resistance: Hidden Transcripts*. New Haven: Yale University Press.
Scott, R.M. 2010. *The Challenge of Political Islam: Non-Muslims and the Egyptian State*. Stanford, CA: Stanford University Press.
Secor, A.J. 2003. 'Belaboring Gender: The Spatial Practice of Work and the Politics of 'Making Do' in Istanbul'. *Environment and Planning A* 35: 2209–27.
——— 2005. 'Islamism, Democracy, and the Political Production of the Headscarf Issue in Turkey', in *Geographies of Muslim Women: Gender, Religion, and Space*, ed. G.-W. Falah and C. Nagel, 203–26. New York: The Guildford Press.
Sen, A. 1990. 'Gender and Cooperative Conflicts', in *Persistent Inequalities*, ed. I. Tinker, 123–49. Oxford: Oxford University Press.
——— 2009. 'Capitalism beyond the Crisis'. *New York Review of Books*, 56(5), March 26 (http://www.nybooks.com/articles/2009/03/26/capitalism-beyond-the-crisis/).
Sharabi, H. 1988a. *Neopatriarchy: A Theory of Distorted Change in Arab Society*. New York: Oxford University Press.
——— (ed.). 1988b. *Theory, Politics and the Arab World: Critical Responses*. New York: Routledge.
Shehata, S. 2003. 'In the Basha's House: The Organizational Culture of Egyptian Public-Sector Enterprise', *International Journal of Middle Eastern Studies* 35: 103–32.
Shenker, J. 2016. *The Egyptians: A Radical Story*. London: Allen Lane.
Sherifa, B. 1999. 'Gender Contradictions in Families: Official v. Practical Representations among Upper Middle-Class Muslim Egyptians', *Anthropology Today* 15(4): 9–13.
Sholkamy, H. 1999. 'Why is Anthropology so Hard in Egypt?', in *Between Field and Text: Emerging Voices in Egyptian Social Science*, ed. S. Shami and L. Herrera, Cairo Papers in Social Science, 22(2), 119–38. Cairo: The American University in Cairo Press.
Shoshan, B. (ed.). 2000. *Discourse on Gender: Gendered Discourses in the Middle East*. London: Praeger.
Sinclair, M.T. 1991. 'Women, Work and Skill: Economic Theories and Feminist Perspective', in *Working Women: International Perspectives on Labour and Gender Ideology*, ed. N. Redclift and M.T. Sinclair, 1–24. London: Routledge.
Singerman, D. 1995. *Avenues of Participation: Family, Politics, and Networks in Urban Quarters of Cairo*. Princeton, NJ: Princeton University Press.
——— 2002. 'Networks, Jobs, and Everyday Life in Cairo', in *Everyday Life in the Muslim Middle East*, second edition, ed. D.L. Bowen and E.A. Early, 199–208. Bloomington: Indiana University Press.
——— 2011. 'The Negotiation of Waithood: The Political Economy of Delayed Marriage in Egypt', in *Arab Youth: Social Mobilisation in Times of Risk*, ed. S. Khalaf and R. Saad Khalaf, 67–79. London: Saqi Books.
Singerman, D. and B. Ibrahim. 2003. 'The Costs of Marriage in Egypt: A Hidden Dimension in the New Arab Demography', in *The New Arab Family*, ed. N.S. Hopkins, Cairo Papers in Social Science, 24(1/2), 80–117. Cairo: The American University in Cairo Press.
Singerman, D. and P. Amar (eds) 2006. *Cairo Cosmopolitan: Politics, Culture, and Urban Space in the New Globalized Middle East*. Cairo: The American University in Cairo Press.
Singerman, D. and H. Hoodfar (eds). 1996. *Development, Change, and Gender in Cairo: A Viewpoint from the Household*. Bloomington: Indiana University Press.
Sirageldin, I. 1995. *Globalization, Regionalization and Recent Trade Agreements: Impact on Arab Economies*, Working Papers Series: Working Paper 9817. Cairo: Economic Research Forum.

Smith, P. and J. Christianson. 2007. 'Stealing Africa: How Capital Flight is Draining Africa's Economies'. Seminar held at the Centre of African Studies, School of Oriental and African Studies, 29 March 2007.

Smith, C. 1984. *Islam and the Search for Social Order in Modern Egypt: A Biography of Muhammad Husayn Haykal*. Albany: State University of New York Press.

Snitow, A., C. Stansell and S. Thompson (eds). 1983. *Powers of Desire: The Politics of Sexuality*. New York: Monthly Review Press.

Snyder, R. L. 2009. *Fugitive Denim: A Moving Story of People and Pants in the Borderless World of Global Trade*. New York City: Norton and Company.

Sonbol, A. el-Azhary. 2000. *The New Mamluks: Egyptian Society and Modern Feudalism*. Syracuse, NY: Syracuse University Press.

——— 2003. *Women of Jordan: Islam, Labor, and the Law*. New York: Syracuse University Press.

Sonneveld, N. 2011. *Khul' Divorce in Egypt: Public Debates, Judicial Practices, and Everyday Life*. Cairo: The American University in Cairo Press.

Sowers, J. and C. Toensing (eds). 2012. *The Journey to Tahrir: Revolution, Protest, and Social Change in Egypt*. London: Verso.

Sparr, P. 1994. 'Feminist Critiques of Structural Adjustment', in *Mortgaging Women's Lives: Feminist Critiques of Structural Adjustment*, ed. P. Sparr, 13–39. London: Zed Books.

Springborg, R. 1975. 'Patterns of Association in the Egyptian Political Elite', in *Political Elites in the Middle East*, ed. G. Lenczowski, 83–107. Washington DC: American Enterprise Institute for Public Policy Research.

——— 1982. *Family, Power and Politics in Egypt: Sayed Bey Marei – His Clan, Clients and Cohorts*. Philadelphia: University of Pennsylvania Press.

——— 1989. *Mubarak's Egypt: Fragmentation of the Political Order*. Boulder, CO: Westview Press.

——— 2003. 'An Evaluation of the Political System at the End of the Millenium', in *Egypt in the Twenty-first Century: Challenges for Development*, ed. R. El-Ghonemy, 183–98. London: Routledge.

Stacher, J. 2012. *Adaptable Autocrats: Regime Power in Egypt and Syria*. Stanford, CA: Stanford University Press.

Standing, G. 1989. 'Global Feminisation through Flexible Labor', *World Development* 17(7): 1077–95.

Stoller, P. 1989. *The Taste of Ethnographic Things: The Senses in Anthropology*. Philadelphia: University of Pennsylvania Press.

Stratton, A. 2006. *Muhajababes: Meet the New Middle East – Cool, Sexy, and Devout*. London: Constable.

Sullivan, D.J. 1990. 'The Political Economy of Reform in Egypt', *International Journal of Middle East Studies* 22(3): 317–34.

Tiano, S. 1994. *Patriarchy on the Line: Labor, Gender, and Ideology in the Mexican Maquila Industry*. Philadelphia, PA: Temple University Press.

Tinker, I. (ed.). 1990. *Persistent Inequalities: Women and World Development*. New York: Oxford University Press.

Toth, J. 1999. *Rural Labour Movements in Egypt and Their Impact on the State, 1961–1992*. Cairo: The American University in Cairo Press.

Tripp, C. 2006. *Islam and the Moral Economy: The Challenge of Capitalism*. Cambridge: Cambridge University Press.

——— 2013. *The Power and the People: Paths of Resistance in the Middle East*. Cambridge: Cambridge University Press.

Tucker, J.E. 1976. 'Egyptian Women and the Female Labor Force: An Historical Survey', *MERIP Reports* 50: 3–9, 26.
——— 1993. 'The Arab Family in History: "Otherness" and the Study of the Family', in *Arab Women: Old Boundaries. New Frontiers*, ed. J.E. Tucker, 195–208. Bloomington: Indiana University Press.
——— 2008. 'Pensee 2: We've Come a Long Way, Baby – But We've Got a Long Way to Go', *International Journal of Middle East Studies* 40(1): 19–21.
Turner, B. 2006. *Suez: The Inside Story of the First Oil War 1956*. London: Hodder and Stoughton.
Tybout, J.R. 2000. 'Manufacturing Firms in Developing Countries: How Well Do They Do, and Why?' *Journal of Economic Literature* 38(1): 11–44.
Uchiyamada, Y. 2000. 'Industrial Sewing Machines, Work-Disciplines and Aesthetics: Of Anthropological Clichés and a Letter from Bohol', *Critique of Anthropology* 20(3): 243–64.
Urry, J.1995. *Consuming Places*. London: Routledge.
Vance, C. (ed.) 1984. *Pleasure and Danger: Exploring Female Sexuality*. Boston, MA: Routledge and Kegan Paul.
van Leeuwen, R. 2000. 'The Lost Heritage: Generation Conflicts in Four Arabic Novels', in *Alienation or Integration of Arab Youth: Between Family, State and Street* ed. R. Meijer, 189–207. Richmond, Surrey: Curzon.
Van Maanen, J. 2001. 'Natives "R" Us: Some Notes on the Ethnography of Organizations', in *Inside Organizations: Anthropologists at Work*, ed. D. Gellner and E. Hirsch, 233–61. Oxford: Berg.
vom Bruck, G. 1997. 'Elusive Bodies: The Politics of Aesthetics among Yemeni Elite Women', *Signs* 23(1): 175–214.
Waldinger, R.D. 1986. *Through the Eye of the Needle: Immigrants and Enterprise in New York's Garment Trades*. Albany, NY: New York University Press.
Waterbury, J. 1984. *The Egypt of Nasser and Sadat: The Political Economy of Two Regimes*. Princeton, NJ: Princeton University Press.
——— 1985. 'The "Soft State" and the Open Door: Egypt's Experience with Economic Liberalization, 1974–1984', *Comparative Politics* 18(1): 65–83.
Ward, G. (ed.). 2000. *The Certeau Reader*. Oxford: Blackwell Publishers.
Ward, K. (ed.). 1990. *Women Workers and Global Restructuring*. Ithaca, NY: ILR Press, School of Industrial and Labour Relations, Cornell University.
Weedan, L. 2008. *Peripheral Visions: Publics, Power, and Performance in Yemen*. Chicago: University of Chicago Press.
Wersh, H.V. 1995. 'Flying a Kite and Losing the String: Communication during the Bombay Textile Strike', in *Bombay: Metaphor for Modern India*, ed. S. Patel and A. Thorner, 64–88. Bombay: Oxford University Press.
Weyland, P. 1997. 'Gendered Lives in Global Spaces', in *Space, Culture and Power: New Identities in Globalizing Cities*, ed. A. Oncu and P. Weyland, 82–97. London: Zed Books.
White, J.B. 1994. *Money Makes Us Relatives: Women's Labour in Urban Turkey*. Texas: University of Texas Press.
——— 2002. *Islamist Mobilization in Turkey*. Seattle: University of Washington Press.
Whitlock, G. 2007. *Soft Weapons: Autobiography in Transit*. Chicago: University of Chicago Press.
Wickham, C.R. 2002. *Mobilizing Islam: Religion, Activism and Political Change in Egypt*. New York: Columbia University Press.
——— 2013. *The Muslim Brotherhood: Evolution of an Islamist Movement*. Princeton, NJ: Princeton University Press.

Williams, C.L., P.A. Giuffre and K. Dellinger. 1999. 'Sexuality in the Workplace: Organizational Control, Sexual Harassment, and the Pursuit of Pleasure', *Annual Review Sociology* 25: 73–93.
Willis, P.E. 1977. *Learning to Labour: How Working Class Kids Get Working Class Jobs.* Farnborough, Hampshire: Saxon House.
——— 1979. 'Shop Floor Culture, Masculinity and the Wage Form', in *Working Class Culture*, ed. J. Clarke, C. Critcher, and R. Johnson, 185–98. London: Hutchinson.
Wolf, D. 1992. *Factory Daughters: Gender, Household Dynamics and Rural Industrialization in Java.* Los Angeles: University of California Press.
Wright, M. 1997. 'Crossing the Factory Frontier: Gender, Place and Power in the Mexican Maquiladora', *Antipode* 29(3): 278–302.
Wright, S. 1995. *The Anthropology of Organisations.* London: Routledge.
Yanagisako, S.J. 2002. *Producing Culture and Capital: Family Firms in Italy.* Princeton, NJ: Princeton University Press.
Yelvington, K. A. 1995. *Producing Power: Ethnicity, Gender and Class in a Caribbean Workplace.* Philadelphia: Temple University Press.
Zaalouk, M. 1989. *Power, Class, and Foreign Capital in Egypt: The Rise of the New Bourgeoisie.* London: Zed Books.
Zakaria, F. 1988. 'The Standpoint of Contemporary Muslim Fundamentalists', in *Women of the Arab World: The Coming Challenge,* Papers of the Arab Women's Solidarity Association Conference, ed. N. Toubia, trans. N. El Gamal, 27–36. London: Zed Books.
Zartman, I.W. 1988. 'Opposition as Support of the State', in *Beyond Coercion: The Durability of the Arab State*, ed. A. Dawisha and I.W. Zartman, 64–87. London: Croom Helm.
Zhang, E.Y. 2001. 'Goudui and the State: Constructing Entrepreneurial Masculinity in Two Cosmopolitan Areas of Post-Socialist China', in *Gendered Modernities: Ethnographic Perspectives*, ed. D.L. Hodgson, 235–66. New York: Palgrave Macmillan US.
Zubaida, S. 1989. *Islam, the People and the State: Essays on Political Ideas and Movements in the Middle East.* London: Routledge.
Zurayk, H.C. and F. Saadeh. 1995. 'Women as Mobilizers of Human Resources in Arab Countries', in *Gender and Development in the Arab World: Women's Economic Participation: Patterns and Policies*, ed. N.F. Khoury and V.M. Moghadam, 35–48. London: Zed Books.

INDEX

A
Abdel Aal, (blog), 137–38n2
Abeer (factory worker), 101
absenteeism, 92, 151
access to factories, for research purposes, 39–41, 45
accountability, of supervisors, 148
age distribution of workforce, 215
Ahmed (factory worker), 113, 115
Akram (supervisor), 144
Ali, Hamida, 104–5, 169, 178
Ali (monitor), 112
ambitions
    of Fashion Express workforce, 126, 127, 151, 200–202
    political, of Qasim Bey, 94–95
Amin, Hanadi, 143, 162, 188
Amin, Hasanat, 127
Amina (machinist), 92
Amira (factory worker), 112
Ammar, H., 138n5
Ammar, Mr., 70
ancestral ties, 62
Anderson, Benedict, 48n15
Ansari, Mr., 58, 59
anthropological research, 3, 4–5
    See also ethnographic research
Arab societies, patriarchal structures in, 56–57
Arab Spring upheavals, 1–2, 47, 195, 207–9, 211
Arab-Israeli conflict, impact on Port Said, 10
arguments on shop floor, 145, 146, 164–65, 168–69, 184–85, 189

'aris wi 'arusa (bride and groom) games, 115–17
arranged marriages, 101, 103–4, 106
Asmaa (factory worker), 104
Asmahan (machinist), 154
assembly, of clothes, 20
authoritarian structures, 56, 141
Awatef (machinist), 144
'Ayiza 'Atgawiz (I want to get married, blog), 137–38n2
ayma (list of possessions upon marriage), 102–3
Ayman (factory worker), 115
Ayubi, N.N., 196
il-ayyn ('requiring an eye', skill), 41, 75
Azima (supervisor), 153
Azmi, Imam, 57, 61–62, 63, 64–65, 69, 150, 191, 193

B
Baron, Beth, 96n6
behaviour, norms of, 36
Beinin, Joel, 2, 47n5, 208
il-beit il-hilw (the beautiful home)/*il-beit yetwadab* (the tidied-up home) ideals, 129
benefits
    BGB management's promises of, 175, 181
    public, 201
BGB management of Fashion Express, 172–77, 191–92, 209–10
    control of workforce by, 180–81, 182–86
    recruitment practices, 177, 178–79, 186–87

resistance from workforce against, 187–89, 190, 191, 192, 210–11
training of new entrants, 179–80
Bill, J.A., 70
Binder, L., 203
bint/ibn il-masna' title (daughter/son of the factory) for supervisors, 153–54, 155, 156, 203
'Biscotta' (factory worker), 149
bizniz women on shop floor, 127
blogs, Arabic, 137–38n2
Bourdieu, Pierre, 199, 201
Braverman, Harry, 21–22
Britain, Fashion Express' relations with, 175–76, 191
British management of Fashion Express *See* BGB management of Fashion Express
Burawoy, Michael, 147, 171n2, 204
businessmen, generosity of, 58–59
Butler, Judith, 37, 168

C

Cairo, 38–39
Cairoli, M.L., 204
capital
flight of, 204
symbolic, 199–200
catalogue vendors on shop floor, 125–26, 127
See also commercial activities on shop floor
CCTV cameras at Fashion Express, 174, 190
Certeau, M. de, 36, 48n15, 202
charity, by businessmen, 58–59
China, factory work in, 96n3
circumcision, female, 130
cities, Egyptian, 5
Civil Association of Investors (Port Said), 196, 197
class
formation, 202
in Islamic society, 87
and power, 38
client-contractor relationships, 18, 24, 48n12, 198
clients of Fashion Express, British, 176, 191

closure of Fashion Express, 192–93, 211–12
co-optation, 195, 196, 203
coercion, and consent, 195, 196, 203
Collins, J.L., 204
commercial activities on shop floor, 99–100, 124–33, 164
BGB clampdown of, 180–81
Commercial District (Port Said), 13, 14
conception, separation from execution, 21–22, 23
consent, and coercion/control, 147, 195, 196, 203
consumers, citizens as, 201
contracts
in garment industry, 18, 24, 48n12, 198
of marriage, 102, 103
control
and consent, 147
by management, 33, 36, 180–81, 182–86
Cornwall, Andrea, 210
corporatism, 195–96
corruption, 211
costs, of marriage, 129
'Cut and Make' contracts, 18, 198
cutting of cloth, 18–20

D

Dagong Laoban, (Factory Boss, Zhang Wei, film), 96n3, 97n12
dancing, at *tangid* parties, 135–36
dating, 119–20
day trips for factory workers, 45
Dayan, Moshe, 10
deadlines, meeting of, 83–84, 89
decision-making, by Qasim Bey, 71
Dedeoglu, S., 38–39
demotion, of supervisors, 150–53
Diab, Amr, 111
discipline, supervisor performances of, 141, 143–48
discourse concept, 35–36, 199
dismissals
of factory workers, 147
of supervisors, 151, 153
docility, female supervisors' rejection of, 205
'Dollar' (factory worker), 149

dress styles
　at weddings, 99
　of factory workers
　　female, 27–28, 108–9, 110, 161, 188–89
　　male, 110–11
　of supervisors, 152, 167
dukhla (celebratory wedding night), 103, 133–34, 137

E
economic policies
　in China, 96n3
　in Egypt, 3, 10–11, 16, 25, 58–59, 126, 195, 201
education
　of Egyptian labour force, 26
　of Fashion Express workforce, 216
　sexual, 130
efficiency, supervisor performances of, 148–56
Egypt
　Arab Spring upheavals in, 1–2, 47, 195, 207–9, 211
　authoritarianism in, 141
　corporatism in, 195–96
　economic development in, 30–31
　economic liberalisation policies, 10–11, 16, 25, 195, 201
　food rationing in, 126–27
　industrial relations/labour unrest in, 2, 3, 97n11, 196
　and Israel, 10, 71
　physical violence avoidance in, 146
　QIZ programme in, 51–52, 96n2, 198–99
　security state in, 3, 196
　state socialism in, 3, 126, 195, 201
　working class in, 202
El-Kholy, H., 38, 138n6
elections for Shura Council, Qasim Bey's candidacy, 94–96
elites of Port Said, 50, 59–60, 200
employment
　declarations of unsuitability for, 147
　private sector, 54, 118
　public sector, 53–54, 118
　of women, 4, 25, 26, 38–39, 205–6
engagements (to be married), 102–3, 118–19, 129
　broken, 104
Enloe, Cynthia, 207
Essam (machinist), 105–6
ethnicity, and power, 38
ethnographic research, 32
　at Fashion Express, 29–30, 33, 41–46, 194, 211–12
　in factories, 30, 38
　of *gihaaz* accumulation, 138n6
　of women's economic roles, 4, 29–30, 38–39
Etrebi, Sawsan, 74–75, 78, 81–82, 93, 128, 159, 184, 189
ETUF (Egyptian Trade Union Federation), 3, 196
evacuation of citizens from Port Said, 12
execution, separation from conception, 21–22, 23
experience, evaluation of, 76
experienced spatial practices, 32
　of management, 32
exploitation, resistance of workforce against, 88–91, 92, 97n11
Export Processing Zones (EPZs)
　corporatism in, 195–96, 203
　labour market in, 49–50, 53, 54–55, 73–74, 91, 193
　of Port Said, 4, 12, 16–17, 40, 49–50, 51–55, 94–95, 196–99
'eye of power' concept, 33–34
'*eyun il-sherka* concept (eyes of the firm), 65, 68

F
factories
　ethnographic research in, 30, 38, 39–46
　in Port Said Export Processing Zone, 16, 197
　reputation of, 55
　spatial organisation of, 31, 32
Factory Boss, (*Dagong Laoban*, Zhang Wei, film), 96n3, 97n12
factory owners, 57, 58, 97n12
　female, 52–53

250 • Index

support for Qasim Bey's political
  ambitions by, 94–95
  See also Fahmy, Qasim (Qasim Bey)
Factory S., 178
factory work, 21, 42
  in China, 96n3
factory workers
  ambitions of, 126, 127, 151, 200–202
  ethnographic research of, 29–30, 43–44
  female, 27–30, 38–39, 54, 204–5
    dress/veiling of, 27–28, 108–11, 161, 163, 188–89
    fear of singlehood, 100–102, 117
    flirtatious behaviour by, 115–16
    respectability/modesty of, 79, 83–85, 121–22, 132–33
    wages of, 124–25, 128
  'floating', 179, 193
  male, 26, 76–77, 109, 128
    dress styles, 110–11
    fear of singlehood, 102
    financial independence sought by, 118
    flirtatious behaviour by, 112–15, 122
    participation in wedding celebrations, 133–34
  relations with supervisors, 143, 144–47, 149–51, 154, 168
  spatial practices of, 33
  training of, 179–80
  views on sexuality, 130–31
  See also recruitment practices; workforce
fahlawi behaviour, 157
Fahmy, Leith, 57, 62
Fahmy, Qasim (Qasim Bey), 4, 42, 49, 199
  and BGB management takeover, 172, 177, 192
  moral force of, 73, 78
  motives of, 199–200
  'proprietor-patriarch' role of, 40, 49, 50, 55, 57–62, 66, 70–72, 91, 153–54, 193
  Shura Council candidacy, 94–96
  workforce loyalty towards, 155, 189–90
Fahmy family, 50, 59–60, 62–63, 94, 173, 200
  evicted from Fashion Express, 178, 185–86

'fair trade and labour' label, 196
'fallen factory' reputation, 50, 55
family
  in Arab societies, 56–57
  recruitment practices among, 57–58, 61
  See also 'firm as family' paradigm
family firms, 4, 55
  women employed by, 38–39
Faruk, Lamya, 143
Fatima (machinist), 122–24
Fatma (supervisor), 135, 158, 160, 182–83, 183–84
female circumcision, 130
female workforce/factory workers *See* women
femininity, 37, 38
  tomcat, 140
feminist scholarship, 206–7
fieldwork, 4–5
  at factories, 30, 38
  at Fashion Express, 29–30, 33, 41–47, 190–91
fighting on shop floor, 146
  See also arguments on shop floor
financial settlements, at marriage, 102
fines, issuing of, 144–45, 184, 187
'firm as family' paradigm, 36, 47
  at Fashion Express, 49–51, 55, 58, 60, 61–72, 81, 85–86, 90–91, 94, 154–55, 199, 201, 202–3, 205, 206
  and BGB management, 171, 185–86, 190
firms *See* factories
flirtations on shop floor, 112–16, 122
'floating' workers, 179, 193
food
  rationing, 126–27
  sold on shop floor, 126
foreign management takeover at Fashion Express *See* BGB management of Fashion Express
formal sector employment, of women, 4, 25, 26, 39, 205–6
Foucault, Michel, 33, 34–36, 199
'Free on Board' (FOB) contracts, 48n12, 198
Free Officers Revolution (1952), 5

Free Trade Zones
  in Port Said, 10, 11–12
  See also Export Processing Zones
Freeman, C., 159
Friedman, Thomas, 1
future, of Fashion Express, 174, 191

G
games, played on shop floor, 115–17, 171n2, 183
garment industry
  client-contractor relationships, 18, 24, 48n12, 198
  female employment in, 204–5
  female ownership in, 52–53
  fluctuations of work in, 4–5, 43, 45
  and globalisation, 204
  of Port Said, 200
  production process, 18–21, 22–23, 24–25, 27–29, 31
  protection of, 197
  See also textile industry
gawasis See spies
Gellner, N., 40–41
gender/gendering
  in Fashion Express workforce/shop floor, 44–45, 76–77, 79–80, 83–84, 137, 170, 214
  performative theory of, 37
  and power, 206–7
  and spatial organisation, 79–80
  at workplaces, 25, 26, 36, 39, 119, 137, 156–57, 159, 170, 205–6
generosity, of businessmen, 58–59
geography, and power relations, 35
gihaaz (trousseau) items
  accumulation of, 99–100, 103, 117, 129, 138n6, 206
  by female factory workers, 125, 128, 129–30, 131–32
  displaying of, 135
  transfer to couple's home, 136–37
giza (fines), issuing of, 144–45, 184, 187
globalisation, impact of, 37–38, 194, 197, 204
Goldberg, E.J., 90
'Gorilla' (factory worker), 150

government bureaucracy, 58

H
Habiba (factory worker), 121–22, 125
hadith, quotations from, 87
hairstyles, of male factory workers, 111
al-Hamalawy, Hossam, 1–2, 211
Hamza (factory worker), 102
haqq (rights) concept, on shop floor, 88–89, 90
haram (forbidden), 122, 159, 161, 163
Hashem (factory worker), 122–23, 124
Hasina (machinist), 85
Hassan (factory worker), 105
Hassan, Nidal, 93–94, 113, 143, 151, 157–58, 170, 187–88
Hatem, M., 156, 171n7
Hatim (factory worker), 116, 147
Hay el Afrangi (Foreign Quarter, Port Said), 13, 15
Hewamanne, S., 38
hijab, wearing of, 27–28, 109–10, 161
Hind (factory worker), 105
Hirsch, E., 40–41
Hoodfar, Homa, 101–2, 109, 138n6
Horeya (supervisor), 76, 92, 93, 109–10, 114–15, 122–23, 132, 141–42, 144, 145–46, 152, 153, 154, 155–56, 158, 164, 165, 166, 169, 170, 183, 191
Hourani, A., 60
housing, in Port Said, 103, 138n3
humiliation expressions, 141, 143
hygiene, feminine, 130

I
Ibrahim, Sonallah, 160
ihtiram (respectability) at Fashion Express, 36, 50, 73, 74, 75–76, 77, 78–81, 84, 124, 151
  material, 132–33
  reassertion of, 188–89
ikhlaas (loyalty), 36, 50, 61–72, 171n3, 185–86
  of supervisors, 154, 155–56
  and *wala'* concept, 178, 193n1
imagined spatial practices, 32, 33

industrial relations
  in Egypt, 3, 196
  See also labour unrest
industrialisation, in Egypt, 30–31
infitah (economic opening) policy (Sadat), 10–11, 25, 58–59, 195, 201
informal recruitment practices, 50, 82–84
informal sector work, by women, 4, 38–39
information flows at Fashion Express, 64–71
institutional power, 33
institutions, regimentation of, 33–34
interviews, with factory workers, 43–44
investors in Port Said EPZ, 198–99, 200
  and labour relations, 196, 197
  support for Qasim Bey's political ambitions by, 94–95
irfa (spirit), of orders, 42
ironing department, 21
Islam/Islamisation
  at Fashion Express, 78–79, 87, 162–64
  and sexuality, 79–80
  and women, 108, 171n7
Islam (supervisor), 144
Ismail, Mr., 172–73, 176, 177, 178, 179, 181, 183, 184, 185, 187, 192
Ismail, S., 39, 58–59
Israel
  Egypt's relations with, 10, 71
  trade relations in Middle East, 51, 198
iterability, 37

J
joker status, 166
Jordan, 96n2
Joseph, Suad, 56

K
Kafr el Dawar, 2
Kandiyoti, Deniz, 55, 171n4, 206–7
katb il-kitab (marriage contract), signing of, 103
kawadir *See* supervisors
Kawakib (factory worker), 113, 121
Khadija (factory worker), 87, 115, 116, 119, 173, 186–87, 191
Khalifa, Mamduh, 165
Kifaya demonstrations, 208

Kimo (machinist), 132–33
kinship ties/networks, 55, 57–58
  in Arab/Middle Eastern societies, 56–57, 70
  metaphorical, 85–86, 90–91, 153–54
  and power relations, 35
  and recruitment practices, 82, 83–84
Kondo, D., 159
Koran verses, decorations/recitations at Fashion Express, 78–79
Korczynski, M., 138n5

L
labour market, 26
  in Export Processing Zones, 49–50, 53, 54–55, 73–74, 91, 193
labour relations
  at Fashion Express, 89, 90–91, 202–4
  Chinese, 97n12
  Egyptian, 3, 196
  in Port Said EPZ, 197
  See also 'firm as family' paradigm
labour studies, 21–22
labour unrest, 2, 3, 97n11
  in Arab Spring upheavals, 1–2, 208
  at Fashion express, 89–91, 202, 208
  See also resistance
laundry department, 21, 83
leadership, female, 203
Lee, C.K., 38, 204
Lefebvre, Henri, 32, 33, 48n15
Lévi-Strauss, Claude, 5
liberalisation policies, 10–11, 16, 25, 195, 201
lingerie items, sold on shop floor, 130–31
Lockman, Z., 30–31, 202
love
  in arranged marriages, 104
  marriages, 99, 104–7
  on shop floor, 98–99, 100–101, 107, 117, 119–24, 137
loyalty *See ikhlaas*; *wala lil-masna'*
lunch-breaks, 28

M
Mahalla strikes, 2, 48n6, 208
mail-order catalogues, on shop floor, 125

Makram, Om, 65–66, 67, 95, 176
male workforce/factory workers, 26, 76–77, 109, 128
  dress styles, 110–11
  fear of singlehood, 102
  financial independence sought by, 118
  flirtatious behaviour by, 112–15, 122
  See also supervisors, male
management, 22, 23, 28, 33, 40, 50, 61–65, 93
  power and control exercised by, 33, 36, 180–81, 182–86
  recruitment of, 57
  relations with supervisors, 140, 146, 149, 150, 151, 157, 159–60, 168–69
  relations with workforce, 63, 194–95
  spatial practices of, 32
  spies (*gawasis*) used by, 34, 64, 65–70, 86–87
  See also BGB management of Fashion Express
Mansur, Kifah, 123–24, 155, 160, 162–63, 166, 184
Manzala, migrant workers from, 92, 102
marriages
  arranged, 101, 103–4, 106
  costs of, 129
  delayed, 159–60
  games on shop floor, 115–17
  of love, 99, 104–7
  prospects, 45, 100–102
  trajectory towards, 102–3, 117
masculine behaviour, by female supervisors, 140, 156–64
masculinity, performance of, 37, 67, 112–13, 140, 167
material respectability, of female factory workers, 132–33
materialist life-styles, of youth, 201
Maymuna (supervisor), 123, 164, 169, 170, 178
meetings, organised by BGB management at Fashion Express, 173–74, 210
mehrem (religiously sanctioned male relatives), 84, 160, 163
Mernissi, F., 79–80, 108
methods, of ethnographic research, 39–46

Middle East, trade in, 51, 198
middle management, female, 159–60
'Mido' (factory worker), 149
migrant labour
  at Fashion Express, 82, 92
    shedding of, 179, 191
  in Export Processing Zones, 54
  female, 84–85, 101
military stores, 126
Mina Clothing Firm, 52
mobility
  social, 126, 127
  of supervisors, 141, 144
  of women workers, 38–39
modernisation
  at Fashion Express, 172, 174
  and authoritarian/patriarchal structures, 56
modesty, of female factory workers, 79, 83–85, 121–22, 132–33
Mohamed, Azima, 113–14, 133–34, 143, 154, 158–59, 161
Mohammed (Prophet), 87
Mohsen (foreman), 77, 149, 150
Mongid (Assistant Production Studies Department), 74, 78
moral respectability
  at Fashion Express, 80–81, 83–84
  importance of, 50, 78, 84–85, 121–22
  See also ihtiram
Morocco, 211
Morsi, Kawsar, 143, 145, 184
Morsi, Mohamed, 209, 211
mu'aksat (flirtation), 112–15
Mubarak, Gamal, 12
Mubarak, Hosni
  deposing of, 195, 207
  economic policies of, 11–12, 201
multazim (consistent with Muslim principles) behaviour, 167
Multi Fibre Arrangement, quota system of, 197
mushrifat See supervisors, female
music, at wedding celebrations, 136, 138n9
Muslim Brotherhood, 208–9, 211
Mustafa (factory worker), 119–20
mutual co-optation framework, 195, 203

'My Way' catalogue, 125

N
Nadia (machinist), 118–19, 120–21, 127
Naguib, Am (cleaner), 183
Naguib, K., 141
names of supervisors, used for production units, 148
Nasser, Gamel Abdel, 3, 5, 97n7
nationalisations, 3
neoliberalism
   in Egypt, 195, 201
   See also liberalisation policies
neopatriarchy, 56
Nermin, Madame, 100, 186–87
networks
   of kinship, 82–84, 85
   of power relations, 35
NGOs, of Port Said, 51
Nile Delta, xv
Niqab, wearing of, 109–10, 162
   See also veiling
niya (good faith) concept, 171n6
norms of behaviour, 36
nouveau rich investors, in Port Said, 40, 198, 200
Nura (factory worker), 100–101, 115, 116, 132–33

O
observations, during fieldwork, 41–43
odit il-ishraf, (female supervisors' room), 44
Osama (factory worker), 128
ostracism, of factory workers, 146–47
overtime, compulsory, 29, 187–88

P
packaging department, 21, 83
participant-observer research, 3, 5, 41–43
participation, 210
patriarchs/patriarchal structures, 55–57
   and power, 70
   women workers' bargaining with, 206–7
   See also 'proprietor-patriarch' role of Qasim Bey
payments
   for shop floor purchases, 131
   of wages, 89–90, 191
performances, 37
   of management, 63
   of masculinity, 37, 67, 112–13, 140, 167
   of supervisors, 141, 143–56
performative theory of gender, 37
physical violence, avoidance of, 146
planning of textile production processes, 22–23
politics
   elite's involvement with, 60, 200
   Fahmy family/Qasim Bey's involvement with, 59–60, 94–96
   of production, 140
Port Said, 3, 5–16, 195
   districts of, 6, 8–9, 13, 14
   elites of, 50, 59–60, 200
   Export Processing Zone (EPZ), 4, 12, 16–17, 40, 49–50, 51–55, 94–95, 196–99
   food rationing in, 126
   Free Trade Zone, 10, 11–12
   gender roles in, 79
   housing, 103, 138n3
   Qualified Industrial Zone of (QIZ), 197–98
   wedding celebrations, 100, 133–37
Posusney, M.P., 97n11
power, 65, 97n7
   Foucault's analysis of, 34–35, 36, 199
   and gender, 206–7
   of informers, 34
   institutional, 33
   of patriarchs, 70
   in production processes, 38, 154
   of supervisors, 145–46, 152, 154, 165–66, 170
PowerPoint presentations, at Fashion Express, 176–77
private sector employment, 54, 118
production
   fluctuations in, 4–5, 43, 45
   habitus, 201
   politics of, 140
   and power relations, 38, 154
   processes, 18–21, 22–23, 24–25, 27–29, 31

quotas/deadlines, meeting of, 28, 83–84, 89, 148–49
units, names of, 148
promotion, to supervisor position, 153, 165–66, 178
'proprietor-patriarch' role of Qasim Bey, 40, 49, 50, 55, 57–62, 66, 70–72, 91, 153–54, 193
and his political ambitions, 94–96
and moral respectability, 73, 78
Public Fee Zones *See* Export Processing Zones
public sector employment, preference for, 53–54, 118
punctuality, emphasise on, 180

Q

qalaq (state of anomy), 137n1
at Fashion Express, 90, 91, 183, 184–85
by being single, 101
Qalyoub, 2
Qasim Bey, *See* Fahmy, Qasim
Qualified Industrial Zones (QIZs) (US programme), 51–52, 96n2
disillusionment with, 198–99
in Port Said, 197–98
quality control
at Fashion Express, 72, 76, 150, 178
in textile production process, 19, 20
Quartier des Affaires (Central Business District, Port Said), 6, 8
Quartier Residentielle (Port Said), 6, 9, 13, 14

R

Rahma (factory worker), 163
Ramadan, compulsory overtime during, 187–88
Rasha (factory worker), 77
Rasmeya (planning monitor), 161–62
ration cards, 126–27
reality, ordered by discourse, 35
reconciliation, after fights/arguments on shop floor, 146
recruitment practices
at Fashion Express, 50, 57–58, 73–78, 81, 82–84
BGB management, 177, 178–79, 186–87
of supervisors, 153, 165–66, 178
in Export Processing Zones, 54–55, 57
raids by competition on workers from Fashion Express, 91–94
regimentation of institutions, 33–34
religion/religiosity
of businessmen, 58–59
at Fashion Express, 78–79, 87–88, 159, 160–64, 167
and power relations, 35
reputation of firms, 50, 55
research
anthropological, 3, 4–5
on Egyptian industrialisation, 30–31
in factories, 38, 39–46
resignations, 153
resistance, 36, 38, 202
by shop floor against BGB management, 187–89, 190, 191, 192, 210–11
by workforce against exploitation, 88–91, 92, 97n11
See also labour unrest
respectability *See ihtiram*; moral respectability; modesty
'The Revolution that wasn't' (article, Roberts), 207
rivalry, in Fashion Express management, 62–63, 69–70
Roberts, Hugh, 207
Rosen, L., 88, 131, 171n6, 211
rotation, of supervisors, 150
rumours, on shop floor, 64–65, 173, 175, 191

S

S., Madame, 52–53, 91–92
Sabah (factory worker), 107
Sabri (supervisor), 154
Sadat, Anwar, 10, 71
Sakina (supervisor), 151–53
Salafism, on shop floor, 162
Salama, Marzuk, 177–78, 187, 189
Saleh, Tewfik, 57, 60, 62, 63, 68–69, 70, 73, 80–81, 95, 114, 185, 188, 189–90, 193n5

Salheya, 101
Salzinger, L., 38
Saviano, Roberto, 204
scholarship, feminist, 206–7
school uniforms, mended on Fashion Express shop floor, 181
Scott, James, 36, 65, 202
Scott, Joan, 156
Scott, R.M., 87
second hand clothes, trade in, 11
second stratum workers, 203
Secor, Anna, 84–85
security
    at Fashion Express, 68, 80–81, 153, 173, 193n5
    state, 3, 196
sewing, 76
sex appeal, workplace personalities based on, 152
sexual education, 130
sexuality
    factory workers' views on, 130–31
    Muslim, 79–80
shaabi music, 138n9
shabka (engagement gift), 102, 103, 106, 118–19
Shaker (head of Planning Unit), 66–67
Sharabi, Hisham, 56
Sharihan (supervisor), 143
Shehata, Samer, 153
shop floor, 4
    arguments on, 145, 146, 164–65, 168–69, 184–85, 189
    and BGB management takeover, 183–89, 191, 192
    commercial activities on, 99–100, 124–33, 164
    BGB clampdown of, 180–81
    games played on, 115–17, 171n2
    globalised, 194
    haqq concept used on, 88–89, 90
    love/romance on, 98–99, 100–101, 107, 117, 119–24, 137
    religiosity displayed on, 161–64, 167
    respectability of, 77
    rumours, 64–65, 173, 175, 191
    supervision on, 147

visits
    by foreign clients, 176–77
    by management/proprietor, 71–72, 149, 150
    See also workforce; workplaces
Shura Council, Qasim Bey's candidacy for, 94–96
shurafa' (honourable) status/class, 59, 200
Sima (factory worker), 163
single women
    disapproval of, 159–60
    fear for status of, 100–102, 117
    gihaaz accumulation by, 125, 128, 129–30, 131–32
    workers, 206
el Sisi, Abd El Fatah, 195, 209, 211
Six Day War (1967), 10
skill levels, 41, 76
Snyder, R.L., 46
social contracts, between workers and employers, 89
social media use, in Arab Spring upheavals, 1–2
social mobility, aspirations of factory workers, 126, 127
social practices, and gender, 37
'social space', 32
societies, Islamic ordering of, 87
Sohair, 136
Soliman, Sheikh (Sheikh 'Yassin'), 79
souk area (Port Said), 13, 14
spatial organisation
    at Fashion Express, 18, 33–34, 44, 64, 86, 148
    of factories, 31, 32
    and gender, 79–80
spatial practices, imagined, 32, 33
Sphinx Clothing, 70
spies (*gawasis*), management's use of, 34, 64, 65–70, 86–87
Springborg, R., 70, 96n5
'Square People', 1
state socialism, Egyptian, 3, 126, 195, 201
statistics
    on Fashion Express workforce, 213–16
    reliability of, 47n5
strategic significance of Port Said, 10

strikes
  in Arab Spring upheavals, 2, 48n6, 195, 208
  at Fashion Express, 89–90
  authorised, 3
  subcontracting chains in textile industry, 24–25
Suez (city), 5
Suez Canal, 6, 7
  and Arab Israeli conflict, 10
supervisors, 28, 34, 44–45, 47, 72, 76, 139–41, 142, 170–71
  and BGB management takeover, 178, 180, 182–84, 189
  demotion of, 150–53
  discipline styles of, 141, 143–48
  efficiency performances of, 148–56
  female, 37, 143–44, 165–66, 170, 203–4, 205
    dress styles of, 152
    masculine behaviour by, 140, 156–64
    and shop floor love/romance, 99, 114–15, 122–24, 137
  male, 140, 144–45, 156, 160, 165–70
  power of, 145–46, 152, 154, 165–66, 170
  recruitment of, 153, 165–66, 178
  relations with management, 140, 146, 149, 150, 151, 157, 159–60, 168–69
surveillance system at Fashion Express, 34, 43, 50, 64–71, 80, 86–87, 164
symbolic capital, 199–200

T
Tahrir Square demonstrations, 1, 2
Tamer (factory worker), 88–89
tangid (quilt fluffing) celebrations, 134–37
taraabut (togetherness) principle, 50, 97n12
  at Fashion Express, 85–89, 91, 124, 189
Tarh el Bahr district (Port Said), 13, 14
tazbitat (work arrangements), 138n7
textile industry, 11, 12, 16, 18
  See also garment industry
theories
  of gender, 37
  social, 32
3arabawy (website), 1–2

Tom wi Jerry (Tom and Jerry) game on shop floor, 183
tomcat femininity, of female supervisors, 140, 158–64
Top Fashion, 53
tourism, in Port Said, 12
trade
  Middle-Eastern, 51, 198
  in second hand clothes, 11
trade unions, 3, 196
training, of factory workers, 76, 92, 179–80
Tukhi, Ismail *See* Ismail, Mr.

U
uniforms
  for Fashion Express workforce, 181–82
  school, 181
United States, trade agreement with Egypt, 96n2

V
veiling, by factory workers, 27–28, 109–10, 161, 163
Village (Quartier) Arabe (Port Said), 6, 9, 13
violence, avoidance of, 146
visibility, in Fashion Express floor plan, 64
visitors, British, to Fashion Express, 176–77
voices, of female supervisors, 143, 144, 163

W
Wafaa (factory worker), 117, 181–82
wages
  of female factory workers, 124–25, 128
  fines deducted from, 145–46, 184, 187
  late payment of, 89–90, 191
  of male factory workers, 118
wala lil-masna' (loyalty to institutional power), 173, 178, 193n1
  BGB management's emphasis on, 174, 210
wealth, of Fahmy family, 60
wedding announcements, 98
wedding celebrations, 100, 103
  of Fashion Express workers, 133–37
White, J.B., 38–39
women
  factory owners, 52–53

factory workers, 27–30, 54, 204–5
   ambitions of, 151
   dress styles/veiling of, 27–28, 108–11, 161, 163, 188–89
   fear of singlehood, 100–102, 117
   flirtatious behaviour by, 115–16
   respectability/modesty of, 79, 83–85, 121–22, 132–33
   wages of, 124–25, 128
   formal sector employment by, 4, 25, 26, 39, 205–6
   and globalisation, 37–38
   informal sector work by, 4, 38–39
   in Islam, 108, 171n7
   leadership styles, 203
   in middle management, 159–60
   supervisors, 28, 34, 44–45, 47, 99, 114–15, 122–24, 143–44, 152, 203–4, 205
   masculine behaviour by, 140, 156–64
   power of, 165–66, 170
workforce
   education levels of, 26, 216
   in Export Processing Zones, 49, 52, 54
   of Fashion Express, 5, 25–26, 47, 213–16
   ambitions of, 126, 127, 151, 200–202
   and BGB management takeover, 174–75, 179–86, 187–89, 210–11
   collective action/resistance by, 89–91, 92, 187–89, 190, 191, 192, 210–11
   as community/family, 50–51, 85–89, 91
   fluctuations in, 81–82
   gender distribution/dynamics, 44–45, 76–77, 79–80, 83–84, 137, 170, 214
   raids by competition on, 91–94
   relations with management, 63, 194–95
   See also shop floor
working class, formation of, 202
workplaces
   gender/gendering at, 25, 26, 36, 39, 45, 77, 119, 137, 156–57, 159, 170, 205–6
   love/romance on, 98–99, 100–101, 107, 117, 119–24, 137
   modus vivendi of, 36
   religion at, 87
   surveillance systems, 34, 43, 50, 64–71, 80, 86–87, 164
   See also shop floor
Wright, Melissa, 147

Y
'Yassin', Sheikh (Sheikh Soliman), 79
yelling, by female supervisors, 143, 144
Yelvington, K.A., 38
youth, materialist life-styles of, 201

Z
Zaim (supervisor), 149, 156, 160, 166–70
Zeinab (factory worker), 77, 88–89, 108, 110, 115, 121, 124, 150
Zhang Wei, 96n3, 97n12
Zizi (supervisor), 70, 77, 113, 120, 124, 130–31, 132, 143, 160, 178, 182, 190, 210
zubbat (officers in the military/police force) cooperatives, 127

www.ingramcontent.com/pod-product-compliance
Lightning Source LLC
Chambersburg PA
CBHW070915030426
42336CB00014BA/2420